PRACTICAL APPROACHES TO CHURCH GROWTH

DAG HEWARD-MILLS

Parchment House

Unless otherwise stated, all Scripture quotations are taken from the King James Version of the Bible.

Practical Approaches to Church Growth

First published 2016 by Parchment House
5th Printing 2017

Find out more about Dag Heward Mills at:

Healing Jesus Campaign
Email: evangelist@daghewardmills.org
Website: www.daghewardmills.org
Facebook: Dag Heward-Mills
Twitter: @EvangelistDag

ISBN : 978-1-61395-563-5

Contents

SECTION 2: THE MEGA CHURCH

SECTION 3: CHURCH GROWTH

Section 1

CHURCH PLANTING

The planting of churches is a phenomenon that is widespread among charismatic ministers. It was a major activity of the early disciples. Successful church planting, however, demands skill and embraces multiple factors. The author analyzes the various components of church planting in this book. It is a training manual for any minister who wants to make church planting his vision for life.

Chapter

1

Church Expansion

CHAPTER SUMMARY

There are times when one wonders whether the church is really advancing or not. There are many activities in the church and many programmes are being held. But is the kingdom of God really marching forward or is it moving in circles? Discover how to expand the kingdom and much more in this chapter.

- **How to advance the Kingdom**

1.1 Follow Christ's instruction.

1.2 Know what a church really is.

1.3 Do not try to impress people.

1.4 Fulfil the Great Comission by evangelism and establishing churches.

1.5 Plant churches in virgin territories.

Sometimes in a large city you see new churches springing up. Often, these new churches become the talk of the town and it looks as though God is doing something new. Everyone flocks to the church and everyone seems to take a liking to this new thing. A closer look at these new movements, however, often reveals that the new congregations are made up of people who simply migrated from another nearby church.

The kingdom of God is full of carnal Christians who are always looking for something new and exciting. Many pastors get excited because they think their churches are growing and there is a revival. In reality, there is little overall growth in the kingdom of God. People are simply rotating from church to church. **The kingdom of God needs to advance in reality.**

Years ago, Europeans sent missionaries to Africa and Asia. Through this act of sacrifice, whole nations have been Christianized. People who were previously pagans have been converted to Christ. Let us not deceive ourselves: there are many more people in the world today. There are also many people who do not have an effective church or pastor. There is an even greater need today for real advancement of the church into un-Christianized territories.

When Europeans sent out missionaries two hundred years ago, there were only one billion people in the world. Today, in the year 2004, there are 6.1 billion people in the world. The secular world always complains about the ratio of doctors to the population.

Does anyone complain about the ratio of pastors to the population? How many evangelists are there compared to the millions of people living today?

How to Advance the Kingdom

The kingdom of God will experience a real advancement when we follow Christ's instruction. Jesus' last command was to go into the world and to make disciples!

And Jesus came and spake unto them, saying, All power is given unto me in heaven and in earth. GO YE THEREFORE, AND TEACH ALL NATIONS, baptizing them in the name of the Father, and of the Son, and of the Holy Ghost: Teaching them to observe all things whatsoever I have commanded you: and, lo, I am with you alway, even unto the end of the world. Amen.

Matthew 28:18-20

In this Scripture, Jesus tells all of us to teach people "the Word of God". There is no way you can teach people unless you regularly gather them together.

What a Church Really Is

A regular gathering of Christians for the purpose of teaching is called "a church". In other words, our Lord was telling us to go into all the world and gather people together regularly in order to teach them the word. God is in the business of creating gatherings of teachable people. God by His Spirit is raising men who will go into all parts of the world to gather people regularly to teach them His word.

The more gatherings and groups there are, the more the Great Commission is being fulfilled. The more groups that are taught, the more the Great Commission is being fulfilled. These groups are the churches that are being planted by obedient servants of the Lord.

■ We Love to Impress People

Unfortunately, because most pastors are so concerned about what people think, they cannot effectively fulfil this Great Commission. We want to have one big impressive gathering for all to see! We want people to think we are great! After all, the more people there are in the congregation, the more important the pastor looks.

> **In the MULTITUDE OF PEOPLE is the king's honour(approval and endorsement) ...**
>
> **Proverbs 14:28**

There is a need to start many gatherings of people in every possible location in order that we fulfil the Great Commission. The vastness of the world and the distribution of people demands that pastors and people move away from the *one congregation church to multiple gatherings in different locations.* If we are really serious about obeying our Lord, then we have no choice than to obey this.

Leaders must be trained. Pastors must be trained. Workers must be trained. The "superstar" mentality of the church must die. This superstar mentality wants us to have one great pastor whom everybody acknowledges and praises.

We are often deceived into thinking that the pastor with the largest congregation will be the greatest in Heaven. This will not be the case. The pastor who will be greatest in Heaven is the most humble and childlike pastor.

> **At the same time came the disciples unto Jesus, saying, WHO IS THE GREATEST IN THE KINGDOM OF HEAVEN? And Jesus called a little child unto him, and set him in the midst of them, And said, Verily I say unto you, Except ye be converted, and become as little children, ye shall not enter into the kingdom of heaven. Whosoever therefore shall humble himself as this little child, THE SAME IS GREATEST IN THE KINGDOM OF HEAVEN.**
>
> **Matthew 18:1-4**

Jesus made it very clear who was going to be the greatest in the kingdom. No one can tell your humility by the size of your congregation. *In fact, pastors with small congregations are likely to be more humble (and therefore greater in Heaven) than pastors with big congregations.*

What we need is more congregations, more churches and more fruit for our Master. Let us plant churches! "A church at every door and in every language" must be the goal of every true servant of God. A gathering at every electric pole or under every tree will make the kingdom go forward.

Let's stop trying to impress people. Let's stop assessing our ministries by the size of our congregations. Let's have the gatherings. Dear church leaders, do not seek for the honour of men but for the honour (approval and endorsement) of God.

> **How can ye believe, which receive honour (approval and endorsement) one of another, and seek not the honour (approval and endorsement) that cometh from God only?**
>
> **John 5:44**

Is Evangelism the Fulfilling of the Great Commission?

Evangelism and crusades are good, as they are the starting point of these teachings. Evangelists must go forth. But are they really fulfilling the Great Commission? Yes and No! YES, because they have started the process and NO, because without the teaching, which comes by establishing churches, the Great Commission will not be truly fulfilled.

Simply put, THE GREAT COMMISSION IS EVANGELISM FOLLOWED BY PLANTING OF CHURCHES. The churches are the gatherings and these gatherings are then taught the Word.

Plant Churches in Virgin Territories

Above all, churches must be planted where the Lord directs us. Churches must be planted in the cities and in the villages.

I see the need for churches to be planted in virgin territories. Most of us concentrate on areas where things are already working. But I tell you, there are many untouched areas where God has called us to. The passion and the commitment to soul winning and church planting must come back into the church and we must sacrifice our young men for this.

Pastors must be concerned that Islam is taking over large sections of Africa and the world, as the church looks on unconcerned. Moslems are sacrificial and do not mind going to the furthermost towns and villages of many nations.

Meanwhile the Christians, who have been commanded to go to the uttermost parts of the Earth, are sitting in the nearest and most convenient cities of the world!

But ye shall receive power, after that the Holy Ghost is come upon you: and ye shall be witnesses unto me both in Jerusalem, and in all Judaea, and in Samaria, and UNTO THE NEAREST, MOST CONVENIENT AND PROSPEROUS CITIES OF THE WORLD! (Which Bible is this?)

Chapter

2

The Mindset of Church Planters

CHAPTER SUMMARY

The following chapter is basically educating you on the importance of the doctrine of church planting. You will be prompted and your ministry will be inspired to engage in the last great apostolic church planting movement.

- **Twelve Ways Your Mind Must Work If You Are To Become A Church Planter**

2.1 Understand that God is monitoring your works.

2. 2 Church planting is the key to going all the way with God.

2.3 You are expected to accomplish certain works whilst on earth.

2.4 Wisdom is to be mindful of Heaven and conscious of approaching eternity.

2.5 You were created to be more than a good person in the society.

2.6 The reason for your salvation is the good works.

2.7 Doing the work helps you overcome your personal problems.

2.8 The strength of a church is measured by its sending capacity.

2.9. Doing the works causes you to overcome the zilch of life.

2.10 Your works will follow you into Heaven.

2.11 You will void becoming critical by planting churches.

2.12 Plant a church because there is a time when God expects you to be a teacher.

> **Let this mind be in you…**
>
> **Phillippians 2:5**

Christ had a way of thinking which made Him do the things He did. "This verse teaches us to think in the same way that Christ thought". This is what "let this mind be in you" means. It is only when your mind works in a particular way that you can accomplish the will of God.

I am writing about how your mind must work if you are to become a church planter. Without this foundation, no one will advance into the very difficult task of church planting.

1. Understand that God is monitoring your works.

Dear friends, your works on earth are being monitored. God is going to require from you an answer concerning what He has put in you. He is going to ask you what you have done with His gifts. God is going to require from you things He has given to you. He will enquire of your works!

It is interesting that in the seven letters written to the seven churches, one phrase was repeated over and over - I know thy works. Which works are these? Whatever these are, it must be important for every church to have these works fully in place. Notice the following verses:

> **I KNOW THY WORKS, and thy labour, and thy patience, and how thou canst not bear them, which are evil: and thou hast tried them which say they are apostles, and are not, and hast found them liars:**
>
> **Revelation 2:2**

> **I KNOW THY WORKS, and tribulation, and poverty, (but thou art rich) and I know the blasphemy of them which say they are Jews, and are not, but are the synagogue of Satan.**
>
> **Revelation 2:9**

> **I KNOW THY WORKS, and where thou dwellest, even where Satan's seat is: and thou holdest fast my name, and hast not denied my faith, even in those days wherein Antipas was my faithful martyr, who was slain among you, where Satan dwelleth.**
>
> **Revelation 2:13**

> **I KNOW THY WORKS, and charity, and service, and faith, and thy patience, and thy works; and the last to be more than the first.**
>
> **Revelation 2:19**

> **And unto the angel of the church in Sardis write; These things saith he that hath the seven Spirits of God, and the seven stars; I KNOW THY WORKS, that thou hast a name that thou livest, and art dead.**
>
> **Revelation 3:1**

> **I KNOW THY WORKS: behold, I have set before thee an open door, and no man can shut it: for thou hast a little strength, and hast kept my word, and hast not denied my name.**
>
> **Revelation 3:8**

"God did not say, "I know thy houses and thy cars". He did not say; "I know thy Mercedes Benz" He said; "I know thy works!" He did not say; "I know thy degrees." He did not say; "I know thy father and thy mother." He said, "I know thy works!"

2. Church planting is the key to going all the way with God.

> **For whosoever will save his life shall lose it; but whosoever shall lose his life for my sake and the gospel's, the same shall save it.**
>
> **Mark 8:35**

In 1985, I took a decision to go all the way with God. I had just finished a very difficult medical school exam. In my opinion, I just scraped through that exam. As I thought of the effort I had put into the exam, and the extra work I had done, I felt in my heart that it was not worth it at all. Why should I suffer so much for medicine? Why should I give my life for such a cause?

I vowed that from then on, my priority would be the work of God. Initially I thought that God was the number one person in my life. I was a very serious Christian leader but I did not realize that God's work was not my number one priority. From that time on, I determined that I had one purpose and that was to do the work of God! All other things became side issues. This was truly a turning point in my life.

From then on, my number one goal was God and the ministry. The Medical School had taken its rightful place as number two or three in my heart. That was probably the time that I entered into full-time ministry.

It is interesting to note that after taking that decision, I began to excel in the Medical School. I had a distinction and I won prizes! To my amazement, I topped my class. My heart was far away from any medical ambitions, yet I was receiving medical laurels. Isn't it amazing that the things you give up are the same things that God gives back to you?

It takes faith to walk with God. The opposite of what I expected had happened. This is what it is like to walk with God. He that loses his life will gain it! He that preserves his life will lose it. There will never be a time when you will not need faith. We will always have to believe.

From that time until now, I have been fully plugged into the ministry. Shortly after that period, I planted my first church, which I am still pastoring. Since then I have been involved in planting over 400 churches. I once made a covenant with the Lord that I would plant at least one thousand churches in Ghana alone. I always pray that God will give me grace to fulfill this covenant. I am going all the way! I am not holding back anymore. Let His will be done in my life!

In 1989, I qualified as a medical doctor. By April 1990 I had finished my housemanship. All my medical mates were on their way to foreign countries. It was quite clear to me that the Lord was asking me to stay in Ghana. There were just a few people in the church but I decided to stay with it. I knew that I had condemned myself to a life of poverty. I talked to my wife and she agreed. She supported me all the way. I knew I would never have a house or anything like that. I just knew it. However, I said, *"Lord, I love you with all my heart, I will do it. I entrust myself to you."*

Many years have gone by and it's been worth it all. He said, *"Seek ye first the kingdom of God and his righteousness and all these things shall be added onto you."*

> **For whosoever will save his life shall lose it: but whosoever will lose his life for my sake, the same shall save it.**
>
> **Luke 9:24**

3. You are expected to accomplish certain works whilst on earth.

> **For by grace are ye saved through faith; and that not of yourselves: it is the gift of God: Not of works, lest any man should boast. For we are his workmanship, CREATED IN CHRIST JESUS UNTO GOOD WORKS, which God hath before ordained that we should walk in them.**
>
> **Ephesians 2:8-10**

God has good works for you to do. That is why you are alive in the first place. Make no mistake, the only reason why you are still alive, is to accomplish certain good works.

The English Taxi-Driver

I was once with a certain English man who was giving me a ride in his taxi. I asked him if he believed in God. He said he did not believe in God and wondered if I believed in such things.

I told him that I did believe in God. Then he asked if I believed in Heaven and Hell. I told him, "I certainly do."

He asked again, "Do you believe that Heaven is a good place?"

I answered, "Heaven is a wonderful place and we are all looking forward to going there one day."

He continued, "Do you think that life in Heaven will be better than life on earth?"

"I'm sure it will be," I responded.

Then he asked a question that I have never forgotten.

He said, "If indeed Heaven is better than this earth, why don't you all just kill yourselves and go to Heaven right away?"

Before I could answer that question, we had arrived at our destination and I had to get down. As I went along, I pondered over the question that this man had asked me. It seemed to make a lot of sense: Why not go to Heaven right now if it is such a great place?

But God's Word shows us why we must still stay on the Earth - we are here to do good works. We are ordained to do certain good works on this Earth! We cannot leave until we have finished our work on Earth.

Kenneth Hagin's Experience

One day Kenneth Hagin had an experience in which he died physically. As his spirit ascended out of his body, he heard a voice saying, "go back, go back, you have not finished your work on Earth." His spirit returned to his body and he lived for many more years, accomplishing the good works that God had called him to do.

Another reason why we do not kill ourselves is because it is a crime to kill yourself. It is against the law and it is against God's will.

4. Wisdom is to be mindful of Heaven and conscious of approaching eternity.

Once, one of my pastors came to the office to say good-bye to me. He wanted me to pray for him. He was going out as a missionary to a foreign country. As he sat next to me, the Spirit of the Lord came upon me and I spoke to him under the anointing. I said, "Always think like a dying man and you will be a wise man. Think about your soon arrival in Heaven and you will be wise." You see, when people are on their deathbeds, they think differently from people who are not thinking of the realities of Heaven and Hell.

I remember talking to my wife. I asked her, "What do you think God will say to me when I arrive in Heaven?" I don't remember the answer she gave me but this is something that bothers me all the time. Is Heaven happy with me? Is God pleased with me? What will Jesus say to me on the day I see him face to face?

Unfortunately, most of us are just thinking about earthly things - money, cars, visas, power, influence and the honour of men. These thinking patterns are not wisdom. If you die without doing His works, you will be a fool on the day of your death.

Don't be deceived; your time on earth is limited. After today, you will have one less day of opportunity. The houses you are building and the things you are acquiring have no real value. Jesus said, **"Do not pile up things on earth."** Why did He say so? Is Jesus against us having nice things? Certainly not! He was giving us the highest kind of wisdom - to live with eternity in mind and to believe in the resurrection. The more eternity conscious we are, the wiser we will be!

Do a little calculation right now; how many more years will you live on earth after reading this book. Compare this with the many years you will spend in eternity.

My father once told me that the way I spend the first twenty-five years of my life would determine how I would spend the next forty-five years of my life. By the age of twenty-five, I was a medical doctor and a pastor. My first twenty-five years have truly affected the years that have followed."

However, I have an even higher piece of wisdom for you: "The way you spend your seventy years on Earth will determine how you will spend millions of years in eternity."

Don't be like the rich young fool who thought that life was only an earthly life. He was planning various things when the Lord said to him, "Thou fool, tonight I require thy soul from thee." That very night, the Lord called him up to Heaven in spite of his earthly plans. God knows the day He is going to call you to account. Get ready with your works. I know thy works!

5. You were created to be more than a good person in the society.

We were not created so that we would just be "good" people. We were created to do certain good works. These good works were ordained by God and not by you. In other words, God has already determined the works that you are supposed to do. No one can do anything to impress God. Your goodness, your morality, your uprightness and your perfection will not impress God. To please God is to do what He says you should do.

After eating of the Tree of Good and Evil, men have become obsessed with what they see as "good or evil'. Obeying God is what is right for us to do. Doing good things, moral things and upright things are not necessarily pleasing to God.

When Satan approached Jesus in the wilderness, he suggested some "good things" for Jesus to do. Jesus was asked to use God's power to turn stones into bread but He did not.

He was also asked to protect Himself with God's power but He did not. These are all "good things" but Jesus did not do them. He knew that the right thing to do was to obey God.

The devil also asks people to do "good things" but there is always a hidden agenda. As soon as you step out of God's commands you are in sin even though you may be involved in a "good thing".

Anomia

Let me help you with a definition of sin. Sin is not necessarily doing something evil. It may surprise you to know that doing a good thing, which is not God's will, is sin. As I said earlier, there were many good things that Jesus simply would not do.

Jesus could have gone on living longer but He accepted His father's will to die on the cross at the age of thirty-three. Would it not have been a good thing for Jesus to have travelled all over the world preaching until He was eighty years old? There are many sick people that Jesus did not heal. Why didn't Jesus heal them? Was it not a good thing to heal the sick?

At this point, we need to understand the essential definition of sin. SIN IS THE REJECTION OF GOD'S WILL. SIN IS THE REFUSAL TO ACCEPT GOD'S PLAN AND GOD'S WILL. It is the substitution of your plans for God's plans. Sin is the substitution of your wisdom for God's wisdom!

That is what "anomia" means. "anomia" is a Greek word. "Anomia" means to reject the law, the will and the way of God. How sad it is that we often think we know better than God.

> **Whosoever committeth sin transgresseth also the law: for sin is the transgression of the law.**
>
> **1 John 3:4**

From this Scripture, we see that transgression of the law is sin. The word "transgression" is translated from the Greek word "anomia". This means "one who acts contrary to the law."

Vine's dictionary declares that this verse gives the real meaning of sin. Vine goes on to say, "This definition of sin sets forth its essential character as the rejection of the law, or will, of God and the substitution of the will of self".

Years ago, I remember telling God about my plans to serve Him. I decided that I would go into the secular world to earn a lot of money to support the work of God. I told God that I would be a high-income earner who would contribute thousands of dollars to the kingdom.

I am not the only one who has had this idea. I have met countless people who have expressed similar ambitions. It is amazing that very few, if any at all of these people actually do bring a lot of money to the kingdom. I am a full-time pastor so I know what people do. Most of the rich people I know do not contribute much to the kingdom. In fact, you virtually have to plead with them to cough up a few of their gold coins.

Can I be honest with you? I think that, if I had gone on that route (which would have been my way instead of God's way) I would have given very little money to the kingdom. I think I would have probably criticized pastors and churches for the way they use money. Mercy Lord!

You see, God knows more than we do and when God called me to full time ministry He knew what He was doing. I remember clearly at the end of 1990 the Lord asked me to stop every other activity and be a full-time ministry worker. My way would have been to give God some money to keep Him quiet. Forgive!

I didn't know about my future ministry. I would have forsaken the ministry and the rewards He had called me to.

The Value of the Thumb

I once met a man whose thumb had been cut off in a factory accident. He showed it to some friends as I looked on with interest. He related what happened and told us how much compensation he was paid for his thumb.

With mixed feelings he stated that he had been paid eight thousand pounds sterling for his thumb. At that time, I had only one pound in my account and I thought to myself, "What a lucky man."

Years later, the Lord reminded me of this man's thumb and asked me to do a calculation:

"If this man was paid eight thousand pounds for just his thumb, how much would two thumbs cost?"

I said; "Sixteen thousand pounds"

Then he asked me; "How much would five fingers cost?"

I said; "Lord about forty thousand pounds"

He continued; "How much would ten fingers cost?"

I answered; "Eighty thousand pounds."

Then the Lord asked me; "How much would an arm cost?"

I answered; "A lot of money"

"What about a leg, a kidney, a heart and a brain?"

"I am not sure"

Finally he asked me; "How much would your whole body cost"

I said, "Millions."

The Lord showed me that no matter how much money I contributed to the kingdom, it would never be up to the value of giving my whole body, spirit and soul to His work. In my limited understanding, I thought that giving a lot of money to God was just as good as giving my whole self to Him.

6. The reason for your salvation is the good works.

We often only preach about money and we teach people how to be successful. However, our salvation was and is for a purpose. The Bible says we were saved by grace through faith and that it is not of ourselves but it is the gift of God (Ephesians 2:8). We are his workmanship created for good works which God has before ordained that we (Christians) should walk in them"(Ephesians 2:10).

This is why we are still alive. There are good works for us to do! One of these good works is the planting of churches. We need to go to the villages and to the towns to preach. God wants people who will go with His message. God is looking for church planters.

These good works are the reason why God gave us a new life in Him. It is so that we would live for Him and do His purposes. Your works are very important to God. This is the reason for our salvation. "I know thy works!"

7. Doing the work helps you overcome your personal problems.

When people preach and teach it does not mean that they do not have problems. As we minister the Word of God, these problems become smaller.

Instead of us focusing on our difficulties, we must lift up our eyes unto the Lord of the harvest and look at what lies before us. Let us stretch out and reach the un-churched people of our day.

God has never used perfect people who have no problems. Noah had a drinking problem but God used him. Abraham had serious marital problems, but God used him. Rahab, the harlot had moral problems but God used her. The fact that God will use you does not mean that you have no problems of your own!

We have "this treasure in earthen vessels" (2 Corinthians 4:7). God's glory and anointing is not in heavenly or angelic vessels, but in earthly vessels. I have always ministered in spite of my personal problems. There are times I have had financial problems, but I did the work of God. There are times I had marital problems, but I did the work of God. There are times I have been sick, and had to be operated upon by surgeons but I still did the work of God.

People look at me and assume that I have never had any problems. Perhaps I even have more problems than the average person. But doing the work of God makes it seem as if I have no problems.

But we have THIS TREASURE IN EARTHEN VESSELS, that the excellency of the power may be of God, and not of us.

2 Corinthians 4:7

Every earthen vessel that the Lord uses is plagued with personal problems. He ministers in spite of these and not because his life is perfect. The good news is that as you focus on the work of God, your personal problems diminish and the excellency of the power of God becomes manifest.

8. The strength of a church is measured by its sending capacity.

The strength of a church is traditionally measured by its seating capacity. The more people the church seats, the greater it is perceived to be. However, the church was born as a sending church. Is your church sending people out? Pastors like to boast about who comes to their churches. They drop names and say "The Minister of the Sun, Moon and Stars comes to my first service. The Deputy Minister for Financial Corruption is on my finance committee." Rarely do pastors speak of the people they have sent forth as missionaries. Notice how the New Testament churches operated.

> **Now there were in the church that was at Antioch certain prophets and teachers; as Barnabas, and Simeon that was called Niger, and Lucius of Cyrene, and Manaen, which had been brought up with Herod the tetrarch, and Saul.**
>
> **As they ministered to the Lord, and fasted, THE HOLY GHOST SAID, SEPARATE ME BARNABAS AND SAUL FOR THE WORK WHEREUNTO I HAVE CALLED THEM.**
>
> **So they, being sent forth by the Holy Ghost, departed unto Seleucia; and from thence they sailed to Cyprus.**
>
> **Acts 13:1, 2, 4**

9. Doing the works causes you to overcome the zilch of life.

> **Therefore I hated life; because the work that is wrought under the sun is grievous unto me: for all is vanity and vexation of spirit.**
>
> **Yea, I hated all my labour which I had taken under the sun: because I should leave it unto the man that shall be after me.**
>
> **And who knoweth whether he shall be a wise man or a fool? yet shall he have rule over all my labour wherein I have laboured, and wherein I have shewed myself wise under the sun. This is also vanity.**
>
> **Therefore I went about to cause my heart to despair of all the labour which I took under the sun.**
>
> **Ecclesiastes 2:17-20**

One of the words Solomon used many times was the word vanity. Solomon discovered after acquiring everything that everything was vanity. God gave him things many human beings could only ever imagine. King Solomon discovered that each and everything was worthless and empty. He said, "Vanity of vanities all is vanity."

Everything is useless. Everything is useless in the context that Solomon was writing; which was the context of "under the sun". "Under the sun" is a commonly used phrase in the book of Ecclesiastes. Under the sun refers to our earthly existence under the influence of the physical sun - zilch.

The earthly existence that we have is useless. That is the reality. Pastors are supposed to teach and preach the truth. We need to be oriented toward Heaven and oriented toward the day of our judgment. A church planter is someone who operates by this wisdom. Planting of churches is not vanity because it will bring us an eternal reward.

10. Your works will follow you into Heaven.

When you die, nothing goes with you. I have conducted many funerals. I have stood over the coffins of people that I have known and loved on this Earth. I have buried people and put them into the ground. I have seen it repeatedly. No one takes anything out of this world. Cars remain behind, houses remain behind and money remains behind.

> **And I heard a voice from heaven saying unto me, Write, Blessed are the dead which die in the Lord from henceforth: Yea, saith the Spirit, that they may rest from their labours; AND THEIR WORKS DO FOLLOW THEM.**
>
> **Revelation 14:13**

Nothing except your works will follow you when you leave this world. You have to get involved with the work of God. You must plant a church in your lifetime. You have to get involved in your church.

God only gives you an opportunity to be involved in His work. God does not need you. He does not need me. He does not even need pastors. If pastors were so important, they would not die. Nobody is of any relevance and significance to God. God's mercy allows us to be involved in His work. Our inclusion in the work is God's mercy towards us!

11. You will avoid becoming critical by planting churches.

It is better to participate than to be an observer. Observers often become critical of everything. After being idle for some time, you begin to see all the faults in your church. You will notice the pastor's mistakes when he preaches. You will notice his mistakes when he quotes Scriptures. You will notice when the anointing is not as strong as it usually is. Before long, you will be familiar with all the shortcomings of your church. You will eventually fall into criticism and become faultfinding. Demons will find in you a haven.

12. Plant a church because there is a time when God expects you to be a teacher.

There comes a time when you should be a teacher of the Word of God. You should teach people, you should give something.

> **FOR WHEN FOR THE TIME YE OUGHT TO BE TEACHERS, ye have need that one teach you again which be the first principles of the**

oracles of God; and are become such as have need of milk, and not of strong meat.

Hebrews 5:12

There is a time when you must become a teacher. If you do not become a teacher when you are supposed to, there is something wrong with your spiritual development.

One day we went preaching and there was a young woman in the group who I asked to preach at an open-air dawn broadcast. She said: "I don't know how to preach. I have never preached before, I don't know enough of the Bible."

Then I told her, "You can preach." I told her to repeat everything I said to her. Before long, she was preaching. She preached a whole sermon that morning. She is still serving the Lord today. You will be surprised at what you can do if you only try.

Chapter

3

The Works of Church Planters

CHAPTER SUMMARY

Works cannot and will never qualify us for heaven. However after we are saved, we are expected to get into the good works that Christ has prepared for us. In this chapter read about the two judgments that await the believer.

- **The Two Judgments**

3.1 The White Throne

3.2 The Judgment Seat of Christ

Let this mind be in you...

> **For by grace are ye saved through faith; and that not of yourselves: it is the gift of God: NOT OF WORKS, lest any man should boast. For we are his workmanship, created in Christ Jesus UNTO GOOD WORKS, which God hath before ordained that we should walk in them.**
>
> **Ephesians 2:8-10**

The Bible makes it clear that our works do not save us. We are not going to Heaven because of our good works. Neither are we saved from Hell because of our good works. We are saved by grace. Our salvation is from the Lord. You cannot do anything to earn salvation. You cannot be good enough to qualify for Heaven! Our best is not good enough. Works cannot and will never qualify us for heaven.

> **As it is written, There is none righteous, no, not one:**
>
> **Romans 3:10**

> **But we are all as an unclean thing, and all our righteousnesses are as filthy rags; and we all do fade as a leaf; and our iniquities, like the wind, have taken us away.**
>
> **Isaiah 64:6**

Notice however that the portion of Ephesians that talks about "salvation not by works" is the same that talks about our being "created for good works." This means that after we are saved, we get into the good works that Christ has prepared for us.

Many Christians relax because they know that they are saved by grace and not by works. They feel that they are already destined to go to Heaven. All we have to do is sit back, relax and enjoy the ride to Heaven. Thank God for the ride to Heaven. But upon arrival, questions are going to be asked!

"Did you do the things I asked you to do? Did you do the good works that I ordained for you?" Jesus will ask.

■ The Two Judgments

God is not going to judge us the way He will judge the rest of the world. He has prepared an extra judgment for believers. The Bible talks about two different thrones of judgment. The White Throne will be the place of judgment for the world. Christians will be judged at a different seat called the Judgment Seat of Christ.

The White Throne is the supreme court of Heaven. This is where the decision to admit you to Heaven or not will be taken. But there is another judgment seat for believers.

1. The White Throne

> **And I saw A GREAT WHITE THRONE, and him that sat on it, from whose face the earth and the heaven fled away; and there was found no place for them.**

> **And I saw the dead, small and great, stand before God; AND THE BOOKS WERE OPENED: AND ANOTHER BOOK WAS OPENED, WHICH IS THE BOOK OF LIFE: and the dead were judged out of those things which were written in the books, according to their works.**
>
> **And the sea gave up the dead which were in it; and death and hell delivered up the dead which were in them: and they were judged every man according to their works.**
>
> **Revelation 20:11-13**

The Book of Life and the Book of Works

It is essential that your name be in the all-important book of life. This determines whether you will enter into Heaven at all.

But the Scripture shows us that there are books that also have the records of all the works we do. This is the book of works! This book will be opened. It contains records of our works. It will show the records of churches that have been planted. The dead will be judged out of these books according to their works.

2. The Judgment Seat of Christ

> **Wherefore we labour, that, whether present or absent, we may be accepted of him. For we must all appear before THE JUDGMENT SEAT OF CHRIST; that every one may receive the things done in his body, according to that he hath done, whether it be good or bad.**
>
> **2 Corinthians 5:9-10**

Mountains of Foolishness

Believers are going to receive judgment for what they do in their bodies. We must work the works of Jesus. The things we treasure are going to lose value in the moment of death. Everything that has been gathered and accumulated will become a mountain of foolishness.

Our accumulated wealth, houses, degrees, clothes and shoes, will stand as testimonies to our faithlessness. We never believed in the resurrection! We never believed that we would resurrect and live again in eternity. Our accumulated perishables will witness against us in that day. They will speak to Heaven and declare "he was faithless. He did not obey you. He did not believe; his heart was on the treasures of this world!"

Baskets of Fruits

One day you will wake up and find that you are in Heaven. On that day, what will you have in your hand? Baskets of fruits for the glory of God, or mountains of foolishness that testify against you? Dear friend only one thing follows you to Heaven - your good works.

And I heard a voice from heaven saying unto me, Write, Blessed are the dead which die in the Lord from henceforth: Yea, saith the Spirit, that they may rest from their labours; and THEIR WORKS DO FOLLOW THEM.

Revelation 14:13

Many years ago in 1982, I was in medical school. I remember going for my first Anatomy lecture. There was so much to write. We wrote down a lot of notes. As the professor continued lecturing, I began to wonder whether I was expected to write everything. I asked myself, "Are all these things important?"

The lecturer continued his extensive and detailed lecture on the Introduction to Anatomy. He taught us different anatomical terms like "pronation, supination, external rotation, internal rotation," etc. My notes that day almost filled my notebook.

During the class, I asked a friend, "Caroline, do you think we are in the right place?"

She said, "No, I don't think so." She told me she was thinking of leaving the school and I said I was also thinking of quitting. We could not imagine seven years of this torture. I thought seven years would never come to an end. We could not wait for seven years: it was too long! But gradually the years came to pass and we finished school. The seven years I thought would never come, have come and gone. Now it's been twenty-two years since I went to medical school. It's twenty-two years since I asked that question.

The point I am trying to make is that eternity, which seems so far, will soon be on us. I thought seven years would never come by. Some of us think eternity will never arrive. We do not believe in the phase two of our lives. We do not believe in phase two of our lives. Our time on earth is short and very soon we will all be in Heaven. We will wonder why we thought we would live on earth forever!

Chapter

4

Church Planting and the Jerusalem Church

CHAPTER SUMMARY

There were two churches worth taking note of in the New Testament, the Jerusalem Church and the Antioch Church. In the following chapters, learn facts about the Jerusalem and Antioch churches.

■ Ten Things Everyone Should Know About the Jerusalem Church

4.1 The Jerusalem Church was the first church.

4.2 The important people were based in the Jerusalem Church. Even the apostles were based in this church.

4.3 They were the church that had first hand instructions from Jesus to go into the entire world.

4.4 They were a very prosperous and flourishing church.

4.5 There was great growth in the church.

4.6 There was great unity in the church.

4.7 God gave them victory over every problem and difficulty they encountered. For example, Peter and John were released from the custody of the chief priest and elders. They miraculously escaped from jail by angelic intervention.

4.8 The power of God was greatly manifested in the church. In the book of Acts, people who lied to the pastors died instantly.

4.9 Unlike many churches today, they cared for the poor.

4.10 But they did not obey the instruction of church planting until catastrophe struck.

■ Ten Things Everyone Should Know about the Jerusalem Church

1. **The Jerusalem Church was the first church.**

2. **The important people were based in the Jerusalem Church. Even the apostles were based in this church.**

3. **They were the church that had first hand instructions from Jesus to go into the entire world.**

4. **They were a very prosperous and flourishing church.**

> **Neither was there ANY AMONG THEM THAT LACKED: for as many as were possessors of lands or houses sold them, and brought the prices of the things that were sold, And laid them down at the apostles' feet: and distribution was made unto every man according as he had need.**
>
> **Acts 4:34-35**

5. **There was great growth in the church.**

> **Then they that gladly received his word were baptized: and the same day there were ADDED UNTO THEM ABOUT THREE THOUSAND SOULS.**
>
> **Acts 2:41**

6. **There was great unity in the church.**

> **And all that believed WERE TOGETHER, and had all things common;**
>
> **Acts 2:44**

7. **God gave them victory over every problem and difficulty they encountered. For example, Peter and John were released from the custody of the chief priest and elders. They miraculously escaped from jail by angelic intervention.**

> **Then the high priest rose up, and... laid their hands on the apostles, and put them in the common prison. But the angel of the Lord by night opened the prison doors, and brought them forth...**
>
> **Acts 5:17-19**

8. The power of God was greatly manifested in the church. In the book of Acts, people who lied to the pastors died instantly.

> **But Peter said, Ananias, why hath Satan filled thine heart to lie to the Holy Ghost… Ananias hearing these words FELL DOWN, AND GAVE UP THE GHOST: and great fear came on all them that heard these things.**
>
> **Acts 5:3, 5**

9. Unlike many churches today, they cared for the poor.

> **…and distribution was made unto EVERY MAN ACCORDING AS HE HAD NEED.**
>
> **Acts 4:35**

10. But they did not obey the instruction of church planting until catastrophe struck.

> **…at that time there was a GREAT PERSECUTION against the church which was at Jerusalem; and they were all SCATTERED ABROAD throughout the regions of Judaea and Samaria, except the apostles.**
>
> **Acts 8:1**

Perhaps all their good characteristics clouded out the reality that they were a disobedient church. When one of the most promising young pastors, probably tipped to be Peter's successor, died suddenly, they sat up.

What a blow this must have been to the Jerusalem church! Everything was going perfectly until this happened. Every problem had so far worked together for good. Somehow every challenge had been overcome by the power of God - until this one. Suddenly they had a dead pastor on their hands.

> **And they stoned Stephen calling upon God…**
>
> **Acts 7:59**

This marked a turning point in the life of the Jerusalem Church. While the church was reeling under this blow, the secular world stepped up their persecution.

> **…And at that time, there was A GREAT PERSECUTION against the church that was at Jerusalem …**
>
> **Acts 8:1**

It was this persecution that made the church finally obey God. It is easy to be deceived by peace and apparent success. After all Bible said, "...when they say peace, peace, then sudden destruction will come upon them"... (1 Thessalonians 5:3). We are not to be led by circumstances or apparent prosperity. These are not indicators of God's blessing. If peace and prosperity were the hallmarks of God's blessing then the Apostle Paul was the greatest sinner because he suffered so much.

Notice how many problems he had in his ministry.

> **Are they ministers of Christ? (I speak as a fool) I am more; in labours more abundant, in stripes above measure, in prisons more frequent, in deaths oft. Of the Jews five times received I forty stripes save one.**
>
> **Thrice was I beaten with rods, once was I stoned, thrice I suffered shipwreck, a night and a day I have been in the deep;**
>
> **In journeyings often, in perils of waters, in perils of robbers, in perils by mine own countrymen, in perils by the heathen, in perils in the city, in perils in the wilderness, in perils in the sea, in perils among false brethren; In weariness and painfulness, in watchings often, in hunger and thirst, in fastings often, in cold and nakedness.**
>
> **2 Corinthians 11:23-27**

Notice Paul's philosophy of life. It is only through tribulation that we will enter the kingdom of God.

> **...WE MUST THROUGH MUCH TRIBULATION ENTER INTO THE KINGDOM OF GOD.**
>
> **Acts 14:22**

Three Funerals

Years ago, I had a terrible experience in my ministry. Within one year, three of my pastors died mysteriously. The first one died on the evening of Friday, 27 October 2000. I had a call from his wife that her husband was ill and in the clinic. Within an hour I had another call on my mobile phone from one of my doctor pastors.

She said, "Bishop, Pastor Charles is dead."

I said to her, "Do you understand what you are saying?"

I remember exactly where I was when I got this call. I couldn't believe my ears. He was a perfectly normal person. He had even had lunch in my house the day before.

I drove straight to the clinic and there I saw his wife of only seven months in tears, sitting outside the ward. She was scared and did not even know what had happened. As I walked into the room, I saw for the first time, one of my own sons in the ministry, a promising young man, just 27 years old, lying dead on the bed.

That was one of the most pitiful and saddest nights of my life. As I watched his wife weep over her husband's dead body, I wondered what we had done to deserve this. At his funeral, we encouraged ourselves in the Lord and tried to reassure his wife. I didn't know that within a year I would be back in the business of burying pastors and comforting their widows.

Two weeks later, I had another call telling me that one of my pastors was very ill. Initially, he was being treated at a private hospital but we moved him to the intensive care unit of a bigger hospital. I remember battling for his life and running around from place to place, trying to get various doctors to attend to him.

I ran around with blood samples trying to save his life. It was all to no avail. Within a few days, he lost consciousness and I eventually had a phone call from the hospital - another Pastor Charles was dead. My heart sunk and depression set in. All strength was gone as I walked home. Another promising young pastor was dead leaving behind a widow with little children.

I thought it was all over, but a few months later, whilst in South Africa ministering, I had a phone call. I had just walked into my hotel room in Pretoria when my Senior Associate Pastor called me from Ghana.

He said, "Pastor Fleischer is dead."

I stuttered, "What.... How... When...?"

By this time, I knew there was something wrong.

You see, in a sense, we were just like the Jerusalem church. Many of the characteristics of the Jerusalem Church could be found in our church. We were blessed, growing, prosperous, powerful, and as they say "we had it going on." It was this event that finally brought my attention to God's plan of church planting for my life.

Do not misunderstand me. God had already used me to establish over two hundred churches. We were into church planting but I had become comfortable with what we had already achieved. I was scared of moving into new territories. I was not so willing to send people anywhere. I had changed, I had backslidden, and I did not even know it.

I was a fearful General, afraid to say to one, "Go and he goeth." I could not bear to send these prosperous pastors and workers to areas that desperately needed churches. My considerations were now different. The "Jerusalem prosperity" had gotten into my head and into my heart. I was thinking of the kind of life people would have in some of these towns and villages. What schools would their children go to? Would these young men ever have enough money to build houses or buy cars?

The Lord asked me, whether those were the considerations I made when I was entering the ministry. The Lord asked me whether our church would be where it is today if considerations of personal well-being and comfort were what had guided us. I knew in my heart that I had backslidden.

Many people think it is hard to be sent. But it is even more challenging to be the one to send people into what may be poverty and death. But I am determined to go all out and not to restrain myself again when it comes to church planting.

I hear the voice of the Spirit saying, *"Send, send, send"*. One time the Lord rebuked me. He said I was training many people but I was not sending them out. He showed me that I needed to balance my training with my sending.

The Jerusalem Church eventually became a church planting ministry but through great difficulty.

> **And Saul was consenting unto his death. And at that time THERE WAS A GREAT PERSECUTION against the church which was at Jerusalem; and they were all scattered abroad throughout the regions of Judaea and Samaria, except the apostles. Therefore they that WERE SCATTERED ABROAD went every where preaching the word.**
>
> **Acts 8:1, 4**

Chapter

5

Church Planting and the Antioch Church

CHAPTER SUMMARY

■ **Seven Things You Should Know about the Church in Antioch**

5.1 The Church in Antioch became the most important church in the New Testament.

5.2 It was in the Antioch Church that believers were first called "Christians".

5.3 The first recorded revival took place in Antioch. Because of this revival, Barnabas was sent to help. The Church in Jerusalem heard of what God was doing in Antioch and was happy to release Barnabas for the Antioch work.

5.4 Barnabas decided to get Paul to join.

5.5 The Apostle Paul made the Antioch Church his home church. He probably felt more at home in The "Antioch Chapel International" than in "Jerusalem Christian Centre".

5.6 There were many prophets and missionary-minded people in Antioch. The Jerusalem church was not so keen on outreaches and missionary work.

5.7 The Antioch Church obeyed the voice of the Holy Spirit without delay. They boldly sent out their best apostles as missionaries to plant churches.

> **Now there were in the CHURCH THAT WAS AT ANTIOCH certain prophets and teachers; as Barnabas, and Simeon that was called Niger, and Lucius of Cyrene, and Manaen, which had been brought up with Herod the tetrarch, and Saul. As they ministered to the Lord, and fasted, the Holy Ghost said, Separate me Barnabas and Saul for the work whereunto I have called them. And when they had fasted and prayed, and laid their hands on them, they sent them away. So they, being sent forth by the Holy Ghost, departed unto Seleucia; and from thence they sailed to Cyprus.**
>
> **Acts 13:1-4**

Seven Things You Should Know about the Church in Antioch

1. The Church in Antioch became the most important church in the New Testament.

Some disciples from Cyprus and Cyrene went to Antioch and started a church there. Initially Antioch was just an offshoot of the ministry in Jerusalem.

> **Now they which were scattered abroad upon the persecution that arose about Stephen travelled as far as Phenice, and Cyprus, and Antioch, preaching the word to none but unto the Jews only.**
>
> **Acts 11:19**

2. It was in the Antioch Church that believers were first called "Christians".

> **And when he had found him, he brought him unto Antioch. And it came to pass, that a whole year they assembled themselves with the church, and taught much people. And the disciples were CALLED CHRISTIANS FIRST IN ANTIOCH.**
>
> **Acts 11:26**

3. The first recorded revival took place in Antioch. Because of this revival, Barnabas was sent to help. The Church in Jerusalem heard of what God was doing in Antioch and was happy to release Barnabas for the Antioch work.

> **Then tidings of these things came unto the ears of the church which was in Jerusalem: and they sent forth Barnabas that he should go as far as Antioch.**
>
> **Acts 11:22**

4. Barnabas decided to get Paul to join.

5. The Apostle Paul made the Antioch Church his home church. He probably felt more at home in The "Antioch Chapel International" than in "Jerusalem Christian Centre".

6. There were many prophets and missionary-minded people in Antioch. The Jerusalem church was not so keen on outreaches and missionary work.

> **Now there were in the church that was at Antioch certain prophets and teachers; as Barnabas, and Simeon that was called Niger, and Lucius of Cyrene, and Manaen, which had been brought up with Herod the tetrarch, and Saul.**
>
> **Acts 13:1**

7. The Antioch Church obeyed the voice of the Holy Spirit without delay. They boldly sent out their best apostles as missionaries to plant churches.

> **As they ministered to the Lord, and fasted, THE HOLY GHOST SAID, SEPARATE ME BARNABAS AND SAUL for the work whereunto I have called them.**
>
> **Acts 13:2**

Paul and Barnabas did not see much power when they were in Antioch. It was when they moved out that they experienced signs and wonders. The miracles we read about in the book of Acts are the miracles that happened when Paul and Barnabas were out planting churches.

The great difference between the Antioch Church and the Jerusalem Church was in their response to the command of Jesus. The Antioch Church heard exactly the same command to plant churches as the Jerusalem Church did. May we follow the example of the Antioch Church. May we promptly obey the instruction to plant churches. There is no need to wait for persecution and trouble before we get involved in church planting.

Chapter

6

Preaching, Teaching and the Planting of Churches

CHAPTER SUMMARY

In the next few chapters, I will be outlining the mysteries of preaching, teaching and healing; the strategy that Jesus Christ Himself used to generate hundreds of thousands of churches in different nations, cultures and languages.

- **9 Suggestions for God**

9.1. Perhaps God would set up several large universities.

9.2 Perhaps God would build the biggest hospital in the world to cater for many sick people.

9.3 Perhaps God would provide potable water for thousands of villages.

9.4 Perhaps God would construct the largest hydroelectric dam to provide electricity.

9.5 Perhaps God would set up relief centres to cater for the refugees and displaced children of the world.

9.6 If God became a man, perhaps He would build many orphanages.

9.7 If God became a man He would probably set up great businesses so that He could finance the work of God.

9.8 If God became a man, He would build schools to cater for all children of school- going age. This would reduce illiteracy in the world and greatly improve the lot of many people.

9.9 If God became a man, He would join some political parties in order to gain influence to help the world. Perhaps He would help the world better by being a president.

■ If God Became A Man

9.10 If God were to become a man, His entry into this world would be unusual. And sure enough, Jesus was born of a virgin amidst many unusual circumstances.

9.11 If God were to become a man, He would probably speak the greatest words ever spoken. His words would probably never be forgotten. This is exactly what has happened. Even though Jesus never wrote a book, or recorded a tape, His words are still echoing through the centuries.

9.12 If God became a man, He would be sinless and perfect. Sure enough, Jesus was the perfect man. He did no sin.

9.13 If God did become a man He would overcome the problems that have plagued mankind through the centuries. He would conquer sickness and disease. That is exactly what Jesus did. All kinds of diseases and sicknesses were banished from the presence of the Lord.

9.14 If God became a man, He would control the elements that He created. That is what Jesus did. He exercised power over the wind and the rain. He even walked on the sea that He had created.

9.15 If God became a man for a brief period, His visit to the Earth, no matter how brief, would always be remembered. It would be referred to as the time God visited us. Surely the visit of Christ has never been forgotten. In fact the entry and exit of Christ are marked annually by the whole wide world. Two thousand years after the visit of Christ, Easter and Christmas are still worldwide events.

9.16 If God became a man, He would overcome man's greatest enemy - Death. The Lord Jesus calmly predicted that He would die and rise up after three days. He seemed to have no fear of death. He conquered death and the grave and Hell for us that we might not have to go there.

9.17 If God became a man we know that He would spend His time doing the maximum good for all mankind.

Preaching, teaching and healing are the key activities that give rise to the formation of churches. Jesus Christ understood that His Father had chosen these little understood methods to establish the church.

Through Jesus' ministry, millions of churches have sprung up virtually everywhere in the world. Truly this is the hand of God and this is God's method of establishing His church.

> **And Jesus went about all the cities and villages, teaching in their synagogues, and preaching the gospel of the kingdom, and healing every sickness and every disease among the people.**
>
> **Matthew 9:35**

The use of much money, administrative techniques, handing out of gifts and building of schools and hospitals has never produced the same results that the three and a half years of Jesus' ministry did.

Indeed, a lasting church has been born. Two thousand years is not enough time to quench the power of three years of preaching, teaching and healing.

As you read the following chapters about preaching and teaching, your duty is to allow God to build faith in you. You must believe in this humble and "foolish" method of church formation. The highest kind of delusion is to think that we can do anything better than Christ did. He said, "It is enough that the servant be as his master".

> **It is enough for the disciple that he be as his master, and the servant as his Lord...**
>
> **Matthew 10:25**

I have often wondered what God would do if He became a man. There are so many problems in the world and not enough solutions. In general, we know that God would do good things and solve people's problems. Here are some ideas about what God could do if He appeared on this Earth for a brief period.

■ 9 Suggestions for God

1. Perhaps God would set up several large universities.
2. Perhaps God would build the biggest hospital in the world to cater for many sick people.
3. Perhaps God would provide potable water for thousands of villages.
4. Perhaps God would construct the largest hydroelectric dam to provide electricity.
5. Perhaps God would set up relief centres to cater for the refugees and displaced children of the world.
6. If God became a man, perhaps He would build many orphanages.
7. If God became a man He would probably set up great businesses so that He could finance the work of God.
8. If God became a man, He would build schools to cater for all children of school- going age. This would reduce illiteracy in the world and greatly improve the lot of many people.

9. If God became a man, He would join some political parties in order to gain influence to help the world. Perhaps He would help the world better by being a president.

But God did become a man. God did take on the form of a man for a brief period.

> **Let this mind be in you, which was also in Christ Jesus: Who, being in the form of God, thought it not robbery to be equal with God: But made himself of no reputation, and took upon him the form of a servant, AND WAS MADE IN THE LIKENESS OF MEN: AND BEING FOUND IN FASHION AS A MAN, he humbled himself, and became obedient unto death, even the death of the cross.**
>
> **...Wherefore God also hath highly exalted him, and given him a name which is above every name: That at the name of Jesus every knee should bow, of things in heaven, and things in earth, and things under the earth; And that every tongue should confess that Jesus Christ is Lord, to the glory of God the Father.**
>
> **Philippians 2:5-11**

How do we know that God became a man? What evidence do we have that God actually became a man? We know for these reasons.

1. If God were to become a man, His entry into this world would be unusual. And sure enough, Jesus was born of a virgin amidst many unusual circumstances.

> **Behold, a VIRGIN SHALL BE WITH CHILD, and shall bring forth a son, and they shall call his name Emmanuel, which being interpreted is, God with us.**
>
> **Matthew 1:23**

Over 109 prophecies were fulfilled by Jesus' coming into this world.

2. If God were to become a man, He would probably speak the greatest words ever spoken. His words would probably never be forgotten. This is exactly what has happened. Even though Jesus never wrote a book, or recorded a tape, His words are still echoing through the centuries.

> **For he taught them as one having authority, and not as the scribes.**
>
> **Matthew 7:29**

3. If God became a man, He would be sinless and perfect. Sure enough, Jesus was the perfect man. He did no sin.

> **Who did NO SIN, neither was guile found in his mouth:**
>
> **1 Peter 2:22**

4. If God did become a man He would overcome the problems that have plagued mankind through the centuries. He would conquer sickness and disease. That is exactly what Jesus did. All kinds of diseases and sicknesses were banished from the presence of the Lord.

> **When the even was come, they brought unto him many that were possessed with devils: and he cast out the spirits with his word, and HEALED ALL THAT WERE SICK:**
>
> **Matthew 8:16**

5. If God became a man, He would control the elements that He created. That is what Jesus did. He exercised power over the wind and the rain. He even walked on the sea that He had created.

> **And when the disciples saw him WALKING ON THE SEA, they were troubled, saying, It is a spirit; and they cried out for fear.**
>
> **Matthew 14:26**

6. If God became a man for a brief period, His visit to the Earth, no matter how brief, would always be remembered. It would be referred to as the time God visited us. Surely the visit of Christ has never been forgotten. In fact the entry and exit of Christ are marked annually by the whole wide world. Two thousand years after the visit of Christ, Easter and Christmas are still worldwide events.

7. If God became a man, He would overcome man's greatest enemy - Death. The Lord Jesus calmly predicted that He would die and rise up after three days. He seemed to have no fear of death. He conquered death and the grave and Hell for us that we might not have to go there.

> **But is now made manifest by the appearing of our Saviour JESUS CHRIST, WHO HATH ABOLISHED DEATH, and hath brought life and immortality to light through the gospel:**
>
> **2 Timothy 1:10**

8. If God became a man we know that He would spend His time doing the maximum good for all mankind.

> **How God anointed JESUS OF NAZARETH with the Holy Ghost and with power: WHO WENT ABOUT DOING GOOD, and healing all that were oppressed of the devil; for God was with him.**
>
> **Acts 10:38**

The Maximum Good

Dear friend, let us ask ourselves what activities Christ engaged Himself in during His brief stay on earth. Was it the building of schools and hospitals? Was it the building of orphanages and providing of electricity and water? The answer is NO! We can find out what Jesus did by reading the four gospels.

In particular, there is a Scripture that summarizes the activities of Christ on earth. I want you to read it carefully.

> **And Jesus went about all the cities and villages, TEACHING in their synagogues, and PREACHING the gospel of the kingdom, and HEALING every sickness and every disease among the people.**
>
> **Matthew 9:35**

This Scripture shows us that the main activities that God engaged in when on Earth were preaching, teaching and healing. These three activities must have been the most beneficial to the human race. "That is why He engaged himself in them." More good was done to this world by the preaching, the teaching and the healing of Christ Jesus. If there were anything better or more helpful, He would have done it. This preaching, teaching and healing has given birth to thousands of churches.

WE CAN SAFELY CONCLUDE THAT THE MOST IMPORTANT AND HIGHEST FORM OF ASSISTANCE GIVEN TO ANY COMMUNITY ON THIS EARTH MUST BE PREACHING, TEACHING AND HEALING. Of course I don't think that any of us would purport to be wiser than God!

I often marvel when people ask me why I have left the medical field for the ministry. I suppose they think that giving out medicine is the highest form of assistance any human being could render to a community.

I agree that the practice of medicine is a very noble and benevolent activity - what would we do without doctors? But Jesus has shown us the highest and the best kind of help you could ever give to mankind.

It is sad that pastors in the ministry are often pressurized to leave their role of preaching, teaching and healing. Subtle psychological pressure is exerted on them until they feel that doing something more secular is more beneficial. The highest form of deception is to think you are wiser than God. The ultimate delusion is to think that you can have a greater impact than Christ did.

It is time to understand that preaching, teaching and healing are what the world needs. The world is waiting for preachers. The world is waiting for teachers. God is raising an army of preachers and teachers who will do His will. By preaching, teaching and healing, the Lord Jesus has brought forth thousands of churches, which have lasted thousands of years.

The church has done more good to this world than the UN, WHO and the UNHCR put together. Definitely the church has done more good to this world than most governments have. All this good is the result of Jesus' preaching, teaching and healing for three and a half years.

I utterly reject the statements of those who say that a church becomes relevant only when it gets involved in social work. The church becomes relevant when it gets involved in preaching teaching and healing. That is what God would have done and that is what we should do. The wisdom of God is foolishness to men. God has chosen that by the foolishness of preaching, man should be saved.

> **For after that in the wisdom of God the world by wisdom knew not God, it pleased God BY THE FOOLISHNESS OF PREACHING TO SAVE THEM THAT BELIEVE.**
>
> **1 Corinthians 1:21**

People used to tell me how helpful I would be to the community as a doctor, but I tell you that I am of greater benefit now that I am a preacher. I believe the greatest calling upon anyone is the call to preach. The best way we can help humanity is to preach, to teach and to pray for healing. That is why you must pray for the power to preach, for the grace to become a teacher and for the grace to heal the sick. When God became a man, He gave Himself to preaching.

Chapter

7

Why Preaching is Powerful

CHAPTER SUMMARY

Preaching ministers life to condemned people! Jesus said, "The words I speak onto you are spirit and life." This and other reasons make preaching very powerful. Find out why in this chapter.

1. Preaching Attacks the Root of Man's Problem

Sin Is the Root of All Our Woes

The world is full of sinners on their way to Hell. No matter how good you are, your sins are manifest to God. Anyone who thinks he is righteous before God is suffering from one of the highest kinds of deception.

The only thing that gives us a right standing before God is the blood of Jesus. Unfortunately some teachings in the body of Christ have led to the deception that we are semi perfect beings who have a right to be in Heaven.

Let me give you a few examples of people I know you respect. You will notice that as they got to know God they became more humble and even uncertain of their standing with God.

Apostle Paul

The Apostle Paul graduated downward in his opinion of himself. He moved from being the highest of the apostles to the worst of sinners. This is real growth in humility.

i. First, he saw himself as not being inferior to any of the apostles.

> **... for in nothing am I behind the very chiefest apostles...**
>
> **2 Corinthians 12:11**

ii. He later considered himself as the least of these same apostles.

> **For I am the least of the apostles, that am not meet to be called an apostle, because I persecuted the church of God.**
>
> **1 Corinthians 15:9**

iii. After a while, he stopped comparing himself with the apostles and likened himself to the least of the saints.

> **Unto me, who am less than THE LEAST OF ALL SAINTS, is this grace given, that I should preach among the Gentiles the unsearchable riches of Christ;**
>
> **Ephesians 3:8**

iv. Finally, at the end of his life and in one of his last letters, he did not bother to compare himself to an apostle or a saint. He had concluded that he was the chief of sinners.

> **This is a faithful saying, and worthy of all acceptation, that Christ Jesus came into the world to save SINNERS; OF WHOM I AM CHIEF.**
>
> **1 Timothy 1:15**

Job

Job was described by God as an upright and perfect man who eschewed evil. However when Job came into contact with the Lord he realized that he was actually a very evil person. He said, "I abhor myself."

> **I know that thou canst do every thing, and that no thought can be withholden from thee. Who is he that hideth counsel without knowledge? therefore have I uttered that I understood not; things too wonderful for me, which I knew not. Hear, I beseech thee, and I will speak: I will demand of thee, and declare thou unto me. I have heard of thee by the hearing of the ear: but now mine eye seeth thee. WHEREFORE I ABHOR MYSELF, and repent in dust and ashes.**
>
> **Job 42:2-6**

Peter

The Apostle Peter was fishing one day when the Lord showed up. When he realized that the one standing by him was Jesus, he was filled with a sense of sinfulness and he said, "I am a sinful man". The presence of God always reveals our deepest corruption.

> **When Simon Peter saw it, he fell down at Jesus' knees, saying, Depart from me; for I AM A SINFUL MAN, O Lord.**
>
> **Luke 5:8**

Daniel

Daniel was a holy prophet greatly loved by the Lord. However when he came into the presence of the Lord, he said "my comeliness has turned in me into corruption". Once again you see a holy man of God who realizes his sinfulness when he is in the presence of God.

> **And I Daniel alone saw the vision: for the men that were with me saw not the vision; but a great quaking fell upon them, so that they fled to hide themselves. Therefore I was left alone, and saw this great vision, and there remained no strength in me: for my "COMELINESS WAS TURNED IN ME INTO CORRUPTION." and I retained no strength. Yet heard I the voice of his words: and when I heard the voice of his words, then was I in a deep sleep on my face, and my face toward the ground.**
>
> **And, behold, an hand touched me, which set me upon my knees and upon the palms of my hands. And he said unto me, O Daniel, a man greatly beloved, understand the words that I speak unto thee, and stand upright: for unto thee am I now sent. And when he had spoken this word unto me, I stood trembling.**
>
> **Daniel 10:7-11**

All this goes to prove that there is none righteous, no not one.

> **As it is written, There is none righteous, no, not one:**
>
> **Romans 3:10**

It is the presence of this pervading sin that is destroying the whole world. Sin is the reason for all the problems in the world. Sin is the root cause of all our woes. That is why preaching is the most important remedy for the problems of mankind. Preaching attacks man's problem at its very root.

Sin Leads All Men to their Death

> **Wherefore, as by one man sin entered into the world, and death by sin; and SO DEATH PASSED UPON ALL MEN, FOR THAT ALL HAVE SINNED: (For until the law sin was in the world: but sin is not imputed when there is no law. Nevertheless death reigned from Adam to Moses, even over them that had not sinned after the similitude of Adam's transgression, who is the figure of him that was to come. But not as the offence, so also is the free gift. For if through the offence of one many be dead, much more the grace of God, and the gift by grace, which is by one man, Jesus Christ, hath abounded unto many.**
>
> **Romans 5:12-15**

Death has passed onto all men because of sin. The sin in our lives leads to death. The Bible also says when sin is finished it brings forth death.

> **Then when lust hath conceived, it bringeth forth sin: AND SIN, when it is finished, BRINGETH FORTH DEATH.**
>
> **James 1:15**

Death is the inescapable end for all human beings. The very fact that we die indicates the presence of sin. Every time you see someone dying, remember that sin has completed its work. Death is the only natural consequence of sin.

Sin Is Behind All the Causes of Death

The presence of sin opens the door to all the known causes of death including the cancers, HIV, incurable diseases, sickness, accidents and old age. The diseases of this world can all be attributed to our sinfulness. As you will notice, none of the human attempts at helping mankind have eradicated the presence of sin and death. So preaching is the only solution that offers life to a human race sentenced to death.

> **In him was life; and the life was the light of men.**
>
> **John 1:4**

No hospital can promise you life. No medical cure can offer you life. The UN cannot solve your problem of death. There is a death sentence on all of us and only Jesus can give us new life. Jesus said, "I came that you might have life".

The Death Sentence

I remember watching a documentary of a young man who had been sentenced to death in America. It was a sad and moving true story of this black man who was alleged to have killed a policeman. He denied ever killing the policeman and many people believed that he was truly innocent. For six long years, legal battles raged, as lawyers, family and friends tried to get him off death row. Finally, his options ran out and there were no further appeals that he could make.

It was an amazing documentary. They filmed this man up until a few minutes before his execution. His family and friends were invited for a last dinner. They all gathered around and had dinner with him.

Finally it was time for them to go and they hugged him one by one till no one was left. He was then escorted to a private room where he had the opportunity to talk to his pastor and then to his lawyer. Within an hour, the execution had been carried out. After the execution his lawyer and his pastor were interviewed. I remember in particular the question his pastor was asked.

"What was the last thing you said to him?" someone asked. The pastor answered, "I told him that all of us were under a death sentence, the only difference is that most of us do not know the day of our execution."

As I pondered over those words, I thought to myself how true they were. We are indeed under a death sentence. All of us will have to die whether we like it or not. It is just a matter of time till the sentence will catch up with us. It is only Jesus who can deliver us from this death sentence and give us new life. He said, "I am the way, the truth and the life." This is why preaching is so important. This is what differentiates preaching from all other kinds of human assistance. Preaching ministers life to condemned people! Jesus said, "the words I speak onto you are spirit and life."

2. Preaching Releases the Power of God

For I am not ashamed of THE GOSPEL OF CHRIST: FOR IT IS THE POWER OF GOD unto salvation to every one that believeth; to the Jew first, and also to the Greek.

Romans 1:16

HE SENT HIS WORD, and healed them, and delivered them from their destructions.

Psalm 107:20

I once had a visiting preacher from Switzerland who made a remark about my church. He said, "Your church is like a giant youth group". He continued, "There are so many young people in your church."

Up until then, I had not really noticed that our church was full of young people. Initially, I thought it was not a compliment for someone to say that my church was full of young people. However, as time went by, I realized that it took the power of God to get young people into church. You see, young people are full of energy and youthful lusts. There are certain desires that are found more in young people. When the church is full of young people, it is a sign that the power of God is present.

The police cannot change young people. Moral codes cannot restrict wild young men. The fear of going to prison doesn't even seem to inhibit people today. However, I know something that has the power to convert the most hardened sinner. Is it not amazing that people who would not listen to anyone - parents, teachers or advisors are "arrested" by the Word of God and are changed forever? Truly, the preaching of the cross is the power of God.

From a very early age I have served the Lord. I have followed Him with all my heart. What could make a young man like me give up his profession and become a preacher? This is the power of God at work. Preaching always releases power and that power has the ability to change people. That is why you must be a preacher. This is because preaching has the ability to release power.

3. Preaching Gives Hope

For whatsoever things were written aforetime were written for our learning, that we through patience and comfort of the scriptures MIGHT HAVE HOPE.

Romans 15:4

Many people come to church with hopeless and discouraging situations hanging over their heads. As the "Word of God" comes to them, discouragement and hopelessness are driven away. Like chaff before a strong wind, discouragement and desperation are forced to fly away. The preaching of the Word of hope keeps men alive.

The Mouse Survived because of Hope

I once read about an experiment in which a mouse was put into a deep bucket of water in a dark room. There was absolutely no light in this room. After about three minutes, the mouse drowned in the bucket. A mouse of similar weight and size was put in the same bucket of water and in the same dark room. This time, a little glimmer of light was allowed to seep through. This second mouse kept swimming for about three days before it finally drowned. What was the difference between the two mice? The thin ray of light that the second mouse saw gave it so much hope. The hope for survival kept the mouse swimming. This is a wonderful story that illustrates how hope can keep a man alive until his miracle comes. We hardly talk about hope, but without hope there can be no faith. Faith is the assurance of the things you are hoping for. As people receive hope through preaching, faith is built up.

4. Preaching Saves Lives.

For after that in the wisdom of God the world by wisdom knew not God, it pleased God by the foolishness of preaching TO SAVE THEM that believe.

1 Corinthians 1:21

God has chosen that by the foolishness of preaching, people should be saved. Preaching saves lives.

The Anointing of Jonah

In the last days, the anointing of Jonah the preacher will be released on men. The anointing of Jonah was sufficient to convert hardened sinners to the ways of God. Nineveh was a city of wicked people and Jonah was initially afraid of preaching there. The entire city was eventually converted when Jonah preached. Jonah did not perform any miracles. He did not slay anyone in the Spirit nor did he have strange manifestations of the Spirit. However, he had a strong preaching anointing and it was strong enough to change an entire city. I see that preaching anointing coming upon your life! You shall preach to thousands! Men's hearts will change when they hear you preaching. People will be saved when they come under your preaching ministry.

The book of Genesis shows us that people lived much longer than they do today.

> **And all the days of Enoch were THREE HUNDRED SIXTY AND FIVE YEARS:**
>
> **Genesis 5:23**

> **And all the days of Methuselah were NINE HUNDRED SIXTY AND NINE YEARS: and he died.**
>
> **Genesis 5:27**

> **And all the days of Lamech were SEVEN HUNDRED SEVENTY AND SEVEN YEARS: and he died.**
>
> **Genesis 5:31**

As sin increased, life became shorter. The Bible is very specific about how God shortened life from hundreds of years to one hundred and twenty years.

> **And the LORD said, My spirit shall not always strive with man, for that he also is flesh: yet his days shall be AN HUNDRED AND TWENTY YEARS.**
>
> **Genesis 6:3**

It seems life was shortened even further from one hundred and twenty years to seventy years.

> **The days of our years are THREESCORE YEARS AND TEN; and if by reason of strength they be fourscore years, yet is their strength labour and sorrow; for it is soon cut off, and we fly away.**
>
> **Psalm 90:10**

The earlier generations were having "four hundred year" birthday parties. They had children when they were hundred and fifty years old. Today we are overjoyed if someone gets to the age of eighty. By the time someone is forty, he seems to be an elderly person. Why has the body begun to give up so early?

> **And it came to pass, when men began to multiply on the face of the earth, and daughters were born to them, That the sons of God saw the daughters of men that they were fair; and they took them wives of all which they chose. And the Lord said, My spirit shall not always strive with man, for that he also is flesh: yet his days shall be an hundred and twenty years.**
>
> **Genesis 6:1-3**

900 years was reduced to 120 years because of fornication with the sons of God! Fornication shortened the lives of the people by 800 years. 90% of their lives were taken away because of fornication. The Bible

declares "when sin is finished it brings forth death." Think about that. Eight hundred years was cut off because of fornication. Do you see how sin shortened our lives?

As you can see, the problem is spiritual and not physical. That is why physical remedies cannot be the solution for mankind. It is a sin problem. And the solution is the preaching of Christ Jesus and Him crucified. When "sin is finished", the agents of death i.e. heart disease, lung disease, cancer, sickle cell disease, skin diseases, HIV, tumors, accidents, fights, kidney failure begin to make arrangements to kill us - whether by making the kidney stop, or by causing a car accident. Everyone has a different method by which the death sentence is carried out.

When Christ came to this Earth, He knew He was dealing with a complex problem. That is why He didn't just heal everyone. He knew that the problem was deeper. He knew why certain ailments had fastened themselves onto certain people. It was not just an issue of being ill. He knew that there was more to it than that!

When the Lord looked at our situation, He thought of the best way to help us, the best way to lengthen our lives. God planned the best way to save us from the things to which we were bound legally. That is why He came around preaching, teaching and healing. It pleased God that by the foolishness of preaching, He would save people.

Preaching and teaching solves your problems. First of all, your spirit is redeemed. You do not have to go to Hell anymore. Thank God that by the power of preaching, your soul will be saved from eternal damnation.

When preaching has powerfully saved your soul, other areas of your life begin to be affected as well. After the soul has prospered, your health will be affected by this salvation. Your financial life is also affected after the salvation of your soul. God's Word begins to heal and solve all problems from within.

> **Beloved, I wish above all things THAT THOU MAYEST PROSPER and be in health, EVEN AS THY SOUL PROSPERETH.**
>
> **3 John 2**

Thinking naturally, you realize that if a person decides to do away with fornication, he reduces his exposure to the HIV infection and therefore death. When you hear the Word of God, and decide to marry instead of running around with different people, you reduce your exposure to many diseases. Preaching and teaching saves our lives in many ways we cannot even imagine.

Because of the Word of God, we decide to stop smoking and drinking alcohol. This extends our lives automatically by many years. You are at far less risk from cancer, heart disease, HIV, gonorrhea and depression when you live in line with the Word of God. A preaching tape can save your life. I believe in listening to preaching tapes. You will discover that the Word you get from the tape is "life to all who find it and health to all your flesh."

> **My son, attend to my words…For they are life unto those that find them, and health to all their flesh.**
>
> **Proverbs 4:20, 22**

Expose yourself to preaching and you will be exposing yourself to many blessings. Jesus came preaching and teaching.

> **He sent his word, and healed them, and delivered them from their destructions.**
>
> **Psalm 107:20**

The healings were just signs. When people came just for signs He told them they were evil. He taught us that loving signs and wonders without loving His preaching is an evil thing.

> **But he answered and said unto them, An evil and adulterous generation seeketh after a sign; and there shall no sign be given to it, but the sign of the prophet Jonas:**
>
> **Matthew 12:39**

Preaching starts churches! God wants more preachers! God wants you to preach! Preaching and teaching will heal your marriage. It will reduce the tendency to fight; it will bring peace. Preaching will prevent divorce. Preaching changes lives!

Chapter

8

Why Teaching Is Powerful

CHAPTER SUMMARY

- **The Differences between Preaching and Teaching**

8.1 When the Word comes to us by preaching, our souls are ministered to.

8.2 When the Word comes by teaching, our minds are largely involved in receiving.

8.3 Teaching has a more lasting effect than preaching does.

8.4 Teaching is sometimes more difficult to assimilate. Preaching enters 8.quickly but fades quickly.

8.5 Preaching is moving and stirring.

8.6 Preaching is more outwardly impressive than teaching.

8.7 Teaching is not as popular as preaching. If I were to put a preacher on the left and a teacher on the right, most people would prefer the preacher.

8.8 Most people would think that a preacher is a more powerful man of God compared to the teacher. If the masses were asked to vote, they would probably choose the preacher because he would be more impressive.

8.9 Teachers usually have churches that grow steadily. This is because the truth is taught line upon line; and precept upon precept. When building a house, the blocks are laid systematically until you get an orderly and lasting structure.

■ Three Direct Effects of Teaching

8.10 The Teaching of the Word Brings Light

8.11 The Teaching of the Word Is the Sword in Action

8.12 The Teaching of the Word Is the Planting of the Seed

One day Jesus was teaching in the temple and a demon shouted, "Leave us alone." The Word is powerful: it attacks demons directly.

> **And they went into Capernaum; and straightway on the sabbath day he entered into the synagogue, and taught. And they were astonished at his doctrine: for he taught them as one that had authority, and not as the scribes. And there was in their synagogue A MAN WITH AN UNCLEAN SPIRIT; AND HE CRIED OUT, SAYING, LET US ALONE; what have we to do with thee, thou Jesus of Nazareth? art thou come to destroy us? I know thee who thou art, the Holy One of God.**
>
> **Mark 1:21-24**

Exposing yourself to the teaching of the Word brings healing to your life. Jesus did not just teach people. The people came to hear Him and after that, to be healed of their diseases.

> **But so much the more went there a fame abroad of him: and great multitudes came together TO HEAR, AND TO BE HEALED by him of their infirmities.**
>
> **Luke 5:15**

There are many accounts in the Gospels where people came to hear Him teach. The reason God is going to raise you up as a powerful teacher is so that you can affect people's lives. God is going to raise you up as a powerful preacher and teacher.

> **And he came down with them, and stood in the plain, and the company of his disciples, and a great multitude of people out of all Judaea and Jerusalem, and from the sea coast of Tyre and Sidon, which came TO HEAR HIM, AND TO BE HEALED OF THEIR DISEASES;**
>
> **Luke 6:17**

Jesus always taught the Word of God before ministering healing. After teaching the Word, He would heal the sick. He did this because the Word of God attacks the source of your sickness. God reaches to the root cause of your poverty. As people are exposed to the Word, healing always comes.

> **My son, attend to my words...For they are life unto those that find them, and health to all their flesh.**
>
> **Proverbs 4:20, 22**

Jesus said, "The words that I speak unto you, they are spirit and they are life" (John 6:63).

Life comes into you as you hear the Word. Thank God that through the teaching of His Word, your spirit comes alive. It is important to continue to expose yourself to the teaching of the Word.

We realize that the Word whether through preaching or teaching, heals us and saves us.

What is the difference between preaching and teaching?

The Differences between Preaching and Teaching

a. When the Word comes to us by preaching, our souls are ministered to.

b. When the Word comes by teaching, our minds are largely involved in receiving.

c. Teaching has a more lasting effect than preaching does.

d. Teaching is sometimes more difficult to assimilate. Preaching enters quickly but fades quickly.

e. Preaching is moving and stirring.

f. Preaching is more outwardly impressive than teaching.

g. Teaching is not as popular as preaching. If I were to put a preacher on the left and a teacher on the right, most people would prefer the preacher.

h. Most people would think that a preacher is a more powerful man of God compared to the teacher. If the masses were asked to vote, they would probably choose the preacher because he would be more impressive.

i. Teachers usually have churches that grow steadily. This is because the truth is taught line upon line; and precept upon precept. When building a house, the blocks are laid systematically until you get an orderly and lasting structure.

Three Direct Effects of Teaching

1. The Teaching of the Word Brings Light

Demons abide in darkness. Demons of frustration, early death and poverty abide in darkness.

Pride is a type of darkness. That is why there are evil spirits where there is pride. Thank God, His Word is light.

> **Thy word is a lamp unto my feet, and a light unto my path.**
>
> **Psalm 119:105**

When the Word is taught, a light comes on in our hearts. Demons, which dwell in darkness, are forced to run away. As the Word is taught, spiritual illumination takes place. That is why people can be healed while teaching goes on. As the Word is taught, your life is transformed. The devil knows this and that is why he does not like you to listen to teaching.

That is why he does not want you to have a tape. A tape can change your life forever. One tape can take you to Heaven. One tape can turn you into a pastor! One tape can turn you from being a divorcee into a happily married person. A tape can give you stability, turn you from madness to sanity and give you health. The devil does not like teaching because of the light it brings.

Years ago, when I was doing my housemanship at the Korle Bu Teaching Hospital, I lived in one of the hostel rooms. There was a time that my room was plagued with rats and mice.

Every night when I got to my room, I would put on the lights and suddenly, these rats would race all over the room and toward a particular hole in the ceiling. It would send shivers down my spine because I hated rats (and these were big ones). These rats were having a field day while I was out and when the lights were off. But as soon as I turned on the lights, they felt exposed and fled.

So it is with us when the light of the Word of God comes on in our lives. Demons are exposed and they are forced to flee. This is exactly how the Word of God operates. The Word throws light on the demons that dwell and flourish in the darkness of our lives!

When the light of the Word of God is off in your life (when you do not go to church, or when there is no Word in your life) demons are free to invade you. Demons look for darkness within human beings. The darkness of unforgiveness, bitterness, hatred, lust, lying, pride, disobedience, sin or anger. That is why the Bible enjoins us not to give any place to the devil. The presence of these dark areas opens the door for demonic maneuvers and operations.

> **Neither give place to the devil.**
>
> **Ephesians 4:27**

You shall be free from satanic oppression when you put on the light of the Word.

2. The Teaching of the Word Is the Sword in Action

> **...and the sword of the Spirit, which is the word of God:**
>
> **Ephesians 6:17**

> **For the word of God is quick, and powerful, and sharper than any twoedged sword...**
>
> **Hebrews 4:12**

Teaching is powerful. It drives away demons, mental diseases, blindness, uncleanness, pride, stupidity, lust, spiritual problems and poverty. The sword pricks the demons and drives them away.

Since the demons do not want to be hurt by the sword of the Word they do all they can to stop you from taking in the teaching. That is why sometimes demons make you sleep in church, lest you hear the teaching. Hearing comes before healing!

> **...which came to hear him and to be healed...**
>
> **Luke 6:17**

3. The Teaching of the Word Is the Planting of the Seed

> **The sower soweth the Word.**
>
> **Mark 4:14**

A seed is planted when you hear the Word. If the preacher says, "you shall be blessed and prosperous," a seed is planted in your life. The words of a teacher are seeds, which grow and become mighty trees.

The reason why many people in my church want to be pastors is because of the seeds I have planted. What you plant is what you reap. Even in ordinary life the things we say about our children come to pass as they grow. As you continue to call your child an angel he grows up to have a sweet spirit and vice versa.

As you tell your congregation that it shall be well with them and that the Lord is their keeper and the shade upon their right hand, these promises come to pass.

The Lord is your helper, you shall live and not die, and it shall be well with you. You shall have the baby you thought you would not have!

Chapter

9

Church Planting and the Tent Ministry

CHAPTER SUMMARY

In the next two chapters, I will be sharing about the tent ministry. As far as I am concerned, it is only through the tent ministry that church planting will be possible on a large scale.

■ Seven Things You Should Know about the Tent Ministry

9.1 The tent ministry is actually the lay ministry.

9.2 It is possible to combine secular work with the ministry.

9.3 The best New Testament example of the tent ministry is the Apostle Paul. The best Old Testament example is the Prophet Daniel.

9.4 Sometimes it is the will of God for you to be a tent minister and sometimes it is the will of God for you to be in full-time ministry.

9.5 The tent ministry will be a prominent ministry in the last days.

9.6 Paul practised the tent ministry so that others would follow his good example.

9.7 The tent ministry can be just as fruitful as full-time ministry.

One of the greatest keys to extensive church planting is the tent ministry. The tent ministry is the sacrifice of pastors and evangelists, who labour without being paid for their services. The enormity of the work is such that, without the strategy of tent ministry, very few churches will be planted. Almost every ministry I know has ground to a halt because of mounting bills, and the high cost of maintaining staff. It is virtually IMPOSSIBLE for the church to employ the people that are needed for the work of God.

The tent or lay ministry is not popular in some circles. In some cultures everybody must be paid for his services. The organist must be paid! The guitarist must be paid! The sound controller must be paid and the pastor constantly seeks a higher salary for his services.

Dear friend, most of the ripened harvest fields are in the poor regions of the world. How will the poor people of the Earth be reached in their poverty? Most of these people cannot pay for the services of good pastors and evangelists. The ministry of unpaid pastors and evangelists is the key to continued church planting.

Where the sacrificial nature of Christianity is compromised, church planting comes to an end. The church was born on the sacrifice of Christ. The church grew through the sacrifice of the apostolic church. Once again, the church will only expand through sacrifice

Seven Things You Should Know about the Tent Ministry

Paul left Athens and went to Corinth, where he met Aquila, a Jewish man from Pontus. Not long before this, Aquila had come from Italy with his wife Priscilla, because Emperor Claudius had ordered the Jewish people to leave Rome. Paul went to see Aquila and Priscilla and found out that they were tent makers. PAUL WAS A TENT MAKER TOO. So he stayed with them and they worked together.

EVERY SABBATH, PAUL WENT TO THE JEWISH MEETING PLACE. He spoke to Jews and Gentiles and TRIED TO WIN THEM OVER.

Acts 18:1-4 (Contemporary English Version)

1. The tent ministry is actually the lay ministry.

It is the ability to combine secular work with real ministry. The best example of the tent ministry was the Apostle Paul's ministry. It is so called because Paul was a tent maker.

2. It is possible to combine secular work with the ministry.

It is a ministry in which you support yourself. You may ask, "Is this the way that God planned for ministry to be?" "Does the Bible not teach that they that preach the gospel must live of the gospel?"

Even so hath the Lord ordained that they which preach the gospel should live of the gospel.

1 Corinthians 9:14

I combined being a medical student with ministry. I know many people who are effectively ministering the Word of God and continuing in their professions.

Paul was the great church planter of the New Testament. He was able to accomplish great things for the Lord whilst he supported himself with the tent making business. The tent ministry is even more vital for church planting today.

3. The best New Testament example of the tent ministry is the Apostle Paul. The best Old Testament example is the Prophet Daniel.

Daniel had three jobs:

i. He was a Member of Parliament for the Babylonian Province.

> **Then the king made Daniel a great man, and gave him many great gifts, and made him ruler over the whole province of Babylon, and chief of the governors over all the wise men of Babylon.**
>
> **Daniel 2:48**

ii. He was the Second Vice President to Belshazzar.

> **Then commanded Belshazzar, and they clothed Daniel with scarlet, and put a chain of gold about his neck, and made a proclamation concerning him, that he should be the third ruler in the kingdom.**
>
> **Daniel 5:29**

iii. He was the Prime Minister during the rule of Darius.

> **It pleased Darius to set over the kingdom an hundred and twenty princes, which should be over the whole kingdom; And over these three presidents; of whom Daniel was first: that the princes might give accounts unto them, and the king should have no damage.**
>
> **Daniel 6:1-2**

4. Sometimes it is the will of God for you to be a tent minister and sometimes it is the will of God for you to be in full-time ministry.

In one breath, the right thing to do is to be fully supported by the ministry, but in another breath the right thing to do is to support yourself. It is important that we follow the leading of the Spirit at all times. Isn't it amazing that the right thing can become the wrong thing ("Anomia"), because God said so? Paul declared that he was instructed by the Lord to be both full and hungry.

> **I know both how to be abased, and I know how to abound: every where and in all things I AM INSTRUCTED BOTH TO BE FULL AND TO BE HUNGRY, both to abound and to suffer need.**
>
> **Phillippians 4:12**

5. The tent ministry will be a prominent ministry in the last days.

Paul's ministry still lives on today. The best way some people can help in the ministry is to be like Paul - secular work during the week and then "reasoning in the synagogue with the Jews on the Sabbath day".

> **And because he was of the same craft, he abode with them, and wrought: for by their occupation they were tentmakers. AND HE REASONED IN THE SYNAGOGUE every sabbath, and persuaded the Jews and the Greeks.**
>
> **Acts 18:3-4**

6. Paul practised the tent ministry so that others would follow his good example.

> **I now place you in God's care. Remember the messages about his great kindness! This message can help you and give you what belongs to you as God's people.**
>
> **I have never wanted anyone's money or clothes. You know how I HAVE WORKED WITH MY OWN HANDS TO MAKE A LIVING FOR MYSELF and my friends. By everything I did, I showed you how you should work to help everyone who is weak.**
>
> **Remember that our Lord Jesus said, "More blessings come from giving than from receiving." After Paul had finished speaking, he knelt down with all of them and prayed.**
>
> **Acts 20:32-36 (Contemporary English Version)**
>
> **For yourselves know how ye ought to follow us: for we behaved not ourselves disorderly among you;**
>
> **Neither did we eat any man's bread for nought; but wrought with labour and travail night and day, that we might not be chargeable to any of you:**
>
> **Not because we have not power, but to make ourselves an ensample unto you to follow us.**
>
> **2 Thessalonians 3:7-9**

I am talking about a fruitful and lasting ministry. Paul was not a reverend minister who did nothing for God. He was indeed an anointed and powerful church planter. It is time for many who are called to follow this good example.

7. The tent ministry can be just as fruitful as full-time ministry.

I do not know of anyone who will say that the Apostle Paul was inferior to any of the other apostles. He laboured more abundantly and travelled more extensively. He planted more churches than any one else did. He was truly an effective, anointed and fruitful pastor.

Chapter

10

How and When to Flow in the Tent Ministry

CHAPTER SUMMARY

■ **How and When to Flow in the Tent Ministry**

10.1 When it is the only way you can live in certain geographical locations and do the ministry.

10.2 The tent ministry helps you avoid becoming a burden.

10.3 The tent ministry will enable you to survive in ministry without being paid by the church.

10.4 The tent ministry enables you to be free from all men.

10.5 The tent ministry enables you to enter the ministry whether finances permit it or not.

10.6 The tent ministry will ensure that you play a part in this great ministry.

10.7 Some people are able to relate better with unpaid ministers of the gospel who maintain their secular jobs.

10.8 To flow in the tent ministry, you need to be sacrificial.

10.9 Selfishness is the greatest hindrance to the tent ministry.

10.10 Laziness is another great hindrance to the tent minister.

10.11 Use a lot of wisdom when practising the tent ministry.

10.12 Become a financial support by engaging in the tent ministry.

10.13 The tent ministry fights idleness in the church.

■ Four Ways that Paying Pastors Can Hinder the Ministry

a. Building projects are slowed down or stopped.

b. The church cannot buy the equipment it needs.

c. Missionaries cannot be sent out.

d. Immature church members who do not understand why pastors should be paid certain amounts of money could cause trouble in a new church. Some people simply do not understand why people who work for God should be blessed. I advise pastors to keep their lives as private as possible.

1. When it is the only way you can live in certain geographical locations and do the ministry.

When missionaries were sent from Switzerland to Ghana two hundred years ago, they had to support themselves on the mission field. Many of them became farmers, teachers etc. There was obviously no way of making bank transfers to these missionaries. It is important for ministers to understand that there are times when secular work gives you the legitimate basis for being in particular places. I have pastors in certain countries that do secular work simply because they need to be able to live in that country legally.

Are we ready to do anything for Christ Jesus our Lord? If you have to hold down a secular job so that you can live and minister in a strange land will you do it? Is that asking too much? How do you think the Prophet Daniel was able to flourish in Babylon? He maintained his job as a Member of Parliament.

2. The tent ministry helps you avoid becoming a burden.

> **Neither did we eat any man's bread for nought; but wrought with labour and travail night and day, THAT WE MIGHT NOT BE CHARGEABLE TO ANY OF YOU.**
>
> **2 Thessalonians 3:8**

There are times when being a full-time minister is a burden to a small congregation. Sometimes a particular person in the congregation is burdened by the fact that he has to support you all the time. There are times I wouldn't want to stay in certain people's homes. This is because I feel that my presence is burdensome to my host.

Once we went out preaching and we got back home very late. It was past midnight. Our hostess came out of her room looking very sleepy and tired.

She said, "Oh, are you guys back?"

"What time is it?" she mumbled.

We found out that it was about one a.m.

"Would you like to eat?" She asked.

I thought to myself, "Of course I would like to eat. I am starving; I haven't eaten the whole day." But I muttered some non-committal and diplomatic answer.

My hostess continued, "I have some fish in the freezer, I can defrost it and make some stew."

I was quiet but she continued, "I have some rice which I can also prepare."

Then she asked again, "Would you like me to make the food?"

I thought to myself, "Should a Christian ask someone to defrost fish and boil rice at one a.m.?" I decided that I didn't want to be a burden to this dear hostess.

I smiled sheepishly and said, "Oh it is alright."

I went to bed on an empty stomach. I simply did not want to be a burden to my hostess.

I have learnt to carry secret supplies of food with me when I travel so that I do not become a burden to people. This is what Paul was talking about. He did not want his ministry to become a burden to anyone.

3. The tent ministry will enable you to survive in ministry without being paid by the church.

> **Neither did we eat any man's bread for nought; but wrought with labour and travail night and day, that WE MIGHT NOT BE CHARGEABLE TO ANY OF YOU:**
>
> **2 Thessalonians 3:8**

Four Ways that Paying Pastors Can Hinder the Ministry

a. Building projects are slowed down or stopped.

b. The church cannot buy the equipment it needs.

c. Missionaries cannot be sent out.

d. Immature church members who do not understand why pastors should be paid certain amounts of money could cause trouble in a new church. Some people simply do not understand why people who work for God should be blessed. I advise pastors to keep their lives as private as possible.

4. The tent ministry enables you to be free from all men.

> **For though I be FREE FROM ALL MEN, yet have I made myself servant unto all, that I might gain the more.**
>
> **1 Corinthians 9:19**

Many times people who give money develop an attitude because of the size of their donations. It is very important for pastors to be free from the negative attitudes of church members. The prophets were warned "don't be afraid of their faces". This is because the facial expression on people's faces often intimidates us. There are times when our being tent ministers eliminates the need for people's gifts and donations hereby eliminating these bad attitudes.

> **For though I preach the gospel, I have nothing to glory of: for necessity is laid upon me; yea, woe is unto me, if I preach not the gospel!**
>
> **For if I do this thing willingly, I have a reward: but if against my will, a dispensation of the gospel is committed unto me. What is my reward then? Verily that, when I preach the gospel, I may make the gospel of Christ without charge, that I abuse not my power in the gospel.**
>
> **For though I BE FREE FROM ALL MEN, yet have I made myself servant unto all, that I might gain the more.**
>
> **1 Corinthians 9:16-19**

5. The tent ministry enables you to enter the ministry whether finances permit it or not.

> **For though I preach the gospel, I have nothing to glory of: for NECESSITY IS LAID UPON ME; yea, woe is unto me, if I preach not the gospel!**
>
> **For if I do this thing willingly, I have a reward: but if against my will, a dispensation of the gospel is committed unto me. What is my reward then?**
>
> **Verily that, when I preach the gospel, I may make the gospel of Christ without charge, that I abuse not my power in the gospel.**
>
> **1 Corinthians 9:16-18**

Paul said, "Woe is me if I preach not the gospel." Sometimes we do not have a choice! We have to do his will whether there is a salary or not.

That is exactly how I feel. I do not think that I have a choice. I am bound to obey God. I feel that if I do anything apart form preaching His Word, God will destroy me. I have heard other pastors say the same thing.

One pastor said to me, "Before I was in the ministry, I knew that God had called me. At one time I felt that God would kill me if I didn't go into the ministry."

He continued, "That is why I am in full-time ministry today."

6. The tent ministry will ensure that you play a part in this great ministry.

> **And this I do for the gospel's sake, that I MIGHT BE PARTAKER thereof with you.**
>
> **1 Corinthians 9:23**

Many of us may never play a part in building the kingdom unless we do it as lay people. Are all apostles? Are all prophets? Are all evangelists? Are all pastors? Obviously not! But thank God you can support yourself and make a significant contribution to the ministry as a tent minister.

7. Some people are able to relate better with unpaid ministers of the gospel who maintain their secular jobs.

God is merciful and He makes a way for all kinds of people to be saved. There are people who have their own impressions of full-time ministers and find it difficult to receive from them. They find it easier to receive from tent ministers who are obviously not in the ministry for the money.

8. To flow in the tent ministry, you need to be sacrificial.

The tent ministry is essentially sacrificial in nature. Unlike what many people think, the ministry is very tiring and stressful. Even paid ministers are often called upon to sacrifice.

Many pastors do not have a normal family life because their family life is constantly interrupted by the incessant demands of the congregation. When it is holiday time, instead of the pastor having time for his family, he has to attend various church and social functions. No one really cares about it until the pastor's children become rebels.

There are many pastors' children who hate the ministry. They feel the ministry steals their parents from them. Besides this, there are many stresses that come to the pastor and his wife by virtue of the position they hold. He is the focus of every spiritual attack; many people do not know this.

One time, when Israel went to war with Syria, the Syrian king gave a very revealing command to his generals and to his captains. He said to them; "do not fight with anyone. DON'T FIGHT WITH THE GREAT AND DON'T FIGHT WITH THE SMALL, FIGHT ONLY WITH THE KING PERSONALLY."

> **But the king of Syria commanded his thirty and two captains that had rule over his chariots, saying, Fight neither with small nor great, SAVE ONLY WITH THE KING OF ISRAEL.**
>
> **1 Kings 22:31**

You can see from this instruction that no target was significant enough except the King of Israel himself. The king represents the leader or the pastor who becomes the focus of the attack.

When a person takes on the sacrifices of ministry without being paid, he makes a double sacrifice.

> **Am I not an apostle? am I not free? have I not seen Jesus Christ our Lord? are not ye my work in the Lord? If I be not an apostle unto others, yet doubtless I am to you: for the seal of mine apostleship are ye in the Lord. Mine answer to them that do examine me is this, HAVE WE NOT POWER TO EAT AND TO DRINK? HAVE WE NOT POWER TO LEAD ABOUT A SISTER, A WIFE, AS WELL AS OTHER APOSTLES, AND AS THE BRETHREN OF THE LORD, AND CEPHAS? Or I only and Barnabas, have not we power to forbear working?**
>
> **Who goeth a warfare any time at his own charges? who planteth a vineyard, and eateth not of the fruit thereof? OR WHO FEEDETH A FLOCK, AND EATETH NOT OF THE MILK OF THE FLOCK? Say I these things as a man? or saith not the law the same also? For it is written in the law of Moses, Thou shalt not muzzle the mouth of the ox that treadeth out the corn. Doth God take care for oxen? Or saith he it altogether for our sakes? For our sakes, no doubt, this is written: that he that ploweth should plow in hope; and that he that thresheth in hope should be partaker of his hope. If we have sown unto you spiritual things, is it a great thing if we shall reap your carnal things? If others be partakers of this power over you, are not we rather?**
>
> **Nevertheless we have not used this power; but suffer all things, lest we should hinder the gospel of Christ. Do ye not know that they which minister about holy things live of the things of the temple? and they which wait at the altar are partakers with the altar? Even so hath the Lord ordained that they which preach the gospel should live of the gospel. But I have used none of these things: neither have I written these things, that it should be so done unto me: for it were better for me to die, than that any man should make my glorying void. For**

> **though I preach the gospel, I have nothing to glory of: for necessity is laid upon me; yea, woe is unto me, if I preach not the gospel! For if I do this thing willingly, I have a reward: but if against my will, a dispensation of the gospel is committed unto me. What is my reward then? Verily that, when I preach the gospel, I may make the gospel of Christ without charge, that I abuse not my power in the gospel.**
>
> **1 Corinthians 9:1-18**

The tent ministry will test your Christian character. Virtues like self-control and temperance will be tested. When I was a medical student and doctor on the wards of the hospital, I had to sacrifice my resting times for the ministry. When people were watching TV, I could not afford that luxury. I didn't have time for useless socializing and chatting. All my spare time was taken up.

9. Selfishness is the greatest hindrance to the tent ministry.

Selfishness is the principal reason why many people do not get involved in the lay or tent ministry. Most people are basically self-centred in their outlook of life; they have no concerns for anyone except themselves. They are engrossed in the little world they have built around themselves. Selfishness speaks of self-centredness, self-concern, self-awareness, self-help and self-gratification.

A selfish person can never be a servant of the Lord. Selfishness makes you think about yourself but ministry makes you think about people you don't even know. The Apostle Paul lamented about this phenomenon. He noted that all men seek for their own welfare.

He said, "No one cares for the things of the Lord."

> **For I have no man likeminded, who will naturally care for your state. For all seek their own, not the things which are Jesus Christ's.**
>
> **Phillippians 2:20-21**

We are all selfish by nature but the deeper we get in the Lord, the less selfish we become. The barrenness of most Christians is a result of the spirit of selfishness.

Who cares if they go to Hell? At least I am going to Heaven. Who cares if there is a village somewhere that has not heard the gospel? At least my family and I are okay. Who cares if somebody is sick and lying on the hospital ward? At least I am well. Who cares if there is some dirty old prisoner languishing in jail? At least I am free! That is the spirit of selfishness at work in the church and the Christian.

If Jesus were selfish, He would not have left His throne in glory and come to this rotten world.

10. Laziness is another great hindrance to the tent minister.

Most people are not prepared to work for anyone much less to work without being paid.

11. Use a lot of wisdom when practising the tent ministry.

> **Behold, I send you forth as sheep in the midst of wolves: be ye therefore wise as serpents, and harmless as doves.**
>
> **Matthew 10:16**

Because of the intrinsic hatred for God and the ministry, many people would like to pick on someone who claims to be a pastor.

> **There was a man of the Pharisees, named Nicodemus, a ruler of the Jews: The same came to Jesus by night, and said unto him, Rabbi, we know that thou art a teacher come from God: for no man can do these miracles that thou doest, except God be with him.**
>
> **John 3:1-2**

People often look out for your faults at work or at school. They say things like, "I am surprised that a pastor would do that. I never knew that pastors also come to work late."

I remember when I worked at the Korle Bu Teaching Hospital, the biggest hospital in my country, as a doctor; I never told them I was a pastor. I knew that at the slightest opportunity they would use it against me. While a student and a pastor, I never indicated that I was even religious. I didn't want them to know anything about me.

It is foolishness to go announcing to the whole world that you are a pastor or a religious leader. Jesus said we should be as wise as serpents. What does it mean to be as wise as a serpent? What wisdom does the serpent have? It has the wisdom to exist quietly in the midst of people who hate it.

The serpent is universally hated and killed on sight, with no questions asked. And yet, snakes flourish all around us. There are millions of snakes all over the world. How has the snake managed to live and multiply in a world that hates it utterly? By discretion, carefulness, judgment, secrecy, prudence and caution!

12. Become a financial support by engaging in the tent ministry.

> **I have shewed you all things, how that so labouring ye ought to SUPPORT THE WEAK, and to remember the words of the Lord Jesus, how he said, It is more blessed to give than to receive.**
>
> **Acts 20:35**

It is amazing that a large amount of financial support comes from my lay pastors. Many times when there is a special appeal for financial support, it is my lay pastors (tent ministers) who often support me most.

When you are involved in the ministry; you know the needs of the ministry. Tent ministers are a good support base for every church.

13. The tent ministry fights idleness in the church.

> **For we hear that there are some which walk among you disorderly, working not at all, but are busybodies.**
>
> **2 Thessalonians 3:11**

After people have been in the church for some years, they seem to know all your sermons. No matter what tricks you use, they are able to see through the message and identify where it is coming from.

I remember preaching a powerful series in church. People were really blessed. Many commented on how powerful the services had been. Then I had a note. This note was from a long-standing church member.

He wrote, "Dear pastor we were tremendously blessed by your message tonight." He continued, "This is exactly what you preached five years ago. You only changed the title". He went further and enumerated the messages from where he claimed I had duplicated my current series. Then to reassure me he said, "We were mightily blessed anyway so keep on doing the good work".

You see, it is important that Christians get involved with the ministry otherwise they become critical busy bodies, analyzing and commenting on things that they do not even understand.

> **LORD, my heart is not haughty, nor mine eyes lofty: neither do I exercise myself in great matters, or in things too high for me.**
>
> **Psalm 131:1**

Chapter

11

Barrenness and Church Planting

CHAPTER SUMMARY

As we study this chapter, God will reveal to us the causes of barrenness in our lives, churches and ministries. There are several Hebrew and Greek words that are translated "barren" or "barrenness". These words throw light on the subject of spiritual and ministerial barrenness.

- **Five Hebrew Words**

11.1 AQAR - (Genesis 11:30; Genesis 25:21; Deuteronomy. 7:14; Judges 13:2, 3; 1 Samuel 2:5;)

11.2 SHAKOL - (Leviticus 26:22; 2 Kings 2:19, Deuteronomy 32:25)

11.3 MELECHAH - (Psalms 107:34; Jeremiah 17:6)

11.4 OTSER - (Proverbs 30:16)

11.5 TSIYAH - (Isaiah 41:18; Psalm 63:1)

- **Two Greek Words**

11.6 STEIROS - (Luke 1:7, 36; Luke 23:29; Galatians 4:27)

11.7 ARGOS - (2 Peter 1:8)

When barrenness is taken away, fruitfulness is always the result. Barrenness is the number one cause for a lack of church planting in the modern Christian church. But God wants us to be fruitful. God wants us to plant churches. In order to be fruitful you must understand what barrenness really is. Some pastors are barren. No matter what they do, their ministries never flourish. This is the problem God wants to deal with in our churches.

In the next few chapters, we will be studying the concept of spiritual barrenness and how it affects church planting. Barrenness is the number one cause for a lack of church planting in our generation. There are a lot of activities and a lot of programmes but there is little or no church planting.

There are several Hebrew and Greek words that are translated "barren" or "barrenness". These words throw light on the subject of spiritual and ministerial barrenness. Let us consider each of these words as definitions of barrenness.

Five Hebrew Words

1. AQAR - (Genesis 11:30; Genesis 25:21; Deuteronomy. 7:14; Judges 13:2, 3; 1 Samuel 2:5;)

This word means "the destruction or removal of generative organs'. It also means "To have non-functioning organs; to be barren or sterile".

It is used in reference to people like Sarah, Zelelponi; the mother of Sampson and Rebecca.

> **There shall nothing cast their young, nor be BARREN (AQAR), in thy land: the number of thy days I will fulfill.**
>
> **Exodus 23:26**

Churches or individuals suffering from "AQAR" barrenness are deficient in the generative aspects of ministry. This means they are deficient in the outreach and fruit bearing aspects of church life. They are unable to give birth to other churches. Such churches have many activities but programmes that generate new churches are absent.

Every minister must consider the outreach aspect of his ministry. Do you have crusades? Do you plant new churches? The absence of crusades, breakfast meetings, witnessing campaigns and church planting, shows a deficiency in the generative aspect of your ministry.

Barren people also receive the Word and probably have the tapes. They may even be involved in other activities of the church. They are seen at prayer meetings and become "fat" spiritually.

However, such people will not be involved in church planting, evangelism or soul winning. They have a deficiency in their spiritual generative organs.

2. SHAKOL - (Leviticus 26:22; 2 Kings 2:19, Deuteronomy 32:25)

This means "to miscarry, to suffer abortion, to be bereaved of children, to be barren, to cast your young, to make childless and to be deprived of children".

> **I will also send wild beasts among you, which shall ROB YOU OF YOUR CHILDREN, and destroy your cattle, and make you few in number; and your high ways shall be desolate (SHAKOL).**
>
> **Leviticus 26:22**

Such churches or ministers cannot keep the souls that God gives them. As you can see, they constantly cast their young and suffer abortions. Such ministers cannot sustain the growth and are unable to continue in the things that God gives to them.

Many churches receive large numbers of visitors and even converts. You must work on keeping these converts. You must make sure that your visitors come again. I always pray over my members. "Lord when they go, let them come back to church. As they come back, let them come with more people." This kind of prayer counteracts "SHAKOL" barrenness. I pray that each member becomes a minister and that each minister gives birth to a church.

Another reason why such churches are unable to break out is that they attack their young leaders. They kill fresh blood. The leaders do not allow mavericks to flourish around them. The anointing on all of us is greater than the anointing on one person. You must allow fresh leaders and pastors to be released under your ministry. The fastest growth always occurs when there are multiple ministers working together.

3. MELECHAH - (Psalms 107:34; Jeremiah 17:6)

This word means "a salted land, a desert or a barren land". It speaks of "no produce" and "no life". The land is dead to any kind of seed.

People suffering from "MELECHAH" are spiritually salted lands. In spite of what you pour into them, they are unable to bear fruit. They are incapable of germinating seeds.

A cursory glance at every congregation will reveal several "salted lands" staring at you. Mercy and atonement! They have been in the church for many years and have heard many sermons. They have been anointed and prayed for specially, but still cannot bear fruit. Much is poured into them but little can be expected from these salted ones.

There are also salted churches. No matter the input, the church does not grow. No new churches are planted from that church. Until the salted land is healed, there will be no fruit.

> **For he shall be like the heath inthe desert, and shall not see when good cometh; but shall inhabit the parched places inthe wilderness, in A SALT LAND and not inhabited.**
>
> **Jeremiah 17:6**

A pastor who is a salted land does not give rise to other pastors of his own kind. He remains in the church he pastors, but cannot bring forth other pastors. Break out of the salted state and start to think of birthing many more churches.

I remember the story of a church that could not grow. No matter what happened and no matter who preached, there was no break through. One day a visiting pastor was waiting on the Lord and he had a vision. Way up in the ceiling he saw a demon sitting above the congregation. This evil spirit had greatly affected the church for many years.

God had opened the pastor's eyes to see the "salt" that was making the church barren. He dealt with the evil spirit and commanded it to leave. After that experience, the church began to grow in leaps and bounds.

I believe there are real salted situations that need the healing hand of God. I see God removing the saltiness from your life, church and ministry!

4. OTSER - (Proverbs 30:16)

This Hebrew word means "to inclose, to hold back and to maintain'. It also means "to close up, to restrain, and retain". In addition, it means "to shut up, to withhold and to stop".

> **The grave; and the BARREN (OTSER) womb; the earth that is not filled with water; and the fire that saith not, It is enough.**
>
> **Proverbs 30:16**

People suffering from this kind of barrenness hold back intentionally. They know a lot, but they hold back and refuse to be fruitful. Pastors with "OTSER" barrenness have the finances and the anointing to plant churches. However, they give their strength to other things like orphanages, schools and social work. Some of them are more concerned with being politically influential and socially acceptable. The drive for church planting is restrained.

Such people can do many things for the Lord but are restrained and hold back their talents. These are usually experienced people in the Lord who could do much more for Jesus.

Often they have decided to give their strength and talents to other things. In your congregation, you will notice people who are leaders of Old Boys Associations or even political groups. They have time for politics, soccer, MBA's, PhD's and other activities. However, when it comes to the work of God, they are inclosed and restrained. They are reserved when it comes to prayer and worship, but vocal when it comes to discussing politics and other issues. These are the people suffering from "OTSER".

5. TSIYAH - (Isaiah 41:18; Psalm 63:1)

This word speaks of being "parched and barren". It speaks of "a drought, a dry land and a wilderness".

> **I will open rivers in high places, and fountains in the midst of the valleys: I will make the wilderness a pool of water, and the DRY LAND (TSIYAH) springs of water.**
>
> **Isaiah 41:18**

This kind of church is often dry of the Spirit. It is a wilderness devoid of worship, prayer and the lifting up of hands. Such churches and individuals are very secular and logical in their approach to life and the ministry. Spiritual dryness and the lack of worship is a true cause of barrenness.

Introducing new worship songs will often fight against this kind of barrenness. Sometimes changing your worship leader will lead to a major change in your church. Changing your choir leader and the type of songs your choir sings can greatly affect your church. Perhaps if the choir were to sing songs about soul winning and reaching the lost, church planting would begin. Do not wait forever to make the changes you need to make.

■ Two Greek Words

1. STEIROS - (Luke 1:7, 36; Luke 23:29; Galatians 4:27)

> **And they had no child, because that Elisabeth was BARREN (STEIROS), and they both were now well stricken in years. And, behold, thy cousin Elisabeth, she hath also conceived a son in her old age: and this is the sixth month with her, who was called barren.**
>
> **Luke 1:7, 36**

This word means "to be stiff and unnatural". It speaks of sterility and barrenness. "Stiffness" speaks of people who are unyielding and disobedient to the Word of God. Such people love to look distinguished and diplomatic. Sometimes they pretend to be spiritual but in reality they are not.

Churches often have these unspiritual and stiff people sitting in the front row. This can prevent growth and induce the "STEIRAS" atmosphere that does not allow growth. You will notice that growing churches are full of lively, exuberant and excited people dancing and praising the Lord. It is time to remove the "deep freezers" from the prominent positions we have given them. The church is not a "who is who" parade.

2. ARGOS - (2 Peter 1:8)

This word means "inactive, unemployed lazy and useless". It also speaks of "being idle, slow and barren". Surprisingly, laziness is one of the principle causes of unfruitfulness in ministry. Lazy people are inactive in church. Their laziness makes them useless to God.

> **For if these things be in you, and abound, they make you that ye shall neither be BARREN NOR UNFRUITFUL (ARGOS) in the knowledge of our Lord Jesus Christ.**
>
> **2 Peter 1:8**

Unfortunately the church is made up of masses of spiritually inactive people. To break this type of barrenness, it is important to preach about diligence. It is important to teach the congregation that they must win souls for the Lord.

Chapter

12

How to Diagnose Barrenness

CHAPTER SUMMARY

One way to diagnose barrenness is to look at how the dictionary defines it.

■ Twenty Definitions of Barrenness

12.1 To be barren means to be unfruitful.

12.2 To be barren means to be sterile.

12.3 To be barren means to be childless, heirless and issueless.

12.4 Barrenness means you are non-productive.

12.5 To be barren means to be deficient in production.

12.6 Barrenness means you are not conceiving at all or producing at all.

12.7 A barren person is someone who produces in very small quantities.

12.8 A barren land is a wasteland.

12.9 Barren trees do not produce the normal fruit.

12.10 Barrenness speaks of bleakness.

12.11 To be barren is to be depleted.

12.12 To be barren is to be deserted.

12.13 Barrenness speaks of dryness.

12.14 A barren thing can be described as not being copious.

12.15 A barren land is a scanty land.

12.16 Barrenness is sometimes dullness.

12.17 A barren individual does not produce after his kind.

12.18 Barrenness speaks of wanting or needing the power of conception.

12.19 Barren places are impoverished.

12.20 Barren places are un-tillable.

It is important to diagnose barrenness when it exists in the ministry. The diagnosis of a problem often leads to the solution. Even in medicine, 80% of our problems are solved when the diagnosis is made.

Many ministries are operating under a spirit of barrenness. Many pastors are unaware that they can have a greater level of fruitfulness. In this chapter, I will show you some signs you must look out for in the ministry.

If Jesus were standing by you, He would say these words to you

> **Herein is my Father glorified, THAT YE BEAR MUCH FRUIT; so shall ye be my disciples.**
>
> **John 15:8**

How to Diagnose Barrenness in the Church

One way to diagnose barrenness is to look at how the dictionary defines it. If you apply these definitions to your church, you will know whether you are barren or not. God will show you if a spirit of barrenness is in operation.

Let us now look at the dictionary definitions of barrenness and see how they apply to ministry.

Twenty Definitions of Barrenness

1. To be barren means to be unfruitful.
2. To be barren means to be sterile.
3. To be barren means to be childless, heirless and issueless.
4. Barrenness means you are non-productive.
5. To be barren means to be deficient in production.
6. Barrenness means you are not conceiving at all or producing at all.
7. A barren person is someone who produces in very small quantities.
8. A barren land is a wasteland.
9. Barren trees do not produce the normal fruit.
10. Barrenness speaks of bleakness.
11. To be barren is to be depleted.
12. To be barren is to be deserted.
13. Barrenness speaks of dryness.
14. A barren thing can be described as not being copious.
15. A barren land is a scanty land.

16. Barrenness is sometimes dullness.
17. A barren individual does not produce after his kind.
18. Barrenness speaks of wanting or needing the power of conception.
19. Barren places are impoverished.
20. Barren places are un-tillable.

Let us now look at the symptoms of barrenness within the church context. Examine your ministry and see whether barrenness exists.

Barrenness in the Church

Barrenness can be said to exist in a church if any of the following exist:

1. If there is no growth in the number of your church members.
2. If there are no converts or, no growth in the number of converts.
3. If there is no growth in church attendance.
4. If there is no growth in the number of full-time staff.
5. If there is no baptism or, no growth in the number of people baptized.
6. If there is the absence of healings and miracles.
7. If there is no growth in the number of leaders in the church.
8. If there is no increase in the knowledge of God.
9. If there is no growth in the depth of relationships.
10. If there is no growth in the number of visions and dreams given by the Holy Spirit or none at all.
11. If there is no programme to send out missionaries or, to increase the number of missionaries sent out.
12. If there is no growth in the finances of the church.
13. If there is no increase in the number of scriptures you know.
14. If there is no growth in your experience in the ministry.
15. If there is the absence of or, no growth in the outreaches of the church.
16. If there is no growth in the length and depth of your prayer or no prayer at all.
17. If there is no increase in challenges and mountains to overcome.
18. If there is no challenge and inspiration to a greater vision.

19. If there is no growth in understanding.

20. If there is no growth in fellowships and branches.

Now that you have diagnosed the problem, receive the prophecy of the Lord for your ministry. Believe that these words are coming to pass in your life.

> **SING, O BARREN, thou that didst not bear; break forth into singing, and cry aloud, thou that didst not travail with child: for more are the children of the desolate than the children of the married wife, saith the LORD.**
>
> **ENLARGE THE PLACE OF THY TENT, and let them stretch forth the curtains of thine habitations: spare not, LENGTHEN THY CORDS, and strengthen thy stakes; FOR THOU SHALT BREAK FORTH ON THE RIGHT HAND AND ON THE LEFT; and thy seed shall inherit the Gentiles, and make the desolate cities to be inhabited.**
>
> **FEAR NOT; FOR THOU SHALT NOT BE ASHAMED: neither be thou confounded; for thou shalt not be put to shame: for thou shalt forget the shame of thy youth, and shalt not remember the reproach of thy widowhood any more.**
>
> **For thy Maker is thine husband; the LORD of hosts is his name; and thy Redeemer the Holy One of Israel; The God of the whole earth shall he be called.**
>
> **For the LORD hath called thee as a woman forsaken and grieved in spirit, and a wife of youth, when thou wast refused, saith thy God.**
>
> **For a small moment have I forsaken thee; but WITH GREAT MERCIES WILL I GATHER THEE. In a little wrath I hid my face from thee for a moment; but with everlasting kindness will I HAVE MERCY ON THEE, saith the LORD thy Redeemer.**
>
> **Isaiah 54:1-8**

Chapter

13

How to Fight Different Kinds of Barrenness

CHAPTER SUMMARY

- **Fighting the Barrenness of Old Age**

13.1 **Do not transfer the duty of outreach and church planting to anyone else.**

13.2 **Do not reject the prophetic Word.**

13.3 **Believe in God, His prophets and in the preaching of His Word.**

13.4 **Take the practical steps that lead to fruitfulness even if it looks like something for younger people.**

- **Fighting the Barrenness of Familiarity**
- **7 Things Everyone Should Know about Familiarity**

13.5 **Familiarity means to know someone or something very well and in such a way as to cause you to lose your admiration, respect and sense of awe. It also connotes a sense of becoming presumptuous, where a person is too confident in a way that shows a lack of respect.**

13.6 **Familiarity was the cause of Michal's barrenness.**

13.7 **Familiarity is still the cause of spiritual barrenness in Christians today.**

13.8 **Familiarity is the greatest block to receiving God's power from God's men.**

13.9 **No matter how great the gift of God, it is neutralized by familiarity. Jesus was the greatest healer and teacher, yet his anointing was neutralized by the presence of familiar people.**

13.10 **Moses who commanded a pillar of fire by night and a pillar of cloud by day could not impress his own sister Miriam. She criticized him about his marriage and suffered for it. My heart is often closed to those who are familiar towards me. I simply do not flow towards them. I can virtually sense the questions in the hearts of people suffering from familiarity.**

13.11 **Familiarity carves out a road of ministry for anointed people. It directs them away from their colleagues, friends and family. It leads them towards the non-familiar, the poor the forgotten and neglected ones.**

Four Groups That Often Suffer from Familiarity

- **Colleagues**
- **Relatives**
- **Pastors' wives**
- **Close friends and Associates**

Twelve Signs of Familiarity

13.12 **Often sitting at the back of the church.**

13.13 **Yawning.**

13.14 **Sleeping during preaching.**

13.15 **Not buying or listening to tapes.**

13.16 **Not buying and reading books written by your man of God.**

13.17 **Discussing the background of the man of God.**

13.18 **Discussing the family issues of the man of God.**

13.19 **Fault-finding and magnifying faults.**

13.20 **Evaluating and rating men of God.**

13.21 **Not believing the man of God's advice.**

13.22 **Having no regard for the anointing.**

13.23 **Not honouring and appreciating your man of God.**

■ Fighting the Barrenness of Old Age

> **Abram married Sarai, but she was not able to have children.**
>
> **Genesis 11:30 (Contemporary English Version)**

> **Now Sarai Abram's wife bare him no children: and she had an handmaid, an Egyptian, whose name was Hagar.**
>
> **And Sarai said unto Abram, Behold now, the LORD hath restrained me from bearing: I PRAY THEE, GO IN UNTO MY MAID; it may be that I may obtain children by her. And Abram hearkened to the voice of Sarai.**
>
> **And Sarai Abram's wife took Hagar her maid the Egyptian, after Abram had dwelt ten years in the land of Canaan, and gave her to her husband Abram to be his wife.**
>
> **And he went in unto Hagar, and she conceived: and when she saw that she had conceived, her mistress was despised in her eyes.**
>
> **Genesis 16:1-4**

We all know the story of Abraham and Sarah. You could consider Sarah as a type of the church. You could also consider her as a type of minister. Sarah could be likened to a pastor who is not bearing as much fruit as he ought to. Sarah could be likened to a wilderness kind of church in which there is no life.

1. Do not transfer the duty of outreach and church planting to anyone else.

The pastor must lead the congregation to win the souls and bear fruit. According to Genesis 16:1-2, Sarah shifted the responsibility of childbearing to someone else. This was an attempt to overcome the barrenness she was experiencing. She tried to overcome barrenness in the wrong way.

2. Do not reject the prophetic Word.

> **Therefore Sarah laughed within herself, saying, After I am waxed old shall I have pleasure, my Lord being old also?**
>
> **Genesis 18:12**

Prophetic messages can make a difference in your ministry. Believe in the Lord and you shall be established, believe in His prophets and you shall prosper. Sarah laughed when she heard the prophecy about Isaac. Receive the visitation of God for your life through revelations, dreams and the spoken Word.

Years ago, I received a message from a prophet. He saw me carrying a flaming torch and leading many people. He gave this message to me in 1980. Twenty-four years have gone by and this prophecy remains in my heart as a true vision. It encouraged me to do the work of God as a student. It encouraged me to persist in the ministry even after school.

3. Believe in God, His prophets and in the preaching of his Word.

> **And God said unto Abraham, As for Sarai thy wife, thou shalt not call her name Sarai, but Sarah shall her name be.**
>
> **Genesis 17:15**

Walk in your calling. You must overcome the greatest enemies of the faith walk. Walking in fear and intimidation will not lead to fruitfulness in ministry.

4. Take the practical steps that lead to fruitfulness even if it looks like something for younger people.

> **For Sarah conceived, and bare Abraham a son in his old age… And Abraham called the name of his son...Isaac.**
>
> **Genesis 21:2-3**

Decide to be youthful, zealous, emotional, exciting, energetic and adventurous again. This will break the spell and curse of barrenness over your ministry. Sarah had sex with her husband at the age of ninety. No matter what prophecy is spoken over your life, there will always be some practical things you have to do. Isaac was not supernaturally conceived as in the case of Christ Jesus. He was conceived by the normal method of sexual intercourse. Sarah had to undress and act like an energetic young lady with a youthful husband. Abraham and Sarah were forced to engage in sexual happiness in their nineties. Can you imagine a ninety year old, menopausal woman acting like a pretty youthful bride again?

Some ministers act and think like people that are too old. Some amount of youthfulness is needed in the ministry. Youthfulness is necessary for fruitfulness.

■ Fighting the Barrenness of Familiarity

Familiarity is the greatest block to the anointing. It cuts off the flow of the anointing that is needed for church planting and church growth. Ministry is a spiritual thing and unless spiritual principles are obeyed, the ministry dries up and barrenness results.

Michal is a type of barren ministry. Michal suffered from familiarity toward her husband. She paid for it by becoming barren. Many people have become barren in ministry because they became too familiar with the man of God.

> **David went home so he could ask the Lord to bless his family.**
>
> **But Saul's daughter Michal went out and started yelling at him. 'You were really great today!' she said. 'You acted like a dirty old man, dancing half-naked in front of your servants' slave girls' David told her, 'The Lord didn't choose your father or anyone else in your family to be the leader of His people.**
>
> **The Lord chose me and I was celebrating in honour of him. I'll show you how great I can be! I'll even be disgusted to myself. But those slave girls you talked about will still honour me'. Michal never had any children.**
>
> **2 Samuel 6:20-23 (Contemporary English Version)**

7 Things Everyone Should Know about Familiarity

1. Familiarity means to know someone or something very well and in such a way as to cause you to lose your admiration, respect and sense of awe. It also connotes a sense of becoming presumptuous, where a person is too confident in a way that shows a lack of respect.
2. Familiarity was the cause of Michal's barrenness.
3. Familiarity is still the cause of spiritual barrenness in Christians today.
4. Familiarity is the greatest block to receiving God's power from God's men.
5. No matter how great the gift of God, it is neutralized by familiarity. Jesus was the greatest healer and teacher, yet his anointing was neutralized by the presence of familiar people.

> **And he went out from thence, and CAME INTO HIS OWN COUNTRY; and his disciples follow him.**
>
> **And when the sabbath day was come, he began to teach in the synagogue: and many hearing him were astonished, saying,**
>
> **From whence hath this man these things? and what wisdom is this which is given unto him, that even such mighty works are wrought by his hands? IS NOT THIS THE CARPENTER, the son of Mary ...**
>
> **And they were offended at him. AND HE COULD THERE DO NO MIGHTY WORK, save that he laid his hands upon a few sick folk, and healed them.**
>
> **Mark 6:1-3, 5**

This Scripture shows us that Jesus could not perform miracles in His hometown. They knew Him too well to receive Him as the Son of God. They had questions about His parents, His family and His background.

6. Moses who commanded a pillar of fire by night and a pillar of cloud by day could not impress his own sister Miriam. She criticized him about his marriage and suffered for it. My heart is often closed to those who are familiar towards me. I simply do not flow towards them. I can virtually sense the questions in the hearts of people suffering from familiarity.
7. Familiarity carves out a road of ministry for anointed people. It directs them away from their colleagues, friends and family. It leads them towards the non-familiar, the poor the forgotten and neglected ones.

This is where the outsiders come in. They often come in to replace people that have become too familiar with the anointed one.

Four Groups That Often Suffer from Familiarity

1. Colleagues

Usually it is people who know you closely who suffer from familiarity. When I started my church as a medical student, very few of my colleagues were able to receive from me. They knew me too well and would say in their hearts, "Is this not Dag? We know him and we know his class. We saw him struggling at an exam last week. We know when he passes and when he fails! How can this lanky boy call himself a pastor?"

2. Relatives

Relatives also suffer from familiarity. They would say. "Is this not Azoyzoy's (my father's nickname) son? We carried him when he was a baby."

They ask, "Do you remember me? I carried you when you were two years old."

They say, "I knew your father very well."

With this background, how can such people receive me as a man of God?

3. Pastors' wives

Pastor's wives often suffer from severe familiarity. Just like Michal, when everyone is impressed, they are not impressed with their husbands. They say things like, "I know you", "No one knows you better than I do", "I am the only one who can tell you certain things!" "I am not one of those people who give you praise and affirmation in the office!", "If people knew how you really were, they would be surprised", "No one knows what you are really like."

In a sense, they are right about all these things, but the fact is that they are also victims of familiarity!

4. Close friends and associates

These people also experience familiarity. They have been around you for so long and they have seen your vicissitudes. It is easy to slip and slide into familiarity. Sometimes it would be better not to know someone closely in order not to develop an air of familiarity.

Familiarity breeds disloyalty. Familiarity created Judas. Judas is referred to, as "mine own familiar friend". When people are familiar, they lose their respect and they cross boundaries they should never cross. Familiarity makes people say things they should never say.

When Michal spoke against David, she stood in the shoes of a rebel fighting and opposing God's anointed. She became a critic of "the man after God's own heart". David had built a tabernacle but she was not impressed. God called him "a man after mine own heart" but she, a mere mortal, despised him. Imagine that God is impressed but you are not impressed. Isn't it amazing?

Familiarity often stems from jealousy and carnality. Michal was jealous of the girls who seemed to appreciate David's ministry. She disliked the fact that David seemed to be impressed with these young whippersnappers.

> **Then David returned to bless his household. And Michal the daughter of Saul came out to meet David, and said, HOW GLORIOUS WAS THE KING TODAY, who uncovered himself to day in the eyes of the handmaids of his servants, as one of the vain fellows shamelessly uncovereth himself!**
>
> **2 Samuel 6:20**

When Miriam criticized Moses, she no longer saw him as God's anointed. She moved into the flesh and became a disloyal rebel.

And Miriam and Aaron spake against Moses because of the Ethiopian woman whom he had married: for he had married an Ethiopian woman.

Numbers 12:1

Judas was the highest kind of traitor. He paid the ultimate price for allowing himself to be deceived by familiarity.

Yea, mine own familiar friend, in whom I trusted, which did eat of my bread, hath lifted up his heel against me.

Psalm 41:9

Knowledge without Experience

I have had different people becoming close to me at different times in my life. Circumstances can sometimes cause people to associate closely with the man of God. Under these circumstances, the person is susceptible to the spirit of familiarity. It takes spiritual discipline not to become familiar. I have noticed in my life and ministry how people become over familiar when given the slightest chance. Let me just remind you of the definition of familiarity.

Familiarity means, "to know someone or something very well and in such a way as to cause you to lose your admiration, respect and sense of awe. It also connotes a sense of becoming presumptuous, where a person is too confident in a way that shows a lack of respect."

One day, a young lady was having a problem in her marriage. Her husband said to her, "I am going to report you to the Bishop".

She retorted, "I don't care. He also has problems".

I smiled when I heard this. I knew that it was only familiarity that was rearing its head. Perhaps I was wrong to have allowed this person to spend a few nights in our home.

On another occasion, another relative who had spent a few days with our family was having some problems. After counseling this relative, she seemed to have understood what I had shared with her. She thanked me and seemed to be blessed.

Unfortunately, I later heard that she had said that I was a man of knowledge and not experience. What she was saying was that I had no experience in the kind of problem she had and that my advice was therefore theoretical.

I thought to myself, "Today, I have become a man of knowledge without experience. It is only because I allowed this person to relate closely to my family and I, that she had the nerve to make such a comment."

Sometimes it is better to know someone from afar so that you can continue to receive from his ministry. When you are too familiar with your pastor, you can mistakenly see him as a man of knowledge without experience.

Assess Your Familiarity Level

In your relationship with a man of God, are you becoming familiar? The following signs will help you determine to what extent you are familiar. Remember that familiarity is the highest kind of anointing killer. It has the highest form of neutralizing the power of God's gift.

■ Twelve Signs of Familiarity

1. Often sitting at the back of the church.

Familiarity is when you are no longer intrigued and excited about the pastor and his preaching. You do not bother to come near anymore. Familiar people just sit at the back and observe from a distance.

Once I attended a Kenneth Hagin conference in Tulsa, Oklahoma. When I came into the hall, the ushers tried to give me a seat at the back.

I thought to myself, "How can I sit at the back when Kenneth Hagin is preaching. I want to be as near as possible!" I negotiated with the usher and even made a friend.

I told him, "Sir, you don't know where I have come from."

I continued, "I have flown thousands and thousands of miles to be here today. I need to be as near as possible. There is no way I can go upstairs or even to the back."

He seemed to understand and eventually I had my way. Unbelievably, I managed to sit on the second row. I was so excited when Kenneth Hagin walked by my seat as he preached.

You see, when you are familiar, seeing a man of God nearby or from afar makes no difference.

Later on, I had a discussion with the principal of their Bible School. I asked him if they had any problems with their students. To my surprise, he did. Their main problem was familiarity. He said to me. "There are some students who do not come for important conferences like these." He lamented, "This is a great prophet and people come from all over the world to receive from him. But right here, there are students who do not bother to cross the road and come to church".

You see, familiarity breeds contempt. Familiarity is all about knowing someone very well. This causes you to lose your admiration and respect.

2. Yawning

Yawning is often a sign of boredom. A familiar person is presumptuous and arrogantly assumes he knows what is coming. Often, people who yawn during the preaching of the Word are saying, "I know this sermon, I know what is coming. I know his line of thought. This man has nothing new to say," Forgive!

3. Sleeping during preaching.

Sleeping occurs when we are tired. But sometimes it occurs as a result of monotony and boredom, when the man of God fails to intrigue you anymore, you may find yourself sleeping as he preaches.

4. Not buying or listening to tapes.

Someone who listens to preaching tapes has not become familiar with the pastor's voice. He sees it as an opportunity to be continuously blessed by the pastor when he is not around. Have you asked yourself why you do not buy tapes anymore? The answer may be familiarity.

5. Not buying and reading books written by your man of God.

I notice how people come from afar to buy my books. There are times people have travelled many miles to acquire and devour large quantities of my books and tapes. Amazingly my own church members often pass by these same books and tapes and instead call for two meat pies and a bottle of Coca Cola. Familiarity causes you to lose your sense of wonder and intrigue.

6. Discussing the background of the man of God.

Every man of God basically, is a "man". Since he is a man, he goes through what all men go through. No man that God ever chose had a perfect life. He has a past! He has a family. He has failings. He has an imperfect marriage. He has challenges just like every one else. It's easy to pick on any aspect of his natural life and neutralize him. Discussing the man of God in a natural way is a sure sign that you have lost your sense of fascination for him. This is the surest way to cancel out the effect of the anointing on your man of God.

Thumos and Ekplesso

When Jesus preached in His hometown, the Scripture says in Luke 4:28, "when they heard these things, they were filled with wrath.' The word "wrath" in Greek is the word "THUMOS". This means incipient displeasure fermenting in the mind, it speaks of fierceness, indignation (as if breathing hard) and wrath. The familiar people were angry with Jesus" sermon.

But when He preached in Galilee according to Luke 4:32 "they were astonished at His doctrine". The word "astonished" is the Greek word "EKPLESSO" which means to be amazed, astonished and struck with terror.

Notice that there are only four verses between THUMOS and EKPLESSO. Notice also that THUMOS took place in Nazareth, Jesus' hometown. EKPLESSO took place in a city of Galilee about two hundred kilometers from Jesus' hometown of Nazareth.

7. Discussing the family issues of the man of God.

> **Is not this the carpenter, the son of Mary, the brother of James, and Joses, and of Juda, and Simon? and are not his sisters here with us? And they were offended at him.**
>
> **Mark 6:3**

By doing this, you are cutting yourself from receiving God's miracle for your life. When Jesus went to his hometown, there was a long discussion as to who he really was. Someone said, "I know that boy, he is my nephew. He and his father have repaired my wardrobes and cupboards for many years".

Jesus could do very few miracles because of the high level of familiarity and doubt in the city. Do not let familiarity cut off your blessing.

8. Fault-finding and magnifying faults.

Whenever you think of the great men of God you respect, you do not often think of their faults. When there is a visiting preacher, no one considers whether he is impatient or easily angered. No one thinks of whether this man is in debt or whether he has an extravagant lifestyle. All we do is to receive the ministry of this man of God.

However, these are thoughts that occur to us about men of God that we are familiar with. We think, "He must be angry today, this man is not patient." As he preaches we say to ourselves, "We understand what he is saying; why does he not progress to the next point?"

I remember years ago, I had a church member who really enjoyed my messages. She recommended me highly to many people who later joined the church. However as time went by, she became familiar with my preaching and me.

One day after church she said to me, "I think you went over last week's point for too long." She continued, "There was very little time for the new points that you brought up."

A few weeks later, she made another remark, "The repetition in your preaching is too much." After this I noticed the frown on her face each time I preached. This lady eventually stopped coming to church.

She might have been right but what she did not realize was that, I was preaching to people who came to church this week and missed the next week. I virtually had a new crowd every week. I might have had my faults, but God has worked through me in spite of them.

Have you removed the log in your own eye? Why are you concentrating so hard on the speck in the pastor's eye? Familiarity has made you critical.

9. Evaluating and rating men of God.

Democracy in its essential nature, calls on us to evaluate our leaders constantly. This is what enables us to vote for the right person. Unfortunately, many are deceived when they think that this same practice of evaluation must be brought into the church.

I was coming home one day after church when someone asked a question in the car. He asked, "How did you find the sermon?"

The car was quiet for a moment then someone said, "I think he did well, I will give him 70%."

Then an older man said, "No, no, no. He deserves about 49%."

Someone asked "Why 49%, the message wasn't too bad?"

I mused to myself, "This poor pastor is being assessed by his congregation."

10. Not believing the man of God's advice.

When you regard someone highly, you cherish whatever advice he has to offer. As familiarity sets in, it becomes more and more difficult to accept advice. Every time advice is given there is a reason not to follow it.

11. Having no regard for the anointing.

When you become familiar, you no longer relate with a man of God spiritually. The fact that he is even anointed does not occur to you. All you see are natural things. If your eyes are on the natural you will see weakness, dishonour and corruption.

> **So also is the resurrection of the dead. It is sown in CORRUPTION; it is raised in incorruption: It is sown in DISHONOUR; it is raised in glory: it is sown in WEAKNESS; it is raised in power:**
>
> **1 Corinthians 15:42-43**

The anointing for ministry is transferred from one man of God to another. The anointing for church planting is transferred from one person to another. Elisha had an exemplary relationship with Elijah. He called him "father" and served him for many years. He did not lose regard for the anointing because of his closeness. He was the beneficiary of a double portion of one of the greatest anointings.

Not every one suffers from familiarity. Some people are able to stay close and still have a high regard for the anointing. I have people around who have seen my human "weakness", "dishonour" and "corruption" for many years and yet they maintain a sense of awe, fascination and respect for the presence of God upon my life. That is what Elisha did for many years and he received the double portion of the anointing that was on the life of Elijah.

Do not be deceived by the apparent weakness of God's men. The weakness is God ordained. It is intended to filter off unworthy recipients of the grace of God.

Jesus taught us to appear weak in the face of arrogant and aggressive people. Turn the other cheek simply means do not fight. It could even mean act weak! Do not mind if they think you have no power. Is it not a "weakling" who would subject himself to more humiliating slaps?

Is it not a weakling who would allow himself to be cheated of his clothes? But this is the Lord's instruction to us.

> **But I say unto you, That ye resist not evil: but whosoever shall smite thee on thy right cheek, TURN TO HIM THE OTHER ALSO.**
>
> **And if any man will sue thee at the law, and take away thy coat, LET HIM HAVE THY CLOAK ALSO. And whosoever shall compel thee to go a mile, GO WITH HIM TWAIN.**
>
> **Give to him that asketh thee, and from him that would borrow of thee turn not thou away.**
>
> **Matthew 5:39-42**

Sick but Anointed

Now Elisha was FALLEN SICK OF HIS SICKNESS WHEREOF HE DIED. And Joash the king of Israel came down unto him, and wept over his face, and said, O my father, my father, the chariot of Israel, and the horsemen thereof.

And Elisha said unto him, Take bow and arrows. And he took unto him bow and arrows.

And he said to the king of Israel, Put thine hand upon the bow. And he put his hand upon it: and Elisha put his hands upon the king's hands.

And he said, Open the window eastward. And he opened it. Then Elisha said, Shoot. And he shot. And he said, The arrow of the LORD's deliverance, and the arrow of deliverance from Syria: for thou shalt smite the Syrians in Aphek, till thou have consumed them.

And he said, Take the arrows. And he took them. And he said unto the king of Israel, Smite upon the ground. And he smote thrice, and stayed.

And the man of God was wroth with him, and said, Thou shouldest have smitten five or six times; then hadst thou smitten Syria till thou hadst consumed it: whereas now thou shalt smite Syria but thrice.

2 Kings 13:14-19

Elisha was sick but anointed. He was dying but he was still anointed. His weakness, dishonour and corruption were apparent to all. He performed his last miracle on his death bed and God moved mightily. One of the highest kinds of deception is to look on outward appearances and pass judgment.

...for the LORD seeth not as man seeth; for man looketh on the outward appearance, but the LORD looketh on the heart.

1 Samuel 16:7b

This is what leads to racism and prejudice of which we are all guilty. Mercy and forgiveness! How often we judge people by what we see on the outside. Our error will be exposed shortly.

Dead but Anointed

And Elisha died, and they buried him. And the bands of the Moabites invaded the land at the coming in of the year. And it came to pass, as they were burying a man, that, behold, they spied a band of men; and they cast the man into the sepulchre of Elisha: and when the man was let down, and TOUCHED THE BONES OF ELISHA, HE REVIVED, AND STOOD UP ON HIS FEET.

2 Kings 13:20-21

You can even be dead and anointed! Believe it or not, the lingering anointing on a dead prophet raised someone from the dead. It is easy to be deceived by the natural weakness of God's servants.

12. Not honouring and appreciating your man of God.

As you get used to your pastor, it is easy to take him for granted. We often neglect those with whom we are familiar.

I remember one pastor who had never been honoured by his congregation. His church was constantly blessing a particular honoured visiting preacher. When this visiting preacher came to hold a convention, the crowds would gather and the people would express their appreciation for the visiting minister. They would bring money and gifts to honour this visiting minister. But the church would never honour its own pastor. The deception here is that the visitor is the one who is sent from God to them. But the reality is that their own familiar pastor is the one who labours over them with love.

I teach my church members that it is biblical to honour and give gifts to the man of God. This is not to enhance the lifestyle of the man of God but it is to honour God's gift and to kill the spirit of familiarity.

Chapter

14

Intercession: The Way out of Barrenness

CHAPTER SUMMARY

The ministries of Paul and Barnabas were born out of intercession. The greatest church planters of the New Testament times were born as they ministered unto the Lord and fasted. A praying church will always lead to new ministries and church growth.

- **Examples of Ministries Born Out of Intercession**

  - **The Church Planting Ministries of Paul and Barnabas**
  - **The Ministry of Hannah**
  - **The Ministry of Elijah**
  - **The Ministry of Jacob**
  - **The Ministry of Moses**
  - **The Jerusalem Church**
  - **The Ministry of Jesus Christ**

■ The Church Planting Ministries of Paul and Barnabas

> **Now there were in the church that was at Antioch certain prophets and teachers; as Barnabas, and Simeon that was called Niger, and Lucius of Cyrene, and Manaen, which had been brought up with Herod the tetrarch, and Saul.**
>
> **AS THEY MINISTERED TO THE LORD, AND FASTED, the Holy Ghost said, Separate me Barnabas and Saul for the work whereunto I have called them.**
>
> **And WHEN THEY HAD FASTED AND PRAYED, AND LAID THEIR HANDS ON THEM, THEY SENT THEM AWAY.**
>
> **So they, being sent forth by the Holy Ghost, departed unto Seleucia; and from thence they sailed to Cyprus.**
>
> **Acts 13:1-4**

The ministries of Paul and Barnabas were born out of intercession. The greatest church planters of the New Testament times were born as they ministered unto the Lord and fasted. A praying church will always lead to new ministries and church growth. The way out of barrenness is the way into church planting. It is the way into evangelism.

I believe that fervent prayer will almost always lead to fruitfulness in a minister's life. A prayerful church almost always becomes fruitful. Churches are planted and ministers are sent out when real prayer begins.

■ The Ministry of Hannah

Hannah is a good example of a barren ministry. Hannah is one of the great examples of someone who broke out of the power of barrenness and became very fruitful. The great key that Hannah demonstrated was again the key of intercession. Evangelists and missionaries are always born out of intercession. Hannah was in serious trouble. She desperately needed a breakthrough. She didn't just doodle and dawdle. To "doodle and dawdle" means to "hang around, loiter, to waste time and to make wavy impressions." She was dead serious about what she wanted from God. Dear pastor, fervent prayer will make you give birth to a new dimension in ministry. Intercession will always lead to new spiritual children.

> **Now Hannah, she spake in her heart; only her lips moved, but her voice was not heard: therefore Eli thought she had been drunken.**
>
> **1 Samuel 1:13**

■ The Ministry of Elijah

Elijah's ardent prayer as he bent over asking for rain, remains the most well known example of fervent prayer.

> **And Elijah said unto Ahab, Get thee up, eat and drink; for there is a sound of abundance of rain.**
>
> **So Ahab went up to eat and to drink. And Elijah went up to the top of Carmel; and HE CAST HIMSELF DOWN UPON THE EARTH, AND**

> **PUT HIS FACE BETWEEN HIS KNEES, And said to his servant, Go up now, look toward the sea. And he went up, and looked, and said, There is nothing. And he said, Go again seven times.**
>
> **And it came to pass at the seventh time, that he said, Behold, there ariseth a little cloud out of the sea, like a man's hand. And he said, Go up, say unto Ahab, Prepare thy chariot, and get thee down, that the rain stop thee not.**
>
> **And it came to pass in the mean while, that the heaven was black with clouds and wind, and there was a great rain. And Ahab rode, and went to Jezreel. And the hand of the Lord was on Elijah; and he girded up his loins, and ran before Ahab to the entrance of Jezreel.**
>
> **1 Kings 18:41-46**

This is the classic example of fervent prayer that was spoken of by James. I see you praying fervently to release the rain of God's blessing on your ministry! Look at the example of Elijah as he prayed to God for rain. Elijah's prayer released the rain of God. When the rain comes, there will be new plants. All the new churches are waiting for the rain. The new things that God has in store will be released through the rain.

> **Ask ye of the LORD rain in the time of the latter rain; so the LORD shall make bright clouds, and give them showers of rain, to every one grass in the field.**
>
> **Zechariah 10:1**

■ The Ministry of Jacob

> **And Jacob was left alone, and there WRESTLED A MAN with him until the breaking of the day.**
>
> **Genesis 32:24**

Jacob's all-night wrestling prayer yielded tremendous results. Jacob was blessed and so was his seed. Several thousand years have gone by but the fruit of this fervent prayer is evident for all to see. Israel still stands as one of the most favored nations on the Earth.

■ The Ministry of Moses

> **Then came Amalek, and fought with Israel in Rephidim.**
>
> **And Moses said unto Joshua, Choose us out men, and go out, fight with Amalek: tomorrow I will stand on the top of the hill with the rod of God in mine hand.**
>
> **SO JOSHUA DID AS MOSES HAD SAID TO HIM, AND FOUGHT WITH AMALEK: and Moses had said to him, and fought with Amalek: and Moses, Aaron, and Hur went up to the top of the hill.**
>
> **And it came to pass, when MOSES HELD UP HIS HAND, THAT ISRAEL PREVAILED: and when he let down his hand, Amalek prevailed.**

> **But Moses' hands were heavy; and they took a stone, and put it under him, and he sat thereon; and Aaron and Hur stayed up his hands, the one on the one side, and the other on the other side; and his hands were steady until the going down of the sun.**
>
> **Exodus 17:8-12**

Moses' burning prayer for victory over Amalek, is another example of fervent prayer. Amalek is a type of demonic force that fights against God's church from behind. The constant attacks by Amalek will distract the church planting drive of every ministry. It is important to rise up in the ministry and deal with Amalek spiritually.

■ The Jerusalem Church

The New Testament Church prayed fervently for the power of the Holy Spirit to be upon their leaders.

> **And being let go, they went to their own company, and reported all that the chief priests and elders had said unto them. And when they heard that, they lifted up their voice to God with one accord, and said, Lord, thou art God, which hast made heaven, and earth, and the sea, and all that in them is: By stretching forth thine hand to heal; and that signs and wonders may be done by the name of thy holy child Jesus.**
>
> **And when they had prayed, the place was shaken where they were assembled together; and they were all filled with the Holy Ghost, and THEY SPAKE THE WORD OF GOD WITH BOLDNESS.**
>
> **Acts 4:23, 24, 30, 31**

God heard their prayer and look at the results. When a church begins to pray fervently there are always results. The Word of God is preached when prayer goes forth. Churches are planted when the Word of God is preached.

It is important to stress that fervent prayer is what makes the difference. Sometimes, I look at people who claim to be having a prayer meeting. Some of them are sleeping and others are just whiling away time. How would you feel if someone fell asleep whilst talking to you? You would think that he is either disrespectful or very uninterested in you.

■ The Ministry of Jesus Christ

Jesus prayed passionately for the will of God to be done in His life.

> **Who in the days of his flesh, when he had offered up prayers and supplications with strong crying and tears unto him that was able to save him from death, and was heard in that he feared;**
>
> **Hebrews 5:7**

The evidence of this was when He began to sweat blood. Fervent prayer always works. The ministry of Jesus was a great success! Two thousand years after these prayers, churches are still being planted. Books are still being written. Songs are being composed about Christ. More people are volunteering their lives to the service of our great God.

You will have great success in your ministry when you learn how to pray fervently. Whenever you don't know what to do, do what Jesus did. Jesus shouted when He prayed! Jesus prayed until He was sweating! Read it for yourself!

> **And being in an agony he prayed more earnestly: and his sweat was as it were great drops of blood falling down to the ground.**
>
> **Luke 22: 44**

Chapter

15

Covenants and Church Planting

CHAPTER SUMMARY

God is a covenant keeping God. There is a little understood revelation on how to move the hand of God, which I call the key of covenant making.

■ **Examples of People Who Covenanted To the Lord**

- **Hannah**
- **Jacob**
- **Jephthah**

Hannah made a covenant to give her child to the Lord. There is no need for anyone to make a covenant before you give your child for the service of the Lord. However initiating a covenant with the Lord can provoke Him to bless you supernaturally; Hannah provoked God to open her womb and to release her children to her. She promised Him the first child even if it was the only one.

Jacob was another person who covenanted to the Lord and by that invoked a great blessing on his life.

> **And Jacob vowed a vow, saying, If God will be with me, and will keep me in this way that I go, and will give me bread to eat, and raiment to put on... then shall the LORD be my God:**
>
> **Genesis 28:20-21**

A final example of someone who covenanted to the Lord was Jephthah.

> **And Jephthah vowed a vow unto the LORD, and said, If thou shalt without fail deliver the children of Ammon into mine hands, Then it shall be, that whatsoever cometh forth of the doors of my house to meet me, when I return in peace from the children of Ammon, shall surely be the LORD's, and I will offer it up for a burnt offering.**
>
> **Judges 11:30-31**

Covenant making is a special kind of prayer in which you engage the Lord in a legally binding agreement. Many people become unfaithful when He honours them in the ministry. The Lord is looking for faithful people who will remain true to His calling as the years go by. Perhaps a prayer of commitment from you to always be faithful to the call of God will release the grace of God that you so desire upon your life. If you will not be faithful to God why will He give you His precious anointing?

All those who made these covenants kept them and the Lord also kept His side of the covenant.

Chapter

16

The Anointing of Rebecca

CHAPTER SUMMARY

As you read this chapter receive the blessing of Rebecca! I prophesy the anointing of Rebecca over your life and ministry! Say it over and over to yourself and believe that the grace for fruitfulness and church growth are released in your life and ministry. It shall surely come to pass! It shall surely come to pass at last!

> **And they blessed Rebekah, and said unto her, Thou art our sister, be thou the mother of thousands of millions, and let thy seed possess the gate of those which hate them.**
>
> **Genesis 24:60**

"And they blessed Rebecca..."

I bless you to become endued with power for ministry!

"... Thou art our sister..."

I declare that you are my brother and colleague in the ministry of the Lord Jesus Christ. We are working together for the Master. We have the victory over the enemy. No weapon formed against us will prosper. One may put to flight a thousand, but two of us shall put to flight ten thousand.

"...be thou the mother of thousands of millions..."

May you be endued with the power for ministry! May you become the father and mother of thousands and thousands of spiritual children! May you have great increase! You will see thousands of thousands coming to the Lord in your ministry! You will experience the things that God has prepared for you!

"...And let thy seed possess the gate of those which hate them"

May you have victory over Satan and demons! May you conquer towns, villages and cities for Christ! May the battle always be in the gates of your enemy and never in your own gate!

Stand and fight, for it is the last battle on this Earth. The gates of Hell have been opened wide but Heaven has also released its forces. We shall surely win for the captain of the host is Jesus.

Many are wounded but many are still strong! Rise from the ashes! Let the wounded join in to fight for the last time. We can win says the Lord! We shall win says the Lord! Your scars shall become the reason for your honour in the resurrection. In that day, the wounds of battle shall make you an honourable warrior. Greater and greater is the glory that awaits my faithful servants!

Your glittering crowns, your beautiful mansions, your precious stones and your unspeakable rewards are piling up for eternity. Fear not for I have determined the time and the hour of your victory!

Chapter

17

Sacrifice and Church Planting

CHAPTER SUMMARY

Sacrifice is the missing ingredient for church planting. This master key will take the average ministry from barrenness to fruitfulness.

- **The Processes that a Missionary / Church Planter Will Go Through When Sent to Plant Churches**

17.1 The falling process

17.2 Dying

i) The Development of a Personal Relationship with God

ii) The Development of Humility

- **The Eleven Complaints of Moses**

i. **And Moses said unto God, "Who am I?" (Exodus 3:11).**

ii. **And Moses said unto God, "...What shall I say unto them?" (Exodus 3:13).**

iii. **And Moses answered, "...They will not believe me ..." (Exodus 4:1).**

iv. **And Moses said, "...I am not eloquent... I am slow of speech, and of a slow tongue" (Exodus 4:10).**

v. **And he said, "O my Lord, send, I pray thee, by the hand of him whom thou wilt send" (Exodus 4:13).**

vi. **And Moses said, "Lord...Why is it that thou hast sent me?" (Exodus 5:22).**

vii. **And Moses spake, "...the children of Israel have not hearkened unto me" (Exodus 6:12).**

viii. **And Moses said, "...I am of uncircumcised lips" (Exodus 6:30).**

ix. **And Moses cried unto the LORD, "...They be almost ready to stone me" (Exodus 17:4).**

x. **And Moses said unto the LORD, "Wherefore hast thou afflicted thy servant?" (Numbers 11:10).**

xi. **And Moses said, "The people are six hundred thousand foot men" (Numbers 11:21).**

17.3 Bearing much fruit

> **And Jesus answered them, saying, the hour is come, that the Son of man should be glorified.**
>
> **Verily, verily, I say unto you, Except a corn of wheat FALL into the ground and DIE, it abideth alone: but if it die, it bringeth forth much FRUIT.**
>
> **John 12:23 -24**

Sacrifice is the key that will transform a reverend minister from an official with a title, to a truly fruitful minister. It will make a church grow from a single church to a chain of churches. It will make a pastor move into church planting.

The readiness to die is a missing ingredient in many good churches. Many of our churches will remain small until we have people who are ready to sacrifice. There comes a time when what is needed is sacrifice. Failure to sacrifice always results in barrenness.

A lot of churches have reached the borderline. Many ministries can do more but they don't. It's because they don't want to sacrifice. They do not lack information or knowledge.

Many people know what I know. If you have read my books, you must have some knowledge. However, knowledge is not enough! You will not have the fruits I have even if you have the knowledge that I have. For you to have what I have, you must pay the price. There is a price for everyone to pay. The price of glory is the same for everyone!

The Scripture says that unless a corn of wheat disappears into the ground and dies, it will be alone.

The corn of wheat symbolizes the missionary. And the missionary is the one who will be sent out to plant the churches. To be alone means to be fruitless. It means to be without members or followers. This dying process in the man of God will eventually bring out much fruit.

Jesus would not have borne the fruit He did if He had not died on the cross. He would have been alone in Heaven with His Father. He could not have saved us if He had not died and gone to Hell. To win followers for Himself and His Father, He had to fall in the ground and die.

The corn of wheat has to fall into the ground and die. When the seed falls into the ground, it disintegrates and decomposes. This is what we call dying. The seed actually goes through a process before it comes out as fruit. That can only take place when it disappears and dies.

The need to "die" is the most important truth to grasp. There are many sincere leaders who know many things. They have heard much and think they are high up in God. Knowledge unfortunately breeds pride.

> **... we know that we all have knowledge. Knowledge puffeth up, but charity edifieth.**
>
> **1 Cointhians 8:1**

The kingdom is more than a school of history and doctrines. It is more than acquiring numerous certificates of Bible knowledge. Knowledge without this process of dying will yield nothing.

Have you noticed that some of the most learned and scholarly Bible expositors are very ineffective at real ministry? In fact sometimes, the more scholarly they become the more faithless and godless they are.

A single corn will become a big tree with many fruits only if it falls into the ground and dies.

The Secondary School of Ministry

It is time to send your young men out. It is time to release those who have been trained into the fields of ministry. The Lord has constantly led me to send my best people out.

One day, a senior pastor who had several junior pastors under him asked me; "How can I improve the quality of my pastors?"

I said, "Send them to the "secondary school" of ministry."

I told him, "Most of the pastors under your care are still in the "primary school" of ministry and they have been there for many years. Instead of releasing them into the next stage of ministry, you have kept them with you and that has destroyed them spiritually."

I explained, "Instead of these ones becoming pastors of hundreds of people, some of them have become guitarists, singers and ushers in your church. They never moved on in ministry."

I continued talking with this pastor, "it is very difficult to send away people you are used to. It is difficult to send away people you love. You even risk destroying your relationship with them as they may develop a spirit of rejection."

I explained; "There are pastors who are very honoured and happy to be overseeing thousands of people today. But when I sent them away from me to begin these churches, they were often sad and felt rejected. I had to counsel and affirm my love towards them many times."

I continued encouraging my friend to send out his best people.

I explained again, "Unless they go through the experience of the dying seed, they will never really bear fruit. They will prance around you and busy themselves with many activities in church, but actually, bear no fruit."

What are the Processes that a Missionary / Church Planter Will Go through When You Send Him to Plant Churches?

1. The falling process

Falling into the ground speaks of a period in a man of God's life in which he is unknown and hidden from the view of the general public. It also speaks of a period of rejection, negative response, refusal, denial and denunciation in his life. Church planters and missionaries will go through this experience many times. Don't worry; isolation, rejection and separation are part of real ministry.

Concerning John the Baptist, the Bible declares that he was hidden in the wilderness until the time of his showing unto Israel. Every pastor must realize that God has a time in his life when he must be hidden. Do not be in a hurry to be exposed since premature exposure leads to destruction.

Jesus Christ was hidden for thirty years before he was exposed to public ministry. His appearance in the ministry surprised those who didn't know that a seed had been in the ground for thirty years.

Moses experienced this falling into the ground. He was utterly rejected by his brethren when he first tried to minister to them. He ended up in the wilderness for forty years. After years of rejection and isolation, he was ready to minister.

Joseph had this same experience of falling into the ground. His visions and dreams were utterly rejected. Then he himself was utterly rejected and dispensed with. He found himself working as a slave and then as a prisoner in Egypt. After several years of separation from his brethren he was finally ready for a great ministry. These are just a few examples of this pattern of falling into the ground. I tell you, no true minister is truly accepted until he has been rejected.

I've Been There

I have experienced this falling into the ground myself. When I started out in ministry I was utterly and totally rejected by the ministers of my day. One minister that I had a good relationship with refused to minister to our group anymore. When I asked why, he said, "I don't sow amongst thorns anymore."

He and other pastors claimed that I was not called by God and had no business starting a church. They felt I was a medical student who should concentrate on his schooling. They told my assistant not to associate with me because it was dangerous to stay with someone who was not called by God.

I told another minister with whom I had a good relationship, that I had started a church. I received an instant rebuke and was questioned as to which Bible school I had attended.

I was discouraged and I went away with my "tail between my legs". To emphasize the rejection, this pastor decided to hold a campaign right where our church was meeting. He held a big programme and showed a very powerful video of his national and international programmes. It was one of the best presentations of that ministry I had ever seen. Our church looked like a group of lame ducks and dwarfs after this presentation. A powerful invitation was then made to me to join this ministry.

After they had left, I asked myself, "Who would want to be with us when there are such powerful and established ministries in the city?" After that programme, we felt demoralized and discouraged. It was obvious that we were a group of struggling students attempting to do ministry work.

I also remember an incident when I met one of these great pastors of an established church. It was at a wedding being held on the university campus.

I went up to him to say hello and he said, "Oh, hello Dag"

Then he paused, looked at me and said, "Pastor!"

As I stood before him, I felt in my heart that he was mockingly referring to me as a pastor. I almost asked him "Sir why are you mocking me?" "Why do you call me "pastor" when you don't believe that I am a pastor?"

I don't know how those words never came out of my mouth. Dear friend, I tell you, that the only thing I felt at that time of my ministry was rejection and intimidation.

I went through a period of utter rejection and I continued the ministry work in virtual separation from most of the ministers I had known. God then taught me to minister through lay people. You see, most of the ministries at that time were based on full- time workers.

Don't be worried when you are not accepted or wanted. Don't be upset when no one invites you. Your day of "showing forth" will come! Today, I am accepted and even respected by some of these great pastors who initially despised me. Perhaps they had no choice but to accept me. After all, I am here even if they don't want me.

> **And the child grew, and waxed strong in spirit, and was in the deserts till the day of his shewing unto Israel.**
>
> **Luke 1:80**

2. Dying

When the seed falls to the ground, it disintegrates and decomposes. It utterly changes in its character and appearance. By the time God is finished with you, your appearance will be different. Your character will be utterly transformed. Allow the dying process to continue. Except the seed dies, it abides alone. Unless these qualities are allowed to develop, your ministry will not develop.

The Development of a Personal Relationship with God

During this period of alienation, many important spiritual traits will be birthed in the man of God. A personal relationship with God is one of the most important things that you will learn when people reject you. Every true minister derives his strength from the Lord directly: You see, many will come in that day and say, "I cast out demons in your name and I did great works in your name". But the Lord will say, "I never knew you". This goes to say that every minister must be very particular with his relationship with the Lord. Rejection stops the horizontal (human) relationships and leaves you to develop the vertical (God) relationship.

The Development of Humility

The rejection by man is intended to make you develop humility. Humility is the highest mantle a minister can wear. The more humble a minister, the higher his standing before the Lord! One of the common deceptions in the church is that the larger your church, the higher your standing before the Lord. That is not the case; Jesus made it clear that the greatest pastor will be the most humble and childlike amongst us.

> **And said, Verily I say unto you, Except ye be converted, and become as little children, ye shall not enter into the kingdom of heaven.**
>
> **Matthew 18:3**

John the Baptist's humility was evident. He made it clear that he was not worthy to unlace the shoes of Jesus. He deferred to the Lord and stated that Jesus must increase as he decreases. How many pastors today want others to increase while they decrease?

> **He must increase, but I must decrease.**
>
> **John 3:30**

The humility of Jesus was evident. He humbled himself and became obedient even to the death of the cross. Moses lost all confidence in himself. The Bible calls him the meekest man on Earth. Wouldn't you be meek after forty years in the wilderness as one of the ten most wanted men in Egypt? When you read about the call of Moses, you see how Moses had zero confidence in himself. He was a great person but his opinion of himself was genuinely very low. Notice Moses' own assessment of himself.

The Eleven Complaints of Moses

1. And Moses said unto God, "Who am I?" (Exodus 3:11).
2. And Moses said unto God, "...What shall I say unto them?" (Exodus 3:13).
3. And Moses answered, "...They will not believe me ..." (Exodus 4:1).
4. And Moses said, "...I am not eloquent... I am slow of speech, and of a slow tongue" (Exodus 4:10).
5. And he said, "O my Lord, send, I pray thee, by the hand of him whom thou wilt send" (Exodus 4:13).
6. And Moses said, "Lord...Why is it that thou hast sent me?" (Exodus 5:22).
7. And Moses spake, "...the children of Israel have not hearkened unto me" (Exodus 6:12).
8. And Moses said, "...I am of uncircumcised lips" (Exodus 6:30).
9. And Moses cried unto the LORD, "...They be almost ready to stone me" (Exodus 17:4).
10. And Moses said unto the LORD, "Wherefore hast thou afflicted thy servant?" (Numbers 11:10).
11. And Moses said, "The people are six hundred thousand foot men" (Numbers 11:21).

Joseph after being a prisoner for some years did not think of vengeance when he saw his brothers. He could see through it all that God had meant it for good. Joseph had become so mature in the things of God that he felt his brothers had done nothing wrong. In fact he felt his brothers were used by God.

After going through all that I have been through, I have come to love and appreciate the people who once rejected me. I feel that God used them to train me in the ministry. I bear none of them a grudge and I value their ministries greatly. Even the bitterest of experiences have worked out for my good.

3. Bearing much fruit

Bearing fruit is a very spiritual thing. Most men of God think that if you have a large church, you have borne much fruit and are pleasing to the Lord. However you will notice that Jesus was pleasing to His father even before He preached His first sermon.

> **And lo a voice from heaven, saying, This is my beloved Son, IN WHOM I AM WELL PLEASED.**
>
> **Matthew 3:17**

You don't have to have a church for the Heavenly Father to say, "This is my beloved son in whom I am well pleased." You don't even have to be a pastor. You don't have to write a book, you don't have to preach a sermon to hear the words, "This my beloved son in whom I am well pleased."

You don't need to be famous to hear the words, "This is my beloved son in whom I am well pleased." Jesus was not famous when this happened. This Scripture shows us that pleasing God is not based on our work per se. Our fruits are actually gifts that are given by the Lord.

Have you ever wondered at the immense fruit that Christ Jesus bore? Have you ever wondered how thousands of churches have been planted as a result of His three years of ministry? Two thousand years have gone by and He has more fruit than He has ever had. What did He do that brought about so much fruit? He did six things: just three years of preaching, teaching and healing, living a life of humility, obedience and the sacrifice on the cross. Significant among these things was His sacrifice on the cross as this opened the door for our salvation. Your obedience and sacrifice to the Lord will give rise to many churches.

This was David Livingstone's philosophy. He allowed himself to be spent so that unsaved tribes and peoples could be discovered and evangelized. I quote from an interview that he had before he died.

David Livingstone: Spend and Be Spent!

At twelve years of age, he showed an anxiety about his spiritual welfare. At twenty he was converted. It was a natural stepping stone from the Christian home to membership in the church.

His folk were worshippers at the Hamilton Church. Two of the elders instructed him in the doctrines. For five months he walked regularly from his home in Blantyre to his little church in Hamilton to be taught by and be prayed with by one of the elders. After this he was duly allowed to become a communicant member. It was then he made the decision to consecrate himself to the service of Christ in some form of missionary effort.

After graduation in medicine and theology, he applied to the London Missionary Society. Could he come down for an interview? He had no money for his fare. Two friends helped him. The necessary probation period in the London school over, he was ready for his life task. China was his choice; but the Opium War had closed the door; his heart was turned to Africa, and to that continent he sailed, and landed at Cape Town in 1849.

What did he look like as he set sail? Moderately tall, slim in build; a wiry, closely knit frame suggesting great powers of bodily endurance.

He gave as his reason: "when first I felt the expansive benevolence of the gospel in my heart, it became an interesting question to me; how can I spend the remainder of my days in bringing my fellowmen to the enjoyment of the same happiness and peace?"

How can I spend my years? ..."SPEND AND BE SPENT" the missionary ideal was constant in all his years. Preaching and teaching, Livingstone was also a physician to the sick. He had a genius for friendship with these Africans. "Love begets love" was his motto. His hands were never idle; bricklayer, carpenter, stones man and general director of the social economy of his settlements he passed his days in intense action.

Spend and be Spent

If you are a senior pastor, don't be afraid to send out the best that you have. God gave His Son and today He has millions of sons. If God has called you to plant a church don't be afraid to die. Unless you die, you will never bear much fruit.

It is time to spend and to be spent for the Lord. Spend your best leaders and workers on the harvest fields of the world. Allow yourself to be spent for Jesus.

The sacrifice of great men like David Livingstone brought about a great expansion of the church into Africa. Truly there is no other way than the sacrificial way laid down by Christ Jesus. The true church is perpetuated by sacrifice!

Chapter

18

Obedience and Church Planting

CHAPTER SUMMARY

Why is obedience to be preferred to sacrifice? When we sacrifice we often know what we are doing and why we are doing it. We know we are going to suffer and we know the reasons for the sufferings. Why is it more desirable, favourable and more acceptable to God when we obey?

■ Why Obedience is Better (Greater) than Sacrifice

18.1 It is greater to obey without fully understanding, than it is to sacrifice.

18.2 It is better to obey a command that you would not naturally do, than it is to sacrifice.

18.3 It is better to obey instructions you do not agree with, than it is to sacrifice.

18.4 It is greater to obey humbling commands, than it is to sacrifice.

18.5 It is better to obey instructions that don't require your wisdom than it is to sacrifice.

18.6 It takes greater faithfulness and diligence to perform duties that do not appear urgent or important.

18.7 The consequence of obeying or disobeying one little instruction can be so great that no sacrifice could ever compensate.

■ Examples of Disobedience:

18.8 The Disobedience of Saul

18.9 The Disobedience of Joshua

■ Joshua's disobedience bred for the following future enemies:

18.10 Gath - where Goliath came from

18.11 Gaza - where Delilah came from

18.12 Ashdod - where Dagon came from

> **And Samuel said, Hath the LORD as great delight in burnt offerings and sacrifices, as in obeying the voice of the LORD? Behold, TO OBEY IS BETTER THAN SACRIFICE, and to hearken than the fat of rams.**
>
> **1 Samuel 15:22**

We often think that the person who sacrifices is greater than the one who obeys. The word sacrifice brings to us, terrifying images of suffering and loss. Obedience seems to be a much milder and less demanding option. In fact, our human analysis would rate sacrifice above obedience any day.

Once again, God's ways are not our ways and His thoughts are not our thoughts. He makes it clear that "to obey is *better* than to sacrifice". The word "better" means "Greater, To be preferred, an improved version, superior, Enhanced, more acceptable, more favourable, higher quality, augmented and more desirable!"

This verse therefore means that "it is greater, to be preferred, superior, more acceptable, more favourable and more desirable" to obey than to sacrifice.

The following reasons will explain why obedience is a greater thing compared to sacrifice.

Why Obedience is Better (Greater) than Sacrifice

1. It is greater to obey without fully understanding, than it is to sacrifice.

The greatest blessings in my life and ministry have come from obeying God rather than sacrificing to Him. Most of the time, it is not easy to understand the implications of what you are doing. As I write this book, there are things the Lord has asked me to do that I don't understand.

The reason why we do not understand is because of our level of growth or our stage of maturity in the Lord. I believe that we will never fully understand what God has asked us to do until we begin to do it. Notice this Scripture. It shows us that it is when you do the will of God that you know His will.

> **If any man will do his will, he shall know of the doctrine, whether it be of God, or whether I speak of myself.**
>
> **John 7:17**

How could I understand the impact of full-time ministry when I was a lay pastor? Many lay people think they understand what full-time ministry is. But I know that they do not appreciate what it is all about. Many lay people think they are serving God just as well as anyone else. It is only in obeying God that I found the importance of full-time ministry.

2. It is better to obey a command that you would not naturally do, than it is to sacrifice.

When the Lord directed me into the healing ministry, I did not fully understand the effect that it would have on my ministry. Until then, I had operated mostly as a teacher and preacher. Naturally speaking I am a more calculating and logical person. It was not natural for me to move by the spirit or minister things that are spiritual. It is one of the most difficult things I have ever done and I am ever grateful for people who helped me cross that barrier. Today I have seen many miracles in the ministry. I can say it is the one thing that has made a great difference in my present ministry.

> **Saying, Father, if thou be willing, remove this cup from me: nevertheless not my will, but thine, be done.**
>
> **Luke 22:42**

It is very unnatural to give yourself to be killed by wicked men. One of the most frightening experiences of mankind is to know that you are going to die. I have had patients who died shortly after being told that they were terminally ill. If you think about it, you would know that it is a terrifying experience.

I remember a lady who had leukemia. She thought she had some kind of fever and was being treated for that. Even though she had a deadly illness she looked and felt quite well. One morning, on a ward round, she asked one of my doctor colleagues where she could get her drugs. My colleague pointed across the road and said, "Oh, you can buy these cancer drugs from the Burkett's tumor department across the road." The lady was silent! She was shocked! Up until this time, she had not been told that she had cancer or any such illness. This lady was so frightened that her condition deteriorated rapidly. I am sorry to say that within a few hours, this lady went into a coma and died.

The knowledge of approaching death is one of the most terrifying ordeals for any man. Mercifully, God rarely shows us our day of departure.

I always remember the blood shot eyes of a thirty-year-old man who was dying of chronic renal failure on a medical ward. He knew there was something terribly wrong with him. One morning as I attended to him, he gripped my hand and said, "Doctor, please help me. I want to go to Germany. I have a brother there who will help me get medical attention." I was scared because I was only a medical student, and I didn't know what to do.

I looked downward and saw his urine bag filled with blood and I knew that only God could save him. I always remember the terror in that man's eyes. I remember the sound of his frightened and pleading voice. "Doctor, please help me."

When I think of my Jesus and how He calmly approached His own gruesome death, I only marvel. When I think of how Jesus prayed for God to take the cup away, I appreciate His obedience to His father.

Dear friend, it is not natural to walk toward your own death. It is not natural to do things that will hurt and destroy you. To obey is better than to sacrifice!

There are many commands of God that will go against your natural mind or way of thinking. It is time to obey. There are people who give extra offerings to the Lord because they are living in disobedience. These extra sacrifices are intended to compensate for their lives of disobedience. Watch carefully every Sunday and you will see many disobedient Christians paying large amounts to the Lord, hoping that these offerings will close the eyes of Jehovah. Mercy!

3. It is better to obey instructions you do not agree with, than it is to sacrifice.

Disobedience often sets in when you do not agree with the instruction given you. When God instructs us to forgive an obviously rebellious person, we may not readily agree. With time, you discover that forgiveness is greater than revenge. Whenever you are wronged, there is a very self-righteous feeling that makes you want to correct and pay back. It is not easy to ignore this feeling! Great blessings have come my way as a result of forgiving the people that wronged me. It is not always easy to agree with God's style of doing things.

> **And it came to pass … that God … said, … Take now thy son, thine only son Isaac, whom thou lovest, and get thee into the land of Moriah; and offer him there for a burnt offering upon one of the mountains which I will tell thee of.**
>
> **And Abraham rose up early in the morning, and saddled his ass, and took two of his young men with him, and Isaac his son, and clave the wood for the burnt offering, and rose up, and went unto the place of which God had told him.**
>
> **Genesis 22:1-3**

I am sure that Abraham didn't agree with the idea to kill his only son but he did what the Lord asked him to do.

4. It is greater to obey humbling commands, than it is to sacrifice.

Many of God's commands humble us. You could say that the number one characteristic of God's instruction is that they humble you. They often make you look foolish in the eyes of men or in your own eyes.

When the Lord led me to be a full-time minister, I looked foolish in the eyes of other doctors. When I receive offerings or do fund-raising, I look foolish in my own eyes and in the eyes of many people.

I planned to make great sacrifices to the Lord when He called me into full-time ministry. I told Him, I would give large amounts of money from the hospital that I would set up. However, the Lord told me that He did not want my sacrifices, but rather He wanted me to work for Him.

The Compensating Lay Pastor

One day I called one of my lay pastors and asked him to come for a ride with me to Kumasi; a city about 250 kilometers from Accra in Ghana.

"Will you come along" I asked

"It would be a privilege to ride with you," He said, "I will slip away from work and join you."

As we drove along, and chatted, I told him something that surprised him.

I said, "You are a very hard working young man."

I continued; "You are always doing extra things for the Lord."

You see, this young man was an architect, and in spite of his job, he was constantly working in the church.

I told him; "You run around the city doing anything that needs to be done. You are one of the most sacrificial and dedicated pastors I have ever worked with."

He smiled gratefully!

I continued; "You have done so many architectural jobs for the church and never charged a penny. Whenever there is any extra pastoral work to be done, it is you I call on".

I explained; "That is why I called you to come along with me on this trip. I knew you would be able to get away from work at short notice."

Then I dropped the bombshell, "But you are in disobedience!"

I continued, "You are disobeying God."

His smile began to fade.

I explained, "The reason why you are so active, so zealous and so sacrificial is because you are trying to compensate for disobeying God. God has called you to serve Him in full-time ministry but you are on the run."

He was shocked. "I never thought about that," he said. "It never occurred to me that I was just compensating for my disobedience."

A few months later, this young man gave up his job and obeyed the call to full-time ministry. May God open our eyes to see if you are disobeying him and trying to compensate!

Oh how we love to compensate for our disobedience! We don't want to humble ourselves before the Lord. We don't want to look foolish before anyone. We want to do our own thing and make a convenient sacrifice to compensate.

> **And being found in fashion as a man, he humbled himself, and became obedient unto death, even the death of the cross.**
>
> **Philippians 2:8**

5. It is better to obey instructions that don't require your wisdom than it is to sacrifice.

> **Provide neither gold, nor silver, nor brass in your purses, Nor scrip for your journey, neither two coats, neither shoes, nor yet staves: for the workman is worthy of his meat.**
>
> **Matthew 10:9-10**

How will I live if I don't provide for myself silver and gold? Walking with the Lord requires that you put aside your own reasoning and trust in His wisdom. To work for God requires faith.

When you see the measly offering baskets with jingling coins, going around from pew to pew, you wonder, "Can I survive on these collections?"

"Is this how God will sustain a full-time pastor?"

Years ago, I visited a church in Europe. The American missionary pastor had a thriving congregation. As I sat in his office, I got to talk about the finances of the ministry.

I told him proudly, "I am not the kind of pastor who depends on offerings."

I continued, "I work as a doctor and do private business. I don't need anyone's money."

He looked at me quizzically and said; "I see the wisdom in what you are doing but God's wisdom is higher than yours."

He explained, "God has a plan and a pattern by which He is building His church. Your plan and your idea will never be superior to His plan."

God's way is simple! "They that preach the gospel must live off the gospel" (1 Cor. 9:14).

He said to me; "You are depriving your congregation of a blessing which they receive when they bless the man of God."

I self-righteously thought to myself; "I don't need any of those offerings."

However, after that conversation I began to consider that I could not be wiser than God.

God must know how to build His church better than I do.

Today, I preach the gospel and I live off the gospel. I humbly depend on the method of sustenance that God has designed for pastors. I am not better than any of God's servants. Instead of sacrificing extra time, doing business and other moneymaking deals, I give myself wholly to the money-making ministry of the Word and prayer. It is better to obey than to sacrifice.

6. It takes greater faithfulness and diligence to perform duties that do not appear urgent or important.

Go ye therefore, and teach all nations, baptizing them in the name of the Father, and of the Son, and of the Holy Ghost:

Teaching them to observe all things whatsoever I have commanded you: and, lo, I am with you alway, even unto the end of the world. Amen.

Matthew 28:19-20

Pray without ceasing.

1 Thessalonians 5:17

Most important things are not urgent. Important things are often unattractive and uninviting. It is difficult to be faithful with what God considers important.

For instance, prayer without ceasing is one of the most important things for us to do. Yet we lack a sense of urgency when it comes to prayer. In times of trouble, you often cannot have faith. While you are in the trouble you will feel like calling on God but fear and anxiety will grip your heart. It is almost impossible to pray under those circumstances. Then you will realize how important it was for you to have prayed.

I have been there in the darkness of life when all theories on faith no longer worked. Have you ever wondered why Jesus did not pray when He was arrested?

It is because He had finished praying before the crisis began.

When Jesus approached the tomb of Lazarus, He wouldn't have said a single prayer before raising him from the dead. He explained that the only reason He was praying was so that those around would know that He had a father.

To preach the gospel and to win the lost is a very important instruction. But often there is no sense of urgency to fulfil that command. The fact that you don't feel any pressure does not mean that it is not important. Pressure does not always signify the importance of a command. It is a great thing to obey the Lord even when we are not under pressure to do so.

7. The consequence of obeying or disobeying one little instruction can be so great that no sacrifice could ever compensate.

Look at the mess we are in because Eve disobeyed the Lord. When the Lord God asked her the question in the Garden of Eden (what is this that thou has done?) He was asking:

What are these wars that you have brought into the world?

What are these sicknesses that you have created?

What is this perversion that you have introduced into the world?

What are these cancers and HIV that you have unleashed on mankind?

Who are these Saddam Hussein, Adolph Hitler and Stalin characters that you have given birth to?

What are all these funerals and deaths that you have released?

What is this fear and self-preservation that is so dominant in the world?

What is this barrenness and pain to women that you have initiated?

What are these hospitals that you have given us a need for?

Who are these handicapped, blind and lame people that you have produced?

Little did Eve know what she was releasing in that one act of disobedience. She could not imagine how much hurt and suffering she was bringing into the world. This is the one thought that keeps me in the ministry. I think about all the people who would perish if I were to disobey God.

Think about Jesus. Think about all the people who were saved through His ministry. By one act of obedience, He has rescued millions from the throes of Hell. Perhaps if He had stayed on for eighty years, preaching in every country, He wouldn't have had the fruits He has today. There is nothing like obedience in the eyes of God. To obey is better than to sacrifice.

> **Therefore as BY THE OFFENCE OF ONE judgment came upon all men to condemnation; even so BY THE RIGHTEOUSNESS OF ONE the free gift came upon all men unto justification of life.**
>
> **Romans 5:18**

This is the most important truth you must learn about obedience.

I remember the story of a lieutenant in the army who had received orders to fire his artillery at a certain target, which were some miles away. As they prepared to fire, the radio operator had a message for the lieutenant to hold his fire. He ran to his officer to tell him the new order. Something had changed: the position, which was formally occupied by the enemy, had been taken up by their own troops.

However the lieutenant was so zealous and eager to fight that he did not listen to the radio operator. He was so bent on getting into the battle that he didn't listen. In the story, the radio operator was struck by a bullet as he pleaded with his lieutenant to listen to the new message. But to no avail. He eventually died before he was able to relay the message. The lieutenant finally opened fire and pounded what he thought was the enemy position. Soon after that, he received word that his own soldiers had suffered many casualties due to the pounding he had given them. It was told him that he had killed many of his own. This man was later court martialled.

From this story; we see how important it is to obey rather than to sacrifice. The young lieutenant wanted to fight at all cost. But the greater thing to do at that point was to hold his fire and not to get involved. Could it be that there are times that we are just to hold our fire?

God is like the general who sees the whole picture. He knows when to sacrifice and when not to, He knows when to fire and when not to fire. I have learnt that to obey is better than to sacrifice.

God has asked us not to do things that we would have traditionally done. Could it be that there will be times that it is more important not to preach, than it is to preach because that is what God says?

The Apostle Paul said he had been given different commands by the Lord. At times, he had been commanded to be full and at other times, he had been commanded to be hungry. Paul was intent on obeying the Lord. If the instruction was hunger, he was prepared for it; if the instruction was fullness, he would obey!

> **I know both how to be abased, and I know how to abound: every where and in all things I AM INSTRUCTED BOTH TO BE FULL AND TO BE HUNGRY, both to abound and to suffer need.**
>
> **Phillippians 4:12**

The Disobedience of Saul

Saul was a classic example of one who thought he was wiser than God and could compensate for his disobedience. No sacrifice, no matter how big is acceptable to God if it is done in disobedience. Read the Bible. There are many sacrifices that God is not pleased with. God is not against sacrifice, but He wants your obedience first.

> **TO WHAT PURPOSE IS THE MULTITUDE OF YOUR SACRIFICES UNTO ME? saith the LORD: I am full of the burnt offerings of rams, and the fat of fed beasts; and I delight not in the blood of bullocks, or of lambs, or of he goats.**
>
> **Isaiah 1:11**

The Disobedience of Joshua

Joshua had a clear mandate from the Lord to wipe out all the heathen nations in the Promised Land. It was explained to him that disobeying this command would result in these very nations becoming a snare onto the Israelites.

> **But if YE WILL NOT DRIVE OUT THE INHABITANTS of the land from before you; then it shall come to pass, that those which ye let remain of them shall be PRICKS in your eyes, and THORNS in your sides, and shall VEX YOU in the land wherein ye dwell.**
>
> **Numbers 33:55**

However, Joshua left the heathen in three key cities. He obeyed God everywhere except in Gaza, Gath and Ashdod. Read it for yourself.

> **Joshua made war a long time with all those kings. There was not a city that made peace with the children of Israel, save the Hivites the inhabitants of Gibeon: all other they took in battle. For it was of the LORD to harden their hearts, that they should come against Israel in battle, that he might destroy them utterly, and that they might have no favour, but that he might destroy them, as the LORD commanded Moses.**
>
> **And at that time came Joshua, and cut off the Anakims from the mountains, from Hebron, from Debir, from Anab, and from all the mountains of Judah, and from all the mountains of Israel: Joshua destroyed them utterly with their cities. THERE WAS NONE OF THE ANAKIMS LEFT IN THE LAND OF THE CHILDREN OF ISRAEL: ONLY IN GAZA,IN GATH, AND IN ASHDOD, THERE REMAINED.**
>
> **So Joshua took the whole land, according to all that the LORD said unto Moses; and Joshua gave it for an inheritance unto Israel according to their divisions by their tribes. And the land rested from war.**
>
> **Joshua 11:18-23**

It is very interesting to note the three groups of people that Joshua left alive: Gath, Gaza and Ashdod. Each one of these three groups of people gave birth to a significant enemy of the people of God. The Lord foresaw this and that is why he gave that instruction.

Theses cities became the breeding grounds for future enemies. The city of Gath produced Goliath. Delilah who was a thorn in Samson's flesh was from Gaza. The god Dagon, into whose temple the Ark of the Covenant was taken, was in the land of Ashdod. These enemies lived to fight God's people and no one has ever forgotten about these three evil agents. Perhaps, by your disobedience, you are giving birth to future enemies of God. A sacrifice will not prevent the emergence of future enemies. Obedience will.

Goliath of Gath

And there went out a champion out of the camp of the Philistines, named GOLIATH, OF GATH, whose height was six cubits and a span.

1 Samuel 17:4

Delilah of Gaza

Then went SAMSON TO GAZA, and … loved a woman in the valley of Sorek, whose name was Delilah.

Judges 16:1, 4

Dagon of Ashdod

And the Philistines took the ark of God, and brought it from Ebenezer unto Ashdod. When the Philistines took the ark of God, they brought it into the house of Dagon, and set it by Dagon. And when they of Ashdod arose early on the morrow, behold, Dagon was fallen upon his face to the earth before the ark of the LORD. And they took Dagon, and set him in his place again.

1 Samuel 5:1-3

May the Lord save us from our own modern day cities of Gath, Gaza and Ashdod!

Chapter

19

Church Planting and the Priestly Ministry

CHAPTER SUMMARY

Read and find out seven important things you should know about the Priestly Ministry. It is the ministry of the priest which counteracts the effects of the devil today.

- **Seven Things That Every Church Planter Should Know About the Priestly Ministry**

19.1 We are priests unto the Lord

19.2 The prayers we offer are incense to the Lord.

19.3 The priest ministers to the Lord and Not for the Lord.

19.4 There is a need for perpetual incense (unceasing prayer) to be offered unto the Lord.

19.5 A priest sins when he does not offer the incense of prayer.

19.6 The priest is able to save (or cause salvation) by intercession.

19.7 Great miracles happen to the priest as he performs his priestly duty.

When pastors become priests, substantial churches are born. Satan's number one ministry is to accuse pastors of evil. He stands before the throne of God and points out our mistakes to us and to the Lord.

This ministry of accusation is so intense that the most appropriate title for the devil today is "the accuser of the brethren". While this ministry of accusation is going on, the ministry of intercession is carried out by the priests of the Lord. It is only the ministry of the priest that counteracts the effects of the accuser.

The accuser is like a prosecutor. If the prosecutor gets his way, judgment will be meted out. If the priestly ministry doesn't go on, the accuser will succeed.

Seven Things That Every Church Planter Should Know About the Priestly Ministry

1. We are priests unto the Lord

> **But ye are a chosen generation, A ROYAL PRIESTHOOD, an holy nation, a peculiar people; that ye should shew forth the praises of him who hath called you out of darkness into his marvellous light:**
>
> **1 Peter 2:9**

> **And hath made us kings and priests unto God and his Father; to him be glory and dominion forever and ever. Amen.**
>
> **Revelation 1:6**

2. The prayers we offer are incense to the Lord.

> **Let my PRAYER be set forth before thee AS INCENSE; and the lifting up of my hands as the evening sacrifice.**
>
> **Psalm 141:2**

> **And the SMOKE OF THE INCENSE, which came with the PRAYERS OF THE SAINTS, ascended up before God out of the angel's hand.**
>
> **Revelation 8:4**

3. The priest ministers to the Lord and not for the Lord.

> **For every high priest is ordained to offer gifts and sacrifices…**
>
> **Hebrews 8:3**

4. There is a need for perpetual incense (unceasing prayer) to be offered unto the Lord.

> **And Aaron shall burn thereon sweet incense every morning: when he dresseth the lamps, he shall burn incense upon it. And when Aaron lighteth the lamps at even, he shall burn incense upon it,**

A PERPETUAL INCENSE before the LORD throughout your generations.

Exodus 30:7-8

5. A priest sins when he does not offer the incense of prayer.

Moreover as for me, God forbid that I should SIN AGAINST THE LORD IN CEASING TO PRAY for you: but I will teach you the good and the right way:

1 Samuel 12:23

6. The priest is able to save (or cause salvation) by intercession.

Wherefore he is ABLE ALSO TO SAVE them to the uttermost that come unto God by him, SEEING HE EVER LIVETH TO MAKE INTERCESSION FOR THEM.

Hebrews 7:25

7. Great miracles happen to the priest as he performs his priestly duty.

There was in the days of Herod, the king of Judaea, A CERTAIN PRIEST NAMED ZACHARIAS, of the course of Abia: and his wife was of the daughters of Aaron, and her name was Elisabeth.

And they were both righteous before God, walking in all the commandments and ordinances of the Lord blameless.

AND THEY HAD NO CHILD, because that Elisabeth was barren, and they both were now well stricken in years.

And it came to pass, that while HE EXECUTED THE PRIEST'S OFFICE BEFORE GOD in the order of his course, According to the custom of the priest's office, HIS LOT WAS TO BURN INCENSE when he went into the temple of the Lord. And the whole multitude of the people were praying without at the time of incense.

And THERE APPEARED UNTO HIM AN ANGEL OF THE LORD standing on the right side of the altar of incense.

And when Zacharias saw him, he was troubled, and fear fell upon him. But the angel said unto him, Fear not, Zacharias: for thy prayer is heard; and thy wife Elisabeth shall bear thee a son, and thou shalt call his name John. And thou shalt have joy and gladness; and many shall rejoice at his birth.

For he shall be great in the sight of the Lord, and shall drink neither wine nor strong drink; and he shall be filled with the Holy Ghost, even from his mother's womb.

And many of the children of Israel shall he turn to the Lord their God. And he shall go before him in the spirit and power of Elias, to turn

the hearts of the fathers to the children, and the disobedient to the wisdom of the just; to make ready a people prepared for the Lord.

And Zacharias said unto the angel, Whereby shall I know this? for I am an old man, and my wife well stricken in years.

And the angel answering said unto him, I am Gabriel, that stand in the presence of God; and am sent to speak unto thee, and to shew thee these glad tidings.

And, behold, thou shalt be dumb, and not able to speak, until the day that these things shall be performed, because thou believest not my words, which shall be fulfilled in their season.

And the people waited for Zacharias, and marvelled that he tarried so long in the temple. And when he came out, he could not speak unto them: and they perceived that he had seen a vision in the temple: for he beckoned unto them, and remained speechless.

And it came to pass, that, as soon as the days of his ministration were accomplished, he departed to his own house.

Now Elisabeth's full time came that she should be delivered; AND SHE BROUGHT FORTH A SON.

Luke 1:5-23, 57

Chapter

20

How to Plant a Church

CHAPTER SUMMARY

Many people are afraid of starting a church because they do not know how to pioneer new work. The art of beginning a church is the art of witnessing, following-up and gathering sheep together.

- **How to Plant a Church**

Avoid these Mistakes:

- **Do not hurriedly appoint people to leadership positions.**
- **Do not be discouraged because of fluctuating attendance**
- **Do not rent an expensive hall.**
- **Do not keep the church's money in your house or in your personal account.**
- **Do not count the money yourself but assign people to do so.**

You Don't Need These Things:

- **You do not need a complimentary card or a briefcase to build a Megachurch!**
- **A constitution is not vital in the early stages.**
- **A church logo is not important, neither is a church flag.**
- **Initially, it may not be necessary to register a church.**

■ Why People Fear to Start Churches

You do not need to break up someone else's church to begin your own! How would you feel if someone was building his house next to yours and decided to break down your house to get some blocks for his? That is madness!

Unfortunately, this seems to be the only way that some people feel they can start a church. From today, do not be afraid of starting out in an honourable way. If God has really spoken to you, it will succeed!

Count the Cost

> **For which of you, intending to build a tower, sitteth not down first, and counteth the cost...**
>
> **Luke 14:28**

Carefully consider the implications of starting a church. It is not going to be easy! Not many people want to identify with a small thing. I learnt many years ago that there are two types of people in the world. There are those who push the canoe from the sand into the sea. Then there are those who jump into the boat when it is safely on the water. When the canoe is on the sand, it is very difficult to push it into the water. When it is on the water it is safer and many more people jump in. That is why it is easier for a large church to grow.

When I began in the ministry I was despised and opposed! Looking back, I am surprised that I was able to survive the storms of beginning a church on my own. At certain times, I felt like giving up. Everyone in the world seemed against me. They called me names and ridiculed me.

When I carried a set of drums from my room in the medical hostel to a nearby classroom, I must have looked like a crazy zealot! "What does this person think he is doing with a few medical and nursing students?"

I had no help from any of the bigger churches of my day. Some of them ridiculed me while others even opposed me. There was no help or approval from any man of God.

Do Not Become Desperate

Do not become financially desperate in the early stages of ministry. Be careful not to become dependent on the church you are pioneering for your financial survival. That is a big mistake! If you do, you will become a desperate man, clutching at every straw for survival.

A small church usually cannot afford to pay the salary of a pastor, much less buy him a car. My advice to anyone who is beginning a church is to find a job and start the church as a lay person. When people see that you are not ministering for financial gain, they will be more interested in your new church.

Too many pastors are desperate for more and more offerings from their few members. Sixteen people cannot look after you. Twenty-one people cannot support your upkeep and your children's school fees. Don't be a desperate pastor! Get a job right now! At the right time, the church will have more than enough money to look after its pastors. I had to invest a lot of my own money to get the church to work. Although I am now in full-time ministry, I was not paid for the first five years of the church's existence.

There is another reason why you should not draw a salary in the early stages of a church. Money will be needed to buy equipment and to pay for other expenses like rent. If you siphon out the lifeblood of the church's money, it will not develop normally.

Two or Three is Enough

How many people are needed to start a church? The answer is in the Bible! Two or three!

> **For where two or three are gathered together in my name, there am I in the midst of them.**
>
> **Matthew 18:20**

Some people have criticized me for having two or three people in a church. Well, such criticism comes from an ignoramus. I would rather hear my dogs barking in the morning than to listen to critical and inexperienced scoffers!

I do not start my churches with half a section of another person's church. If I have one pastor who is ready to obey God, all I need to do is to send him and he will start the work. The Lighthouse Cathedral was started with as few as five people.

When I went to Zürich to start a church, I knew only one person. Today that church has several hundred people in it. One pastor who did not know anybody in South Africa, but was willing to do the work of God, started our church in South Africa. You do not need more than one person to start a church. I have churches that have only three people, and I am not ashamed to say it. Do not try to impress anyone; just do the work of God! Sometimes people are afraid to pioneer a church because they do not know how to do basic Christian tasks. What do I mean by the basics? The basics are praying, witnessing and following up converts.

The Megachurch Had One Member!

One day, one of my pastors went to church and only one person came. He told me that he was very discouraged and depressed. He led that one person in worship. Then he preached to that one person. Afterwards he took an offering from that one person and then closed the service. He narrated to me how he went back home to his apartment in the deepest and blackest depression of his life. I am happy to tell you that today his church is a Megachurch and is still growing.

If you are truly called of God then the only person you need is yourself! All churches which began in this way have grown to become great trees. The Bible says that the kingdom of God is like a mustard seed.

> **...The kingdom of heaven is like to a grain of mustard seed, which a man took, and sowed in his field: Which indeed is the least of all seeds: but when it is grown, it is the greatest among herbs, and becometh a tree, so that the birds of the air come and lodge in the branches thereof.**
>
> **Matthew 13:31, 32**

What does that mean? Whereas an Old Boys Association or a Keep Fit Club may begin with quite a number of people, the beginnings of a church are like insignificant seeds. But they can grow, and they will grow. Many of my pastors are surprised when their churches grow. They cannot believe that the church will work. The beginning looks so miserable, yet that is how the kingdom of God is.

Don't Be in a Hurry

There isn't any tree that grows from a seed into a large tree overnight. No human being grows to be six feet tall in one year. No two-year old grows into an eighteen-year old within six months. If you have a hasty spirit, you will not be successful in starting a church.

> **He that hasteth to be rich hath an evil eye, and considereth not that poverty shall come upon him.**
>
> **Proverbs 28:22**

In fact, when you are in a hurry, you are likely to cut corners, break someone else's church and criticize those ahead of you. You will commit dangerous sins in the early days of your fledgling ministry. Do not expect much within a year. Don't be surprised if you only have twenty people after two years. The mustard seed will surely grow into a Megachurch!

Pray for and Recruit Pillars

Pray for labourers. Ask God to give you helpers. Then go out and recruit pillars. Jesus called individuals to follow him. Jesus recruited Simon and Andrew. Then He also recruited James and John.

> **Now as he walked by the sea of Galilee, he saw Simon and Andrew his brother... And Jesus said unto them, Come ye after me, and I will make you to become fishers of men.**
>
> **Mark 1:16, 17**
>
> **And when he had gone a little further thence, he saw James the son of Zebedee, and John his brother... And straightway he called them and they left their father... and went after him.**
>
> **Mark 1:19, 20**

These people later became pillars in the church.

> **And when James, Cephas, and John, who seemed to be PILLARS...**
>
> **Galatians 2:9**

Sometimes you need to travel quite far in order to convince certain important pillars to join your church. Be extra careful that you do not break down somebody else's church in the process of building your own.

Making an open invitation to all is different from coercing people to leave their church to join you. The very existence of a church is an open invitation. Remember that you will reap what you sow (Galatians 6:7). If you pressurize pillars in another person's church to leave, it will happen to you one day.

One important aspect in recruiting people is to pray for labourers. Let it be your daily prayer topic. Ask God for workers and committed people. Pray for people who will be loyal to you in everything that you do. Pray for people who will support you.

> **Pray ye therefore the Lord of the harvest, that he will send forth LABOURERS into his harvest.**
>
> **Matthew 9:38**

Lay a Foundation of Prayer

I recommend an average time of prayer and fasting of three weeks or more. Pray for the future of the church. Do not expect results next week. The answer to these prayers will be seen in the years ahead.

When I first came to Korle-Bu (the area in Accra where our church is located), I would go at ten o'clock every night with four other medical students to the beach to pray. We would pray up until midnight. As I stood on the rocks near the seashore, my prayer was simply, "Lord, let your will be done. Do whatever you want to do with my life." As the years have gone by, the Lord has answered this prayer beyond my wildest imagination.

I believe in laying a solid foundation of prayer and fasting at the beginning of every church. The church is a spiritual entity and not a social club. It must be established on scriptural and spiritual foundations.

Some useful Scriptures in praying for church establishment and church growth are:

> **...Thy will be done...**
>
> **Matthew 6:10**
>
> **Thy kingdom come...**
>
> **Matthew 6:10**
>
> **Ask of me, and I shall give thee the heathen for thine inheritance...**
>
> **Psalm 2:8**
>
> **...enlarge my coast...**
>
> **1 Chronicles 4:10**
>
> **...increase them with men like a flock.**
>
> **Ezekiel 36:37**
>
> **...for as soon as Zion travailed, she brought forth her children.**
>
> **Isaiah 66:8**
>
> **...I travail in birth again...**
>
> **Galatians 4:19**

Be a Motivational Leader

After gathering a few people into a room, you will need to greatly encourage them, including yourself. People will be thinking in their minds, "Are you out of your mind? Is this what you call a church?" You must learn to do what David did when faced with discouragement. Encourage yourself first.

> **...but David encouraged himself in the Lord his God.**
>
> **1 Samuel 30:6**

Then you must encourage the people. Tell them that though the beginning seems to be small, the future is going to be great!

> **Though thy beginning was small, yet thy latter end should greatly increase.**
>
> **Job 8:7**

Tell them not to despise the small start. Explain to them that the end is always better than the beginning. When they see that you are encouraged, they will be motivated to continue with the church.

> **Better is the end of a thing than the beginning thereof...**
>
> **Ecclesiastes 7:8**
>
> **For who hath despised the day of small things?...**
>
> **Zechariah 4:10**

Tell them that they are privileged to be founding members of a great church. Explain that the foundation of a building is the most important part of a building. Therefore, they are the most important members that the church will ever have. Tell them that Jesus always had a special place and reward for the apostles because they were his foundational members.

> **And are built upon the foundation of the apostles...**
>
> **Ephesians 2:20**

Do not make the mistake of rebuking and shouting at them. Do not vent your frustration on your few members. It is not their fault that the church is small in the beginning stages. Preach faith! Preach hope! Preach stabilization! Preach about a better tomorrow! People love to hear that tomorrow will be better than today. You must be bold and shameless in your preaching.

> **I say unto you, Though he will not rise and give him, because he is his friend, yet because of his importunity [shamelessness] he will rise and give him as many as he needeth.**
>
> **Luke 11:8**

In the above passage, the Greek word Anaideia translated importunity, also means shamelessness. The shamelessly persistent person gets results. Let's face it! There is some amount of shame in beginning a ministry with a few people. That is why people despise small beginnings!

Shamelessness (Anaideia) must characterize all that you do when you begin a church. Shamelessly invite people to join you on Sunday morning. When they see that you are not shy of your church, they will be interested in coming. Shamelessly advertise your church.

People will believe what you say about your church. If you have an assistant, he must say good things about the preaching and about the church in general. All of these things help to create a good atmosphere for church growth.

Witnessing and Follow-Up

This must be predominant in all of your church activities. You must boldly enter into the houses of your city and preach Christ to the people. You must shamelessly lead people to Christ in their living rooms. Pray for them and invite them to church.

Stand on the street and talk to passers-by about Jesus Christ. If you cannot shamelessly do street evangelism, then you cannot be a pastor. Lead the congregation in inviting people to church every Sunday. Do not be depressed if most of the visitors do not come back. Most of them will not stay anyway. God will supernaturally bring the increase. Pastors must realize that there is a spiritual principle of sowing and reaping. Whatever you sow is what you will reap.

> **...for whatsoever a man soweth, that shall he also reap.**
>
> **Galatians 6:7**

If you sow seeds through invitations and witnessing, you will reap from it one day. My experience is that after a crusade or an outreach we initially have very few results. However, after awhile we begin to have people coming from the very place we did the outreach. Usually they are not the people we witnessed to. But God divinely sends them to us from that place. Use all of the principles of anagkazo (For further study see the book, "Anagkazo" by Bishop Heward-Mills).

Avoid these Mistakes

Do not hurriedly appoint people to leadership positions. Allow time to pass before you make definite appointments. Many of the people who are with you in the beginning will leave anyway. Do not be discouraged because of fluctuating attendance. Do not be discouraged because of a rotational shift of the members, i.e., half attend this week, the other half next week. That is how sheep behave. Take no notice of them!

Do not rent an expensive hall. Do not keep the church's money in your house or in your personal account. One day somebody will accuse you of stealing, although you may have contributed a lot to the church. Do not count the money yourself but assign people to do so.

You Don't Need These Things

Contrary to what people think, several things are not necessary when starting a church. You do not need a complimentary card or a briefcase to build a Megachurch! A constitution is not vital in the early stages. What is important is to have members and a regular congregation. A church logo is not important, neither is a church flag.

Initially, it may not be necessary to register a church. Many countries allow freedom of association and freedom of religion. Just build the church and fill it with people. Pray for them, preach the Word, visit the sheep and trust God! Since the greater one is in you, you cannot fail!

Chapter

21

Planting a Network of Churches

CHAPTER SUMMARY

Every pastor can expect the Lord to use you to plant more than one church. After a period you will have a network of churches. These churches will have to be managed. Managing a network of churches involves training, encouraging and guiding a team of ministers as they work. Discover how in this chapter.

■ Three Keys to Planting a Network of Churches

21.1 **Key No. 1 - Teaching on How to Do the Work of Ministry**

21.2 **Key No. 2 - Teaching on Loyalty**

21.3 **Key No. 3 - Teaching on Church Administration**

■ The Advantages of a Network of Churches

21.4 **History has proved that the networks of churches or branches are very successful. These networks of churches are sometimes called denominations.**

21.5 **There are several well-known networks of churches in the world today. These networks are often the most stable and established**

congregations everywhere. The Assemblies of God Church, the Church of Pentecost, Church of God in Christ are but a few notable examples of these networks. The largest church in the world, pastored by David Yonggi Cho, belongs to the Assemblies of God Church network.

21.6 History has shown that belonging to a network of churches can give rise to very large stable congregations. It may be the key to church growth for your congregation.

21.7 Belonging to a network of churches sometimes eliminates the instability that characterizes young independent churches. The institutional stagnation that sometimes develops in a network of churches may be much less of an evil compared to the advantages that come with it.

21.8 In a network of churches, there are tried and tested principles which are passed on to sister churches.

21.9 In a network of churches, the already existing name serves as publicity and attracts people to the churches. This name becomes like a franchise and serves as a powerful asset. The good name of a network of churches also has spiritual significance that cannot be quantified.

21.10 In a network of churches, trained members benefit from an established and respected system of pastoral recommendation and appointments.

Three Keys to Planting a Network of Churches

Key No. 1 - Teaching on How to Do the Work of Ministry

The first key to planting a network of churches is the TRAINING of ministers. The congregation is a field in which you plant seeds. If you plant seeds of leadership and inspire the members to do pastoral work, they will do it. The more you teach on how to do the work of the ministry, the more potential ministers will be released.

When you teach your leaders, you are actually teaching many more people. You are also teaching the followers of this leader. Pastors must know the principle of explosive growth: if you want GROWTH, teach your members, if you want EXPLOSIVE GROWTH, teach your leaders!

Teaching leaders establishes authority over the leaders who work under you. This is because the authority over the leaders is demonstrated by your ability to feed them. Teaching ordinary members is an investment into the church today. Teaching leaders is an investment into the future when you are gone. Success without a successor is failure!

Every pastor must teach leaders because Jesus Christ taught leaders all the time. Pastors must spend more time teaching leaders than teaching ordinary church members. This is the pattern set by Christ Jesus. Teaching leaders is your greatest key to true expansion. You will not have anyone to delegate if you have not trained leaders.

Every pastor must teach his leaders because the leaders will never know what to do unless you teach them. Many pastors assume that the potential leaders around them will acquire vital knowledge by osmosis. People feel that leadership is for special people who are born that way. Osmosis is not the key to leadership - teaching is!

I have written many books on these subjects which I recommend to you: "Lay People and ahe Ministry", "The Mega Church", "Transform Your Pastoral Ministry" etc. As you teach your members these materials, you will be surprised at what they will become.

Key No. 2 - Teaching on Loyalty

The second key to planting a network of churches is LOYALTY. Loyalty is essential for maintaining a network of churches. The churches you will plant will not be in the same location. It is therefore necessary for people to be loyal wherever they are situated. I have taught a lot on loyalty. I have also written two books on this subject "Loyalty and Disloyalty" and "Leaders and Loyalty". I recommend that you read these books, as they will be a blessing to your ministry.

I once heard of someone criticizing me for teaching on loyalty.

He said, "Why should you teach on loyalty and disloyalty?"

He went on to say that loyalty is not something that is taught but is something that people are inspired to do because of your leadership. I was not surprised that this dear critic of mine had not planted a single branch of his church but was criticizing someone who had planted over four hundred churches.

On another occasion, a dear pastor criticized me for teaching on loyalty. However when his church split, he became an avid reader of my books and even promoted them to other ministers. Loyalty is a key subject which must be taught until the culture of faithfulness and loyalty is established!

Key No. 3 - Teaching on Church Administration

Church administration involves the managing of the churches that have been created. It involves managing a combination of secular and spiritual issues. It involves balancing natural things with supernatural things.

Church administration involves the blending of hierarchical leadership and a democratic form of government. Both of these styles are biblical. The Bible has examples of committees being formed as in Acts chapter 6. As in the case of Paul and Timothy, the Bible also has examples of an autocratic style of leadership with direct instructions being handed down.

Church administration requires combining the power of God and the wisdom of God. See my book entitled Church Administration.

Without good church administration everything that you build will eventually collapse. You need to master church administration otherwise your ministry will be likened to a rocket that shoots out and falls apart shortly after take off.

> **But unto them which are called, both Jews and Greeks, Christ the power of God, and the wisdom of God**
>
> **1 Corinthians 1:24**

The Advantages of a Network of Churches

1. History has proved that the networks of churches or branches are very successful. These networks of churches are sometimes called denominations.

2. There are several well-known networks of churches in the world today. These networks are often the most stable and established congregations everywhere. The Assemblies of God Church, the Church of Pentecost, Church of God in Christ are but a few notable examples of these networks. The largest church in the world, pastored by David Yonggi Cho, belongs to the Assemblies of God Church network.

3. History has shown that belonging to a network of churches can give rise to very large stable congregations. It may be the key to church growth for your congregation.

4. Belonging to a network of churches sometimes eliminates the instability that characterizes young independent churches. The institutional stagnation that sometimes develops in a network of churches may be much less of an evil compared to the advantages that come with it.

5. In a network of churches, there are tried and tested principles which are passed on to sister churches.

6. In a network of churches, the already existing name serves as publicity and attracts people to the churches. This name becomes like a franchise and serves as a powerful asset. The good name of a network of churches also has spiritual significance that cannot be quantified.

7. In a network of churches, trained members benefit from an established and respected system of pastoral recommendation and appointments.

8. The network of churches can benefit from each other financially. You are not likely to get financial support outside your network. Through a system of brotherly interdependence, churches are able to accomplish much more.

9. Church members readily flow between churches belonging to the same network. The network of churches is therefore to keep members within the fold.

10. Churches within the network easily benefit from anointed senior ministers of that network. They do not have to go through the protocol or experience the cost of having such ministers.

11. Pastors within the network of churches can receive fatherly counsel and encouragement from seniors. Pastors of independent churches are usually suspicious and wary of external ministers who parade as fathers. There is little trust because independent churches often compete with one another rather than support each other.

12. Churches within a network operate under a particular spiritual covering. The same anointing runs through the entire network because it is really one church.

Section

2

THE MEGA CHURCH

"...Go out into the highways and hedges, and compel them to come in. THAT MY HOUSE MAY BE FILLED" Luke 14:23. The heartcry of God is for the world to be saved, and for His house -the church- to be filled! From this revelation was born this section. Your church and ministry will never be the same again after reading this!

Chapter

22

Twenty-Five Reasons Why You Must Have a Mega Church

CHAPTER SUMMARY

- **25 Reasons Why You Must Have a Mega Church**

22.1 You must desire to have a mega church because that is the most appropriate vision and goal for a pastor.

22.2 You must desire to have a mega church because the desire for a mega church will lead you on a journey that will make your church grow.

25.3 You must have a mega church because the prophetic destiny of every church that the Lord builds is to have a greater end than the beginning.

22.4 You must have a mega church because most pastors are deceived into thinking that the work is being done when it is not being done.

22.5 You must have a mega church because God's will is that "His house may be filled." Most churches are not filled because they are not mega churches.

22.6 You must have a mega church because your harvest field is the world.

22.7 You must have a mega church because the biblical example of churches had thousands of members.

22.8 You must have a mega church because having a large church means that more souls have been won to the kingdom.

22.9 You must have a mega church because in a mega church more workers and labourers are released to work for God.

22.10 You must have a mega church because through a mega church more ministers of the gospel, full time pastors and bishops are appointed and released into the harvest field.

22.11 You must have a mega church because in a mega church more people are involved in prayer against the power of the prince of the air.

22.12 You must have a mega church because a mega church generates large crowds and large crowds create great expectation.

22.13 You must have a mega church because in a mega church you will have a greater manifestation of miracles because of the greater crowds and greater expectation.

22.14 You must have a mega church because more evangelism is possible through a mega church.

22.15 You must have a mega church because a mega church has a larger and greater income that can be used for the work of God.

22.16 You must have a mega church because special ministries which take care of special needs will develop within a mega church.

22.17 You must have a mega church because it shows that you have made full proof of your ministry.

22.18 You must have a mega church because in a mega church there are more "beloveds" (potential marriage partners).

22.19 You must have a mega church because in a mega church more marriages and more weddings take place.

22.20 You must have a mega church because there are more contacts and connections through the people in the mega church.

22.21 You must have a mega church because in a mega church there is always a large pool of employers who can help the church members.

22.22 You must have a mega church because all the different needs of the congregation can be met through the mega church.

22.23 You must have a mega church because a mega church is more likely to accomplish the 25% biblical quota of souls won from the community.

22.24 You must have a mega church because a mega church is a force to reckon with and it becomes a nation within a nation.

22.25 You must have a mega church because the glory of the end time church will be greater than the glory of the early church.

Twenty-Five Reasons Why You Must Have a Mega Church

1. You must desire to have a mega church because that is the most appropriate vision and goal for a pastor.

The best vision and burning desire for every pastor is the vision for a large church. Why not have a large church if you are going to have a church?

> **Where there is no vision, the people perish: but he that keepeth the law, happy is he.**
>
> **Proverbs 29:18**

2. You must desire to have a mega church because the desire for a mega church will lead you on a journey that will make your church grow.

Having a desire for miracles will lead to the specific result of having miracles in your ministry. Having a desire for the anointing will lead to the specific result of having the anointing. The desire for church growth will lead you on a journey of discovery that will make your church grow.

> **Therefore I say unto you, what things soever ye desire, when ye pray, believe that ye receive them, and ye shall have them.**
>
> **Mark 11:24**

3. You must have a mega church because the prophetic destiny of every church that the Lord builds is to have a greater end than the beginning.

Do not be discouraged about the smallness of your church today. It has been predicted that the end of your ministry will be much more glorious than the beginning. Because the word of God prophesies that the glory of the latter house shall be greater than the glory of the former, you must expect something more glorious than what you saw at the beginning. God will do something great and He will increase the congregation.

> **Though thy beginning was small, yet thy latter end should greatly increase.**
>
> **Job 8:7**

4. You must have a mega church because most pastors are deceived into thinking that the work is being done when it is not being done.

During the time of His ministry, Jesus made a very important statement.

> **...The harvest truly is plenteous, but the labourers are few...**
>
> **Matthew 9:37**

This means there are plenty of winnable souls. There is plenty of work for us all. There are plenty of people to fill our churches.

Many pastors are deceived by the fact that their little halls are full. Many ministers feel that they have "arrived" in ministry. You receive a nice salary and have a nice car. God has blessed you and all your expenses are paid for. This does not mean that you have "arrived". Do not let the devil blind your eyes to the real work we have to do. It is Satan who fans the church to sleep!! He whispers to the hearts of many ministers: "Everything is O.K." "This is it." "You have made it." "This is how far you can go." "This is everything you can achieve for God!" Such ministers have had their spiritual and visionary eyes blinded by Satan. The enemy whispers to their heart, "Everything is okay. This is it! You have made it!"

Satan wants your church to remain small. The fewer people you have in your congregation the more captives he has. The size of your church shows you to what extent you are depopulating Hell. When you have a megachurch, it means that you are establishing more souls. It also means that more souls have escaped from the clutches of the devil.

5. You must have a mega church because God's will is that "His house may be filled." Most churches are not filled because they are not mega churches.

> **And the lord said unto the servant, Go out into the highways and hedges, and compel them to come in, THAT MY HOUSE MAY BE FILLED.**
>
> **Luke 14:23**

In Luke 14, the Lord gave us an important revelation. The master said to his servant, "I need my house to be filled." The master in this story represents Jesus. Jesus wanted His house to be filled. In other words, Jesus wants His churches to be filled. God wants full churches! The master in this story was not content with having just a few people at his party. He could have had the party anyway, but he wanted many more people. And more especially he wanted the house to be filled. Through this story, God is showing His will for the church. His will is more people! His will is filled rooms! His will is overflowing churches! His will is the MEGACHURCH!

6. You must have a mega church because your harvest field is the world.

God did not send us to a suburb of your town. Neither did He send us to a few villages. He sent us to the whole world. If we had a small field to harvest from, then we could not expect a large quantity of harvested fruits.

> **And he said unto them, Go ye into all the world, and preach the gospel to every creature. He that believeth and is baptized shall be saved; but he that believeth not shall be damned.**
>
> **Mark 16:15-16**

The fact that the entire world is to be reached implies that the harvest of souls that we will bring in must be very large. It will definitely be a major portion of the world's population. If a major section of the world's population is to be saved through the preaching of the gospel, then every church should be bursting at the seams for lack of space. Remember that there are over six billion souls out there waiting for us to reach them with the Gospel.

7. You must have a mega church because the biblical example of churches had thousands of members.

Is the early church not the best example for us to follow? If the early church had three thousand and five thousand people, should these numbers not serve as a guiding post for us? Indeed, these numbers are recorded in the bible so that we may know what to aim for.

> **Those who believed what Peter said were baptized and added to the church--about three thousand in all. They joined with the other believers and devoted themselves to the apostles' teaching and fellowship, sharing in the Lord's Supper and in prayer.**
>
> **Acts 2:41-42 (NLT)**
>
> **But many of the people who heard their message believed it, so that the number of believers totaled about five thousand men, not counting women and children.**
>
> **Acts 4:4 (NLT)**

8. You must have a mega church because having a large church means that more souls have been won to the kingdom.

In a large church there will be more services, more altar calls and more opportunities to be saved than a small church. Is it not the aim of every minister of the gospel to win souls to the Lord? Is it not an extra added blessing that a mega church leads to the salvation of many people who join it?

9. You must have a mega church because in a mega church more workers and labourers are released to work for God.

> **He said to his disciples, "The harvest is so great, but the workers are so few. So pray to the Lord who is in charge of the harvest; ask him to send out more workers for his fields**
>
> **Matthew 9:37-38 (NLT)**

There will always be a certain percentage of the flock who are real labourers. No matter what you do or say, a certain percentage of the church will not get involved in the real work of ministry. There will always be the spectators and observers. There will always be the commentators. The labourers will always be in the ministry. The larger the crowd you have, the more labourers will be sent forth. And the more easily you will be able to finance them.

10. You must have a mega church because through a mega church more ministers of the gospel, full time pastors and bishops are appointed and released into the harvest field.

In a large church there is always a training programme that produces ministers. A ten thousand member congregation will therefore produce more pastors than a hundred member church. Indeed, the pastor of a smaller church is not likely to have enough people who want to be ministers of the gospel.

11. You must have a mega church because in a mega church more people are involved in prayer against the power of the prince of the air.

For we wrestle not against flesh and blood, but against principalities, against powers, against the rulers of the darkness of this world, against spiritual wickedness in high places.

Wherefore take unto you the whole armour of God, that ye may be able to withstand in the evil day, and having done all, to stand.

Stand therefore, having your loins girt about with truth, and having on the breastplate of righteousness;

And your feet shod with the preparation of the gospel of peace; Above all, taking the shield of faith, wherewith ye shall be able to quench all the fiery darts of the wicked. And take the helmet of salvation, and the sword of the Spirit, which is the word of God:

Praying always with all prayer and supplication in the Spirit, and watching thereunto with all perseverance and supplication for all saints

Ephesians 6:12-18

When you have a megachurch, more prayer will go forth unto the Lord. Therefore, more people will be saved and established. When the Lord sent me to establish churches in Europe, He showed one key role that we were going to play in rebuilding His kingdom in that continent. You see, Europe has virtually become a continent of atheists. They have put God out of their minds. Many Europeans do not believe that God even exists.

Years ago, Europe sent out missionaries to the world. But now, they have fallen to the lowest state of demonic blindness and godlessness. The Lord showed me that one of our duties as a church was to release prayer into the atmosphere concerning the Church in Europe. Our presence in countries like Switzerland, The Netherlands and England, has resulted in much more intercession being made in those nations.

Our church in Geneva has all-night prayer meetings every Friday, praying from midnight until 6 a.m. They engage in spiritual warfare in a land where God is forgotten. As more churches like ours go into the nations, then more prayer will take place. This is one of the primary reasons why a large and branching church is important.

When the church I pastor, The Lighthouse Cathedral, grew to a certain size, we were able to successfully have all-night prayer meetings everyday. We had so many small groups within the church that it was possible to set up a rotation so that one of these groups could have an all-night prayer meeting everyday. Thus, we had a different group praying every night.

The larger the church, the more prayer groups are created. More prayer is possible in a megachurch! That is why the devil wants the church to remain small!

12. You must have a mega church because a mega church generates large crowds and large crowds create great expectation.

> **And as the people were in expectation, and all men mused in their hearts of John, whether he were the Christ, or not.**
>
> **Luke 3:15**

Through experience I have noticed that the larger the crowd, the greater the expectation. When there is a large gathering of God's people, there is an air of excitement, expectation and real faith. Why is this? This happens because the faith of everyone is heightened by what they see. The sight of a large crowd inspires faith and creates excitement. The combined faith of the crowd is greater than the faith of just one person. That helps to draw out the gift of God from the minister.

I have preached to small groups and to very large crowds. The spiritual atmosphere of these two situations is often different.

13. You must have a mega church because in a mega church you will have a greater manifestation of miracles because of the greater crowds and greater expectation.

> **Then Philip went down to the city of Samaria, and preached Christ unto them. And the people with one accord gave heed unto those things which Philip spake, hearing and seeing the miracles which he did. For unclean spirits, crying with loud voice, came out of many that were possessed with them: and many taken with palsies, and that were lame, were healed. And there was great joy in that city.**
>
> **Acts 8:5-8**
>
> **And they went forth, and preached every where, the Lord working with them, and confirming the word with signs following.**
>
> **Mark 16:20**

Whenever there is great faith, you can expect more power and miracles of healing. Jesus often said, "Your faith has made you whole." It is faith that generates the miraculous! I know some people will misunderstand me on this. I am not saying that God does not move in small congregations. I often minister in small congregations, and I see God moving in a wonderful way. God certainly does miracles in small churches. All I am saying is that, generally speaking, when there are more people, there is more faith, more expectation and therefore, more miracles. I think even the simplest Christian can understand this simple logic.

A bigger church means more people, which means more faith, which means more power, which means more miracles, which results in more testimonies!

Don't you want more glory, power and anointing to flow in your congregation? Dear pastor friend, believe God for a bigger church. With a bigger church, many more blessings will flow from the throne of God to his people.

14. You must have a mega church because more evangelism is possible through a mega church.

> **And now the word of the Lord is ringing out from you to people everywhere, even beyond Greece, for wherever we go we find people telling us about your faith in God. We don't need to tell them about it,**
>
> **1 Thessalonians 1:8 (NLT)**

One of the side effects of having a larger church is that more evangelism takes place. Our Cathedral is divided into about fifteen chapels. Under each chapel, there are several ministries and under each ministry several fellowships.

It is our policy that every ministry has at least one major outreach during each month. Since our church has many ministries, it is possible that fifty different outreaches by fifty different groups will be taking place at the same time at many different locations!

More soul winning has taken place simply because the church has grown larger. It is God's will for your church to grow larger so that more souls will be won for the Lord.

15. You must have a mega church because a mega church has a larger and greater income that can be used for the work of God.

> **Neither was there any among them that lacked: for as many as were possessors of lands or houses sold them, and brought the prices of the things that were sold, and laid them down at the apostles' feet: and distribution was made unto every man according as he had need.**
>
> **Acts 4:34-35**

Having more people also means having a higher church income. If a church has a good pastor, the money of the church will be used for the right things. Unfortunately, some pastors are more like vampires – they suck the blood of the church rather than pour their lives into the ministry.

A higher income means many more spiritual goals are achievable. Money is not an evil thing. Money is neutral! It is the love of money that is evil! Money is a weapon in the hand of man. If a good man has money he will use it to do good things. A good minister will use the income of a mega church to build the church and promote the gospel!

I had a dream that we would one day have trucks driving around the nation, holding crusades in every town and village. Once upon a time, that was just a dream. Now, with a larger church we have been able to purchase a truck and have begun crusading all across the nation. How was that possible? We had more people and therefore more money, and we could do more for God!

16. You must have a mega church because special ministries which take care of special needs will develop within a mega church.

It is important to desire to have a large church. Pastors must dream of having large congregations. A large church results in the multiplicity of many ministries. It results in the multiplication of several important activities in the church. For instance, it multiplies the ministry of music.

Initially, our church had only one choir. Now we have no less than six choirs in addition to numerous other singing groups. What does this mean? It means that a large church has resulted in vital multiplication. It is the will of God that more of His children sing for Him. The more singing groups we have, the more God is glorified. The number of choirs you have depends on the number of people in the church.

As the church grows, it becomes more diverse in its composition. This results in specialist ministries being developed. When you have a small church, there will usually be very few special ministries like a ministry to the poor, refugees, and to orphans. As the church becomes larger it is possible to get involved in some of these other areas. When a church is able to be involved in these special areas, many blessings are released! Look at the blessings that are available to churches that minister to the poor.

> **Blessed is he that considereth the poor: the Lord will deliver him in time of trouble. The Lord will preserve him, and keep him alive; and he shall be blessed upon the earth: and thou wilt not deliver him unto the will of his enemies.**
>
> **Psalm 41:1, 2**

These are powerful blessings for those who are able to grow to the point where they minister to special needs. Often when a church is small, it does not have the capacity to reach out in these areas. Have a vision of building a megachurch. Other special areas of ministry will develop within it. You will have people with the ministry of giving being released. There are churches which have men and women with a heart for financing the gospel.

> **...he that giveth, let him do it with simplicity;**
>
> **Romans 12:8**

It is rare to come across church members who have the ability to make a difference in the church through their giving. Every pastor would love to have members who take care of major expenses for the church.

In the earlier stages of our church's life, I had no one who could do things like that. But now, there are people who have the ability and the ministry of giving.

Other special areas that can develop are ministries to the poor and to the disabled. I have a dream to establish an orphanage. I've had this dream for a long time. But, it will take a large and strong church to be able to support such a venture. If you have a hundred orphans in your orphanage, you have to pay for three hundred meals a day. You also have to buy clothes for a hundred people. You then have to pay the hospital bills for a hundred children. After that you have to pay several professionals to care for these motherless and fatherless people. I think that you will agree with me that it will take a truly megachurch to set up such a ministry.

17. You must have a mega church because it shows that you have made full proof of your ministry.

Many ministers do not do a thorough job of being pastors! Many ministers only touch the surface of their calling! Many ministers are a phantom of what they could be! Most churches have the potential of growing larger. Often, the growth does not come because the pastor does not do a thorough job of pastoring the church. Every field of endeavour has greater or lesser dimensions. You must aim for the greatest possible dimension in pastoral work.

> **But you – keep your eye on what you are doing; accept the hard times along with the good; keep the Message alive; do a thorough job as God's servant.**
>
> **2 Timothy 4:5 (The Message)**

18. You must have a mega church because in a mega church there are more "beloveds" (potential marriage partners).

> **For there was not a needy person among them, for all who were owners of land or houses would sell them and bring the proceeds of the sales**
>
> **Acts 4:34 (NASB)**

Years ago, when our church was much smaller, a young lady said to me, "My type of man is not in this church." When I looked throughout my congregation, I realized that what she said was true. There was no suitable person for this woman to marry. Some years later she went ahead and married an unbeliever.

At another point another lady said, "There is no man who is old enough to marry me. So I'm going to a larger church where I can find a man to marry me." You see, she was thirty-nine years old and there were no forty-year-old bachelors in the church. All of the bachelors we had in our church were in their twenties and thirties. In a mega church there are brides and grooms of all ages. In a megachurch, even people over the age of seventy can become bridegrooms and brides.

19. You must have a mega church because in a mega church more marriages and more weddings take place.

People love to get married in church. Marriages and weddings are a spicy blessing for every congregation. The congregation always loves to hear of the announcement of upcoming marriages. They get excited and hope and pray that it will be their turn soon. You will be blessed with more weddings when you have a mega church. A healthy growing church is one that has numerous marriages taking place. I always pray that there will be more weddings and marriages in my church.

20. You must have a mega church because there are more contacts and connections through the people in the mega church.

> **As we have therefore opportunity, let us do good unto all men, especially unto them who are of the household of faith."**
>
> **Galatians 6:10**

The larger the church the more contacts and "connections" can be made. Let's face it, many things in this world depend on "who you know!" You may get a breakthrough just because you belong to a certain church. I have employers in my church to whom I can recommend potential employees. When our church was smaller, it was only full of students. Now, many people can find jobs through the church.

People like to stay in a place that has added blessings and security. The church members love these fringe benefits of making contacts and connections with others.

21. You must have a mega church because in a mega church there is always a large pool of employers who can help the church members.

In a large church you will have more people who are substantial enough to provide jobs to help the congregation. In a mega church you will have the added benefit of being able to fight the scourge of unemployment in your congregation.

> **And the congregation of those who believed were of one heart and soul; and not one of them claimed that anything belonging to him was his own; but all things were common property to them. And with great power the apostles were giving witness to the resurrection of the Lord Jesus, and abundant grace was upon them all. For there was not a needy person among them, for all who were owners of land or houses would sell them and bring the proceeds of the sales**
>
> **Acts 4:32-34 (NASB)**

22. You must have a mega church because all the different needs of the congregation can be met through the mega church.

A congregation is a group of people with varied needs. When I stand before large crowds asking them to lay hands where they have a need, everyone prays fervently because everyone has a need. If there are a thousand people, there are a thousand different needs. A mega church affords you the chance to meet many of these different needs. If there is a small church and someone needs a lawyer's advice it is not likely that he will find one. But in a large church, you are likely to find a lawyer, a doctor, an engineer, a pharmacist or even a psychiatrist.

> **And all those who had believed were together, and had all things in common; and they began selling their property and possessions, and were sharing them with all, as anyone might have need.**
>
> **Acts 2:44-45 (NASB)**

23. You must have a mega church because a mega church is more likely to accomplish the 25% biblical quota of souls won from the community.

> **And when he sowed, some [25%] seeds fell by the way side... some [25%] fell upon stony places... some [25%] fell among thorns... But other [25%] fell into good ground and brought forth fruit...**
>
> **Matthew 13:4-8**

The Bible teaches us that the sower went out to sow the Word of God in a city. The result was that, one out of four (25%) of his seeds yielded good results. If we win only a quarter of our cities to Christ, I can assure you that there will be no more half-filled churches. It is time for the Church to achieve its biblical quota of twenty- five percent of the population. How many people are there in your city?

There are about four million people in the city of Accra, Ghana. According to my little theory, at least twenty-five percent of them should have responded to the Word of God. This means that at least one million of these people should be safely established in the Church. However, I wonder how many people darken the doorways of church buildings in Accra every Sunday morning. Several thousands do, but I doubt whether it reaches our biblical quota of twenty-five percent of the population.

If the church of God attains the twenty-five percent goal, there will be many many large churches scattered all over the city. Every church will have multiple church services from morning to evening. Calculate it for yourself! You will see that the Church is no where near attaining that twenty-five percent goal. How many born again Christians attend church on a Sunday morning in your city? What is the population of your city?

Total citywide born again church attendance **= 25% ??**

Total population of your city

When I did this calculation for my own city, I realized that we were far from achieving the results of that "sower who went out to sow". But I prophesy that churches shall be filled in the last days. The land shall be filled with megachurches. God wants big churches because He is expecting at least twenty-five percent of the population to respond positively to our preaching.

24. You must have a mega church because a mega church is a force to reckon with and it becomes a nation within a nation.

As the church increases in size it will become a powerful community. It virtually becomes a nation of its own. Governments begin to fear the power and influence of a mega church, but they despise small churches. Governments know that a large church means a lot of people, which means a lot of votes. The politicians fear the power of the masses. They know that popular opinion keeps them in power. They know that pastors are influencing people's minds. Small things are easy to despise. The Bible says,

> **For who hath despised the day of small things?**
>
> **Zechariah 4:10**

Politicians can no longer despise the reality of the Kingdom of God when it is massive! They cannot attack the pastors in the churches when they know the number of people they lead.

Our church was once attacked and the walls around us broken. The people behind the attack thought that they could get away with it easily. They did not appreciate the magnitude, strength and scope of influence of the church they were attacking. The "people behind the scenes" were very surprised when the attack led to a nationwide crisis. Several churches and the general public rallied together against the perceived attackers. The politicians had to act quickly to prevent nationwide demonstrations and civil unrest.

As you read this book, I want you to believe God for a megachurch. I want you to receive the anointing to rise out of smallness into the largeness that God has destined for you.

25. You must have a mega church because the glory of the end time church will be greater than the glory of the early church.

> **The glory of this latter house shall be greater than of the former, saith the Lord of hosts...**
>
> **Haggai 2:9**

The Bible predicts that the glory, which means beauty, of the latter day church, will far exceed the glory of the former one. I believe that we are in that latter day. When I consider what the Lord has done in Ghana over the last fifteen years, I realize that God is bringing a greater glory to His end-time Church. The largest churches some fifteen years ago would be the youth groups of some of the megachurches that God has raised up today!

Let me share with you a very important secret. God does not work with only one person. The Spirit of God does not move in only one church. If a pastor has been able to achieve great growth in your city, it is a clear sign that the grace of God is abundant for the work of church growth there.

People who think that God is only using one man are deceived!

The Lord ministered powerfully to Ahab the king through Elijah the Tishbite (1 Kings 17, 18, 21). But there was another powerful prophet called Micaiah who was used to rebuke Ahab the king. God does not limit Himself to one man.

Elijah made the mistake of thinking he was the only one who was faithful to God.

> **And he said, I have been very jealous for the Lord God of hosts: because the children of Israel have forsaken thy covenant, thrown down thine altars, and slain thy prophets with the sword; and I, even I only, am left...**
>
> **1 Kings 19:14**

But the Lord showed him that He had seven thousand other faithful prophets.

> **Yet I have left me seven thousand in Israel, all the knees which have not bowed unto Baal, and every mouth which hath not kissed him.**
>
> **1 Kings 19:18**

Many big churches are springing up. God is raising up men and women of integrity to pastor His people. Flow in it. Catch the spirit! You will also walk in the glory of the latter church. Learn the strategies of church growth. Obtain the power and the wisdom of God. Walk in love towards the brethren. Love even those who slander and betray you. Every great work of the Holy Spirit is as a result of love, unity and teamwork.

I really want to emphasize and stress this great truth that God does not work with one isolated person. Did you know that when Ezekiel was prophesying between 622-600 B.C., Daniel the prophet was also raised up and prophesied between 616-536 B.C.

It was a time when God was moving through great prophets – people who yielded themselves to the call were used greatly in the ministry. Interestingly enough, Jeremiah also ministered between 685-616 B.C. You will notice that the time periods often overlap. This is because the Spirit of God does great works with many people at the same time.

Isaiah (792-722 B.C.), Nahum (786-757 B.C.) and Micah (772-722 B.C.) were raised up in the ministry around the same period of time. You must buy into the move of God when the season comes. Zechariah and Malachi both prophesied about the end-times. Their ministries, interestingly enough, spanned the same period of time 557-525 B.C.

What am I trying to say? I am showing you that God is using many people to do the same thing in a particular season. He is building megachurches now! Jump on the train and become the pastor that God wants you to be. Did you know that God moved in a spirit of reform during the sixteenth century? Did you know that He did not only work through Martin Luther in Germany?

At the time the spirit of reform was flowing through the ministry of Martin Luther, the spirit of reform was also flowing through a man called Zwingli in Switzerland. If Martin Luther had thought he was the only anointed reformist he would have been making a big mistake! God moves in waves! There is a wave of church growth right now. There is a wave of massive harvesting of souls! Get in on this move of God! Allow God to use you to build a megachurch!

Be open to learn new things that you do not know. A common statement in my church is, "You don't know everything! You and I are learning. Everyday of our lives should be a living classroom. Everyone you meet can teach you something!" As we study the subject of church growth through the power and wisdom of God, decide that you can do it. Do not let the failures of yesteryear keep you down. Be a "Can-do man". Rise up in your spirit and say, "We are able to possess the land. We can do it!"

> **...Let us go up at once, and possess it; for we are well able to overcome it.**
>
> **Numbers 13:30**

When you say, "I can," the Holy Spirit will rise up to perform that which He has called you to do. Remember, you did not call yourself. Faithful is He that called you and He will do it. You are the believer and God is the doer.

I remember when our church had only one member that owned a car – me! I prayed that we would have more people in our church with cars. I confessed and believed that we had ten people in our church who owned cars. After some time, I received what I believed God for. Believe that the God who called you, will do it.

> **Faithful is he that CALLETH you, who also will DO it.**
>
> **1 Thessalonians 5:24**

I recall walking up and down the streets adjacent to the canteen we had rented for our church services. I spoke to the street and said, "Be filled with cars." I spoke to the empty benches and said, "Be filled with members." Today there are countless numbers of cars and members in our church.

Chapter

23

How to Measure Church Growth

CHAPTER SUMMARY

There are seven types of counting that I have observed in the Body of Christ; and I think it will do us all some good to know which type of counting is being used.

■ 7 Types of Counting

23.1 **Type 1 counting: The number of human beings physically present at a particular meeting.**

23.2 **Type 2 counting: This is the total number of people on the church register.**

23.3 **Type 3 counting: It is the cumulative count.**

23.4 **Type 4 counting: This is where the seating capacity of the building is used to estimate membership.**

23.5 **Type 5 counting :This is when pastors give rough estimates.**

23.6 **Type 6 counting: 'wild and unreasonable guessing' .**

23.7 **Type 7 counting: This type of counting aims at outdoing everyone else.**

3 Dangers of Counting

- **The pressure to impress, lie and exaggerate**
- **Self-deception and complacency**
- **Discouragement**

4 Advantages of Numbering

- **Numbering lets you know where you are.**
- **Numbering helps to check backsliding.**
- **Numbering stimulates growth and generates a new vision and compassion for the lost.**
- **Numbering the sheep has been a valuable tool to help monitor the increase and decrease of the church.**

■ Fourteen Important Numbers

23.8 The number of people physically present on Sunday mornings (Type 1 Counting of Sunday service)

23.9 The number of people present at a weekday service

23.10 The number of people present at small group or fellowship meetings

23.11 The number of people who attend fasting and prayer sessions

23.12 The number of people at a convention

23.13 The number of people absent at each church service

23.14 The number of people in the choir of the church

23.15 The number of people in the city where your church is located

23.16 The number of people who give their lives to Christ every Sunday

23.17 The percentage of people who were saved in the church

23.18 The number of new converts who are still in the church after two months

23.19 The number of lay workers in the church

23.20 The number of people who pay tithes

23.21 The number of people who attend the 31st December night service

I believe in real numbers and I have learnt that many people count the same thing differently! If I gave you a number of the members in my church, you may not know exactly how I arrived at that figure. Consequently, I may end up giving you the wrong impression.

It is important for the credibility of pastors that we say what we mean and mean what we say. I used to get confused by the numbers that certain pastors claimed to have in their churches.

I have visited these churches at night and counted the chairs in their halls (I am an expert at counting chairs quickly). I would ponder, "How can they claim to have so many thousand members in their church?"However, as I checked and rechecked the number of chairs, I realized that there was no way that those numbers could be accurate. Even with the addition of canopies and multiple services, there was no way that I could correlate the numbers that I heard with what I had actually seen. Maybe they were counting all the people who were present in spirit, but not in the flesh. After all, Paul claimed that he attended the Corinthian church in spirit.

> **For I verily, as absent in body, but present in spirit…**
>
> **1 Corinthians 5:3**

I could not bring myself to believe that the pastors were telling lies. I prefer to think that they were just counting in a different way. I realize that there are different ways of counting. There are seven types of counting that I have observed in the Body of Christ. And I think it will do us all some good to know which type of counting is being used.

7 Types of Counting

1. Type 1 counting

'Type 1 counting,' is the counting of the number of human beings *physically present at a particular meeting.* It is the headcount of people in *attendance.* This is the headcount. **I believe this type of counting is the most informative of all the types of counting.** However, it is probably the least used way of counting because it is usually the lowest!

When I ask my data officer for numbers in the church, I get the *Type 1 numbers.* I need to know the *Type 1 figures.* I work best with *Type 1 Counting.* The fact is that only a fraction of your members come to church on Sundays. If you use the *Type 1 Counting,* you are only talking about a fraction of the real number of people that God has given you to look after. In spite of this, I still prefer to work with *Type 1 Counting* because it provokes me to work harder.

2. Type 2 counting

This is the total number of people on the church register. Many churches quote this *Type 2* number as their membership. The *Type 2* Counting is larger or smaller depending on how far back the church will go in counting its registered members. The figure also depends on whether the church updates or revises its membership lists frequently. It also depends on how a church revises the membership list. Some churches have what we call 'active members'.

For some people, an active member is someone who attends a service at least once a month. For others it is someone who attends every Sunday service. I consider an active member to be someone who comes to church during the week, i.e., not only on Sundays. For others it is someone who belongs to a smaller cell group.

All of these can vary the eventual outcome of the *Type 2 Counting.* What this means is that my ten thousand figure may be different from your ten thousand figure. That is why I prefer to stay with *Type 1 Counting* because there can be no variation in the method of counting heads who are actually present.

Some pastors give a *Type 2* figure as their regular attendance. When you attend their church and see the actual number of people, you may be very disappointed.

There is often a sharp contrast between the number of people physically present and the number of people the pastor claims to be his members. You may even think the pastor has a problem with lying or exaggeration.

I have seen situations where the *Type 1 Counting* is as low as ten percent of what they claim to be their membership. The church may claim to have ten thousand members, but only one or two thousand are present in the service.

3. Type 3 counting

This type of counting is often used during conventions and crusades that run over a few days. It is the cumulative count. The total number of people who attend the meetings is counted. For instance they could say that the convention was very successful and that, ten thousand people were in attendance.

What they actually mean is that two thousand people came each night for five days! This type of counting is often misleading, as it does not give an accurate picture of the truth.

4. Type 4 counting

This is where the seating capacity of the building is used to estimate membership. Sometimes a building has a maximum capacity of three thousand. During a programme, the pastor could say that there were three thousand people in church. This is because the whole church looked full, so the assumption was that three thousand people were there. This is a wrong assumption.

A *Type 1 Counting* could have easily revealed that only two thousand people were present. A hall, that is capable of seating three thousand people, can "look" full when only two thousand people are present. Once again, this is why I feel that *Type 1 Counting* will help us all to know where we are and where we need to go.

5. Type 5 counting

This is when pastors give rough estimates. They try to give a reasonable assessment of the crowd. The pastor thinks he can assess the numbers present in the crowd. He makes estimates based on experience, and concludes for instance that there are about three hundred people present. Sometimes these rough estimations are quite accurate but at other times they can be totally misleading.

The pastor of the local church is likely to give a higher Type 5 Counting than the pastor of a sister church who is visiting and observing. The local pastor would say, "There are about two thousand people present." The visiting minister would say, "I think there are about one thousand two hundred people present." The visiting minister would not like his rival's church to look too big, so his figure would therefore be much more modest.

6. Type 6 counting

Type 6 Counting is what I call 'wild and unreasonable guessing'.

> *Some years ago when we had about eight hundred people attending our church, I met someone in London who told me, "I heard you had a convention and there were seven thousand people present."*
>
> *I asked him, "Who told you that?" He gave me the name of the woman who had said that.*
>
> *She had said, "I was in the meeting myself and there were about seven thousand people present."*
>
> *I always wondered "How did she get the figure 'seven thousand'?" She must have had a shot at Type 6 counting – wild guessing!*

7. Type 7 counting

This type of counting aims at outdoing everyone else. A pastor mentions a figure that is higher than any other figure being mentioned in town. If the largest church in town is said to be around five thousand, he will always have around six or seven thousand members. This pastor is suffering from the spirit of lying and exaggeration.

■ Is it Scriptural to Count?

We need to ask ourselves – is all of this counting biblical? Is it scriptural to be concerned about numbers? Should we not be concerned about quality and not quantity? The answer is implicit throughout the Scriptures.

Numbering was done in the Old Testament. There is an entire book in the Bible dedicated to numbering – the Book of Numbers. In that book, the number of people, the number of soldiers and the number of tribesmen were recorded.

However, there was a time when God was angry with King David because he had numbered the people. It is clear from this that when numbering is done for the wrong reason it displeases God. For instance, if you put your faith and trust in your numbers, you are making a grave mistake.

> **...for there is no restraint to the Lord to save by many or by few.**
>
> **1 Samuel 14:6**

God will pull down whatever you put your trust in. He wants you to have your faith in Him and Him alone.

In the New Testament, different reports of numbering were mentioned. Everyone knows that Jesus had only twelve disciples. We know that Jesus sent out seventy disciples. It was reported that Jesus appeared to five hundred people after He rose from the dead. We also know that one hundred and twenty people were waiting for the Holy Spirit in the Upper Room. The Book of Acts records that Peter ministered to three thousand people at one time. At another time, we know that five thousand responded to an altar call at Peter's crusade.

If these numbers were not important, then why were they recorded in the Bible? God through the Holy Spirit was teaching us that the numbers of people involved in any spiritual event is a significant indicator. The numbers are important. The Bible says that God will reward us for the quality of work we have done.

> **Every man's work shall be made manifest… of what sort it is.**
>
> **1 Corinthians 3:13**

But Luke 19 shows us that God will judge us for how much we have done in His name.

> **...A certain nobleman went into a far country…when he was returned, having received the kingdom... then he commanded these servants to be called unto him, to whom he had given the money, that he might know how much every man had gained by trading.**
>
> **Luke 19:12, 15**

God is interested in what sort of work you are doing. But He is also interested in how much.

■ 3 Dangers of Counting

1. The pressure to impress, lie and exaggerate

Many pastors are under pressure to say things that sound impressive. If everyone around you claims to have so many thousand members, you can look foolish if you just have a few hundred. It's almost as though you have not been called by God. *God is not going to reward us because of the number of people in our churches. He is going to reward us for our faithfulness to Him.*

> *I once attended a convention of a great church. I counted all the people that were seated there. As I said, I have become an expert at counting seats and human beings very quickly. There were a few thousand people present. Later, I heard a claim from the pastor who had held that meeting, that several thousand people had attended the meeting. This pastor was probably under the pressure to impress and to exaggerate. I was there myself! I counted the human beings present, personally. Yet I heard a figure for that meeting which was several times more than the facts.*

Perhaps the other thousands were present in spirit. If the people you are counting are there in spirit, please tell us so that we stop looking for them in the physical!!

2. Self-deception and complacency

It is easy to deceive yourself if you use the wrong counting method. I heard one minister say, "The whole area outside the building was full." He continued, "People were sitting under canopies."

That is how he knew that things were getting better. But that is deception. I have learnt not to trust this type of counting. I don't want to be self-deceived. I want to know the reality. When you are self-deceived, you think you are what you are not! You think of yourself more highly than you ought to, but this will lead to your downfall.

> **...to every man that is among you, not to think of himself more highly than he ought to think...**
>
> **Romans 12:3**

3. Discouragement

You can also be discouraged when you count too often. Counting should be done so that you have a baseline figure you can use as a reference point. This will help you to know whether things have gotten any better over the months.

However, if you want to put on weight, for example, I would not advise you to weigh yourself everyday. You will become depressed because you will not notice any change. Growth should not be and cannot be measured so frequently.

Church attendance can fluctuate so much that following it on a weekly basis can lead to a weakening of the pastor's heart. I have the head usher or data officer in my church do a *Type 1 Counting* every Sunday. But I only ask for the figures after several months have passed. This helps me to see if there is any improvement.

4 Advantages of Numbering

1. Numbering lets you know where you are.

When you know where you are, you can more readily plan your future. (When you know where you are, you know where you want to go.) It helps you to see the reality of what you are doing. It is easy to deceive yourself. Checking the true numbers will help you to move forward with God.

2. Numbering helps to check backsliding.

There is a law of degeneration at work in this world. Everything starts to decay the moment you take your eyes off it. The Bible teaches that you should look diligently to know the state of the flock.

> **Be thou diligent to know the state of thy flocks, and look well to thy herds. For riches are not for ever...**
>
> **Proverbs 27:23, 24**

Numbering is a diligent way of knowing the state of the flocks. When you are fed with information that things are decaying, you will sit up! When you are stimulated by the veritable facts, it generates a greater vision within you to do God's work. It makes you rise up to build the Kingdom of God.

One day I asked my data officer to tell me the attendance for that Sunday. He told me how many people were in attendance on that day. I was very discouraged because I thought it was a very small number after all my years of hard work. However, when he added the total number of satellite and branch churches, the real fruit of the ministry became clearer to me and I was a bit more encouraged. I decided to start more churches and press on for more growth in the central church.

3. Numbering stimulates growth and generates a new vision and compassion for the lost.

You become dissatisfied with smallness. It leads you to pray. Knowing the true number of people in my ministry has always made me pray more, fast more and seek God more often. You know that prayer changes things, and prayer can change those ugly numbers.

4. Numbering the sheep has been a valuable tool for me to help monitor the increase and decrease of the church.

It will guide you when you need to emphasize on visitation and when you need to judge yourself in areas that may be hindering growth.

■ Fourteen Important Numbers

There are some important figures that every pastor must always be constantly aware of. Each of these figures has some significance. I have discovered that each meeting has its special role to play in the life and development of the church.

1. The number of people physically present on Sunday mornings (Type 1 Counting of Sunday service)

This number is only a percentage of your true membership. In a normal church a large number of people are absent on some Sundays. This is why the number can fluctuate so much. The Sunday service attendance is the best number to use for monitoring progress in a general way.

2. The number of people present at a weekday service

This tells you the number of the very committed members you have. Most serious Christians make time to attend church during the week. You will find that the anointing and flow of the Spirit is different on a weekday service. A corporate anointing manifests because of the gathering of faithful ones. Lukewarm and religious attendees do not dilute the atmosphere.

3. The number of people present at small group or fellowship meetings

This number shows you how developed the internal structure of the ministry is. There are some churches which can command thousands of people for a special convention, however they are not able to mobilize fifty people on a regular basis for small group meetings. It is important to have these small groups so that they can meet the needs of the members at a personal level.

4. The number of people who attend fasting and prayer sessions

This tells you the number of spiritual soldiers you have. This is very different from the swelled up convention attendance. It should be the goal of every pastor to build up a large core of spiritual warriors. These people may be more dependable.

5. The number of people at a convention

The convention crowd contains many people who are moved by excitement. There are many "miracle seekers" and "sign watchers" in attendance.

6. The number of people absent at each church service

This is a very important number. It tells you how many people are falling away. It is probably an indication of how hard the pastors and shepherds are working. Perhaps they are not being prayed for and they are not being visited.

7. The number of people in the choir of the church

The choir of a church is like the flower of a plant. It is often the part of the church that the outside world sees. It is often a reflection of the organizational skills of the church. It tells us how well the pastors are making use of the talents within the congregation.

8. The number of people in the city where your church is located

A church's size is always related to the size of the city in which it is situated. The largest churches in the world are found in the largest cities in the world. For example, if 0.1 % of people in Accra (a city of 4 million) are in the Lighthouse; then our church population would have to be four thousand. If the membership shoots up to six thousand, we would still form only 0.15% of the population. This figure makes us relatively insignificant.

The figure must be determined every year for us to know how great an impact we are making in the city. If this percentage is insignificant, it must motivate us to have more visitations, more prayer, more fasting and more witnessing. It means that we must have more pastors, more shepherds, more churches, more ministries and more fellowships. We must invite more people, do more follow-up, have more crusades and release more power.

9. The number of people who give their lives to Christ every Sunday

This tells you how conscious of lost souls the pastor is. It shows you whether members are inviting non-Christians to church. It tells us whether the church is fulfilling the Great Commission in getting people born again.

10. The percentage of people who were saved in the church

Occasionally, it is interesting to find out how many people got saved in the church. This tells you how original the church is. Many of my members were saved at the Lighthouse Cathedral. Some churches are made up of breakaway members of other churches. Since this was the source of the majority of their members, they often don't know how to win souls for themselves. Every church must know how to intentionally win souls and assimilate new converts.

11. The number of new converts who are still in the church after two months

This tells you whether follow-up is being done.

12. The number of lay workers in the church

This shows you how involved the general congregation is in the ministry. It tells you what percentage of the church is asleep. *When a human being is asleep only eight percent of his body is at work. If only eight percent of your members are active, it means your church is asleep.*

13. The number of people who pay tithes

This is a reflection of the number of truly loyal people you have. The Bible says, "For where your treasure is, there will your heart be also." It tells you how many people in the crowd have their hearts solidly planted in the church.

14. The number of people who attend the 31st December night service

Traditionally, this is a very well attended service. From my experience, it is the best attended service in the whole year. Superstitious people run to the church so that God will see them in church as the new year dawns. All of those you haven't seen throughout the year may finally show up on 31st December. The pastor is usually encouraged by the 31st December crowd. This swollen number usually regularizes within a few weeks.

Chapter

24

How You Can Receive the Anointing

CHAPTER SUMMARY

In this chapter, I will introduce you to the most important factor that will make you start out and accomplish something substantial for God.

- **8 Different Ways the Anointing Is Released**

24.1 Terminated transferred anointing

24.2 Living transferred anointing

24.3 Anointing sharing

24.4 Modified anointing transfer

24.5 Diminishing anointing transfer

24.6 Enhanced anointing transfer

24.7 Former anointing reintroduced

24.8 A new and original anointing

> **...Not by might, nor by power, but by my spirit, saith the Lord of hosts.**
>
> **Zechariah 4:6**

One thing all of us must realize is that ministry is different from any other secular job. In the secular world, many things are important for success. Zerubbabel was trying to build the temple. We are trying to build the Church. Building the church and building the temple are one and the same thing. The instruction that applied to Zerubbabel applies to us.

The Bible is making it clear that it is not by any form of power that the Church will be built. **The Church will be built by the power of the Holy Spirit – *end of story!***

Some people who look at me and say, "Oh, he's succeeding because he's educated." But it is not by the power of education. There are educated people in the ministry whose churches have not amounted to a "hill of beans". It is not by education, it is by the anointing.

The Handsome Pastor

I read a newspaper article which said, "The pastor of the church is so handsome. That is why so many young ladies go there." But I know that there are pastors who are not handsome per se, whose ministries have grown into thousands.

Still others say, "Oh, it is their background." "Oh, it is the location of the church." "Oh, it is the wealth of the members." "Oh, it is the exciting music." "Oh, it is the instrumentalists." Everybody tries to give a reason why something does or does not work. There are pastors who have said to me, "You have the strategies!" They think I have loads of hidden tactics to make my ministry work. Some people think I am an expert administrator, that is how come things are working.

I believe in education. I believe in administration. I believe in strategies. But above all, I have come to the conclusion that the Prophet Zechariah came to – *it is not by any form of might, it is not by any power, it is by my Spirit says the Lord.*

This Spirit is the same thing as the anointing. The Bible says in Acts 10:38, "How God anointed Jesus of Nazareth with the Holy Ghost and with power." You will see from this Scripture that the substance that God anointed Jesus Christ with, was the Holy Spirit. Therefore, we can conclude that the anointing is the Holy Spirit.

We need the anointing to do the work.

The ministry is not a human or natural thing. As soon as all ministers get that in their minds, the better it will be for them. When you see a successful minister, look beyond the physical and see into the realm of the spirit. Observe the anointing at work. There is an invisible cloak over that person which allows him to succeed at what he is doing. That invisible mantle is what I call the anointing. It explains why some people succeed and some don't. It explains why some people have greater degrees of success under exactly the same circumstances.

A pastor cannot oversee a very large church, unless he is anointed to do so. I have been in the ministry for nearly twenty years and I know from the Word and by experience that it is by the anointing and nothing else! Jesus told Pilate that all the power he possessed was what God had allowed him to have. Nobody can have power unless God gives it to him.

> **...Thou couldest have no power at all against me, except it were given thee from above...**
>
> **John 19:11**

I believe that God selects people and specifically anoints them to accomplish certain purposes. When I look back on my life, I can see that I was specifically anointed to do what I'm doing. This is different from a genuine in-filling of the Holy Spirit which every Christian has. Since the anointing is so important, we must ask ourselves, "How do we get this vital ingredient?"

It is very important to realize that the anointing is not *taught* it is *caught*. How does this special ingredient come onto a person? Is it something that we can all have or is it reserved for the special few? God is the one who introduces the anointing into the earth. He does it in His own sovereign way. I have noticed different ways by which the anointing is released on the earth.

■ 8 Different Ways the Anointing Is Released

1. Terminated transferred anointing

In this type of transfer, a man of God's life is terminated and his anointing is transferred to someone else. The person who has received the anointing usually starts ministering after the death of the originally anointed vessel. A good example of this is Joshua. Joshua became anointed to lead the people of Israel after Moses' life was terminated.

A transferred anointing is something that is moved from one person to another. **This transfer can occur when a man of God dies or leaves the scene. His mantle then falls directly on someone else.** The departure of Elijah from the scene resulted in the anointing on his life being transferred to Elisha. This resulted in the same anointing being present on the earth, but operating through another human being.

God is concerned about finishing His work and will use which ever vessel is available. I call this *terminated transfer* because death terminates the life and ministry of one man and the anointing is transferred to another. This also happened under the ministry of Jesus. As soon as Christ was off the scene, the anointing that operated through Him whilst He was on earth began to function through His disciples. People were amazed. The only explanation that they could give for Peter and John's new charisma, was their association with Christ.

> **Now when they saw the boldness of Peter and John,... they marvelled; and they took knowledge of them, that they had been with Jesus.**
>
> **Acts 4:13**

2. Living transferred anointing

The next type of transfer is *living transferred anointing.* **In this case, the anointing on one person is transferred to someone else whilst that man of God is alive.** A man of God who is blessed with long life may see the anointing that is on his life working through others.

For example, the anointing departed from Saul and was replaced by an evil spirit. Meanwhile, his successor, David, was anointed while Saul was alive. Saul saw the anointing to be king on another man and was afraid of him. **This is a common occurrence in the ministry.** Even the Prophet Samuel was afraid to anoint David while Saul was yet alive. He knew that it would provoke much jealousy and hatred.

> **And the Lord said unto Samuel… fill thine horn with oil, and go, I will send thee to Jesse the Bethlehemite: for I have provided me a king among his sons. And Samuel said, How can I go? if Saul hear it, he will kill me...**
>
> **1 Samuel 16:1, 2**

Some older men of God can see that their anointing has left them and moved on to another person. This sometimes leads the older man of God to fight the new one upon whom he sees the anointing. Have you not seen this in your city? The older and insecure men of God fight to keep their position, whilst God works through others. God allowed Saul to fight David in order to test David's character. All things do work together for good to them that are called.

3. Anointing sharing

This is when God takes the anointing on one man and shares it with several other people at the same time. You will notice several men of God in the same era, operating in a similar way. In Bible times, several of the prophets lived and prophesied around the same time. God took of the anointing that was upon Moses and shared it amongst seventy people.

> **...Gather unto me seventy men… and I will take of the spirit which is upon thee, and will put it upon them...**
>
> **Numbers 11:16, 17**

All seventy men were anointed. They shared in Moses' anointing and accomplished God's will. I have seen the anointing on my life being shared to many of my pastors. I can see them operating under the same anointing. I have watched them catch the anointing.

4. Modified anointing transfer

The next type of anointing transfer is what I call a *modified anointing transfer.* **In this case, the anointing is transferred from one individual to another but in the process, it is modified.** In such a case, the recipient of the anointing may be notably different in ministry from the one from whom the anointing was transferred. An example of this can be seen under the ministry of Moses and Joshua. It was Moses who laid hands on Joshua and imparted the Spirit (anointing).

> **And Joshua the son of Nun was full of the spirit of wisdom; for Moses had laid his hands upon him…**
>
> **Deuteronomy 34:9**

Basically, Joshua was anointed to do battle and take over new lands. Moses did not conquer any new lands, however you could see a similarity between Moses and Joshua. Joshua crossed the River Jordan using the "Red Sea crossing anointing" which he had received from Moses. He ruled the people with the authority of Moses. But apart from this and a few other occurrences, Joshua was quite different from Moses.

5. Diminishing anointing transfer

The *diminishing anointing transfer* occurs when the anointing from one is passed to another, but is reduced in its strength and glory. It is often God's way of fading out a particular ministry.

You will see a clear example of this under the ministries of King David and King Solomon. David's kingly anointing was transferred to his son Solomon and then to Rehoboam and Jeroboam. Solomon's sons did not have the grace of God on their lives to rule over all of the twelve tribes of Israel. We cannot even remember the names of the other kings who lived after Solomon.

This is because the kingly anointing was fading as the years passed by. God showed Solomon before he died, that the anointing on his son Rehoboam would be greatly diminished.

> **But I will take the kingdom out of his son's [Rehoboam] hand, and will give it unto thee, even ten tribes. And unto his son will I give one tribe...**
>
> **1 Kings 11:35, 36**

Some American universities started out as Christian institutions with a Christian vision. Today, there is not even a trace of Christianity in some of those colleges. The initial anointing is diminished!

6. Enhanced anointing transfer

This is when the anointing transfer from one person to the other is upgraded. For example, Elisha had twice as much of the anointing that Elijah had and performed twice as many miracles. This type of anointing transfer is unusual. You will notice that Elijah told Elisha that he had asked for a hard thing; that is, to have an *enhanced anointing transfer.*

> **…Thou hast asked a hard thing…**
>
> **2 Kings 2:10**

7. Former anointing reintroduced

This type of anointing transfer can be seen in the case of John the Baptist and Elijah. God decided to reintroduce the *Elijah anointing* through a man called John the Baptist. This is because God was doing a work, which needed a dramatic Elijah-type of ministry.

> **And if ye will receive it, this [John] is Elias, which was for to come.**
>
> **Matthew 11:14**

I believe that some of the apostolic and prophetic anointings of the early Church are being reintroduced into the Church at this time.

There is therefore a resurgence of the miraculous and the prophetic. There are much more larger churches with ministers preaching to three thousand and five thousand members like Peter did in the Book of Acts.

The Bible predicts that two prophets with a peculiar anointing will arise in the Last Days to challenge the Anti-christ. The Bible says that these two prophets will do certain things. A closer look at the ministry of these two Latter Day prophets reveals a great similarity between their anointings and those of Moses and Elijah. Once again, this is the principle of the *reintroduced anointing* at work.

These two prophets will have power to call down fire from heaven. They will also have power over the weather to prevent it from raining for three and a half years. This sounds very much like Elijah. The Bible also says that they will have power to turn water into blood and command plagues to appear at random. Once again this sounds like the anointing that was on Moses.

> **And I will give power unto my two witnesses, and they shall prophesy a thousand two hundred and threescore days, clothed in sack cloth. These are the two olive trees, and the two candlesticks standing before the God of the earth. And if any man will hurt them, fire proceedeth out of their mouth, and devoureth their enemies: and if any man will hurt them, he must in this manner be killed. These have power to shut heaven, that it rain not in the days of their prophecy: and have power over waters to turn them to blood, and to smite the earth with all plagues, as often as they will.**
>
> **Revelation 11:3-6**

Once again, it looks like God is reintroducing a former anointing in order to do a vital job. The anointing on Moses' life was introduced to fight against a despotic and repressive Pharaoh. The anointing on Elijah's life contended with one of Israel's most detestable and incorrigible kings, Ahab.

The Antichrist, one of the most tyrannical and evil men the Bible speaks about, will need to be trounced by a combination of these two strong anointings. Perhaps the Antichrist himself will combine the evil spirits that worked through both King Ahab and Pharaoh.

You will learn from this study, that God does specific things for specific reasons. You may want a miraculous ministry to impress people but God wants to fulfil His purpose. He may not want you to do any miracles. All He may want you to do, is to teach His Word. John the Baptist did not perform any miracles but he fulfilled his ministry. He prepared the way for Christ. Jesus said John the Baptist was the greatest prophet.

> **...Among them that are born of women there hath not risen a greater than John the Baptist...**
>
> **Matthew 11:11**

You can only line up with God's purpose. God will not do anything outside His purpose. When you fulfil God's purpose for your life, Jesus will call you "great". Find out the purpose of God and flow with it. It is the purpose of God that will be achieved at the end of the day, and not your purpose.

This is the purpose that is purposed upon the whole earth: and this is the hand that is stretched out upon all the nations.

> **For the Lord of hosts hath purposed, and who shall disannul it? and his hand is stretched out, and who shall turn it back?**
>
> **Isaiah 14:26, 27**

8. A new and original anointing

In this case, a person comes on the scene and God anoints him to do new things. This is not very common! A study of the Bible will show you that God rarely introduces a new and original anointing. The more common way by which God introduces anointing, is through people. Elijah the Tishbite is somebody who appeared with what I believe was a new and original anointing.

Two other people, Elisha and John the Baptist, have operated in the same anointing that was on Elijah. The difference was that, Elijah was walking in a new and original anointing! Elisha was walking in an enhanced transferred anointing and John the Baptist was walking in a reintroduced anointing.

Chapter

25

How to Understand the Anointing

CHAPTER SUMMARY

It should be the desire of every real minister to catch the anointing. Without the anointing, your ministry is reduced to philosophy and your church to an ideological institution. Learn some important facts to catch an anointing.

- **Five Important Facts about the Anointing**

25.1 It is difficult to get an anointing.

25 2 You must have a strong desire for the anointing.

25 3 Jacob desired the anointing.

25 4 God anoints the desirous.

25 5 You can desire another minister's anointing.

It should be the desire of every real minister to catch the anointing. Without the anointing, your ministry is reduced to philosophy and your church to an ideological institution. If you want to have a big church, you need an anointing. If you want to teach the Word, you need an anointing. If you want to be a prophet you need to be anointed. Without the anointing, you are no nearer being a minister than I am to becoming the Prince of Wales.

There are a few important facts that people need to know about catching the anointing.

Five Important Facts about the Anointing

1. It is difficult to get an anointing.

> **...Elijah said unto Elisha, Ask what I shall do for thee, before I be taken away from thee. And Elisha said, I pray thee, let a double portion of thy spirit be upon me. And he said, Thou hast asked a hard thing...**
>
> **2 Kings 2:9, 10**

Although this Scripture is usually referred to in terms of being anointed with a double portion, I believe that it also refers to the act of receiving an anointing. **It's a hard thing because few people have the anointing.** Many people try to get it, but few succeed. I can see why it is a hard thing.

Why is it that there are few doctors (relatively speaking) in the whole world? The answer is simple. It is because it is a "hard thing" to become a doctor. Many would like to be doctors, but few end up becoming doctors. In Ghana, like other countries, it is only the very best students who gain entry into the medical schools.

As I look around, I realize that there are not so many "truly" anointed ministers. Many may call themselves pastors, but few are really anointed to stand in that office. If they were anointed we would both know and see it. Though many have certificates and qualifications from Bible schools, few are actually anointed. This leads us to ask, "Why is it such a difficult thing to be anointed?"

2. You must have a strong desire for the anointing.

I want to show you why it is such a difficult thing for you to be anointed. **One reason why God does not readily give His anointing to just anyone is because the anointing is the Holy Spirit (God Himself).** The Holy Spirit is a precious gift from God to the Church. However, God does not haphazardly bestow that higher anointing needed for ministry on anyone. God does not cast His pearls before swine – you wouldn't!

If you don't value the anointing, God will not give it to you!

I once had an old car that I had used for a number of years. I wanted to give it to somebody. I searched earnestly for someone whom I could give it to. I knew that the car was very valuable and would cost millions of Ghanaian cedis (thousands of dollars) on the open market. However, because the car was slightly used I knew that if I gave it to the wrong person, he could mistakenly think I was getting rid of a worthless wreck. He would not appreciate it at all. Because of this, it took me a long time to decide whom to give it to.

There were many around me who desperately needed a car. But because I wasn't sure whether they would appreciate it or not, I decided to give it to a particular person. When I eventually gave the car away, I was happy with his response to the gift. I felt that he genuinely appreciated it. I am sure there were people who wondered why I didn't give the car to them.

God has a very precious commodity! He is looking for someone who really wants it and will appreciate it. Often, those who should be obvious recipients miss out on the blessing. The anointing then passes on to someone else, to the surprise of others.

Many wonder why God anointed someone like me. A visiting pastor once stood in my pulpit and overwhelmed by the huge crowds. He said, "The tables are turning. Many people are asking, *"Why Dag? Why is God using Dag?"* He was surprised that God had given me an anointing. Perhaps, in his estimation I shouldn't have received it.

Have you ever asked yourself why God loved Jacob and hated Esau?

3. Jacob desired the anointing.

> **As it is written, Jacob have I loved, but Esau have I hated.**
>
> **Romans 9:13**

Was Jacob not a heel snatcher and a deceiver? He was, but he desired the anointing. Often other earthly desires drown the desire for the anointing. You may be surprised that not meeting this qualification (of desiring the anointing) eliminates many people, as it did with my car gift.

Jacob strongly desired the birthright (anointing), but Esau did not care much about it. Something that should worry us is the fact that God hated Esau. If God hated Esau, then it is possible that God can hate you! If God hated Esau because he didn't care about the gift, then God can hate you because you don't care about the gift of His anointing. People have wondered why God used Kathryn Kuhlman, a healing evangelist. She married someone's husband and later on divorced him. I believe that she strongly desired the anointing.

4. God anoints the desirous.

God will pass over a thousand people who don't care much for the anointing and will give it to a person who strongly desires it. I see God passing over many people to get to you now!

Did you know that Elijah's first servant was not Elisha? Did you know that Elijah's first servant was bypassed when it was time to be anointed? This servant was active in ministry but he was not chosen to be anointed by God. It was this servant who Elijah sent seven times to see if the rain clouds had appeared.

> **...And Elijah went up to the top of Carmel; and he cast himself down upon the earth, and put his face between his knees, And said to his servant, Go up now, look toward the sea. And he went up, and looked, and said, There is nothing. And he said, Go again seven times.**
>
> **1 Kings 18:42, 43**

Why did this servant not receive the anointing? Why did Elisha, who was not even in the ministry, receive the anointing? Elisha was involved in business. He was plowing a field with his other business partners.

> **So he departed thence, and found Elisha the son of Shaphat, who was plowing with twelve yoke of oxen before him, and he with the twelfth…**
>
> **1 Kings 19:19**

What happened to the servant? Why wasn't he anointed? Why didn't he become the next great prophet? Please learn this important principle right now! God will pass over a thousand people who don't care much for the anointing and will give it to a person who strongly desires it.

Desire the anointing more than anything else in this world. That is the first step to becoming "anything" in the Kingdom of God. God told Pastor Timothy to look for people with a *desire* to be bishops. **It is people with strong desires who get spiritual gifts.**

Paul said,

> **Follow after charity, and desire spiritual gifts [anointing]...**
>
> **1 Corinthians 14:1**

If we could paraphrase this, it would say, "desire the anointing".

> **But covet [desire] earnestly the best gifts...**
>
> **1 Corinthians 12:31**

5. You can desire another minister's anointing.

I have learnt that you can specifically desire the anointing you see on a particular man of God. You can covet the gift that God has given to him. This is possible because Elisha specifically requested for the anointing that he saw on Elijah. Look around and see which man of God's ministry or gift you would like to have. I see that gift coming on you now!

Why would God tell you to desire something you cannot have? **The anointing is the principal tool for ministry. Without the anointing, all of your Bible school knowledge and certificates are useless.** You need an anointing. Anointing does not come by going to school. *Anointing is not taught, it is caught!*

When I was coming up in ministry, I did not know what I am teaching you now. God led me personally into this revelation. I loved the ministries of certain men and I followed hard after them. The anointing that I unknowingly coveted began to operate in my life. I will share more about this later. God often uses a man or several different men to impact your life with the anointing.

When you have decided which gifts and anointing to covet, there are several hard steps or filters that you will have to go through. I call them filters because as people go through them, many "drop out". There are people who desire the anointing but never get it. It is because they are not able to pass through these tests. The steps are filters, which differentiate between the receivers and all others.

Chapter

26

Steps to the Anointing

CHAPTER SUMMARY

- **7 Steps to the Anointing**

26.1 The principle of vessel change

26.2 Servanthood

- **13 Signs of a Servant**
  - **A servant has a master.**
  - **A servant is at the beck and call of his master.**
  - **A servant is one who executes the command of another.**
  - **A servant cannot be inconvenienced by any job or task.**
  - **A servant does not see himself as equal to his master.**
  - **A servant carries out the wishes of his master.**
  - **A servant cannot be embarrassed by his job.**
  - **A servant does menial jobs: picking up crumbs, serving food..**

- **A servant promotes his master while he stays below.**
- **A servant does not expect thanks or acknowledgment.**
- **A servant does what his master wants in the way his master wants it.**
- **A servant ministers to his master of his substance.**
- **A servant has a reward.**

26.3 Receiving a father

26.4 Follow the man of God closely

26.5 Spiritual ministrations

26.6 The passage of time

26.7 Minister to the man of God

■ 7 Steps to the Anointing

1. The principle of vessel change

The anointing is like liquid that is poured into a vessel. Every liquid has a corresponding bottle or vessel. For instance, *Coca-Cola* will only be found in *Coca-Cola* bottles. *Sprite* has its own bottle. In order to be filled with Sprite you need to be a Sprite bottle. This is because specific fluids are associated with specific bottles. It is the same thing with the anointing. **Specific anointings are associated with certain types of people.** An evangelistic anointing will go with a certain type of personality and character. A pastoral anointing will fit into a certain type of vessel. The Bible says that in a large house there are many types of vessels. You and I are those vessels.

> **But in a great house there are not only vessels of gold and of silver, but also of wood and of earth; and some to honour, and some to dishonour.**
>
> **2 Timothy 2:20**

If we want to be filled with a Coca-Cola anointing we need to be Coca-Cola bottles, so that the anointing will fit into us. If you study the Prophet Elijah, you will see a particular kind of anointing on his life. The prophetic anointing (1 Kings 18:36) on Elijah's life led him to do certain things. The anointing allows you to achieve certain things. He rebuked the kings of his day (1 Kings 21:17-20), fought with religious leaders (1 Kings 18:20-24), challenged sins and evil, was dramatic (1 Kings 18:30-39), and had his ministry ended by a woman, Jezebel (1 Kings 19:3,14,16).

The Bible tells us that John the Baptist operated in the same prophetic anointing as Elijah (Luke 1:76). We therefore see John the Baptist, rebuking the king of his day (Mark 6:17-20), confronting religious leaders (Matthew 3:7-10), fighting sin and evil and having a very dramatic ministry (Luke 3:7-14). We also see his ministry terminated by a woman, Herod's wife (Matthew 14:6-10). This was the anointing of Elijah at work.

Elijah's anointing operated in John's life because he was changed into a vessel that could receive it. Note that both John the Baptist (Mark 1:4) and Elijah (1 Kings 19:4) lived in the desert. Both Elijah and John the Baptist ate weird things – locusts (Matthew 3:4) and worms (1 Kings 17:6). Both John the Baptist (Matthew 3:4) and Elijah (2 Kings 1:8) wore clothes made of camel's hair.

To receive such a heavy prophetic healing anointing such as that on Elisha, a person cannot have problems such as lying, stealing and covetousness. The anointing of Elisha does not fit into lying and covetous vessels.

Unfortunately, Gehazi did not pass the test of lying and stealing. He lied and misrepresented Elisha! If a prophet is a liar, how will you know when he is speaking the Word of God? How would you know when he is speaking his own mind? Although Gehazi was close to the anointing, he did not obtain it! Elisha eventually cursed Gehazi for his unethical behaviour as a prophetic student.

> **The leprosy therefore of Naaman shall cleave unto thee, and unto thy seed for ever. And he went out from his presence a leper as white as snow.**
>
> **2 Kings 5:27**

If you desire a particular anointing, God will mould you into the type of vessel that can contain that anointing. If God wants you to be a great pastor, He may work on your education. He may work on your knowledge of administration and law. To receive the anointing you must allow Him to work on you!

Some people are not educated, nor do they educate themselves by reading. Yet, they desire the anointing to be leaders of large numbers of people. Don't you know that pastoring a large number of people means that you will have several highly educated people in your congregation? How will you relate with all of these people?

God may be working on your language. He may try to polish your manners and general etiquette! He may send you to a Bible school for training. He may send you off to a secular university for molding. I've had seven years of university training. Those years molded me into a suitable vessel. 'God may take you through various humbling experiences. All He is doing is preparing a vessel that can handle the anointing. This is the principle of vessel change.

If you desire a strong prophetic anointing, God is likely to require of you a life of solitude. You cannot have such an anointing if you do not make time to wait on the Lord.

You see, many changes may have to take place in your character and moral life if God is to use you for great achievements. **Those who refuse to change and to modify are refusing to be recipients of the anointing.** This first step alone can explain why many people desire the anointing but never get it. Nobody pours *Coca-Cola* into a fuel tank. It is only petrol that is poured into a fuel tank. **If you are a fuel tank, you will never receive Coca-Cola – you will receive fuel!** There are different containers for different anointings. Please accept this simple reality.

2. Servanthood

Throughout the Bible, those that received an anointing were servants. Joshua was a servant of Moses.

> **Now after the death of Moses the servant of the Lord it came to pass, that the Lord spake unto Joshua the son of Nun, Moses' minister, [servant]...**
>
> **Joshua 1:1**

Elisha was a servant of Elijah.

> **...Here is Elisha the son of Shaphat, which poured water [servant] on the hands of Elijah.**
>
> **2 Kings 3:11**

Peter, James and John were the servants of Christ.

> **HENCEFORTH I CALL YOU NOT SERVANTS [the disciples were ushers, bodyguards and errand boys]; for the servant knoweth not what his lord doeth: but I have called you friends...**
>
> **John 15:15**

The position of a servant is a humbling one. You do not have your own mind! You must work for your master, taking him to be right all the time. When you become a servant, you are like a grown up child, ready to receive every instruction that is meted out to you.

No one is above the Word of God. **If Joshua had to be a servant before he became an anointed General, so will you!** This is another reason why some people never become anointed. They are simply too big to ever become servants of anyone. They are too conscious of their age and position in society. They feel that their status must be constantly recognized. No wonder God has raised up many young people to receive an anointing. Many old dogs could not be taught new tricks.

Although God has given me several thousand people in my ministry, I have been a servant for many years. **I have served as an usher, drummer, arranger, sound technician and organist.** There is hardly any department of the church, in which I have not been a servant.

I marvel at those who want pastoral positions based on their having a Bible school diploma. They are no nearer to becoming pastors than I am to living on Mars. Some people just attend services and want to be appointed elders in the church, without serving their way to the top. These are the signs of a servant. Ask yourself if you are a servant or a boss.

13 Signs of a Servant

- A servant has a master.

> **A son honoureth his father, and a servant his master…**
>
> **Malachi 1:6**

- A servant is at the beck and call of his master.

> **For I am a man under authority, having soldiers under me: and I say to this man, Go, and he goeth; and to another, Come, and he cometh; and to my servant, Do this, and he doeth it.**
>
> **Matthew 8:9**

- A servant is one who executes the command of another.
- A servant cannot be inconvenienced by any job or task.
- A servant does not see himself as equal to his master.

He doesn't say things like, "We are all classmates. We are all engineers. We all have children."

> **Who, being in the form of God, thought it not robbery to be equal with God:**
>
> **Philippians 2:6**

- A servant carries out the wishes of his master.

> **Exhort servants to be obedient unto their own masters, and to please them well in all things; not answering again;**
>
> **Titus 2:9**

- A servant cannot be embarrassed by his job.

> **And being found in fashion as a man, he humbled himself, and became obedient unto death, even the death of the cross.**
>
> **Philippians 2:8**

- A servant does menial jobs: picking up crumbs, serving food..

> **When they were filled, he said unto his disciples, Gather up the fragments that remain, that nothing be lost.**
>
> **John 6:12**

> **...Elisha the son of Shaphat, which poured water on the hands of Elijah.**
>
> **2 Kings 3:11**

- A servant promotes his master while he stays below.

> **He must increase, but I must decrease.**
>
> **John 3:30**

- A servant does not expect thanks or acknowledgment.

> **So likewise ye, when ye shall have done all those things which are commanded you, say, We are unprofitable servants: we have done that which was our duty to do.**
>
> **Luke 17:10**

- A servant does what his master wants in the way his master wants it.

> **...Behold, to obey is better than sacrifice, and to hearken than the fat of rams.**
>
> **1 Samuel 15:22**

- A servant ministers to his master of his substance.

> **And certain women, which had been healed of evil spirits and infirmities, Mary called Magdalene, out of whom went seven devils. And Joanna, the wife of Chuza Herod's steward, and Susanna, and many others, which ministered unto him of their substance.**
>
> **Luke 8:2, 3**

- A servant has a reward.

> **Wherefore God also hath highly exalted him, and given him a name which is above every name:**
>
> **Philippians 2:9**

> **Looking unto Jesus the author and finisher of our faith; who for the joy that was set before him endured the cross, despising the shame, and is set down at the right hand of the throne of God.**
>
> **Hebrews 12:2**

3. Receiving a father

When God leads you to follow a man of God, (like Elisha followed Elijah) it is important for you to receive him as a father. You will notice from the story of Elisha that he had an earthly father called Shaphat.

> **...Here is Elisha the son of Shaphat...**
>
> **2 Kings 3:11**

However, by the time Elijah was taken away, Elisha referred to Elijah as his father. He did this effortlessly and naturally.

> **And Elisha saw it, and he cried, My father, my father...**
>
> **2 Kings 2:12**

Why is it important to receive your man of God as a father? What does it mean? I want to bring to your attention two very important reasons why you must receive him as a father.

Two Important Reasons for Receiving the Man of God as a Father

1. Firstly, a person who does not have a father is very different from someone who has parents.

A person with a father receives guidance and direction in life. A fatherless person has a life full of struggles.

I never worked whilst I was in university. My father provided for me fully until I became a doctor. The money he gave me each month as a student was even more than my salary when I became a doctor. My father bought me a brand new car when I was in the fifth year of medical school. I was really blessed to have a good father looking after me. **My life as a student was struggle free because I had a father!** However, the same cannot be said for many people. I have met countless people who did not receive guidance in life. They threw away their talent and became non-entities in life, because there was no father to guide them. I know many people who do not even know their fathers.

The situation is worse for an orphan! Struggles abound for orphans. The future of an orphan is very uncertain. It is the same thing in ministry. When you have no one to influence you in the right way, your ministry is full of various struggles. Although I have had different fathers in ministry, there are times I have been fatherless as far as developing into a pastor was concerned.

I have had fathers in ministry from afar. I have gone through various struggles because I have not received support from nearby and potential fathers. Many of the struggles and frustrations I've experienced in ministry are because I had no one to help me in starting a church. In fact, people who should have been fathers to me when I was beginning my church, were more of outright enemies. They opposed my cause and fought against me. Today, some of these people are always eager to claim fatherhood over my life because I am successful in ministry.

2. The second reason why it is important to have a father is because inheritance flows naturally from a father to his children.

In the ministry, spiritual inheritance flows naturally from the fathers to the sons. When my father died, his Will was read in court. He left his properties to his children. Although he had many employees and friends, he didn't leave anything to them – it all went to his children. Dear friend, that is the reality of life. Inheritance usually goes to children. There is something known as a *spiritual inheritance* (Ephesians 1:18). **This spiritual inheritance of anointing and gifts passes naturally from fathers to sons.** It does not pass from father to equals, colleagues and friends. It does not even pass from father to servants. It passes from fathers to sons.

Hello Boss!

I used to have a junior pastor who preferred to call me "boss". I always felt uneasy when he called me "boss", but I didn't know why. You see, when someone calls you "boss", it means that he sees himself more as a hired hand. A few years later this pastor departed under unpleasant circumstances. Then I realized why I had felt uneasy.

A servant or an employee does not stay around forever. He's only there for awhile and will leave when it suits him.

> **And the servant abideth not in the house for ever: but the Son abideth ever.**
>
> **John 8:35**

So, if you have a relationship with a man of God which becomes a father-son relationship, then you can expect a spiritual inheritance of anointing to flow effortlessly from him to you.

■ How to Receive a Father

How do you receive someone as a father?

1. When someone is your father, he can speak freely into your life and you trust what he says.

A child usually believes that his father really cares for him, no matter how much the father disciplines him. If you have doubts in your mind about someone, or are suspicious of him, that person cannot be a father to you. A pastor can be a good man of God to some people, but to others he becomes a father. When a person becomes a father to you, one of the main features is an attitude of fullest trust in him.

That attitude makes you admire and open up to him. You can never really open up your spirit to someone unless you trust him.

2. Maintain great respect and admiration for anyone you want to receive as a father.

Our father which art in heaven, hallowed be thy name (Matthew 6:9). Let the will of your father in ministry be done. If he tells you to pray and to fast, because you believe it is for your own good, allow that thing to happen.

3. Accept the father's position and authority.

Every time we pray the Lord's Prayer, we end it by saying, "thine is the kingdom, the power and the glory." We constantly affirm the position of our heavenly father. In the same way, every son must overcome the temptation to fight his father's authority and rule. Never fight a father, it is a dangerous violation. Instead, give the honour to the fathers.

> **The eye that mocketh at his father, and despiseth to obey his mother, the ravens of the valley shall pick it out, and the young eagles shall eat it.**
>
> **Proverbs 30:17**

4. Follow the man of God closely

Another important step is to follow the man of God closely. All the examples of people who received anointing, stayed close to their mentors. Elisha stayed with Elijah to the very end. Elijah tried on many occasions to get Elisha to stay behind, but he followed him to the very end. It was at the end that he caught the anointing. There are three ways you can follow a man of God closely.

■ 3 Ways to Follow the Man of God

1. Physical association and close interaction

The first way is through physical association, close interaction and personal acquaintance with the anointed servant of God. Joshua associated with Moses as his personal servant and minister.

> **...Joshua the son of Nun, Moses' minister...**
>
> **Joshua 1:1**

Elisha desired a double portion of the anointing on Elijah's life. He knew that through service to the man of God he could obtain the anointing he desired.

Elisha became known as the person who physically washed the hands of Elijah. Close association of this sort may lead to a transfer of anointing.

> **...Here is Elisha the son of Shaphat, which poured water on the hands [cleaned and ministered] of Elijah.**
>
> **2 Kings 3:11**

2. Follow his words closely.

The second way by which you can follow a man of God is to follow his words closely. Not many people will have the privilege of interacting personally with their mentors. So how can anyone catch the anointing on a great man of God? The answer is simple. Is it the pouring of water or the doing of menial jobs that leads to a transfer of anointing? The answer is no! **The physical interaction exposes you to his words.**

Jesus said to His disciples, the words that I speak to you, they are Spirit (anointing) and life. **The anointing is in the words.** The disciples of Jesus soaked in the words of their master until He left them. **They took His words seriously because He had told them that the anointing was in the words.** Thank God that today the words of anointed ministers are available in books, tapes and videos.

> **...the words that I speak unto you, they are spirit [anointing], and they are life.**
>
> **John 6:63**

The anointing enters you as you listen to the Word. The Word is not just some philosophical discourse. It is different from a lecture in college. The Word is able to impart an anointing into your life. Look at this amazing Scripture in Ezekiel! The prophet said he could feel the anointing enter him as the Lord spoke to him.

> **And the spirit entered into me when he spake unto me...**
>
> **Ezekiel 2:2**

I have always wanted the opportunity to live and serve certain men of God. But that opportunity was never practical. However, following some of these men through videos, tapes and books has greatly blessed my life and ministry. The fact that you are reading this book is evidence that an anointing I received some years ago is real.

The Bible records that Elisha soaked in the words of his spiritual father. Elisha didn't just wash Elijah's hands. He didn't just wash and clean in the house. Just like Jesus and the disciples, Elisha and Elijah engaged in lots of important conversation.

> **And it came to pass, as they still went on, and talked...**
>
> **2 Kings 2:11**

3. Decide to stay close to the very end until the anointing which you desire is flowing through your ministry.

Elisha walked so closely to Elijah that God had to separate them Himself. Don't allow anyone to separate you from your spiritual father. Do not allow circumstances to keep you away from your man of God.

> **...there appeared a chariot of fire, and horses of fire, and parted them both asunder...**
>
> **2 Kings 2:11**

5. Spiritual ministrations

We must be careful not to make any mistakes. God will give you the anointing. No man can give you the anointing. Yet, He does it through men. It is important to pray and ask for the anointing.

> **If ye then, being evil, know how to give good gifts unto your children: how much more shall your heavenly Father give the Holy Spirit to them that ask him?**
>
> **Luke 11:13**

Another way you can receive the anointing is through the *laying on of hands.* The laying on of hands is a foundational doctrine of the Church. It is the principal way in which an impartation or gift is given. It is such an important procedure that God tells us not to hurriedly impart gifts through the laying on of hands.

> **Lay hands suddenly on no man, neither be partaker of other men's sins: keep thyself pure.**
>
> **1 Timothy 5:22**

Timothy, the pastor, had hands laid on him and he received spiritual gifts. The Bible plainly declares that he received the gift of God through the laying on of hands.

> **Wherefore I put thee in remembrance that thou stir up the gift of God, which is in thee by the putting on of my hands.**
>
> **2 Timothy 1:6**

This means that the manifestation of the gift and anointing must have begun to operate in Timothy's life after hands were laid on him. Thank God for the preaching of the Word of God. There is a place for the laying on of hands. The disciples received an anointing when Jesus breathed on them and said,

> **...Receive ye the Holy Ghost:**
>
> **John 20:22**

These different spiritual ministrations are ways by which God can impart His gift to you.

6. The passage of time

Time is a very important element in the development of any ministry. The Word of God teaches us that Jesus adds to our gifts when He recognizes that we are faithful to what He has given to us.

> **He that is faithful in that which is least is faithful also in much: and he that is unjust in the least is unjust also in much.**
>
> **Luke 16:10**

With the passage of time your faithfulness will be tested. Your faithfulness will provoke God to give you additional gifts and a greater anointing. You will discover that certain realms are inaccessible to you until "time" elapses. Unfortunately, there is no substitute for the test of time.

Some years ago, I tried to raise the dead but I did not succeed. I often wondered why God did not honour me then. If He had, I probably would have backslidden by now. I now see certain things happening in my ministry, which I didn't see before. If I had had that level of anointing some years ago, it could have destroyed me. It is important to trust God to allow time to pass so that He Himself can lift you up at the right time.

7. Minister to the man of God

The last but not the least step I want to share with you is about ministering to the man of God with your substance.

> **And certain women, which had been healed of evil spirits and infirmities, Mary called Magdalene, out of whom went seven devils, And Joanna, the wife of Chuza Herod's steward, and Susanna, and many others, which ministered unto him of their substance.**
>
> **Luke 8:2, 3**

You must be able to minister to the man of God out of your own substance. If money is a problem to you then you cannot be a minister. The Bible teaches that people who have been taught should share their good things with those who teach them.

> **Let him that is taught in the word communicate unto him that teacheth in all good things.**
>
> **Galatians 6:6**

The man of God will minister spiritual things to you and you will minister back to him in physical things. The anointing is provoked when you minister to the man of God. Anytime I have had the opportunity to be near those who have been a blessing to me, I have ministered to them out of my substance.

When the woman with the alabaster box of ointment ministered to Christ, He said that she would be remembered. When you pour an "alabaster box" on a man of God you will provoke a blessing and be remembered. **Your ministry will have a longer life span as you decide to honour those before you. Your ministry will be remembered by many.** You will provoke the favour and anointing of God over your life.

Notice what great men like Abraham did when they met with greater men of God. They immediately ministered to the man of God out of their substance.

> **And Melchizedek king of Salem brought forth bread and wine: and he was the priest of the most high God. And he blessed him,... And he [Abraham] gave him tithes of all.**
>
> **Genesis 14:18-20**

Chapter

27

What it Means to Catch the Spirit of the Ministry

CHAPTER SUMMARY

To effectively build the house of God it is important to recruit people who have caught the spirit of the ministry. There is simply no other way. In this chapter discover the eight things in a ministry you must catch and how to catch them.

■ **Eight Things You Must Catch**

27.1 The vision of the house

27.2 The principles of the house

27.3 The philosophy of the house

27.4 The standards of the house

27.5 The doctrines of the house

27.6 The procedures of the house

27.7 The emphasis of the house

27.8 The anointing of the house

Your aspiration for church growth will naturally lead you to work with many different people. It is only understandable that in a larger ministry you will need more "hands on deck". The act of recruiting new people often leads to the destruction of the ministry. Be careful that you do not end up destroying what you are trying to build. It is important to recruit people who have what I call the spirit of the ministry.

> **And I will come down and talk with thee there: and I will take of the spirit which is upon thee, and will put it upon them; and they shall bear the burden of the people with thee, that thou bear it not thyself alone.**
>
> **Numbers 11:17**

Please notice the revelation that God gave Moses. He said, "I'm going to take of the spirit or anointing that is upon you and that same anointing will be transferred to other people." It is only then that they will be able to work with you. It is only then that they will be able to help you.

God could have simply given these seventy people an anointing for leadership, but He didn't. **God did not give them a general anointing for leadership! Neither did He give them a special anointing of management and wise judgement! He simply gave them Moses' anointing.** What was the spirit upon Moses? It was the special gift of ministry given to Moses to lead the people. This is what those seventy pastors received.

There is an anointing on every ministry. That is why people can start out in a ministry of their own and have only twenty people after ten years. Were these people to operate under a certain ministry, they would not have only twenty people after ten years. They may have a thousand. This is because different ministries have different anointings over them.

I am not saying that you do not have to start something new, not at all! I am saying that God gives certain gifts to certain men. Those who find themselves planted under such men find that they are catching the same spirit of ministry. They will find themselves doing great things or even greater things than he is doing.

There Is a Difference!

Catching the spirit of the ministry is a little different from catching the anointing. When you join a new church, you will notice that it is different from any other church. **Understand that every church is different and has its own culture.** Every minister has a peculiar anointing on his life. This leads to a unique ministry. When you join up with this unique ministry, you must adapt and flow with it. Understand that every church is different. When you join a church, you have to acclimatize and re-learn certain things. It is the senior pastor's duty to prevent anyone from becoming a minister without adapting fully to the culture of the church.

It is the trainee's duty to learn, imbibe, observe and adapt to the spoken and unspoken philosophies of the church. Study the culture. Flow with it. Do all you can to fit in. When you fit in, that peculiar anointing will also fit into you and operate through you. It is possible and it is necessary if you want to be fruitful in the context of a particular church.

If you do not adapt, the anointing will not be able to fit into you because it was meant for a particular type of vessel. You will run into problems if you choose to ignore the standards accepted and used by the general leadership. **When people do not operate under the same Spirit (anointing), they create conflict.**

The leaders become disunited and each one thinks he is right. The church begins to disintegrate behind the scenes and soon this comes into the open.

How to Catch the Spirit of the Ministry

To catch the spirit of the ministry, you have to company with the church and its leadership. There is simply no other way. You have to know what they do, and watch them do it! You have to accept it in your mind and believe in it in your heart. The standards and principles in the church must become yours. They must no longer be "their" principles.

When you think like the leadership, you have caught the spirit of the ministry.

The anointing makes you think in a particular way. The anointing makes you act in a particular way.

I learnt long ago that I should not accept people who do not really fit in as sons, into my ministry. Someone may be a well-qualified minister with great credentials, but if he does not have the spirit of the ministry, it is no use taking him on. The few conflicts that I have experienced in the Lighthouse denomination have been through and from people who did not fully catch the spirit of this ministry. It looked as though they fitted in, but in reality, they were not a part of us.

After Jesus ascended into Heaven, a replacement was sought for Judas. They chose someone who had the spirit of Jesus' ministry. Someone who knew them through and through. They needed someone who had accepted the standards and philosophies of Christ. They did not want to introduce somebody who would create confusion within their ranks.

> **Wherefore of these men which have companied with us all the time that the Lord Jesus went in and out among us, Beginning from the baptism of John, unto that same day that he was taken up from us, must one be ordained to be a witness with us...**
>
> **Acts 1:21, 22**

You will observe in the above Scripture that they chose somebody who had been with them long enough to catch the spirit of the ministry. They didn't care whether the person had the gift of prophecy or the gift of leadership. It is better to be safe than sorry. Go for those you know and avoid unknown elements!

There are three groups of people I do not often consider for employment. These are not "bad" people! They are good people but they need to catch the spirit of the ministry.

Three Groups of People I Will Not Employ

a. A Bible school graduate seeking employment in the church

Graduating from a Bible school means very little to me. All it means is that you have a piece of paper showing that you have studied some courses. Those courses may be different from the courses I teach in my church. Even if they are the same, they may have a completely different orientation. I ask such people to simply join the church and become a part of the church family. They must then go through the ranks like every other church member. *If and only if he is able to catch the spirit of the ministry, can he be part of its leadership.*

b. An experienced and seasoned minister

There is a saying, "You can't teach an old dog new tricks". This saying is not in the Bible but it is often true. When a tree is young, you can bend it. But when a tree is old, you must break it in order to get it to bend! Usually, people who have been in the ministry for years feel that they know all about the ministry. Such people have problems fitting in. After being a part of your system for a while, they will say, "I was a pastor before I joined you", "I was a minister in my own right before I came here." They will add, "I had a ministry before I came here and I just decided to place it under your ministry." **Such people do not fit in because they are not prepared to be trained or retrained.**

I have learnt from painful experience to train up my own sons and daughters in ministry. They are to me, like the disciples were to Jesus. I can trust them and I can leave my ministry in their hands wherever they are in the world. Jesus left His ministry to twelve men and they handled it perfectly. When you have people who have caught the spirit of the leadership you can leave things with them and not worry. They will not rebel.

c. A pastor of a small church who wants to join a largernetwork

This is even more dangerous! When the church begins to grow under a new name and new anointing, the pastor will begin to have thoughts of breaking away. He will say, "I had a church with members before I joined up with you. I want to change the name back to what it was before." This often leads to painful splits and breakaways. At this point, no one will know who is really right or wrong.

My policy is to encourage such individuals to continue independently in ministry.

If he insists, the way forward is for him to close down his church and join the bigger network as an ordinary member. With the process of time, such a person may become a minister within the network and start a church again. However, it takes a lot of humility to do something like that.

It is important for senior pastors to know when people have caught the spirit of the ministry. It is important for up-and-coming ministers to understand how to catch the spirit of the ministry.

■ Eight Things You Must Catch

In every church, you must endeavour to catch the *vision, principles, philosophy, standards, doctrines, procedures, emphasis* and the *anointing* of the house. To illustrate this better I will just use Lighthouse Chapel International as a model.

1. The vision of the house

Generally speaking, the vision of Lighthouse Chapel International is soul winning and church planting. Many pastors do not have a vision for soul winning. We have a strong vision for soul winning. If you are not oriented towards the harvest, you will be a misfit in such a church.

Everyone is taught and motivated to save the lost and to be involved in practical ministry. No one is left out, including professionals and businessmen. **We believe that every member can be a minister.** It may sound strange, but that is our vision. Some churches have a vision for prosperity. Others have a vision for dominion over the works of darkness. Others have a vision for deliverance. Whichever church you decide to be a part of, you must learn to catch the vision of that house. No one vision is right or wrong. The vision depends on the call that God has given to the man. Leave the judgement of that to the Lord.

2. The principles of the house

The principles of LCI are the principles in the Word of God. One of our principles is that everything must be founded on the solid foundation of the Bible. It is our principle to reject things that are not firmly based on the Word of God.

We have principles of loyalty. People who break these principles cannot fit into our ministry. I am loyal to my pastors and I expect them to be loyal to me. We believe in principled leadership where everyone can climb to the highest position in ministry.

3. The philosophy of the house

The philosophy of the house refers to the general trend of thinking. Our church believes that lay people must do the work of ministry. We believe that the educated can also be in ministry.

We believe that church buildings are very important for the establishment of the church. We believe that church buildings bring stability and permanence. Church building projects allow church members to know that their money is being "put to good use". We also believe in frugality. There are many ways by which we save money. Ironically, this makes people think that we are rich.

Another important philosophy of LCI is that we are pro-marriage. We encourage people to marry, and to do so at a young age. We feel that it is the biblical pattern for young people to marry and stay pure, rather than to live in sin and hypocrisy. Any leader within our system must have these ideas as *his own* ideas.

4. The standards of the house

In our church, we expect people to be faithful to their marriage partners. We expect ministers to lead honest lives and to have financial and moral integrity. We do not compromise on these standards! We do not expect people to be perfect, but we do expect them to be honest.

A lowering of the standards of any church will lead to a gradual and complete deviation from the original vision of the church. It is because of the lowering of standards that gay and lesbian priests and even bishops are now a part of church life. Some priests are officiating the marriages between two men. They are thereby claiming God's approval on homosexuality. This is Sodom and Gomorrah coming into the church. How did it get there? It got there by gradually changing the standards of the Church of God.

5. The doctrines of the house

Within every church there are certain beliefs based on the Bible. A doctrine is a trend of teaching. One of our doctrines is the doctrine of loyalty.

We teach extensively on this. *(For further study see my book **Loyalty & Disloyalty**).*

Another doctrine we have is what we call, Anagkazo. This Greek word means something to every leader in our church. It teaches about compelling souls to come to Christ. You cannot be a minister in our church if you do not understand and believe in Anagkazo.

6. The procedures of the house

The way things are done in every church is different. In our church, a person becomes a pastor by rising through the ranks. One must first be a shepherd before being promoted to a lay pastor. That is just the way things are done here. We have very few full-time ministers.

We believe that you must first be successful as a lay pastor before becoming a full-time minister. This may be different from the way you do things in your church, but if you want to be in a particular ministry, you must accept the procedures of that house.

You cannot be a leader in the church if you do not pay tithes, or what we call First and Best Fruits. That is just the way we do things. Every Lighthouse church takes two offerings on Sundays. In our church, you must have extensive counselling before getting married. These are just some of the procedures we do not intend to alter. Anyone who is going to be a leader of the church has to accept these procedures and flow with them.

The church has a system of small groups involving fellowships, ministries and chapels. This system has worked for us throughout the world, wherever Lighthouse churches have been established. That is the way we do things. That is our procedure. Welcome to the house.

7. The emphasis of the house

Every ministry has a peculiar emphasis. We emphasize the preaching and the teaching of the Word of God.

Some emphasize prosperity and healing. Some emphasize the anointing. We emphasize the winning of souls and the establishing of the church. Mind you, we believe in miracles, and we experience great moves of the Spirit, but our emphasis is the Word. If you accept this emphasis then you can be with us.

8. The anointing of the house

This is the anointing that we have been talking about in the earlier chapters. Apart from getting the natural and physical aspects like the procedures and standards, you need to get this spiritual component.

There is nothing like the anointing. Without it, you can do nothing in ministry. Once you have tasted the anointing and the difference it makes to ministry, you will not like to do anything without it. If you are within a particular church, the principal anointing that you should desire is the anointing on your leader. This is because you are working under his ministry.

Chapter

28

Fight for Commitment

CHAPTER SUMMARY

The key to increasing in size is to have more and more very committed people.

■ Four Main Types of Commitment

28.1 Fair weather commitment

28.2 Situational friendship commitment

28.3 Non-situational friendship commitment

28.4 Marital commitment

If you want your church to grow you must fight to have more committed members. Committed members are the building blocks of a large church. Let's consider for example if you are in a situation where you are building a house. Supposing you laid a hundred blocks on your building foundation everyday. At the end of the day you might look at the work done and say to yourself, "Things are getting better. The building is coming up nicely!"

How would you feel if you noticed that seventy of those blocks were missing every morning? You would feel very frustrated because your building project would progress at a much slower rate. The building would still develop, however at a much slower rate. This is because of the regular loss of the building blocks. In the case of a church, the building blocks are the members. The missing blocks are the uncommitted members who disappear ever so often.

In order to develop committed members, every pastor must know about the different levels of commitment each member may have. Do not be deceived by a large crowd. **A large crowd consists of people with different levels of commitment. You must press for the highest level of commitment possible from every one of your members.** Over the years, I have observed four main types of commitment.

Four Main Types of Commitment

1. Fair weather commitment

The lowest type of commitment is Fair Weather Commitment. This consists of those who are committed when things are going well. The Bible says a rich man has many friends, but a poor man does not have many friends.

> **Wealth maketh many friends; but the poor is separated from his neighbour.**
>
> **Proverbs 19:4**

When I started out in ministry, I had few friends. When the ministry became large and successful, many people claimed to be my friends. Many spoke of imaginary assistance they gave me in my early days. Senior ministers have sworn that they never said negative things about me (although I know they did). When things are not going well, people don't want to know you. But when the sky is clear, they all claim to be your friends.

Fair weather church members are people who are committed only when things are going well. They form the crowds that come when the church is flourishing and successful. Such people fall away when a crisis or problem arises. You cannot rely on such people when building a Megachurch. People with fair weather commitment are usually not aware of their low level of commitment. Therefore, the pastor must preach and teach against being committed only when things are going well.

2. Situational friendship commitment

The next type of commitment is what I call situational *friendship commitment.* Friends are committed to each other to some extent. There are also two levels of commitment between friends, *situational friendship commitment and non-situational friendship commitment.*

There are two types of friends in the world. There are friends, who are friends because the *situation* permits. In school, for instance, different situations bring people together and make them friends. Everyone has friends like that. You had to sit in the same classroom for some years and you became friends because of the circumstances. However, when you left school or didn't see these friends anymore, you stopped relating with them. I have many friends like that.

Some people are only committed to their church when the situation permits. They may live near the church or there may be no other church nearby. However, if another church were to start in the vicinity they would go there. You may have many people in your church, but they are only members because of their circumstances. Such people cannot be relied upon. You must press for a higher commitment.

Aim to get all of your members to be committed irrespective of their circumstances. That is *non-situational commitment.* They are committed to you irrespective of the situation. Some children come to the church because their parents do so, however, if their parents were not to come anymore they would stop coming to church.

Attack Sunday

Our church was once attacked by traditional practitioners. On that Sunday morning an armed mob of people invaded the church, threw rocks at the church and physically assaulted several of our church members and pastors. I believe they were hunting for me on that fateful morning. The attack so startled us that it has been ingrained in our memories. After the attack, we had to wash away streams of blood from the church grounds.

Many of our church members were hurt and the entire incident was broadcast on national television. As you would expect, this caused the "fair weather" and "situational friendship" members to vanish for several weeks. Someone whose commitment is deep, will not be moved by such attacks.

On that Sunday, many cars were vandalized, with their windscreens smashed. However, the next Sunday, the committed members were back in church with their cars. They were members, whether they were attacked or not. In fact, some have expressed their commitment to die for the church if there is any further attack.

Members whose commitment is at the level of *"fair weather"* and *"situational friendship"* are not of much use to the church in times of crisis. The pastor must preach to raise the level of commitment of all members.

3. Non-situational friendship commitment

When your church members have graduated to this level of commitment, they are not moved by hurts, separation, conflicts or distance. You can rely more on such people. The commitment is one of deep friendship. It is not affected much by circumstances. Pastors should aim at moving their members to at least this level.

I have friends I don't see often. For instance, one of my university roommates, "Dr. Nosh", is a non-situational friend. That means he's my friend whether I see him or not. We live in different parts of the world, yet our friendship is not affected by distance or separation. I know he's my friend and he knows I am his friend. He can depend on me and I can depend on him. Like Jonathan and David, their friendship became a bond between them.

> **And Jonathan caused David to swear again, because he loved him: for he loved him as he loved his own soul.**
>
> **1 Samuel 20:17**

4. Marital commitment

There is an even higher level of commitment – *marital commitment.* In marital commitment, the individuals are committed as though they are married. In marriage, there should be no thought of divorce, but rather a spirit of permanence. There are no more options left.

You cannot decide to stay or leave. You must stay; it is as simple as that! You are in it for good. There may be conflicts, challenges and even disappointments, but this will have no ability to shake the commitment of a married couple.

Like everyone else, I have had challenges in my marriage. I have had happy times and not so happy times. Nevertheless, I never consider the option of divorce. That option has been ruled out by the Word of God and by my level of commitment. Nothing can and nothing should be able to separate a married couple. **Our commitment to Christ is at the marital level of commitment.** The Bible teaches that we are supposed to be married to Christ.

> **Wherefore my brethren…that ye should be married to another, even to him who is raised from the dead, that we should bring forth fruit unto God.**
>
> **Romans 7:4**

When the commitment to the church rises to the level of marital commitment, the Bible teaches that we will begin to bring forth fruit unto God. The higher the commitment, the more the fruit. **It is only when a man and woman have marital commitment that they can successfully bring forth fruit (children).**

This is the type of commitment I expect from all pastors, leaders and mature members in the church. I am committed to them for life and I expect them to be committed to me for life. When a church has a pastor who is unstable, the congregation can feel the instability. The church members are not ready to give their best if they feel that the pastor is there for just a season.

Preach marital commitment. Teach marital commitment. The commitment of your members will rise. They will become solid building blocks of your mega church. Anytime you speak to a church member, assess his or her level of commitment. Try to place him in one of these four levels. Then you must work on him or her for a higher level of commitment. If your members are very committed, no one can invite them away or steal them from you.

The Temporary Associate

One day I was visited in my office by a senior pastor and his associate. I asked him, "How is the ministry?"

"We're not doing badly," he said. "We are having a few struggles though."

They continued, "As you know, our church has been going through one crisis after another."

The senior pastor continued, "It has not been easy. One person after the other keeps leaving the church."

Out of curiosity, I asked the associate, "Do you have any plans of starting your own ministry one day?"

"Certainly!" he said. "I am just working with this man for a while, then I will launch out on my own."

"Oh, I see."

I told him (in front of his associate), "If I were you, I would not like to work with someone who is using me as a springboard to start his own ministry."

I warned him, "When this pastor eventually leaves you, it will cause a lot of pain and conflict in the church."

"Really!" he exclaimed.

I advised him, "I personally do not believe that your closest associate should have such a low level of commitment. I think a pastor in the church should have the highest level of commitment. I believe he should have what I call marital commitment."

"I only want to work with people who are committed. This is because I can then pour out my life into them."

I explained further, "Take a young man and a young lady who are courting each other. A decent young woman would not be prepared to undress and perform acts of great commitment with her fiancé. However, if this young man takes his fiancée to the marriage altar and signs a legal contract, then he can expect the highest level of commitment (till death us do part) from her. That same decent young lady would then be prepared to give her utmost commitment and flow into the deepest level of involvement."

"Do you understand what I am saying," I said to this pastor.

He seemed to understand what I was saying.

"I would not like to get deeply involved with people unless they guarantee me the highest level of commitment," I added.

Not long after, this senior pastor called me saying, "Just as you predicted, my associate has left me suddenly and it has caused me a lot of pain."

At the time I had the conversation with him, he had about seventy members in his church. However, after the associate left the church, he was left with only twenty people. The lack of a high level of commitment from associates and pastors is very damaging to a church. The congregation follows what they see the pastors do. If they see shallow commitment, they in turn will have a low level of commitment.

Let's be committed to one another. I am the type of person who gives my utmost to help people. I do not want to pour out my life and soul into people only for them to despise and destroy me.

For I am persuaded, that neither death, nor life, nor angels, nor principalities, nor powers, nor things present, nor things to come, Nor height, nor depth, nor any other creature, shall be able to separate us from the love of God, which is in Christ Jesus our Lord.

Romans 8:38, 39

Chapter

29

How to Develop Devoted Members

CHAPTER SUMMARY

In this next section, I want to share with you a few keys on how to develop devoted membership. The first important thing is that you the pastor, be devoted.

- **3 Different Types of Members**

29.1 Deer stage members

29.2 Goat stage members

29.3 Sheep stage members

- **Ten Keys for Developing Devoted Members**

29.4 Be a devoted pastor!

29.5 Say positive things about the church.

29.6 Say positive things about the pastors.

29.7 Say good things about your church members.

29.8 Encourage employers to hire church members.

29.9 Encourage members to apply for work from within the church family.

29.10 Encourage church members to marry each other.

29.11 Encourage members to socialize and fraternize.

29.12 Develop smaller church families within the big church.

29.13 Become a father or mother to your church.

A person goes through three stages when he is becoming established as a member of your church. As a shepherd, you must be able to distinguish between the different types of members that you have.

> **...he shall separate them one from another, as a shepherd divideth his sheep from the goats.**
>
> **Matthew 25:32**

3 Different Types of Members

1. Deer stage members

When a person is initially converted, he behaves like a deer: untamed, swift-footed and difficult to keep in one place. You have to track them down through the mountains and the forest. They are difficult to handle. It is important to move your members out of this stage. When you visit them, they play "hide-and-seek" with you. Deer are nimble creatures.

The Deer and the Assistant Deer

Seventeen years ago I visited a deer stage member called Adelaide. Somehow, she did not want to see her shepherd at all. This was one of the deer in my fellowship. I was trying to convert her from the deer stage to the sheep stage. I remember one evening when I knocked on her door in Volta Hall of the University of Ghana.

A voice from within answered, "Who is there?"

"It's me Brother Dag. I'm looking for Sister Adelaide."

After a few moments her roommate said, "Come in." This roommate happened to be her sister Irene.

"Hello. I am looking for Adelaide. Is she in?"

The roommate smiled sweetly, "Sorry, she's not in."

"Oh, I see. Where did she go?"

"I'm not sure, she just went out."

"Alright, please tell her I came by to check on her."

"Okay," she smiled again sweetly. "When she comes back I'll tell her you were here."

Each room had its own balcony, and unknown to me Adelaide was hiding there. I was a shepherd who was dealing with a deer and an assistant deer. Only deer dodge and hide. However, I worked on them until they became sheep. Today, they are stable "sheep" members.

2. Goat stage members

Goats are a little better than deer. They are far more domestic and easily accessible. However, a goat is much more independent than a sheep. They do what they want to do and are less likely to follow. When a church member graduates from the deer stage, they move on to the goat stage. As soon as a deer sees a human being, it takes off, whereas a goat remains. **Goats are friendlier than deer, though they can often have traces of stubbornness.**

3. Sheep stage members

Sheep are the best of the three groups. Your goal as a pastor should be to have your church full of devoted sheep. These people follow the shepherd. They stay together and move with the group. Such members are much easier to pastor. Sheep are often devoted, committed, faithful, dependable and loving members. If your church is full of devoted sheep, you will be a happy pastor. They will stay near you always, and receive your ministration.

■ Ten Keys for Developing Devoted Members

They devoted themselves to the instruction given by the apostles and to fellowship...

Acts 2:42 (Moffatt translation)

And they continued steadfastly in the apostles' doctrine and fellowship...

Acts 2:42

They devoted themselves to the apostles' teaching and to the fellowship...

Acts 2:42 (New International Version)

The number one task of a shepherd is to transform the members from deer to devoted sheep. How is this possible?

But we all...are changed into the same image from glory to glory...

2 Corinthians 3:18

Now the word "change" comes from a Greek word *metamorphoo*, which means metamorphosis. The word metamorphosis always reminds us of a dramatic transformation that occurs inside a cocoon when a larvae changes into a butterfly. When you see a butterfly elegantly fluttering around, you have no idea what it used to be like. There has been a drastic and major change – *metamorphosis*.

It is this same kind of *metamorphosis* that can take place in the members of a church. People change because of the ministry of the Word. They are transformed by the renewing of their minds. Loose and dodgy Christians can become devoted and committed zealots.

Devotion is a spiritual thing, it can be perceived. There are three main areas in which you can develop devoted membership: who you are, what you say and what you do.

1. Be a devoted pastor!

The pastor must be devoted to his church and his church members. Devotion is a spiritual thing. It is transmitted sometimes by osmosis – from person to person. *The unspoken commitment and sacrifice of the leadership is contagious; it passes from one member to another without speaking.* Why do I say this? Because not all pastors are committed to their churches.

I began my ministry as a medical student. In 1987, I was already struggling as a pastor/medical student. The tradition for newly qualified doctors in Ghana is for them to travel to America to seek "greener pastures". Medical doctors earn thousands of dollars in America, England and South Africa.

My fledgling church was full of people watching to see whether I would remain in Ghana or move out of the country. When the time came for the decision to be made, I declared boldly to my members that I was staying with them. I wasn't going to leave them. From that time onwards, I noticed a dramatic change in the commitment of the members to the church.

The sheep can sense the pastor's commitment. No one wants to follow someone who will abandon him midstream. In addition to the senior pastor being devoted, associates and assistants must be equally committed and devoted. The assistant pastors must be devoted to the senior pastor as well as to the church members.

The seed of devotion leads to a harvest of multiplied commitment from the church members.

2. Say positive things about the church.

Everybody wants to be part of a good thing. That is human nature. People are more likely to be devoted to something that is successful than to something that is failing. I have learnt that you can make your church flourish by *using your mouth.* If you want your church to grow, tell the members that they are part of a good church. Speak positively about the other pastors in the church. Do not criticize the pastors of the church.

That is why we call the Lighthouse Chapel International, *The Megachurch.* I am aware that this worries some people. It is just our faith confession! We know we have a long way to go. We know that we are still learning. But we believe that we have a mega ministry with a mega impact in a lost and dying world!

3. Say positive things about the pastors.

The associate pastor must say positive things about the senior pastor. He must say things like, "This is some of the best teaching you can get anywhere in the world." You must tell the church, "We are blessed to have such a man of God as our pastor." The Book of Acts, chapter two says that they continued steadfastly in the apostles' doctrine (teaching). One version puts it this way,

> **And they steadfastly persevered devoting themselves constantly...**
>
> **Acts 2:42 (Amplified version)**

You can make your church members become devoted to your teaching. Let them hear that it is the best they can get anywhere. The assistant pastor must constantly make the church aware of the precious gift that God has graciously given to them in their senior pastor.

I Am the Best Preacher for My Church

I believe I am the best preacher for my church. This is not vanity, it is biblical commonsense. I am their shepherd and I know what is best for my people. When God gives a woman a baby, He fills her breasts with milk for her baby. God does not fill another woman's breast with milk for that baby.

Similarly, God has filled my spirit with the Word of God for my sheep. My spiritual breasts are full of spiritual milk for my spiritual children. That is why I preach all the time to my church members. **I have other pastors, but I do ninety percent of the preaching and teaching. This is because I am the shepherd and God gave me the duty of feeding the sheep.**

Pastors ought to take charge of the pulpit and discharge their duties honourably. Thank God for visiting ministers. Many have ministered at my church and have been a blessing, but I am the best shepherd for my sheep.

In various ways, I make my church members become devoted to my teaching and preaching. I let them know that it's the best thing for them. If your members are not devoted to your preaching and teaching they will be devoted to someone else's ministry, and your church will not grow.

I have watched how visiting preachers are appreciated more than a resident pastor. This is unfortunate! Visiting pastors are often hailed as superheroes, whilst their resident pastors are ignored. The church members should not be deceived into thinking that the visiting minister has more to offer than their own pastor. He does not! He may have something different but he does not have anything better! It is only because the pastor from the church has fed the sheep so well, that there is a congregation groomed enough to receive a visiting minister.

One translation of Acts 2:42 says that they were devoted **"to the teaching of the apostles and to fellowship with one another."** In Bible times, the Christians were devoted to two principal things:

- Their pastors' teachings.
- Fellowshipping with one another.

Read Acts 2:42 for yourself! Read it from different versions of the Bible. It is crystal clear! Any simpleton should be able to understand these two strategic keys of church growth. Get your church to be like the New Testament Church and you will have the thousands that are spoken of in the Book of Acts. **If you don't have an associate pastor who says good things about your teaching, then get one who does!**

4. Say good things about *your church members.*

In order to encourage inter-sheep relationships you must speak good things about your church members. Some people say things like, "I don't trust these church members." "I don't want any church member in my house." Although some church members may disappoint you, do not maintain a negative attitude towards all other members. That would be a big mistake!

I have heard Christians say, "I'd rather employ a Muslim than a Christian." That is unscriptural! The Bible teaches us to do good to Christians, especially your church members.

> **As we have therefore opportunity, let us do good unto all men, especially unto them who are of the household of faith.**
>
> **Galatians 6:10**

The fact that you have had unpleasant experiences with Christian men does not mean that you should marry an unbeliever. You are reacting in the wrong way. You are moving into foolishness!

Speak positively about Christians, especially your own church members. This will cause your church members to interact with each other. If you say evil things about them, new members will not form vital bonding relationships.

There is a principle at work here. **People are often attracted to the church by the pastor, but they often remain in the church because of the internal relationships they establish.** Never forget this! People stay in a church because of relationships they have in the church. It is the duty of the pastor to create interaction between members of the church.

This is a very important key to implement, if you really desire to have a large church. The Bible says that they were devoted to the fellowship. Members must be devoted to the fellowship of Christians in the same church. If you have members who hardly know each other, then introduce and influence them to develop relationships.

Encourage them to be committed to the church. Teach them that it is important to attend church all the time. **Teach them not to make a habit of hopping from church to church, just to see what is happening elsewhere.** Explain to them that it is only the devil who goes "to and fro" (Job 1:7).

5. Encourage employers to hire church members.

Practically speaking, you can also encourage the members to be devoted to one another's fellowship in many different ways. When I have a church member who is an employer in a strategic position, I encourage him to consciously help other members to get jobs. Do not think that this will happen naturally, the pastor's involvement is important.

When one Lighthouse member secures a job in a company, you will often find several other members finding their way there. Nowadays, this often happens naturally without my involvement. However, in the beginning I had to encourage this interaction. Many people were put off by the bad behaviour of some church members. Do not overreact to the disgraceful behaviour that some church members display when they are employed. Church members are human beings. Keep on recommending in the Spirit of love and forgiveness.

One employer said that he would not employ a member of the church because the church member would arrive at work late, claiming he went witnessing early in the morning. That is nonsense! Witnessing is not supposed to make you arrive late for work. I would encourage you to sack such a person. Church members are supposed to be disciplined!

6. Encourage members to apply for work from within the *church family.*

When you have a member who needs a job, direct him to other church members that can help him to get a job. This increases the members commitment because the sheep will see that you really care for them. The church then becomes an important family to belong to.

7. Encourage church members to marry each other.

Have you ever noticed how a young lady seems so committed to a church? Many of them have relationships within that church. Often it is their fiancés that act like glue which fixes them to the church. They are cemented to the church by their relationships. This is what I call *shepherdorial cement.* As I said earlier, they may be attracted initially to the church by the charismatic man of God, but they remain because of the relationships they acquire within the church!

I repeatedly tell my church members that the person they want to marry can be found within our congregation. If they want a tall, short, fat, skinny, fair or dark person; they can find their choice within the congregation! Of course, it is not a sin to marry from outside your own church. Many people in my church do that! All I am saying is that I encourage my church members to intermarry.

Anytime one of our "daughters", in whom we have invested, is married and taken to another church, we lose a church member. However, if this member stays on in the church, she will contribute to church growth. The couple will also have children who will become members of our children's church, and eventually our adult assembly. You may want to argue with my theory, but it's working very well for me!

8. Encourage members to *socialize* and *fraternize.*

The New Testament church was devoted to fellowshipping with one another! Sometimes people will accuse us of sticking to ourselves and not interacting with outsiders. However, that is not our intention at all! Our intention is also to interact with outsiders in order to win souls.

But make sure you encourage your church members to have their friends from within the church. **If your church members' friends are within the church, they will have two reasons for coming to church.** Firstly, they will come for spiritual nourishment. Secondly, they will come to meet with their friends. You can easily lose members whose friends are mainly people outside the church.

9. Develop smaller church families within the big church.

My church is made out of many small groups. Some groups have ten members, five, and even others have fifty.

It is these small groups, called ministries and fellowships, which form the nucleus of family relationships in our church. You may be surprised to discover that people are more committed to these smaller groups than to the big church. When there is a wedding or funeral, it is usually the concern of these smaller groups. Even when there is a social event, most of the friends are drawn out of these same groups.

10. Become a father or mother *to your church.*

Some pastors never develop beyond being a teacher of doctrines and truths. Chicks gather around the mother hen because of her motherly security.

> **...I have gathered thy children together, even as a hen gathereth her chickens under her wings...**
>
> **Matthew 23:37**

If you want your church to grow, develop fatherly or motherly attributes. Be everything to your sheep. Be a friend. Be a brother.

Be a father. Show concern for your flock. Show interest in things that concern them. Be interested in their school. Ask for details concerning their businesses. Help them in their marriages. Correct them when they are wrong. Rebuke them and discipline them when they need it. Don't just give them good teachings. Become a mother or a father to your flock. **The anointing to be a father or mother is the anointing to *gather*.**

> **To the weak became I as weak, that I might gain the weak: I am made all things to all men, that I might by all means save some.**
>
> **1 Corinthians 9:22**

Chapter

30

Retention Evangelism

CHAPTER SUMMARY

One of the secrets of church growth is the secret of "retention evangelism". Retention evangelism is the art of winning souls and retaining them. Every pastor must learn to keep what he already has – at all costs.

- **Three Vital Strategies for Retaining Church Members**

30.1 Strategy 1: Follow-up Brings Retention

- **Three Principles for Follow Up**

  - **Pray for visitors and converts**
  - **Visit new converts and visitors**
  - **Do not waste your time**

30.2 Strategy 2: Concentrate to Retain

30.3 Strategy 3: Devotion Brings Retention

One of the secrets of church growth is the secret of "retention evangelism". *Retention evangelism is the art of winning souls and retaining them.* Every pastor must learn to keep what he already has – at all costs.

> **...Gather up the fragments that remain, that nothing be lost.**
> **John 6:12**

Jesus did not waste any of His blessings. He wanted to save as much as He could.

The same applies to church growth. Our problem is not one of bringing new people to the church, but one of getting them to stay! If we can retain all the visitors and souls who come in through the front door, we will build a megachurch for Jesus.

A megachurch pastor is interested in what others despise. **Be interested in every single member.** Jesus collected the fragments.

If the fragments were important to the Lord, then the fragments must be important to you. Every member, big or small, rich or poor, must be important to you!

> **...Of them which thou gavest me have I lost none.**
> **John 18:9**

Let me share with you three vital strategies for retaining church members.

Three Vital Strategies for Retaining Church Members

Strategy 1: Follow-up Brings Retention

Many years ago, I learnt a simple truth which has stayed with me ever since. This truth has helped me greatly in the ministry. It is the secret of retention through follow-up.

My physics teacher once showed me a graph of the population of a poultry farm. The graph showed that the population of fowls remained constant at a low level for a long period. At a point, the fowls began to multiply and the farm population increased greatly. Something had happened to make the fowls multiply.

I then looked at the population of the world which had remained constant up until the beginning of the twentieth century. At the turn of the century, the population of the world began to expand greatly.

The question was: "What caused the sudden increase of the fowl population on the farm?" The other question was: "What made the population of the world increase so radically?"

The answer was simple. When the fowls in the poultry farm received the right medication and stopped dying from epidemics, the number of fowls suddenly increased. With the world's population, the pattern was the same. The reason for growth in the world's population was not the result of people having more babies. In fact, the number of births had been relatively the same. The reason for the growth was that the mortality rate had reduced. People's lifespan had been expanded due to medical science.

Medical science has improved remarkably from the beginning of the twentieth century. Diseases that have killed human beings for many years are now treated with one injection. Children no longer die from tuberculosis and malaria as they used to.

There is a great revelation to be derived from these two graphs! **If we can prevent a large number of converts from dropping out, then the church will experience the growth of the poultry farm.** If we can prevent many Christians from falling away, perhaps we will experience sudden accelerated growth like the world population did.

The Population/Follow-up Graph

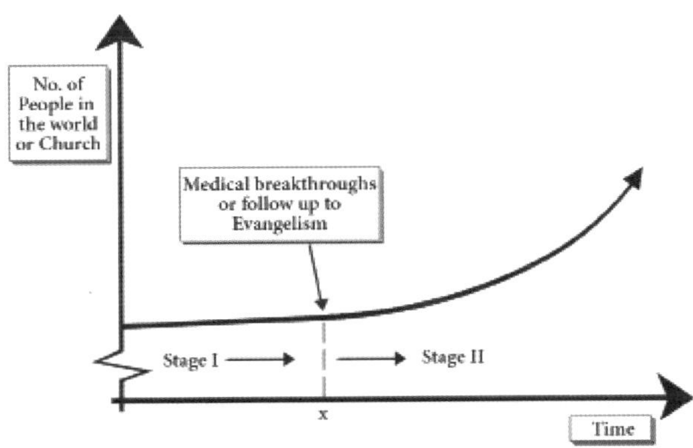

Stage I

® Mortality rate is high.

® No medicines, no medical answers.

® The growth of the population was very slow.

Stage II

® At time “x” there was a medical revolution.

® Mortality rate was greatly reduced: fewer people were dying.

® Suddenly, the population began to shoot up very rapidly.

® If a church is at Stage I, there is little or no growth. When a church begins follow-up, it is able to retain the people it gets from evangelism from a certain point “x” onwards. Notice how growth of the church occurs at Stage II.

This can be the graph of your church’s membership. The turning point, as you can see, is the point at which retention begins. I see your church multiplying greatly in Jesus’ name!

Every successful pastor must have the picture of this Follow-up Graph firmly imprinted in his spirit. The follow-up ministry is important because without it, our fasting and praying for church growth is in vain. Without follow-up, all of our efforts are useless! Without follow-up, all evangelism is worthless! Let's not make fools of ourselves. If we evangelize and invite people to church, why don't we follow them up? I believe that every new convert must be followed-up.

■ The Art of Follow Up

You must bear in mind that the follow-up ministry is both a physical and spiritual exercise. It consists of three main components: prayer, visitation and teaching. Always remember that the church is not a social club. It is a spiritual organism, which operates through prayer and the Word of God.

Three Principles for Follow Up

1. Pray for visitors and converts

Pray that all visitors and converts will come back to the church. Declare that they will return the following week. Prophesy that when they go back home, they will return the next week with more people. Pray that when they return, they will come back with their families. Pray that they will become established in Christ! You travailed for them to be born again, now travail for Christ to be formed in them!

> **My little children, of whom I travail in birth again until Christ be formed in you.**
>
> **Galatians 4:19**

Without prayer, you are wasting your time. I really want to emphasize that prayer is important in order to achieve anything for the Kingdom of God. Pastors must emit spiritual energy whenever they speak or minister. Lead your entire church in prayer for the establishment of visitors and converts in the church.

2. Visit new converts and visitors

It is important to visit all new converts and visitors. This is an area where many of the church members can get involved. Churches are full of sleeping and lazy Christians who contribute nothing to the work of God. One person cannot effectively visit many people. However, one hundred trained workers can do a great deal more. I involve many people in following-up new converts.

There are three types of visits that church members must be trained to participate in.

Three Types of Visit

IDL visit

This is done to Identify and Locate the homes of converts. I encourage church members to accompany new converts to their homes after the service. This first visit is to locate their homes. Sometimes the official address does not correspond to the reality on the street. Physically going to homes for identification is a powerful first step in the visitation process.

WELP visit

This visit is done to minister the Word. You must Encourage the new converts. This second visit will demonstrate that you really Love them. Finally, you must Pray with them for the establishment of their soul and for their general welfare.

ABA visit

This involves *anagkazo, biazo* and *anaideia.* Sometimes you must visit your members and physically bring them with you to church. Demonstrate that you care by patiently waiting for them as they get ready for church, and take them to church. Many inactive Christians will become active if they find something to do in the church. Teach these three types of visitation for following-up new converts and you will discover how many more of your members will become active Christians.

3. Do not waste your time

You will have to be careful not to waste your time on non-serious converts. The Bible teaches us that we should commit things to faithful people. In other words, do not waste too much time on unfaithful people.

> **And the things that thou hast heard of me… commit thou to faithful men…**
>
> **2 Timothy 2:2**

The word faithful means constant and reliable. When a new convert says that he will be there and does not show up, this may be a sign of unfaithfulness. **Learn to distinguish between faithful and unfaithful converts. Then direct your time and investment to the faithful ones.**

On several occasions, I have wasted my time on non-serious converts (they probably weren't even born again). With time, I have learnt to distinguish between people who are serious with God and those who are just playing games. When you have many converts, you really have to learn to distinguish between who is serious and who is not. This is more crucial when your converts outnumber your lay workers. **In that case, you should only follow-up those who are serious.**

Strategy 2: Concentrate to Retain

Retention evangelism requires concentration. In every city, there are many different churches and pastors. Though many of these pastors and churches interact, they often end up having all sorts of conflicts. Unfortunately, in the real world, you will see competition between churches and pastors.

There will always be one or two pastors fighting for supremacy over the Body of Christ in their city. Who is the father and leader of us all? Some will claim, "I am the father and leader of all Christians in this city."

Others will take sides and join one faction or the other. I want to tell you right here, that your church will not grow if you involve yourself in these things.

Politics consumes both time and energy. **Church growth requires concentration.** The rays of the sun shine on us everyday, yet none of us catches fire. If you were to take a magnifying glass and concentrate the rays of the sun on one spot, you could set a piece of paper on fire. The principle at work here is the principle of concentration. *When the rays of the sun are not concentrated, they have no power to light a fire.*

Direct your spiritual energy towards your calling.

Our principal goal must be to fulfil the call of God on our lives. A prophet related a vision he had had to a friend of mine. He saw a world famous man of God standing on a platform.

Behind the platform were two electric generators. One of the generators was on and the other was off. The voice of God came loud and clear in this vision, "This man of God has neglected one half of his ministry." He had set aside the power and evangelistic dimension of his call and was only doing half of what he was called to do.

Two weeks after this revelation, this world famous man of God died suddenly. That was a real shock to everyone, including me. Failing to concentrate can cost you your church. It can cost you your ministry. It can even cost you your life!

Strategy 3: Devotion Brings Retention

Another essential method for retaining your membership is to teach devotion in the church. You must teach them to be devoted to the pastor's teachings. You must teach them to be devoted to one another's fellowship. We have discussed this at length in a previous chapter.

It is also very important for the pastor to be devoted to his members. When a pastor is devoted to his members it leads to retention. Anytime there is a wedding, funeral, baby dedication or some crisis in your church member's life, you have a chance to practise devotion. That is your golden opportunity to devote yourself to your sheep. Stand by them at the graveside. Be there in their deepest sorrow. Attend their important events.

This demonstrates your devotion to them. You are fulfilling a principle: whatsoever a man sows he shall reap. **You will reap the devoted membership of your church members.** Many years ago I heard a seasoned pastor say, "If you stand by your members in their time of need, they will stand by you in yours."

Chapter

31

How to Have Permanent Church Members

CHAPTER SUMMARY

No good person enters a marriage with the mind that "I am in this marriage for just a few years." Who would like to marry such a person? Likewise, **the best type of church member is a permanent church member.**

- **Eleven Reasons Why Your Congregation Must Be Permanent Members**

31.1 They are part of a family.

31.2 They are part of a building.

31.3 They are part of a garden.

31.4 They are part of a tree.

31.5 They will flourish if they are planted.

31.6 They can invest freely when they are permanent.

31.7 They will have a family to celebrate their victories.

31.8 They will see the fruit of their labour.

31.9 They will avoid the deception of short relationships.

31.10 They will have consistent pastoral care.

31.11 They will be rewarded for faithfulness.

The Lord emphasized to me the need to have permanent church members. I realized that many of the young church members were vacillators. **The best type of church member is a permanent church member.** A permanent member is unmovable, stable and dependable throughout the years. A very important characteristic of that member is that his mind and heart are saying, *"I am here, and I am here forever."*

I am not a fool! Of course I know that not everybody is going to stay forever. Yet, it is important for people to have the mind of staying around forever. I am not God. If God, by His Spirit, would lead someone away from our church, there is nothing I can do about it. It is the same thing with marriage.

My Famous Announcement

One day I told my church, "I have decided to go to America to study cardiothoracic surgery." I announced, "I am going to be a heart surgeon."

I went on to explain, "The course will last for about five years after which I will need to gain some experience on the job. That will last for another five years, making the trip a total of ten years."

The whole congregation was shocked. "Ooooooh," they said, "It can't be possible." They all looked very sad.

"Why are you sad?" I asked, "Don't you want me to go away?"

I asked them, "How many of you would like me to be here in three years' time?" Everybody raised their hands.

I asked again, "How many of you here would like me to be here in seven years' time?" Again, they all raised their hands.

"So you don't want me to go," I said.

They all shouted, "No!"

I began to laugh. Then I told them, "I was just joking. I'm glad you want me to stay! I realize that you want me to stay permanently!"

I went on, "If you would like me to be here in seven years' time, I would also like you to be here seven years from now. Just as you want me to be your permanent pastor, preaching to you and praying for you, I also want you to be permanent members for me!"

I believe in permanent members and permanent commitment. I would strongly recommend all pastors to teach their congregations about being permanently joined to the church. Listen to me, faith comes by hearing and hearing by the Word of God (Romans 10:17). *What you teach your people is what they will believe.* If you want them to be a permanent part of the ministry, teach them and they will be!

The church members want a permanent pastor and we the pastors want permanent members. I am going to give you several reasons that you can share with any congregation as to why they should become permanent members of the church. If you teach these things, your members will stop jumping around from church to church.

Eleven Reasons Why Your Congregation Must Be Permanent Members

1. They are part of a family.

> **Of whom the whole family in heaven and earth is named...**
>
> **Ephesians 3:15**

The first reason why people must be permanent part of the church is because they are part of a family. When every church member is taught that the church is a family, they will be less willing to leave. Every family has its problems! In every family, you have conflicts and misunderstandings. But there is simply no way you can leave your family. You are simply a part of that family whether you like it or not.

A misunderstanding with your uncle does not lead you to change your name. Teach the church members that misunderstandings and hurts should not make them change their churches. Family members belong together in a lifetime commitment. Church members must belong to the same family in a lifetime commitment.

2. They are part of a building.

> **For we are labourers together with God: ye are God's husbandry, ye are God's building.**
>
> **1 Corinthians 3:9**

The second reason why people need to be permanent is because they are part of God's building. The Bible clearly teaches that we are God's building. Every Christian must know that he is part of God's building, which is the church. You cannot easily remove the blocks of a building. Blocks are a permanent part of the structure. **How would you feel if you came home and your bedroom had moved to the next house?** Sections of buildings do not move around!

I teach my church to see themselves as permanent building blocks in the building called Lighthouse Chapel International. I tell them that I have never seen a building block walk out of a building before. Such an occurrence would be magical. I trust that there is no magician amongst the members.

3. They are part of a garden.

> **And now go to; I will tell you what I will do to my vineyard: [garden] I will take away the hedge thereof, and it shall be eaten up; and break down the wall thereof, and it shall be trodden down...**
>
> **Isaiah 5:5**

Throughout Scripture, we see believers being referred to as a garden. If we are like a garden, then each of us is like a plant in the garden. If you uproot a plant and replant it in another spot, you endanger the life of that shrub. In fact, if you do this repeatedly, you will kill the plant.

It is a common fact that planting and replanting kills plants. God has no plan for planting and replanting His people in different churches every few years. If every time your roots go a little deeper you move around, you will kill yourself spiritually. I have noticed that Christians who are planted and replanted in different churches often do not survive spiritually.

When the Lord asked the devil where he had been, the devil replied that he had been roaming in the earth. The devil does not sit still, he moves "to and fro" and "up and down" in the earth. If you move to and fro, from church to church, your lifestyle resembles the devil.

> **And the Lord said unto Satan, Whence comest thou? Then Satan answered the Lord, and said, From going to and fro in the earth, and from walking up and down in it.**
>
> **Job 1:7**

4. They are part of a tree.

> **I am the vine, ye are the branches: He that abideth in me, and I in him, the same bringeth forth much fruit: for without me ye can do nothing.**
>
> **John 15:5**

Another important revelation is that you are a part of a tree. Jesus said that He is the vine and we are the branches. Everyone knows that a branch cut off from the tree is dead. Branches are intended to be permanently fastened to bigger branches or tree trunks.

If you are indeed a branch, have no plans of moving anywhere. People who move from church to church often do not flourish in the Kingdom of God. They experience stunted growth and some even backslide and go to Hell.

Pastor Turns Rasta

Recently I was speaking with a prophet of God. He told me how the Lord had shown him a dream, about how a pastor who had been moving from church to church, had backslidden and had become a Rastafarian. This prophetic dream was predicting that the vacillating pastor was going to fall. This was a warning to the unstable pastor.

Cutting yourself off and attempting to re-attach yourself is risky business. I believe in permanent membership. I teach permanent membership. I campaign for permanent members. My people want a permanent pastor, and I want permanent members.

5. They will flourish if they are planted.

> **Those that be planted in the house of the Lord shall flourish in the courts of our God.**
>
> **Psalm 92:13**

The next reason for permanent membership is so that you will flourish. You will notice that I have a scriptural basis for each of these points. What I am sharing with you is sound biblical doctrine. I am not saying that there are no grounds for a person to leave a church. Not at all! What I'm saying is that you must teach people to be permanently attached and permanently planted for their own benefit. Sheep will follow and obey what their shepherd tells them.

The Bible tells us plainly that those who are planted will flourish. I have watched Christians and pastors who move around from place to place. **You cannot compare a planted member to a roving member.** Stay in one place. Develop roots and flourish!

As you remain in one place, you will develop businesses and business contacts. Members of the church will begin to rely on you for their business. You will develop lasting friendships that may help you during your lifetime. Staying in one place for only a couple of years does not allow you to develop the sort of relationships that you need for a blessed life.

6. They can invest freely when they are permanent.

It is very convenient to live in one's own house. It is very different from renting a house. When you live in your own house, you can invest freely. You can pour in your money, your time and your life. Why is this? Because it is yours and you are going to be there permanently. No one wants to spend any money on a house that doesn't belong to him. After all, he is only going to use the place for a few months.

> *When we acquired our own church building, we invested freely into the structure. One day the contractor told me, "I want to construct this building as perfectly as possible because I am going to be here for life."*
>
> *"I want the floor to be smooth and perfect because I intend to die as a member of Lighthouse," he added.*
>
> *He continued, "One day when I am dead and my coffin is being carried into the church for the funeral service, I will not want anyone to trip and fall over an uneven floor."*
>
> *I laughed. Though this was a joke, he was also making a serious point. He had planned to be there for life. In other words, he had opted for permanent membership.*

Permanent members will be encouraged to give their money freely. They know that they are building a church for their children's weddings and will see the fruit of their investments.

7. They will have a family to *celebrate their victories.*

I preach faith and hope for the future. I tell my members that things are going to get better. Many poor people come to the church. As they hear the Word, their faith rises and they begin to see better things ahead.

If they are permanent members, they will live to celebrate their victories in the church. If they are not permanent, in the day of their victory, they will have no one to rejoice with. *Remember that joy shared is double joy and sorrow shared is half sorrow.*

> **Rejoice with them that do rejoice...**
>
> **Romans 12:15**

They will have a family to rejoice with as their new houses, new cars and new babies are dedicated. You will stand together and remember how the Lord took them from the beginning and brought them so far!

I have often reminisced with my friends about the ministry. We ponder over how the Lord has been kind to us. We laugh about things that threatened us some years ago. We say like the psalmist,

> **When the Lord turned again the captivity of Zion, we were like them that dream. Then was our mouth filled with laughter, and our tongue with singing: then said they among the heathen, The Lord has done great things for them.**
>
> **Psalm 126:1, 2**

Who will you sit down with to quote this Scripture to one day? Will you have abandoned all the friends with whom you struggled in the early days? A permanent relationship will give you people to rejoice with in the day of rejoicing. Better days are ahead. I teach my church that our better days are yet to come. I want them to stay around to see the better days of this ministry.

I remember when I used to speak about miracles. It was more like a dream. Today we have real miracles abounding in our midst. The Lord has been good to us. We are seeing better days. When you are permanent, you will have a family to go through your mourning with you. Joy shared is double joy, and sorrow shared is half sorrow.

8. They will see the fruit of *their labour.*

It is important for Christians to know that harvest time is coming in the future. What is the use of labouring in a church for years, only to leave just before harvest time? Some of the people who were with me in the days of real struggles are no longer around to enjoy the blessings. That is a pity! That is the price you pay for not being permanent.

Anyone who is double-minded about his commitment becomes unstable in other areas of his life. The Bible states that such a person is unstable in *all* his ways. Be stable. Be permanent. Be blessed.

> **A double minded man is unstable in all his ways.**
>
> **James 1:8**

9. They will avoid the deception of *short relationships.*

Short relationships are sweet while they last. There are no quarrels, no emotional disturbances, no worrying comments or misunderstandings. Long relationships have often been through much testing.

Long relationships that have survived the tests of time are better. Greater trust develops. You also know what to expect in the relationship. I prefer to work with someone I have known for a long time rather than with someone I have just met.

Joshua Made That Mistake!

Joshua made the mistake of forming an alliance with someone he didn't really know. He thought the Gibeonites were ambassadors from a far country.

Little did he know that they had lied to him in order to secure a peace treaty. He later discovered their true identity. But it was too late! He was already bound to the peace accord, although it was done under a cover of deception.

> **...And Joshua said unto them, Who are ye? and from whence come ye? And they [Gibeonites] said unto him, From a very far country... And it came to pass at the end of three days after they had made a league with them, that they heard that they were their neighbours, and that they dwelt among them.**
>
> **Joshua 9:8, 9, 16**

What I am saying is that longer relationships are safer relationships. Permanent members will be able to develop genuine relationships with genuine people. As the years go by, the members will know whether they have a genuine pastor or not and they will be more committed.

10. They will have consistent *pastoral care.*

The church, like a hospital, cares for you. Your permanent pastor can cater for you better because he has been with you for a long time and knows your history better. He is better equipped to minister to you.

Church members often leave churches when they think the pastor has discovered their secret sins. You must want your pastor to have access to your life so that he can minister in the area where you really need help.

11. They will be rewarded for faithfulness.

The next important reason for being a permanent member is that God will reward His children for faithfulness.3 Faithfulness means loyalty, constancy and permanence.

> **Well done, good and faithful servant...enter thou into the joy of thy Lord.**
>
> **Matthew 25:23**

Please note in this scripture that, the servant is recommended for his faithfulness. He is not recommended for his charisma or his gifting. Being a permanent member is part of the life of faithfulness. Be faithful. Be permanent. One day, Jesus will tell you, "Enter thou into the joy of thy Lord." That is the day I am waiting for. I just want to hear Him say, "Well done, good and faithful (permanent and loyal) servant!"

Chapter

32

The Secret of Industrialization

CHAPTER SUMMARY

As I pondered over the future of the church, the Lord told me that one way I could secure the future was to develop a culture of industrialization. When a church is industrialized, even when the charismatic leader is no more, the church will continue to grow on its own accord. Why industrialize? So that we may increase and not diminish.

I like to think of the future and how things will be like in some years to come. I have often wondered what our church will be like in a few years.

> *God instructed me to industrialize my church. He showed me how our nation, at that time, was only importing goods from western countries and reselling them at a profit. "There is no future in this," the Lord said. "Have you noticed that the richest nations of the world are all involved in producing important products?"*
>
> *"Yes," I replied. God showed me that the richest nations of the world produce cars. The best cars come from the richest countries of the world. These countries are rich because they produce something.*

The church will be rich in souls if we begin to be spiritually industrialized!

Just as the success of the nations of the world depends on their producing something, the success of the church depends on her producing souls. An industry is an organized system of producing goods and services regularly.

An industry is a deliberately (intentionally) organized system. It comes out with a well-defined product on a regular basis. It does not only produce its products when it is convenient nor does it produce goods accidentally. An industry is also very profit-oriented. Any nation that does not establish industries is doomed to buy secondhand things forever. It is doomed to be at the mercy of those who produce goods and services.

When I speak of industrialization, I am not speaking of making money. I am talking about churning out souls deliberately and regularly. I am a "businessman" for God, and my currency is human souls. Your church will have reached an industrialized stage when it begins to churn out souls regularly and systematically. The important word here is regular. I know of some car factories that produce one car every three minutes.

Jesus said in Luke 19:13, "Occupy (do business) till I come." That is, industrialize and commercialize with diligence until I come. In other words, Jesus expects us to take the business of soul winning as a very serious enterprise. Soul winning should be intentional and not incidental.

Many pastors are afraid of starting churches because they do not know how to win souls. Others don't know how to follow-up and establish converts in the Lord. They only know how to break churches and take away half of somebody's church members. No industry turns out a car accidentally. It is a deliberate planned exercise. It is time for us to deliberately win souls with the regularity of a factory.

God showed me how to set up the church and ministry to deliberately and regularly win souls every month. My church is divided into chapels, ministries and fellowships. Each ministry is supposed to have a regular monthly outreach.

The Lord showed me that it is important for the ministries to develop the habit of having a monthly outreach without needing a special exhortation to do so. Car factories do not need a charismatic manager to preach about the importance of producing their product for the month! In contrast, churches and ministries seem to need a special emotional seminar on soul winning. Without this, everybody forgets about the harvest. Surely this is not an industrialized church.

That is why I initiated ministries and fellowships, so that we would win some souls every month. I am not directly involved in the winning of those souls. It is done at the ministry and fellowship level. I do not have to go and whip up enthusiasm for the winning of souls before it happens. It just happens automatically.

An Industry Is Profit-Conscious

> **Again, the kingdom of heaven is like unto a merchant man, seeking goodly pearls [souls]:**
>
> **Matthew 13:45**

An industrialized church is concerned with the number of people converted every month. It is biblical to be interested in the number of souls that are being added to the church daily, weekly or monthly.

> **...And the Lord added to the church daily such as should be saved.**
>
> **Acts 2:47**

It is interesting to note how many pastors rarely do altar calls. Many ministers do not care about the lost souls. Instead, they care about how impressive they were and how powerfully they ministered!

After ministering at a convention, the host pastor said something to me that struck my heart. He said, "You are the only minister who made an altar call during this convention." I asked myself, "Have altar calls for salvation become obsolete?" How sad! The primary job of the church is being relegated to the background.

Altar calls for salvation are compulsory in every service we have. I make altar calls at all weddings and funerals. Industrialize your church – regularly and deliberately conduct outreaches. I see you increasing as you industrialize your church!

> **Build ye houses, and dwell in them; and plant gardens, and eat the fruit of them; Take ye wives, and beget sons and daughters; and take wives for your sons, and give your daughters to husbands, that they may bear sons and daughters; that ye may be increased there, and not diminished.**
>
> **Jeremiah 29:5, 6**

Chapter

33

Principles for Church Growth

CHAPTER SUMMARY

The following are principles that I have discovered for building successful and large churches. I advise you to carefully consider them and allow the Lord to give you a deeper understanding of what I am teaching in this chapter.

- **Fourteen Principles for Church Growth**

33.1 The principle of the multiplied senior pastor

33.2 The principle of maximized Sunday usage

33.3 The principle of smaller sub-divisions

33.4 The principle of the Person X oriented church

33.5 The principle of catering for group A and group B members

33.6 The principle of multiple services

33.7 The principle of dynamic church services

33.8 The principle of using technology and research

33.9 The 80-20 principle

33.10 The principle of the scholarly pastor

33.11 The principle of having a power ministry

33.12 The principle of pastoral individuality: fulfil your call

33.13 The principle of massive organized prayer

33.14 The principle of using lay people to do the work

■ Fourteen Principles for Church Growth

1. The principle of the multiplied senior pastor

I have discovered that if you could multiply the senior pastor by twelve, it would mean that you had twelve pastors at work. Logically, you could do twelve times as much work. I taught my assistant pastors to do whatever I do. If I meet people after church, they should also meet people after church. If I am able to counsel ten people and twelve other pastors are able to counsel ten people, that makes it one hundred and thirty people who are being attended to.

There are some churches in which the senior pastor is a "superman". He is the only one who does anything important – and that is a sure recipe to keep your church small. One person can only attend to a certain number of people. If you try to visit, counsel and help everybody, you will go crazy! There is a limit to what you can do. That is why I have many branches and many pastors. I believe that many of the people I preach to can also preach. I believe that many of the people who are receiving the Word now, are capable of rising up into the ministry.

Do not be an insecure senior pastor. Don't be afraid to trust people. It is true that many people will betray your trust, but if you live in fear, Satan will have access to your life and ministry. I have been hurt by some people, but I have decided to still trust others to help me. If they betray me one day, I will take it in stride and keep on trusting some others.

One of the reasons why some people cannot trust is because they do not believe that people can do a good enough job. In the medical field, young doctors are being trained all the time. Some people are always attended to by inexperienced student doctors under supervision. As the young doctors are allowed to have a go, they learn and soon they are just as good. It is the same thing in the ministry. People must be trusted with responsibilities under supervision. **They must be allowed to do important things.** This will multiply the number of capable pastors in the ministry.

2. The principle of maximized Sunday usage

This principle has been stretched to its fullest at the Lighthouse Cathedral in Accra. The principle of using Sunday to its fullest is effective because traditionally, people have dedicated Sunday to both resting and going to church. Since so many of the church members are available on Sunday, it is only wise to use Sunday to its fullest. Sunday is a full working day for me. Jesus worked on Sundays and I would like to follow His example.

> **And therefore did the Jews persecute Jesus, and sought to slay him, because he had done these things on the sabbath day. But Jesus answered them, My father worketh hitherto, and I work.**
>
> **John 5:16, 17**

Sunday is a full working day for all lay pastors in our church. We work hard from Sunday morning until late Sunday evening. We are able to accomplish a lot of counselling because people are free on Sundays. Visitation is also very effective on Sundays because many people are at home on Sunday afternoons. We conduct Bible schools for lay people on Sunday afternoons. Many people are able to attend because they don't have much to do on Sundays.

Decide to utilize your Sundays. I don't know what pastors are doing in their homes at two o'clock on Sunday afternoon when most of the church members are available to be ministered to. Take advantage of this opportunity. Lay pastors and shepherds will be able to do more work for the Lord.

Although some people find it difficult to accept, I emphasize to all the people I work with, that Sunday is a full working day for me and my church. I am not an accountant or a computer programmer. My working hours are not Monday to Friday from nine to five. I work on Sundays and I rest on Mondays. We do not start work at eight o'clock in the morning. I see no reason to go to work at eight o'clock in the morning. We stay late in the evenings because that is when many lay people are available for us to minister to them.

Our office is usually closed on Mondays, and all of our staff, except the security officers, have a day off. Pastors and churches must not allow the world to impose its schedule on us. When airplane pilots go to work at odd hours no one complains. Everyone accepts that their work demands a different type of work schedule. Pastors and non-pastoral people must realize that the work of the ministry is peculiar and goes with its own special working hours.

Begin to consider what you can do with your Sundays. Think of how many more people you can attend to if your Sundays are used for ministry instead of being used for sleeping and having lunches in the afternoon.

3. The principle of smaller sub-divisions

Smaller sub-divisions within the church allow for better pastoral care, which eventually leads to church growth. Questions that cannot be asked in a large Sunday service can be addressed in the small groups. The small groups become the family units to which church members belong.

I have several smaller groups within the church. I have always believed that every Christian can and should actively serve the Lord. These smaller groups allow for all Christians to get involved.

As your church becomes mega, it will remain small enough to meet the needs of all the people. As it is said, "Large enough to include you, and small enough to know you."

Some people's churches are like large convention centres. People come in, hear the Word, and go away. No human being likes to feel that he is not known. People are not numbers they are human beings. **Nobody wants to be reduced to a numbered article or a countable commodity.** People want to feel important. People want to feel necessary. People want to feel loved. You may preach a powerful sermon but, they still need to belong to a little family.

Your church can be broken into cells, divisions or departments. Our church has chapels, ministries and fellowships. I am always encouraging my members to get involved in one ministry or the other. How can I know all the people who come to church? How can I know what they think or feel? How can I know their problems and how can I help them?

If you think that God is going to give you a word of knowledge about these people everyday, you are making a mistake. God expects you to break up your church into smaller divisions so that the people can receive adequate pastoral care.

4. The principle of the Person X oriented church

What on earth is a "person x" oriented church? I define "person x" as a new convert or a new member. **Most churches are oriented towards established members.** A "person x" oriented church is very concerned about new people and visitors.

Treat your visitors well. We make song sheets so that the new people can get involved during the praise and worship. After the service, we host a reception to allow our new members to feel at home. We also give gifts to new converts.

Recently, the Lord directed me to direct my most senior associates to handle all new converts. God told me that if new converts were important to me, then I should allow senior ministers to take care of them rather than junior leaders. This has helped tremendously to establish many new people in the church. When a church is "person x" oriented, it is on the road towards increase because, growth will come through new members and converts.

> **And those members of the body, which we think to be less honourable, upon these we bestow more abundant honour...**
>
> **1 Corinthians 12:23**

Most people think that growth comes because more people visit the church. This is not necessarily the case. Some people also think that growth takes place because more converts are won. History has shown that the population of this world has increased because people are being kept alive and not because more people are being born. If we want our churches to grow, we have to sustain and maintain our new members and converts.

5. The principle of catering for group A and group B members

Every church can be divided into group A and group B members. Group A members are the more reliable people; they attend church twice or more a week. They are often involved in other small group activities in the church life. Thank God for Group A members. We really appreciate their input.

Group B members on the other hand, are the once-a-weekers, non-small group members, early service lovers, short sermon lovers, mind drifters, day dreamers, Bible forgetters, non note-takers, non tithe payers, clock-watchers and the church-near-me attendees.

These group B members will form an important segment of your church, as it becomes a larger entity. You will have to accept them as part of the family. **You can choose your friends, but you cannot choose your brothers.** Not everybody is going to be a prayer warrior.

In fact, in a large church many of the people fall into group B. Love them anyway. Preach sermons that they can also appreciate. Pray for them. The Spirit of the Lord will work on them. Sometimes when you organize a social event like a beach party, the group B members will flood the place. Use such opportunities to minister to them.

If you try to filter out your group B members, you may be left with nothing at the end of the day. Jesus said that the harvest is plenteous but the laborers are few. Jesus didn't say that there were few members, He said that there were few labourers (Group A members).

6. The principle of multiple services

Nobody ever told me that multiple services lead to church growth. I discovered it almost by accident. Well, now I am telling you that multiple services lead to church growth.

We have seven different services every Sunday morning. It is very tiring and draining, but our church attendance is better because of these multiple services. As the church grows, people with all sorts of needs come into the church.

Some pastors give the impression that they conduct multiple services because they have such a large crowd. This is true to some extent. But I do not have multiple services because the building can be filled four times over. Not all the services are full. Each service has a different level of attendance. I have never seen multiple services where all the services have the same attendance. **I conduct multiple services primarily to make a variety of convenient services available to my members.**

I am always amazed at why people will want to come to church at 6 o'clock in the morning. I always ask myself, "Can't they come to church a little later?" Human beings are so varied. **Once you are dealing with a large number of people you are dealing with variety.** If you don't make variety available, you will lose those for whom you have nothing to offer.

Accept the reality of variety and flow with it. You will notice that different types of people come to each service. Some of the services are more formal whilst others are more relaxed. The type of people who attend each service determines the type of atmosphere you get. We have services for the youth and for the children. We have services for different languages. We have several services for English speaking members. Each of these services is different and there are people to fit into all of these services. **God will bless your church as you provide variety for more people.**

7. The principle of dynamic church services

You must have a goal for each service you conduct. When determining the goal of the service, you must ask yourself, "What am I trying to achieve with this service?" Are you planning to raise the dead, to heal the sick, or to preach and teach? In the Lighthouse Cathedral, our Sunday morning services are teaching and worship services. We do not usually pray for the sick on Sunday mornings. We pray for the sick on other days.

How much time have you allotted for each service? How long should the service be? Our services are one and a half hours and two hours each. Within two hours, you can do everything that you need to do for a church service.

Many years ago, I attended a church whose services began around eight o'clock in the morning and ended at about three o'clock in the afternoon. After attending twice, I decided that the service was too long. Today, that church is non-existent. When your Sunday services are too long, you will drive away all of your members. You cannot achieve everything on a Sunday morning. We conduct miracle services which can last for several hours. We have camp meetings at which I can preach for more than twelve hours in a day. At the last Shepherd's Camp Meeting of my church. I preached from 6:30 a.m. to 12:30 a.m. on one of the days with only two short breaks. I know how to have long meetings, but I'd advise you not to use your Sunday services for such things.

What type of meeting place do you have? Man looks on the outward appearance, so it is important to decorate your church nicely. Even if you do not own a church building, let your place of meeting attain a certain standard. **Remember that you have only one chance to give a first impression.** Make use of flowers, baskets, curtains or anything that would improve the physical appearance.

Sometimes the pastor does not have very good taste. How can you know if you do not have good taste? He would have to rely on others in the church to help in enhancing and brightening his corner.

It is important that every church tries to acquire its own place of meeting. Owning your own facility introduces more stability to the church.

How do you present yourself? God looks on the heart, but man looks on the outward appearance. Man cannot see your heart. Man can only see your outward appearance. That is why your outward appearance is also important. We must seek to put up a good outward appearance in addition to preparing the right heart for the Lord. Everyone who plays a part in the service must be well dressed. Male pastors must be formally dressed and neatly shaved. Female pastors must be properly dressed and must not wear suggestive or indecent clothing.

In some churches the musicians look like agents from the world who have been temporarily contracted to help God. These instrumentalists often come in with the attitude and culture of secular pop groups. That is why I insist on all my musicians dressing like pastors. If they cannot afford it, we buy clothes for them!

Altar calls should be made at every service. This important and good habit must be maintained at all costs. New converts and visitors must receive a warm welcome. Remember these are the "person x" members. The assisting pastor should take over and briefly emphasize the message of the senior pastor. He should also encourage the congregation to buy tapes.

Pastors must not run off after church. They must stay and mingle with the congregation for some time after the service. I question the call of someone who says he's a pastor but does not want to mingle with his congregation after the service. The shepherd's place is in the field amongst the sheep. **A true shepherd smells of sheep.** I remember meeting a frustrated congregant in a church. This man had travelled many miles to attend a conference. He wanted to have a chance to say hello to the great man of God. He was so frustrated that he became bitter. I met him in a lift and he said to me bitterly, *"Is this man a prime minister or a pastor?"*

But I have been to other conferences where the men of God made the effort to stay around and mingle with the sheep. Some people just want to shake your hand. Give them the opportunity to get near if you can. A pastor's wife must help with the interaction and must be seen to be a warm and friendly person. All these things contribute to building the mega church we all desire.

8. The principle of using technology and research

As the number of passengers on different airlines has increased, their efficiency has improved. This is because air line industries have used technology to help them in their work. Whilst the membership of most churches has increased over the past few years, the pastor's ability for handling larger crowds has not been developed.

In our church, we try to keep an accurate data and statistics department. We maintain accurate counts and figures of everything. We have developed our own pastoral care monitoring system which we call the "Pastoshep".

In spite of the limitations due to limited addresses and telephone numbers in Ghana, our Pastoshep has become a reliable and technological method of assessing the work of all pastors and shepherds alike. Without being there to physically see what people are doing, my computer tells me what everybody is doing. I decided long ago to allow technology to help me to do the work of God.

Too many pastors say things like, "The whole of the outside was full." They say things like, "Thousands of people were here today." Whereas in reality, just a few hundred were present. Let's have real numbers!

We sometimes do surveys in the church to find out different interesting things. For instance, we did a survey to find out how many members of the church had ever been visited by a pastor. The results of that study were certainly revealing!

9. The 80-20 principle

This rule teaches us that eighty percent of your increase comes from twenty percent of the people. This means that eighty percent of church growth is as a direct result of the work of twenty percent of your members. Therefore, it is important for every pastor to spend more time with the twenty percent who will bring church growth.

Often the leaders, teachers and pastors make up this twenty-percent. They are the most important people in the church. More time, personal interaction and prayer with this twenty percent will give you amazing results that you never expected. Some pastors spend most of their time with the rich and influential. They do not know that they are spending time with the wrong group. **Spending time with rich people does not make your church grow.** It rather makes the rich people more important than they really are. It can make the rich people stubborn and difficult to pastor!

A church with a future will identify potential leaders and put them to work. When you do

this, you are looking out for the twenty percent who can bring about sustained church development.

When I visit our churches outside the headquarters, I spend more time with the leaders and pastors than with the rest of the church. Often I just minister in one service. Afterwards, I have various meetings, spending several hours with the pastors and shepherds. This style of activity does not come naturally. It is born out of the knowledge of the 80-20 Principle.

When you implement the 80-20 Principle, you may initially think that you are doing the wrong thing, but that is not the case. You will soon discover that this simple principle is a secret of church growth.

10. The principle of the scholarly pastor

By this, I simply mean that pastors should develop themselves academically. I have never been to Bible school; I only attended medical school. Yet, I have learnt so much about the ministry by reading.

I always have several books that I am reading at the same time. I believe in reading, studying and acquiring knowledge. How could I rise above the handicap of having no formal pastoral training? Only by reading!

There is a difference between ministers who read books and those who do not. **Those who do not read are no better than those who cannot read! Those who do not read are doomed to be ruled by those who do read.** Paul the apostle was a reader of books and parchments. He deemed his books so important that he asked Timothy to bring them to him.

> **...when thou comest, bring with thee, and the books, but especially the parchments.**
>
> **2 Timothy 4:13**

Prophet Daniel read the books that Jeremiah wrote.

> **In the first year of his reign, I Daniel understood by books the number of the years, whereof the word of the Lord came to Jeremiah the prophet, that he would accomplish seventy years in the desolations of Jerusalem.**
>
> **Daniel 9:2**

People like Daniel and Paul read books. It is no surprise that they went far in ministry. There are many ministers who also need some secular education. They would do well to educate themselves in important subjects like administration, law, medicine and history. Administration is important in a church because many aspects of the church have to be run in a secular way. Things have to be managed properly. Accounts have to be prepared. Salaries have to be determined and paid. People have to be employed and dismissed. Things simply have to be done properly. A good study of administration and management will do the church of God a lot of good.

The study of law is also important for pastors and churches. Churches enter into contracts and the law of contract becomes important. There are laws that affect property acquisition. The law of property then becomes important to the pastor. There are laws that concern marriage. Pastors have to be well versed in the laws that exist. God does not want His ministers to be ignoramuses. I am not a lawyer, but I know quite a bit about law because I have taken an interest in it for my own sake.

A good understanding of medicine is also important. A pastor, like a doctor, often deals with terminally ill people. There is no use in a pastor not appreciating the conditions of their members. It is important to have a basic understanding of what is going on around you. I have seen pastors declaring healing based on ridiculous and presumptuous premises. How absurd we sometimes look to the professionals of this world! They know we are completely unlearned in certain areas.

Another area that pastors need a bit of education in is history and politics. History shows the rise and the fall of tyrants. It shows trends which keep repeating themselves. The Bible says that there is nothing new under the sun. In fact, the Bible predicts that the past will repeat itself over and over again. For those of you who want to know the future – it is basically the past repeated.

> **The thing that hath been, it is that which shall be; and that which is done is that which shall be done: and there is no new thing under the sun. Is there anything whereof it may be said, See, this is new? it hath been already of old time, which was before us.**
>
> **Ecclesiastes 1:9, 10**

11. The principle of having a power ministry

If you cut out all the Scriptures on healing and miracles from your Bible, you will discover that your Bible is totally destroyed! You will be destroying the Word of God. When you take out the Scriptures concerning the power of God, you are left with a book on philosophy.

It is not only the teaching and preaching which helps God's people. God's children also want to receive a touch of His power. **It is important to add on the power dimension of miracles, healings and deliverance.**

The Holy Spirit wants to manifest Himself and bless the people of God. You will discover that your people love to be prayed for. It is important for you to pray for your sheep and minister God's power to them.

12. The principle of pastoral individuality: fulfil your call.

It is very important for every pastor to fulfil his individual call. Don't look to the crowd. Don't think about what others are doing.

Many years ago when I started out in ministry, many people laughed at me. One pastor ridiculed me as I encouraged my members to go out and witness door-to-door. He sneered at me and said, "What is witnessing? What is door-to-door witnessing? We have moved on into higher realms of ministry!"

I answered, "It is an important Christian activity."

I stressed, "No matter how big you become in the ministry, it is important to preach the gospel from house-to-house."

Today, that pastor who scoffed at me is struggling at the bottom of the ministerial ladder. Please do not allow anyone to drown your convictions. Be a man of conviction. Follow the plan that God has given to you. Comparison is one of the dangerous practices of certain ministers. Please do not compare yourself with anyone else, it is too dangerous.

For we dare not make ourselves of the number, or compare ourselves with some that commend themselves: but they, measuring themselves by themselves, and comparing themselves among themselves, are not wise.

2 Corinthians 10:12

God told me not to compare myself with anybody. He showed me how certain ministers were uneducated and that His expectations of different people varied. He also showed me that my background of prolonged education made Him give me a different standard. He told me that I would be wrong to compare myself with anyone else. The Lord also showed me that if I used other ministers as a standard, I may do far less for Him than I am supposed to. The Lord showed me that I would mistakenly think that I had "arrived" because I had used certain low standards that had been set by others. It is indeed a dangerous thing to compare yourselves with others. Paul said that he dared not compare himself with others.

13. The principle of massive organized prayer

Massive organized prayer involves gathering all of your leaders and/or members for intensive prayer. I do massive organized prayer on three levels. At the highest level, I frequently organize the senior ministers away from the city to pray for a few days.

At the level of cell leaders, we often decree what we call prayer sentences. Sometimes we "sentence" the shepherds to twenty hours of prayer within a three-week period. This means that they have to meet as a group and pray for twenty hours spread over three weeks. This is massive organized prayer – organizing prayer on a massive scale.

Finally, we involve the whole church in prayer. There are times we have all-night prayer and fasting meetings everyday for an entire week. I am always surprised when on a weekday the church is full at 2 a.m. Working people gather to pray intensively for church growth and breakthroughs.

There is no other way to make any progress in the ministry than to work in the realm of the spirit. The Bible says, "Epaphras was always labouring in prayer." The principle of massive organized prayer is what you need to bring about a breakthrough in your ministry.

> **Epaphras...always labouring fervently for you in prayers, that ye may stand perfect and complete in all the will of God.**
>
> **Colossians 4:12**

There are some people who see me as an administrator and a strategist. Anyone who knows me closely knows that as I write this book, I do not even have a desk or an office. But I do have a study where I pray and I do have places where I spend time praying. There is no shortcut in the ministry. There is no other way than that which has been set by the Lord. There is no other example than that which has been set by Jesus. Peter said that he wanted to give himself to prayer and the Word. Prayer and the Word are more important than administration and strategies!

> **But we will give ourselves continually to prayer, and to the ministry of the word.**
>
> **Acts 6:4**

14. The principle of using lay people to do the work

One of the great secrets of a large church is in the use of lay people or voluntary church workers. These volunteer workers can do most of the church work.

I have several pastors who are not paid a dime for all of their hard work. The Lord pays them Himself. They work very hard on Sundays and other evenings. They make huge sacrifices in their private lives in order to be pastors and shepherds. Many very big churches use this principle and are succeeding. May the Lord give you understanding and revelation concerning this vital principle.

I am always saddened when I see a small church of one hundred people employing seven full-time pastors. I often ask myself, "How much will one pastor be paid? Do the wives of these pastors work? Do they make enough money to survive?" Such environments are the breeding grounds for discontent and rebellious elements! Many church rebellions are related to money. When money is left out of the ministry, people are able to concentrate on the work of the Lord because they love God.

Many pastors in my church are doing well as lay pastors. If some of them were to come into full-time ministry, things may change. The church may be able to pay them enough money, but they may not be at the stage where they are ready for full-time ministry. New problems relating to salaries and income levels may arise. These problems have the potential to disrupt the work of ministry.

I suggest this to every senior pastor: analyze the church conflicts you have ever had. Aren't most of them related to money? **Make use of unpaid people. They are the key to a peaceful and stable church environment!**

I see a ministry growing! I see your ministry growing! I see you rising up in the Kingdom of God! I see you taking your place! I know the Lord is going to use you! He has determined to use you! The mega church is for you! The anointing is yours! Rise up with wisdom and possess what the Lord has placed before you!

Section

3

CHURCH GROWTH

We know that church growth is elusive and difficult to achieve. All pastors wish their churches would grow. This book is the answer to your quest for church growth. You will understand how "many different things work together" to achieve church growth. As the words and anointing of this book find their way into your heart, you will experience the church growth you have been praying for.

Chapter

34

Church Growth and a Burning Desire

CHAPTER SUMMARY

As the years have gone by, I have realized that the vision you have must be a burning vision. You cannot have a superficial vision for a large church. A shallow vision will not make your church grow. In this chapter learn about:

- **How a vision really leads to church growth**
- **Why your vision must be a burning vision**
- **How a burning vision affects the invisible engine of Church Growth**
- **How external influence cannot make you a Mega Church Pastor**
- **What a vision can make you do**

> **Where there is no vision ...**
>
> **Proverbs 29:18**

Does a Vision Really Lead to Church Growth?

Many years ago, I read from David Yonggi Cho's magazine about how it was important to have a vision and a dream for church growth. I never understood why and how a vision was necessary for church growth.

Dr David Yongi Cho, the pastor of the largest church in the world and propagator of the concept of church growth, said something else that I did not understand. He said, "Your vision makes you. You do not make your vision." I also did not understand this.

Honestly, I assumed that the subject "having a vision" was always mentioned as a standard opening point for all teachings on leadership.

As I listened to people teaching about the importance of having a vision, writing down goals, etc., I still did not understand how it brought about church growth. Every pastor who attended church growth conferences seemed full of visions and desires for church growth.

I thought to myself, "But all pastors have a desire for their churches to grow, but their churches still do not grow. If it were desires and visions that led to church growth, then every church would be a big church!"

Your Vision Must Be a Burning Vision

The vision must eat you up and burn within your soul. Then, all the things Dr Cho said will happen. That burning vision will literally make you into a mega church pastor.

Actually, in the absence of a burning vision for a large church you will never have real church growth.

The way a burning vision causes church growth is by inspiring and leading you on the difficult road to real church growth in a way that no human being can.

A Burning Vision Becomes the Invisible Engine of All Church Growth

It is a long and tortuous journey to become the pastor of a large church.

A burning vision and dream is the invisible engine that drives a minister on that journey from being the pastor of a small church to becoming the pastor of a mega church.

Some pastors do not have that internal engine that is needed to make them do the many hard and difficult things necessary for church growth.

External Influence Cannot Make You a Mega Church Pastor

There is no external advice or input that can sufficiently drive an individual on that difficult road to becoming a mega church pastor. All external influences will fade out long before you become a mega church pastor. External advice, encouragement and counsel are too short-lived to cause any minister of the gospel to survive on the road to church growth.

What a Vision Can Make You Do

There is something that a burning internal vision and dream does for you that no human being can do for you.

The internal burning vision and dream makes you humble enough to do all the things that you must to have church growth.

A burning vision and dream for a large church makes you pray for church growth. Without a burning vision and dream you will never pray hard enough to attract God's attention.

A burning vision and dream for a large church makes you seek the wisdom and strategies needed for church growth. Without a burning vision and dream, you will not spend the time needed to seek the wisdom that brings church growth. You will soon be irritated with the strategies that are taught by church growth pastors. Without a burning vision you will say that these teachings do not work.

The internal burning vision and dream will cause you to keep reading and re-reading the same things until something works.

Without a burning vision and dream for a large church, you will have no time to read the books that lead to church growth.

A burning vision and dream for a large church will drive you to meet the people who will help you to have church growth. It will make you humble enough to relate with and fellowship with the right people until their influence and anointing rubs off on you.

Without a burning vision and dream for a large church you will not listen to the messages that bring church growth. You will criticize the very thing that you need most and even make fun of it.

A burning vision and dream is the only true source of the staying power, stamina and persistence needed for the long journey towards church growth.

Chapter

35

How You Can Achieve Great Things through Lay People

CHAPTER SUMMARY

History teaches us that great things can be accomplished through people who "lack skills". A quick glance at the achievements of lay people or common people will inspire you to use them to make your church grow.

- **Great Achievements in the Church World**

35.1 Lay people were the pillars of the great reformation of the church.

35.2 Lay people are the pillars of the great Methodist Church.

35.3 Lay people were the pillars of the largest single church in the world.

35.4 Lay people are the pillars of huge networks of churches originating from Nigeria and Ghana.

- **Great Achievements in the Secular World**

35.5 The great government system of democracy was birthed through lay people.

35.6 The great super-power was given birth to through lay people.

35.7 The great election victory came through lay people.

■ Laikos – The Layman

The word layman comes from the Greek word laikos which means "having no skills". The following are a few definitions of the word layman.

1. A layman is an ordinary person.
2. A layman is a normal person.
3. A layman is a commonplace person.
4. A layman is a usual person.
5. A layman is a regular person.
6. A layman is a common person.
7. A layman is an everyday person.
8. A layman is an average person.
9. A layman is someone who is not a professional.
10. A layman is someone who is not an expert.
11. A layman is someone who is not specialized.
12. A layman is someone who is not skilled.
13. A layman is someone who is not trained.
14. A layman is someone who is not certified.
15. A layman is someone who is not licensed.

■ Great Achievements in the Church World

1. Lay people were the pillars of the great reformation of the church.

Martin Luther's translation of the Bible into the language of the common people changed the world. Instead of just being in Latin, the Bible was made more accessible to the common people.

Once the common/lay people had revelation knowledge in their hands they changed the world. Realising that salvation was available to all men through the grace of God they rose up and championed what we now know as the Reformation.

2. Lay people are the pillars of the great Methodist Church.

By the middle of the 20th century, Methodism was the largest Protestant denomination in the United States. The great Methodist church has ridden on the backs of lay people.

A very early tradition of preaching in the Methodist churches was for a Lay Preacher to be appointed to lead services of worship and preach in a group of churches called a "circuit".

The lay preacher walked or rode on horseback in a prescribed circuit of the preaching places according to an agreed pattern and timing. After the appointment of ministers and pastors, this lay preaching tradition continued with "Methodist Local Preachers" being appointed by individual churches, and in turn approved and invited by nearby churches, as an adjunct to the minister or during their planned absences.

3. Lay people were the pillars of the largest single church in the world.

One of the foundational principles on which the Yoido Full Gospel Church is built is the principle of working through lay people.

The Yoido Full Gospel Church, founded by David Yonggi Cho and his mother-in-law, Choi Ja-shil, both Assemblies of God pastors held its maiden worship service on May 15, 1958 with four other ladies in the home of Choi Ja-shil.

Membership of the church had reached fifty thousand by 1977, a figure that doubled in only two years. On 30 November 1981, membership topped two hundred thousand. By this time, it was the largest single congregation in the world and was recognized as such by the Los Angeles Times.

In 2007 its membership stood at 830,000, with seven Sunday services translated into sixteen languages.

4. Lay people are the pillars of huge networks of churches originating from Nigeria and Ghana.

Both The Redeemed Christian Church of God with its home in Nigeria and The Church of Pentecost with its headquarters in Ghana are known to make good use of lay people. Both of these ministries have huge networks of churches and regularly employ the services of lay people for preaching and pastoring.

The Church of Pentecost was founded by an Irish missionary sent by the Apostolic Church, Bradford, UK to the then Gold Coast.

It has grown to have a membership of over 1.7 million members; the Church of Pentecost has over 13,000 churches in 70 countries across all the continents of the world.

In 1952, the Redeemed Christian Church of God was founded in Nigeria by Pa Josiah Akindayomi. Under the leadership of its General Overseer, Reverend E.A. Adeboye, it has grown to have churches in more than 140 countries, with millions in attendance. Truly, these are great achievements and they have been made possible through the inputs of lay people.

■ Great Achievements in the Secular World

1. The great government system of democracy was birthed through lay people.

Democracy is giving common people the opportunity to act and change the government if they wish.

Democracy is the common man's power to refuse to live under unacceptable conditions.

Democracy is the common man's participation and influence in a country.

Democracy is built upon the principle of equal opportunity given to all common people.

2. The great super-power was given birth to through lay people.

The American Revolution is a classic example of the power of the common or lay people in shaping history.

The common man gave birth to a superpower. At the turn of the last century, the American Revolution was a successful experiment that marked the transition of a world controlled by a few to a world controlled by the many. The Revolution was largely shaped by small revolutionary organizations such as the Sons of Liberty. These organizations were not controlled by the rich and powerful landowners but common people of average social status came together to plant the seeds of the Revolution.

3. The great election victory came through lay people.

In May 2008, Barack Obama first black president of the United States of America, clenched the Democratic nomination for the presidency of the United States.

Even though the country's rich and influential Democrats were Clinton supporters and provided the millions of dollars, Obama raised more than any other presidential candidate in history by using the power of the common person. Obama raised over $80 million in his campaign, most of which came from common people making small individual contributions.

Chapter

36

How Lay People Have Helped Churches to Grow

CHAPTER SUMMARY

I have experienced two worlds of ministry — full-time ministry and lay ministry. Most pastors are only aware of the existence of the full-time dimension of ministry. My intention is to help you to discover the reality of how lay people can cause the church to grow. This chapter reveals:

i) **Why lay people can do the work of the ministry**

ii) **Why there must be a revival of the lay ministry in the church**

iii) **The two keys to being in lay ministry - Sacrifice and Wisdom**

iv) **The work of a pastor**

A lay person is someone who maintains his secular job and yet is active in the ministry of the Lord Jesus. A full-time minister is someone who has abandoned his secular job to concentrate fully on the ministry.

Many ministers who are in full-time ministry are not comfortable with the idea of lay people participating in the ministry. This is because they want to maintain the ministry as the exclusive preserve of a few "called" men of God.

Some full-time ministers do not want to accept the reality that lay people are capable of making a substantial (non-financial) contribution to ministry. Many full-time ministers are happy to maintain their lay people as mere financial supporters.

Pastors want to feel special as they perform their exclusive ministerial duties. "Why should a lay person do what I do?" they say. They think, "After all, if you can do the job I'm doing, what makes me special? What makes me (the pastor) different if lay people can do the things I do?"

Many ministers are not convinced that lay people can do the work of the ministry. I have had pastors ask me, "Will they have time to attend to the needs of the flock?", and "Can they handle emergencies?" "Can they minister powerfully the way we do?"

The answer to these is very simple - a resounding YES! I have been in the lay ministry for many years and have found it to be practically possible.

I'm writing this book to introduce you to an alternative to the traditional concept of full-time priests who only wait on God in the temple. The lay ministry is a key to church growth. Churches that have experienced phenomenal growth have all employed the principle of using lay people for the ministry. I believe that it is the key to fulfilling the Great Commission.

There is no way we are going to win this world with a few priests and pastors. Everyone must get involved. Many people must get involved at a higher ministerial level. There must be a revival of the lay ministry in the church.

There is such a thing as a lay pastor, i.e., a pastor who combines both his secular job and does the ministry as well. Ninety percent of the pastors in my church are lay pastors.

Full-time pastors must be secure in their positions in order to encourage lay people to get involved. There is nothing mystical about the ministry! There are pastors who want the ministry to be shrouded in mystery so that their members feel dependent on them.

It is time to demystify the art of shepherding and pastoring people. It is something that many can get involved with. What a blessing it is for lay people to discover that they can be useful in the ministry! What a blessing for the pastor when he discovers that the contributions of lay people can make his church grow.

I am not saying that there is no need for full-time ministers. I am myself a full-time minister. There is a great need for full-time ministers to be one hundred percent involved in ministry work.

There are things that only full-time ministers can do.

I Was a Lay Pastor

At the age of about fifteen, in secondary school, I met the Lord. From the day I gave my life to Christ, I became very active in ministry. I was involved in soul winning and following up converts. I was also involved in singing and playing musical instruments for the Lord.

In the first phase of my Christian life, I was not a traditional Sunday morning church attendee. In fact, I hardly went to church on Sundays. My Christian life was so active from Monday to Saturday that I ended up resting on Sundays! On Mondays and Wednesdays I had a prayer meeting and Bible study. On Tuesdays and Thursdays I had music rehearsals. On Fridays we had fasting and prayer meetings. And then on Saturdays we would have a retreat from ten in the morning until six in the evening.

Whilst I was involved in these activities I never gave up my schooling. I completed my GCE 'O' levels and passed with a distinction - I had seven ones (one is the highest mark of distinction). That was a great accomplishment by any standards. In my GCE 'A' levels I topped my class and was one of the only people from my school admitted into the medical school. Throughout this period, I was fully involved in ministry. I preached! I won souls! I visited people in their homes! I counselled many people! I fasted and prayed! At one point, I fasted so much that I became as thin as a rake. Someone even asked me, "Do you think that you will get to Heaven by being a skeleton?"

Never did it occur to me that I had to be paid for the ministry work that I was involved in. By the time I was nineteen years old, I was fully involved in the ministry. I had many sheep who looked up to me for direction and prayer. By 1980 I was a strong preacher and leader of the Scripture Union fellowship. The point I am making is that ministry is possible alongside other pursuits.

I entered the university in October 1982. I was privileged to be studying medicine - one of the most difficult and time-consuming courses. Whilst in the university I began a Christian fellowship that is still in existence today.

During my fourth year, I began to establish the foundations for a church. I then became a pastor and was acknowledged as such whilst I was still a medical student.

During this time I was not being paid by anyone to do the work of the ministry. Neither did I slacken in my academic work. On the contrary, I did extremely well and won prizes in the medical school. I applied wisdom and sacrificed my leisure time so that I could be involved in ministry.

Sacrifice and Wisdom

These are the two keys to being in the lay ministry - *sacrifice and wisdom.*

What is the main task of a pastor? Is it to perform funerals and to officiate weddings? Certainly not! These are certainly duties of a minister but they are not main duties. If your ministry has deteriorated to the point where your main functions are to conduct marriages and bury people, then you need to read your Bible again! The main duty of a minister is to fulfil the Great Commission.

> **Go ye therefore, and teach all nations, baptizing them in the name of the Father, and of the Son, and of the Holy Ghost: Teaching them to observe all things whatsoever I have commanded you: and, lo, I am with you alway, even unto the end of the world. Amen.**
>
> **Matthew 28:19, 20**

The reason why it is called the Great Commission is because it is the great commandment to all ministers. It is sad to see ministers of the Gospel who have become mere social functionaries. Sometimes pastors are under pressure to be accepted by society.

As a result, they want to do nice things that relate to health, education, etc., so that they may gain the approval of society. Apostle Peter came under the same pressure to leave his principal duties and to perform mainly social tasks.

> **And in those days, when the number of the disciples was multiplied, there arose a murmuring of the Grecians against the Hebrews, because their widows were neglected in the daily ministration. Then the twelve called the multitude of the disciples unto them, and said, It is not reason that we should leave the word of God, and serve tables. Wherefore, brethren, look ye out among you seven men of honest report, full of the Holy Ghost and wisdom, whom we may appoint over this business. BUT WE WILL GIVE OURSELVES CONTINUALLY TO PRAYER, AND TO THE MINISTRY OF THE WORD.**
>
> **Acts 6:1-4**

You can see from this Scripture that Peter's main duty was to pray and to minister the Word. This is something that can be done by lay people.

Lay people can be taught to visit and counsel younger Christians!

Lay people can be taught how to preach!

Lay people can be taught how to witness!

Lay people can be taught how to minister the Word with power!

Lay people can be taught to make spiritual gains through prayer!

What I have just described is the work of a pastor. Any honest reader will agree that a lay person can become a lay pastor. What you need is a systematic way of training your lay people to become ministers. Do not limit your lay people because they are professionals in other fields. Do not say that your doctors, lawyers, architects, carpenters, engineers, tailors, masons, nurses and secretaries, cannot be pastors. They can!!

I remember visiting one of our churches that was pastored by a female nurse. There were hundreds of people in the church and I gave glory to God for that. In a large house there are many vessels. God is using all kinds of people. Do not limit God to what you have been used to.

> **But in a great house there are not only vessels of gold and of silver, but also of wood and of earth; and some to honour, and some to dishonour. If a man therefore purge himself from these, he shall be a vessel unto honour, sanctified, and meet for the master's use, and prepared unto every good work.**
>
> **2 Timothy 2:20, 21**

When I was in my first year at the university, I was told by the Christian fellowship that *I could not be a leader because I was a medical student.* Medical students were considered too busy to be involved in ministry work. How unfortunate! They had effectively eliminated a whole group of potential leaders from the fellowship.

This is what many pastors do. They look at the doctors in the church and think to themselves, "Sit down quietly, receive your Sunday sermons and pay your tithes. Be a nice principled Christian doctor who does not perform abortions and you will please God!!" I want you to know that a doctor can also please God by winning souls. It is true that God wants principled doctors. But God also wants doctors who will win souls and do the work of ministry. Today, I have doctors who own clinics and at the same time pastor churches with hundreds of members.

There are many architects who do full-time architectural work and are very fruitful in ministry. There are pastors who work in banks but pastor large churches. I have seen teachers, pharmacists, university lecturers, accountants, students, doctors, nurses, army officers, civil servants, air conditioner repairers, computer scientists, computer technicians, businessmen, and lawyers become great lay pastors.

Many people cannot believe that our long lists of pastors are lay people who are not paid by the church. If pastors understand that their lay people can do much more than just give money to the church, they would help themselves and their churches a great deal. That is what this section is about - showing how lay people can help the church to grow. Please do not misunderstand me; not every layperson must become a pastor. Some of the lay people can function as ordinary shepherds (cell leaders). But there are others who have the call of God upon their lives and who will become pastors.

The Pineapple Patch

One day as I was walking on a hillside I saw something that I want to share with you. I was praying in tongues and walking along a footpath on one of the hills in Ghana. The entire hillside was covered with wild bushes and tall untamed grass. As I walked along, I saw a section within the wild grass measuring about 20 meters by 20 meters. In that particular section there were neatly planted pineapple plants. I could see the baby pineapples sprouting. That section of the hillside was very different from everywhere else.

The Spirit of the Lord spoke to me and said, "That section of the hillside is different because certain seeds have been planted there. That area of the hillside is different because some special investment has been made on that patch of ground."

The Lord told me that the rest of the hillside can be likened to the general congregation which receives seeds of normal preaching. The special patch of ground that was yielding pineapples could be likened to the part of the church that received the special seeds of leadership and pastoral training. If you sow the seeds of pastoral training you will soon have many more pastors and leaders around you.

Many people do not invest the seeds that give rise to leaders, pastors and shepherds. If you sow the seeds that train leaders, you will harvest a crop of well-seasoned leaders. I spend more time with my leaders than I do with the general congregation.

The teachings in this book are examples of some of the things I have taught ordinary people over the years. This investment has turned many people into shepherds and lay pastors! Invest specially in leaders and potential pastors and they will grow up to become great ministers!

I have heard people criticizing me for starting churches with people whom they consider not to be pastors. Do not criticize someone who has been holding Shepherds' Camps to train people. Criticize yourself for not having spent hours training your own lay people to be in the ministry.

You must encourage your lay people to become something more than principled citizens of the country. You must encourage them to become soul winners for Jesus. You must want them to be shepherds of God's flock. You must want them to fulfil the Great Commission.

Dear pastor friend, I wrote this book for you! God told me to write it so that you will understand that lay people can and will help you to build your church. Dear lay person, I wrote this book for you as well! God has a ministry for you. Please do not go to Heaven and discover that you did not even start your ministry before you died! Take what you are reading seriously and learn the art of shepherding and pastoring. Discover for yourself the joy of serving God as a layman.

Chapter

37

Why You Must Share the Burden with Lay People

CHAPTER SUMMARY

"And the Lord said unto Moses, Gather unto me seventy men of the elders of Israel, whom thou knowest to be the elders of the people, and officers over them; and bring them unto the tabernacle of the congregation, that they may stand there with thee. And I will come down and talk with thee there: and I will take of the spirit which is upon thee, and will put it upon them; and they shall BEAR THE BURDEN of the people with thee, that thou bear it not thyself alone."

Numbers 11:16, 17

Join me discover from this all important scripture, why you must share the burden with Lay People.

And the Lord said unto Moses, Gather unto me seventy men of the elders of Israel, whom thou knowest to be the elders of the people, and officers over them; and bring them unto the tabernacle of the congregation, that they may stand there with thee. And I will come down and talk with thee there: and I will take of the spirit which is upon thee, and will put it upon them; and they shall BEAR THE BURDEN of the people with thee, that thou bear it not thyself alone.

Numbers 11:16, 17

One of the most difficult tasks in life is to "lead" people. Moses delivered the Israelites from bondage but struggled to lead them to the Promised Land. They were too difficult for him to handle. Moses' job of leading difficult people is the job that all pastors have to do.

God graciously gave Moses spectacular and sensational miracles. These signs and wonders helped to establish his authority over God's flock. In spite of this, the burden of leading the people was more than he could carry. The Bible calls it a burden - and that is what it is! Moses eventually succumbed to the pressures of leading difficult people and lost his chance to enter the Promised Land.

■ There Is a Real Burden

If you have a pastor's heart and love people, you cannot disassociate yourself from their problems. Their problems will become your problems and their burdens will affect you!

When God uses you to minister to a large number of people, he expects you to share the burden. Failure to share this burden simply means that you may collapse or come to a standstill in ministry. There are many standstill churches around. They grow to a point but can grow no further. The reason is that they fail to share the burden of ministry. A balanced church is one that has people of all sorts within it; young, the old, educated and uneducated, rich and poor, and male and female. All these people must be drafted in to the share the burden.

■ Don't Exclude Anyone

I notice that most churches exclude the educated and the rich from ministry. Usually, the rich are expected to contribute money whilst the educated enhance the image of the church. However, I have found that both the rich and the educated can be spiritually useful.

There are many medical doctors, carpenters, plumbers, specialists, lecturers, architects, and engineers, who serve as lay pastors. These lay pastors share the burden of ministry. The burden of the ministry cannot be borne by one person. It is simply impossible.

■ Share the Burden and Have a Larger Church

If you want to have a greater ministry than what you currently have, you must share the burden. Sometimes people do not share the burden because they want to take all of the glory for themselves. They want people to feel that they are the only ones with a supernatural gift. They want people to show appreciation to them alone. Others are afraid of rebellion in the camp. How common is the story of associate pastors rebelling. Many senior pastors fear their assistants will outshine them one day. Fear not, only believe! You cannot expand without trusting people. The work is so great that you will never ever be able to do it all alone.

Chapter

38

How Lay People Will Help to Bring Church Growth

CHAPTER SUMMARY

- **How Lay People Will Help to Bring Church Growth**

38.1 Lay people will help you deal with ungrateful and forgetful sheep.

38.2 Lay people will help you overcome disloyalty in the congregation.

38.3. Lay people will help to deal with disrespectful and rebellious church members.

38.4 Good lay people encourage others to respond positively to the Word.

38.5 Lay people will cause the church to expand by becoming part of the workforce.

38.6 Lay people will help you with prayer, visitation, counselling and interaction.

38.7 Lay people will help you to account for the sheep on the Day of Judgment.

1. Lay people will help you deal with ungrateful and forgetful sheep.

> **...in the last days... men shall be... unthankful...**
>
> **2 Timothy 3:1, 2**

There will always be lay people who are very grateful for your ministry. They will love you and appreciate your efforts for them. These people will help to neutralize the presumption that is common in the congregation. Their grateful speeches will neutralize rebellion in the camp.

You will notice ungratefulness in people by the way they complain. Moses led the Israelites out of bondage and slavery and yet they murmured and complained bitterly against him. Aaron even had to make a golden calf to calm them down.

If something ever goes wrong, you will be surprised at the reactions of people you have ministered to. Many quickly forget what you have done for them.

The things a pastor does are not physically tangible, but spiritual. Many therefore think that the pastor has done nothing for them.

Church members can sin against you after you have been a blessing to them. Don't be shocked! The prophet Jeremiah experienced the same thing from his people. He said, "Shall evil be recompensed for good?..." (Jeremiah 18:20).

The Sin of Hezekiah

Once, a pastor told a very disturbing story. He said that he was surprised when one of his church members came to his house one night to assault him. He couldn't believe that this young man whom he had led to Christ, trained up in the Lord; whose marriage he had blessed and helped through various crises would attack him in that manner.

Dear friend, do not be surprised! Do not expect gratitude from man; expect your rewards from God. Hezekiah was blessed. But he did not "render again". That means he did not show gratitude for all the blessings he had received.

> **But Hezekiah RENDERED NOT AGAIN according to the benefit done unto him...**
>
> **2 Chronicles 32:25**

This is the nature of man. This is the nature of the people God wants you to lead.

2. Lay people will help you overcome disloyalty in the congregation.

With the help of lay people, you will be able to fight disloyalty in the church. The presence of zealously committed lay workers always inspires more loyalty in the ranks. Lay people, who do not earn money from the church, are a great support to every pastor. Lay people who are loyal will report what is going on in the congregation.

Though Judas walked and ministered with Jesus for three years, he eventually betrayed him for a small amount of money. Betrayal is a part of ministry. It is also a part of life. If you have yet to experience betrayal, I can assure you that you will. The disturbing thing about betrayal is that it comes from people who are supposedly close to you.

You are not greater than your master Jesus! The fact that someone may betray you one day makes it very difficult for you to happily interact and flow with the people. Look closely at the ministry of any great man of God. You will discover that they have all had their fair share of traitors. All of this contributes to the burden and difficulty of ministry.

> **Yea, mine own familiar friend, in whom I trusted, which did eat of my bread, hath lifted up his heel against me.**
>
> **Psalm 41:9**

Paul experienced sudden desertions by some of his colleagues, like Demas. I remember one young man whom I trained. He was about to take up an important position in the ministry that we had been preparing for, for over a year. On the day he was to fill the position, he suddenly informed me that he was leaving the country. I couldn't believe my ears! All of our months of preparation meant nothing to him. He just abandoned ship without notice. These experiences are all part of the ministry. Abandonment also occurred under the ministry of Apostle Paul.

> **For Demas hath forsaken me…**
>
> **2 Timothy 4:10**

Because people can abandon you at any time, it is burdensome to lead them. The presence of committed lay people will always help to share the burden of abandonment. God wants us to be involved in His work. God wants us to be shepherds!

3. Lay people will help to deal with disrespectful and rebellious church members.

> **And Miriam and Aaron spake against Moses … Hath the Lord indeed spoken only by Moses? HATH HE NOT SPOKEN ALSO BY US?...**
>
> **Numbers 12:1-2**

There are lay people who will sort out disrespectful and rebellious church members for you. You always need people on the ground to deal with church members who make light of pastors. There are people who think their money and status in the secular world gives them a right to say and do anything in the church.

Miriam and Aaron (the closest assistants and closest relatives) spoke against Moses. They most probably said things like, "God also speaks by us" and "Are you the only one God uses?" With time, familiarity creeps in and arrogant people now consider you as an equal. They tend to think, "We can all do it. What's the big deal? You are no different from us!"

This is unfortunate, but real. People easily take you for granted. They murmur and complain against you, forgetting all that you have done for them. When some church members lose their temper, they will speak to you as though you are a little child.

"You Remind Me of My Father"

One church member approached her pastor after Sunday service. The pastor thought she was about to compliment him for the powerful sermon he had just preached.

She started, "Pastor, you know something? I felt I should tell you that you remind me of my father."

"Oh really?" the pastor responded. He thought he reminded her of some good traits in her father.

She continued, "He was so full of himself and so are you!"

The pastor was taken aback but had to smile and continue as though he had received a compliment. This church member was telling the pastor exactly what she thought of him. Moses also experienced rebels who thought he was "too big" for his shoes. Moses also had people who wanted to cut him down to size. That is why Moses had to share the burden with seventy other elders.

Now Korah ... and Dathan ... and Abiram ... and On ... rose up before Moses ... and said ... wherefore then lift ye up yourselves [Moses and Aaron] above the congregation of the Lord?

Numbers 16:1-3

4. Good lay people encourage others to respond positively to the Word.

When any one heareth the word of the kingdom, and UNDERSTANDETH IT NOT...

Matthew 13:19

The domino effect is when one thing leads to another. When one layperson responds positively to your teaching, others are inspired to do the same. It is always a blessing to have ordinary congregants who are outspoken in their support of you. Sometimes large sections of the congregation do not understand the Word.

Often they do not understand why you have to do fund-raising. Consequently, many do not respond in giving. Many times, I have to explain that they are giving to build a nice church where they can have their weddings, their baby dedications and their ceremonies. Leading people who have all the above characteristics: ungratefulness, disloyalty, etc., is a major task.One person cannot do it alone. The burden must be shared with others. Sharing the burden is hard work.

5. Lay people will cause the church to expand by becoming part of the workforce.

The use of lay people as part of the workforce is the secret to unlimited expansion of the church. Sometimes people think that lay people cannot do much ministry work. Do not be deceived--try using lay people and you will discover how much work they can do. Lay people can join the pastors to share the burden of the people. Let your lay people know that they are called to share the burden of ministry with you. They will share the burden on earth and they will share the burden of accounting for the sheep in Heaven.

When we established churches in the universities, we entrusted the preaching and pastoring responsibilities to students. I am very proud of these student ministers because of the great job that they have done on the different campuses. I don't have to rush to the different universities every Sunday morning to minister the Word. Ordinary saints have joined in to help. These saints must be perfected (prepared, trained) to do the work of the ministry. Ordinary saints can do the work.

> **For the perfecting of the saints, for the work of the ministry, for the edifying of the body of Christ:**
>
> **Ephesians 4:12**

The principal strategy for distributing the burden is to involve lay men and women in ministry. No church is capable of employing an endless number of people. Every church has a limit to its resources. It is not possible to pay salaries and rent an unlimited number of houses for the staff of the ministry. Full-time staff are limited in the amount of work that they can do.

6. Lay people will help you with prayer, visitation, counselling and interaction.

Lay people can help you with the burden of praying, visiting, counselling and interacting with the sheep. Moses was breaking down under the burden of having to pray, visit, counsel and interact with so many people. God saw a disaster waiting to happen and decided to take of the "spirit" that was on Moses and put it on the seventy leaders "to bear the burden" with him.

> **And the Lord said unto Moses, Gather unto me SEVENTY MEN of the elders of Israel ... THAT THEY MAY STAND [work] THERE WITH THEE.**
>
> **Numbers 11:16**

Involving students, workers, and professionals helps to distribute the burden to all saints in the church. The Lord wants everyone to be fruitful no matter what they do in life.

7. Lay people will help you to account for the sheep on the Day of Judgment.

> **... for they watch for your souls, AS THEY THAT MUST GIVE ACCOUNT, that they may do it with joy...**
>
> **Hebrews 13:17**

The burden of answering for the sheep cannot be borne by one person or a few people who supposedly have a "call". The burden of accounting for hundreds of different people cannot be borne by one person. When I stand before the judgment seat and God asks me about certain souls, I intend to refer to the lay pastors and shepherds I put in charge of these souls.

When the Lord asks me about some souls in the church, I intend to find out who was in charge and tell the Lord to ask that person. I cannot possibly answer for all these different people personally.

Every pastor will have a lot to answer for when he stands before the Lord in Heaven. Your burden is to be able to lead all your sheep to Heaven. Make sure you lose none of them. Every pastor must hope to say, "Of all that you have given me, I have lost none!" Jesus said this phrase in three different places – John 6:39, John 17:12; and John 18:9.

Chapter

39

Five Evils that Evolve When Lay People Are Not Involved in the Ministry

CHAPTER SUMMARY

- **Five Evils that Evolve When Lay People Are Not Involved in the Ministry**

39.1 If you do not allow lay people to work in the ministry you will kill the Christian principle of sacrifice in the church.

39.2 If you do not allow lay people to work in the ministry you will remove the opportunity for them to demonstrate faithfulness.

39.3 If you do not allow lay people to work in the ministry you will employ people to do jobs that do not occupy them fully.

39.4 If you do not allow lay people to work in the ministry everything done in the church will be related to money.

39.5 If you do not allow lay people to work in the ministry they will not learn the importance of obedience and submission.

1. If you do not allow lay people to work in the ministry you will kill the Christian principle of sacrifice in the church.

> **Then said Jesus unto his disciples, If any man will come after me, let him deny himself, and take up his cross, and follow me.**
>
> **Matthew 16:24**

The symbol of Christianity is the cross. The cross speaks of suffering and dying. God spoke to Abraham and asked him to give up his most treasured possession––his son. Don't listen to anyone who tells you that the day of suffering, sacrificing, losing and dying is over. The day of sacrificing, losing and dying has come. God is requiring us to give up our treasured possessions so that we can serve Him. The church is being filled with people who are not aware that God is calling them to sacrifice. Christianity is a religion of sacrifice. Christianity is based on the cross. Christianity is based on losing your life so that you gain a new life.

Different Sacrifices for Different People

But some people have the mistaken view that God asks everyone to sacrifice their "Isaac". But God did not ask Joseph to sacrifice his sons. Neither did He ask Jacob or Isaac to sacrifice their sons. King David was a man after God's own heart, but God did not ask David to sacrifice his son.

God deals with everyone differently! What God requires of me may be different from what He requires of you. God has asked me for my profession. Perhaps God will not ask you for your profession. But He will ask you for something and you will have to give it up.

Christianity always involves sacrifice. If you do not allow lay people to work in the ministry, they will never learn to give up the smallest things for Christ. If they cannot give up their time, their evenings and their leisure for Christ what will happen if the Lord asks them for their "Isaac"? It is important to expose the lay people in your church to this basic principle of sacrifice.

2. If you do not allow lay people to work in the ministry you will remove the opportunity for them to demonstrate faithfulness.

The Bible teaches clearly that he that is faithful with little will be faithful with much.

> **He that is faithful in that which is least is faithful also in much: and he that is unjust in the least is unjust also in much. If therefore ye have not been faithful in the unrighteous mammon, who will commit to your trust the true riches? And if ye have not been faithful in that which is another man's, who shall give you that which is your own?**
>
> **Luke 16:10-12**

If somebody is not faithful as a layperson, how will he be faithful when he is in full-time ministry?

Many people are not doing well in full-time ministry because they did not do well as lay people.

Did you work for the Lord as a layperson who did not need supervision?

Did you need anybody to tell you to get up to pray?

Did you need anybody to tell you to study your Bible?

Were you faithful when you were in school?

My Lay History

I was a committed worker in the Scripture Union fellowship in my school. I was heavily involved as an organist in a Christian singing group to which I belonged.

I was a drummer and pianist for Victory Church in London.

I was involved with the fellowships in the university. Yet it never once crossed my mind that I should be paid for these things.

This lay ministry is an important background for a future full-time ministry. He that is faithful with lay ministry will be faithful with full-time ministry. Many people who have worked as lay people work even better as full timers.

3. If you do not allow lay people to work in the ministry you will employ people to do jobs that do not occupy them fully.

Not every ministry needs a full-time pastor. Many churches can be pastored by unpaid lay pastors.

If there are only twenty-five people in the church, it is obvious that it cannot sustain and does not need a full-time minister. Many of the church members secretly ask, "What does the full-time pastor do all day?"

Many people think that pastors sleep from morning to evening. The fact is that there isn't so much to do with a congregation of thirty. The ministry has to develop to the point where it needs a full-time worker. The other reality is that most of the members are at work during the day and only become available in the evenings.

Pastors are not bankers, accountants or pharmacists. They are shepherds who are supposed to look after sheep. Working hours are different for different professions! I do not work from nine to five everyday because I am not an accountant. I am a pastor! When the sheep become available in the evenings I become very active. That is why I work late into the night. Some pastors become idle and lazy as they wait for Sunday when they can deliver their next sermon.

For we hear that there are some which walk among you disorderly, WORKING NOT AT ALL…

2 Thessalonians 3:11

Let us be honest! Let us be realistic! Does your church need so many full-time pastors? Does it need even one full-time pastor? Can the income of the church sustain the pastor and his family? Can the pastor not find a secular job to do? Pastors are frustrated and fearful because they are not sure whether they will be able to survive until the next month.

You can overcome that frustration today! Get a job and pastor the church on the side until it grows and demands your full attention! The Swiss missionaries who were sent to Ghana many years ago were sent as self-sustaining ministers. They came equipped with skills that would enable them to work in Africa as they did their ministry work. That is a good example to follow. We need self-sustaining ministers today more than ever before. Most churches cannot bear the burden of maintaining so many full-time pastors. You must keep your ministry staff as small as possible so that you can pay them properly. You must not have idle and discontented people around you. Idleness leads to laziness and laziness leads to discontentment and discontentment leads to disloyalty.

> **And withal they learn to be idle, wandering about from house to house; and not only idle, but tattlers also and busybodies, speaking things which they ought not.**
>
> **1 Timothy 5:13**

4. If you do not allow lay people to work in the ministry everything done in the church will be related to money.

> **He that loveth silver shall not be satisfied with silver; nor he that loveth abundance with increase: this is also vanity.**
>
> **Ecclesiastes 5:10**

The ministry is not an alternative source of employment for anyone. It was never intended to be! It is a special job that God gives to those whom He has called. **As the church becomes larger, it often deteriorates into a source of employment for the unemployed.** This attracts many people who have no better options. What happens to the church? It becomes full of seekers of wealth and lovers of silver. The church is filled with pastors who constantly fight for better salaries and conditions of service.

I Never Knew Anyone Earned Money for Preaching

I started ministry as a layperson, so the idea of being paid in full-time ministry came up much later. I started my church as a medical student and found myself pastoring while at the same time practising medicine. Later on, I went into business and combined it with pastoral work.

At the end of 1990, the Lord told me to leave everything I was doing and enter into full-time ministry. It was not an easy decision for me. Since January 1st, 1991 I have been full-time in the ministry for the Lord Jesus.

There are many people who are in full-time ministry who should not really be there. There are many people who I believe should find secular jobs! How can a church with sixty members sustain eight full-time pastors and their families? Yet, this is the case in many ministries. Success in the ministry requires both power and wisdom.

> **But unto them which are called, both Jews and Greeks, Christ the power of God, and the wisdom of God.**
>
> **1 Corinthians 1:24**

Many pastors see the ministry as a way to travel around the world and to drive nice cars. I did not enter the ministry in order to drive a nice car. I do drive a nice car now but I did not come into the ministry because I wanted to have the nice things of this world. In fact, coming into full-time ministry was, for me, the end of all hopes of ever having the nice things of this world.

> **Yea doubtless, and I count all things but loss for the excellency of the knowledge of Christ Jesus my Lord: for whom I HAVE SUFFERED THE LOSS OF ALL THINGS, and do count them but dung, that I may win Christ,**
>
> **Philippians 3:8**

A minister who is going to serve God properly must have died to the love for silver and gold. Why is this? The Bible teaches that those that love silver are never satisfied with silver. The more you give them, the more they want. Why is it that the richest people in this world are often the biggest thieves?

Is it because they are poor? Is it because they are in need? Certainly not! It is because of the greed for more and more and more!

You cannot satisfy people with more and more money. From experience, whenever I have felt under pressure to raise salaries, I have often discovered it does not solve the problem!

Senior pastors, if you feel under pressure to raise salaries and give more and more benefits, you will discover that the problem never goes away. Full-time ministers must be people who just want to serve the Lord at heart. This does not mean that people will be poor but it means that the heart is not craving endlessly after more and more.

Soon the church becomes unionized with the workers against the management, and the management against the workers! The "management" are often the senior pastors who make decisions and the "workers" are the other pastors and workers who are not involved in the decision-making. You should see the bitterness, petty jealousies and bickering amongst the full-time staff of many churches and ministries. This often extends to their families and pastor's wives pick up quarrels with other pastor's wives.

I would rather have one or two workers with peace than to have a hundred unhappy and discontented full-time staff.

5. If you do not allow lay people to work in the ministry they will not learn the importance of obedience and submission.

As you enter into full-time ministry you must be open for whatever the future will bring. You may be rich or you may be poor. You may have abundance or you may live in the "want of all things". Are you ready for anything?

> **Verily, verily, I say unto thee, When thou wast young, thou girdedst thyself, and walkedst whither thou wouldest: but when thou shalt be old, thou shalt stretch forth thy hands, and another shall gird thee, and carry thee whither thou wouldest not. This spake he, signifying by what death he should glorify God. And when he had spoken this, he saith unto him, Follow me.**
>
> **John 21:18-19**

Jesus told Peter to be ready for anything. Be ready to be carried anywhere. It will no longer be your will, but God's will. You are not the commander, you are just one of God's workers. One of the reasons why I am in the ministry is because I have no choice.

> **...woe is unto me, if I preach not the gospel!**
>
> **1 Corinthians 9:16**

There are detractors, faultfinders, analysts and commentators who talk about me all the time. I have no time for empty chatter. I prefer to hear my dogs barking in the morning than to listen to their hateful and sarcastic comments. I must continue doing what God has called me to do. Some people love me for what I do and others hate me. I thank God for them all. But I press on for the mark of the prize of the high calling.

I am totally surrendered to fulfilling the call of God upon my life, so help me God!

Chapter

40

The Art of Wielding a Rod and a Staff

CHAPTER SUMMARY

Without the ability to use your equipment you cannot achieve church growth. A shepherd must know how to use his rod and his staff. The equipment of a good shepherd are his rod and his staff. Indeed, every profession has its tools.

■ How to Use Your Rod and Your Staff

40.1 The rod and staff are used to lead and to rule.

40.2 The rod and staff are used for a way-making ministry.

40.3 The rod and the staff are used for taking territories in ministry.

40.4 The rod and staff are used to comfort people.

40.5 The rod and staff are used for self-assessment.

40.6 The rod and staff are used in correcting people.

40.7 The rod and staff are used to feed the sheep.

■ The Equipment of a Shepherd

> **... thy ROD and thy STAFF they comfort me.**
>
> **Psalm 23:1, 4**

Without the ability to use your equipment you cannot achieve church growth. A shepherd must know how to use his rod and his staff. The equipment of a good shepherd are his rod and his staff. Indeed, every profession has its tools.

Guns are the equipment of soldiers with which they kill and destroy. The stethoscope is one of the key tools of a doctor.

■ How to Use Your Rod and Your Staff

1. The rod and staff are used to lead and to rule.

> **And out of his mouth goeth a sharp sword ... and he shall rule them with a ROD OF IRON...**
>
> **Revelation 19:15**

You must learn to wield the rod and the staff as tools for ruling. The traditional perception of a pastor is of someone who is soft, kind-hearted, compassionate, poorly paid, available at all times, and a never-complaining doormat. This is not a picture of a ruler but rather a picture of one who is ruled. I believe that a pastor must be kind-hearted and patient, but one of his cardinal roles is to lead and to rule. A pastor is the head of the local church. A head must take decisions.

> **The Lord is my shepherd... HE LEADETH ME beside the still waters.**
>
> **Psalm 23:1, 2**

A true shepherd leads sheep to the place where they need to go. You cannot be a good leader if you are weak. Every church needs a strong voice that is confident and bold in the Lord. The sheep are looking for someone with direction, who knows where he is going. A pastor must lead the people spiritually and in other areas such as in the family and social dimensions.

When the church does not have a strong capable leader, something is wrong. Learn to speak to your sheep with authority. I do not mean you should dominate their lives. Lead them with a high level of confidence and control. Sheep are meant to be led. You have authority over the sheep God has placed in your care. You will answer for their souls one day.

A leader who refuses to take important decisions is doomed to failure. A good leader takes decisions when all necessary information has come to him! These decisions may be hard and painful. If you, as the shepherd do not take them, your church is doomed to wither.

Just look around and see how many churches are dead and lifeless. They are a far cry from what their founders had envisaged. This is because as wrong things began to creep in, the leaders were afraid to rock the boat and take important decisions.

Sometimes when I look at some hopelessly incompetent government corporations and agencies, I just marvel. They make huge losses, and generate a lot of waste in the system. I have been to government offices where I see everyone reading newspapers. Sometimes you see twenty secretaries in one office with one typewriter. They have nothing to do, yet they are paid with the taxpayers' money every month. What a pity! They sleep, eat and chat all day. Their managers are afraid to take the decision that nineteen out of the twenty typists must be laid off.

The country becomes poorer and poorer and people wonder why. The reason is simple. The leaders have refused to assess the situation and take a strong but hard decision. They are refusing to rule. The fear of losing political power makes democratic leaders become liars and hypocrites.

I am not afraid of taking such decisions because I realize that the church will deteriorate if I do not. Remove stagnating leaders and replace them with willing and capable workers. I make the necessary changes in my staff and with my lay pastors when I realize a change must be made.

Don't be afraid of changes. Sometimes, it is only a big change that will lead to a big breakthrough. **A minor change will take place when you take minor decisions. But a major transformation will occur when you are bold enough to take a major decision.** Be a strong ruler and lead your sheep to green pastures. Lady pastors can learn to be strong firm leaders without being ill-natured and quarrelsome. Lady shepherds should be gentle and effective, without being cantankerous.

2. The rod and staff are used for a way-making ministry.

> **And the Lord said unto Moses ... But LIFT THOU UP THY ROD, and stretch out thine hand over the sea, and divide it: and the children of Israel shall go on dry ground through the midst of the sea.**
>
> **Exodus 14:15, 16**

You must learn to wield the rod and the staff as tools for making a way. As a leader, God will tell you to speak to His people, giving them many instructions. After you have given instructions to the sheep, you must help them to obey the Word. A true shepherd loves his sheep and tries to help them to obey God.

Moses was the shepherd of the people of Israel. His instructions were to cross the Red Sea. After receiving that command he stretched forth his rod and made a way where there was no way. That is what I call the way-making ministry of the pastor.

Every full-time minister or lay pastor must learn to make a way where there seems to be no way for the people of God. When some of your sheep think that their house is too far away from the church, go and visit them wherever they live. This will prove to them that their homes are not too far.

My Visit Produced a Pastor

I knew a family that lived about a two-hour train ride from one of our churches. When I called them, they said it was too far to attend church. So one Saturday, I took a car and together with another pastor, we drove all the way to their house. They were so surprised to see us visiting them.

This is one thing that visits do. It establishes the fact that people are not too far away. From that day, the entire family decided to come to church, taking the train and travelling two hours to church. They did this for a number of years, and today one of them is a pastor. Make a way for your sheep. Help them to see that it is possible to obey the Word of God. Sometimes when they don't have money, give them some money to help them attend. You may not be able to give them money all the time, but the fact that you did it once or twice encourages them and shows that you really care. This is the pastor's heart.

Make a Way for Your Sheep to Get Married

As a pastor, it is easy to see that your sheep are looking for husbands or wives. Don't just look on unconcerned and preach about how good it is to be married. Discuss the practical issues of choosing a partner with them. Help them to notice one another. That is what we call "Shepherdorial Linking."

Teach your members that they can find a good partner within the church. Some people may not like that idea, but it works and it stabilizes the sheep. Of course, do not force people to marry each other.

You must warn them that happiness is not guaranteed just because they marry a person you recommended. This is because marriage is complex and you don't want anyone cursing you for the rest of their lives.

Make a Way for Sheep to Find Jobs

I preach to my members about prosperity. After I've done that, the way-making anointing comes upon me and I help them to get jobs. If one of my church members is strategically positioned as an employer, I would speak to them about a sheep who needs employment.

Sometimes a person you have recommended will disgrace you. But do not let that deter you from making a way for other good sheep. It is not good enough to say "Cross the Red Sea"; you must make a way for them to cross!

Make a Way for Your Sheep to Attend Programmes in Church

I have often changed meeting times or rehearsal times so that one person could attend. I am a pastor and I want all of my sheep to attend the meetings. Schedule reasonable meeting times. *Make things possible for people.* That is the way-making ministry in action.

Schedule fewer meeting times without compromising the number of meetings. Sunday is a good time to meet and counsel your sheep. You can always combine meetings. Don't let people travel to church twice when they could have come once.

Be an expert at overcoming the excuses of church members. When they say that church services are too long, point out to them how many hours they spend watching television. When they say that the church is too far from their homes, ask them how far their jobs are from their homes. When the church member doesn't have shoes, get him a pair. Be a way-maker. Be like Moses. Make a way through the Red Sea with your rod and your staff.

3. The rod and the staff are used for taking territories in ministry.

You must learn to wield the rod and the staff as tools for taking territories. If you have a burning vision for a mega church you will always want to take more territory for Christ. **You can take more territory for God through prayer and fasting.** You can lead your people into spiritual warfare.

I always have a new vision for my church. When I had twenty members, I had a vision to have fifty. When I had fifty people at the Korle Bu Teaching Hospital, I dreamed of the day when I would see a hundred people sitting in church on Sunday morning.

When I had five hundred, I dreamt of a thousand. Mega Church Pastor, you must have dreams for greater territories for the kingdom of God. We are not a social club. We are not fighting a psychological warfare. We are into spiritual warfare.

> **And Moses said unto Joshua, Choose us out men, and go out, fight with Amalek: tomorrow I will stand on the top of the hill with the ROD OF GOD in mine hand. And it came to pass, when Moses held up his hand, that Israel prevailed: and when he let down his hand, Amalek prevailed.**
>
> **Exodus 17:9, 11**

People who take new territories are people who fast and pray. I believe in praying for long periods. I believe in fasting as the Spirit leads. Moses, the shepherd of God's people, stretched out his rod in warfare against Amalek. Moses' rod symbolized the power of intercessory prayer. It is the art of travailing in prayer for the ministry.

What you see happening in the physical is only a manifestation of what has taken place in the spiritual realm.

Anyone who calls himself a pastor must learn to fight with prayer in the realm of the spirit. If you want to have a big church, you must learn to fight for it in the spiritual realm. Every territory is occupied by evil spirits who dominate the area. When I travel from place to place, I can virtually feel the difference in the spiritual atmosphere. When I am in Ghana, I sense a lighter and easier spiritual climate. When I am in Germany I sense the presence of many marauding evil spirits.

Develop the art of intercession for taking more territories for God. That means you must develop several important prayer skills.

4. The rod and staff are used to comfort people.

> **...thy rod and thy staff they comfort me.**
>
> **Psalm 23:4**

You must learn to wield the rod and the staff as tools for comforting the sheep. One of the principal ministries of a shepherd is to comfort the sheep. Every sheep should be able to say to his shepherd, "Your rod and your staff comfort me." Some people do not know why their churches do not grow.

The shepherd must genuinely love the sheep and care for them when they are in trouble. Never lose the opportunity to be by your sheep's side in their time of difficulty. The duty of the lay pastor is to stand by his sheep in the time of their greatest need and greatest joy. It is not an option! Remember that, sorrow shared is half sorrow, and joy shared is double joy. The sheep want to share their sorrows and their joys with their pastor.

It is the duty of the shepherd to comfort the sheep. The comforting ministry starts by showing interest in things that are important to the sheep. Be interested in all of their major events; especially the birth of a child, marriages, sickness and funerals. God expects you to be there!

What is important to your sheep must be important to you. If you claim to be a pastor, what are you doing to show real love to your sheep? Shepherds, if you genuinely do not love your people, they will not respond to your good preaching. The Bible says that God is angry with the shepherds because they have not ministered to the sheep under the comforting ministry.

> **The diseased have ye not strengthened, neither have ye healed that which was sick, neither have ye bound up that which was broken, neither have ye brought again that which was driven away, neither have ye sought that which was lost; but with force and with cruelty have ye ruled them.**
>
> **Ezekiel 34:4**

The sheep often know the Word before you preach. What they want is some love. Everybody responds to love. It is only demons that cannot be loved! Remember that love never fails. The Bible does not say, "Preaching never fails" or, "Teaching never fails". The Bible says, "Love never fails". The comforting ministry is love in action.

5. The rod and staff are used for self-assessment.

One of the principal duties of a shepherd is to do what I call measuring the temple. Measuring the temple helps you to know where you stand.

> **And there was given me a reed like unto a rod: and the angel stood, saying, Rise, and MEASURE the temple of God, and the altar, and them that worship therein.**
>
> **Revelation 11:1**

This involves a critical analysis of the way things are going. Pastors need to take time off to analyze themselves and to see whether things are being done according to the vision that God gave. You must constantly measure yourself. Ask yourself, "Am I doing what God called me to do?" The reason why I am writing books now is because I believe it is in obedience to God. No matter what I do, I am constantly trying to fulfil the specific call of God on my life.

Only Twenty-five Members after Twelve Years

I was chatting with a pastor who had been in the ministry for twelve years. After being in the ministry for twelve years, he only had twenty-five members in his church. His church was in a city where there were many large churches.

After many years of hard work there was little growth. Anything that is alive and healthy grows. If this pastor were to have analyzed his ministry properly, he would have come up with some important decisions. For instance, he may have realized that he was better suited to be an assistant than to be a head.

Perhaps he would have discovered that he lacked a genuine call of God. Perhaps he would have realized how he needed to close down the church. Analysis and self-assessment are very important in ministry. They help you to make vital mid-stream corrections.

He Returned to the Ministry

Some years ago, I spoke to a pastor friend of mine. I had known this pastor for several years. He had been actively pastoring a church in a large city.

Due to circumstances beyond his control, he found himself in another city. There he just attended a dead church. He was no longer actively involved in the ministry. He was just a church attendee.

I spoke to him and said, "If you are called of God to the ministry, then wherever you are and whatever your circumstances are you must fulfil your ministry." I impressed upon him to analyze his condition (measuring ministry) as a pastor and take the important decisions that would bring him to a place where he was fulfilling his divine call. I'm happy to say that he did. Today, he is overseeing many churches.

EXAMINE YOURSELVES, whether ye be in the faith; prove your own selves…

2 Corinthians 13:5

Examine yourselves to see whether you are within your call and whether there is anything that you have to change.

Can you imagine if the Mercedes-Benz car that is being sold today is exactly the same as it was fifty years ago? Can you imagine what it would be like if these car makers were to carry on for years without making changes? But that is how many churches are. They carry on for years without trying to make improvements

Our churches and ministries must be - continually upgraded and improved.

We must compare what we are doing to what is in the Bible. If you see something in the Bible that is not in your church, strive to attain that biblical standard. I always marvel at people who fight against miracles and prophecies. Prophecies and prophets are in the Bible. The entire Bible is full of testimonies of supernatural and spectacular miracles.

If you have no miracles in your church, please do not say that the day of miracles has passed.

Just work on yourself until you have the miraculous operating in your ministry.

Accept the fact that there are biblical standards to attain! It is because we don't measure what we are doing, that we continue in the wrong thing for a long time.

Ask yourselves, "Am I a good person?" Ask your wife or husband what she/he thinks about you. Ask yourself, "How many people should there be in the church at this stage?" Measure your performance and analyze your duties! If you assess yourself, God will not have to judge you.

But he that is spiritual judgeth all things, yet he himself is judged of no man.

1 Corinthians 2:15

6. The rod and staff are used in correcting people.

> **...SHALL I COME UNTO YOU WITH A ROD, or in love, and in the spirit of meekness?**
>
> **1 Corinthians 4:21**

You must learn to wield the rod and the staff as tools to correct people. Some people do not like it when the pastor points out evil and corrects it. The worst type of pastor is the one who cannot correct things that are going out of line. It is important to purge out certain things from the flock. When your sheep realize that you are a weak leader, they will take you for a ride.

Black Beauty

Many years ago, I went for a ride on a horse called Black Beauty. This was at Burma Camp, a military riding school in the city of Accra. I was a new rider and the horse soon realized that I was a novice. Our instructor was taking us on a ride through various fields in the countryside.

When we got to the boundary of the riding school, the horse didn't feel like going out for the ride so it stopped at the gate. I had a whip in my hand so I hit the horse several times and it began to kick and jump.

Soon, it knew that I was afraid of it. Some of the more experienced riders in the group came alongside and encouraged me to control my horse and bring it out into the field.

Would you believe that the horse calmly turned around and took me back to its stable? It utterly refused to go out on a ride that afternoon. I would say that the horse rode me; I didn't ride it! Some months later after I became experienced, this horse was no match for me. I could make it do anything I wanted it to do.

That is how the pastor must be with the sheep. If the people you are leading feel that you are weak, they will lead you. When they realize that you are strong, they will stay in line. Identify disloyal people and remove them from the fold. Rebuke people publicly when you have to.

Strength to Drive out Thieves

One Tuesday night, during a church service, my associate pastor invited a church member to come up on stage. This young man was notorious for stealing.

The associate pastor announced to the church that the young man was a dangerous thief who was going about taking things from church members. He went on to say that everybody in the church should be careful of him and not believe his lies anymore.

The church was dead calm for a second and then suddenly burst out in thunderous applause. The young man had thought that he could take us for granted. He thought that because we were a church we would allow him to do anything he wanted. That was his mistake and the sheep appreciated the strong leadership of the pastor.

...Know ye not that a little leaven leaveneth the whole lump? Purge out therefore the old leaven...

1 Corinthians 5:6, 7

To some of the sheep, you must be gentle and say things like:

"I am disappointed in you."

"I wasn't expecting this from you."

"I was expecting something better from you."

"Let this never happen again."

"Shame."

"I give you 20% for your Christianity."

And of some have compassion, making a difference:

Jude 22

Correcting the sheep does not mean you should disgrace them. You can correct them without disgracing them. If you do not correct them, that thing will begin to spread among the congregation.

The "Ruby, Walk Out!" (RWO) Treatment

To some of the sheep, you must be rough and hard. With others, you must actually dismiss them from the church. I remember one pastor who stood in the pulpit and looked at two giggling girls and shouted from the pulpit, "Ruby, Walk Out!" She had no choice but to walk out, never to return.

Cast out the scorner, and contention shall go out; yea, strife and reproach shall cease.

Proverbs 22:10

I call this the RWO treatment. Some people need to be dismissed from the church. Their presence in the church is not desirable or helpful, so get rid of them. It's as simple as that!

7. The rod and staff are used to feed the sheep.

You must learn to wield the rod and the staff as tools for feeding the sheep. It is a principal duty of a shepherd to feed his sheep. Everything else comes after he has done this principal duty. The authority to lead is given to those with the ability to feed.

FEED THY PEOPLE WITH THY ROD, the flock of thine heritage, which dwell solitarily in the wood, in the midst of Carmel: let them feed in Bashan and Gilead, as in the days of old.

Micah 7:14

I have people in my church who are older and wiser than I am in many respects. Yet in the church, I am their leader and I minister to them. Where would I get the authority to advise someone who could be my father or my mother? This authority is found in the ability to feed.

Where does your earthly father get his authority from? It comes from the fact that he has fed you for years and continues to feed you. When your parents no longer feed you, the authority they have over your life reduces.

Jesus said to Peter three times, "Feed my sheep". It is very important to the Lord that His sheep are well fed on the Word of God.

> **...Jesus saith unto him, Feed my sheep.**
>
> **John 21:17**

The principal duty of all ministry offices is to preach and to teach the Word of God.

> **And Jesus went about all the cities and villages, TEACHING in their synagogues, and PREACHING the gospel of the kingdom...**
>
> **Matthew 9:35**

Paul was an apostle and a prophet. He called himself an apostle to the Gentiles.

> **Paul, AN APOSTLE of Jesus Christ by the will of God...**
>
> **2 Timothy 1:1**

Paul went on to say in verse eleven,

> **Whereunto I am appointed a PREACHER, and an apostle, and a TEACHER of the Gentiles.**
>
> **2 Timothy 1:11**

It should be clear to every minister that our main resolve is to preach and teach the Word. What did Paul tell Timothy?

> **I charge thee therefore before God, and the Lord Jesus Christ... PREACH THE WORD...**
>
> **2 Timothy 4:1, 2**

Paul predicted that a time would come when people would not want the Bible to be preached.

> **For the time will come when they will not endure sound doctrine; but after their own lusts they shall heap to themselves teachers, having itching ears; And they shall turn away their ears from the truth, and shall be turned unto fables.**
>
> **2 Timothy 4:3, 4**

I believe that time has come now! Many prefer to be prophesied to. They want a quick, "bless me" prayer and some anointing with oil. Pastors, develop your ability to feed and to preach. It is your one great asset. Look around you and observe the great men of God you know. You will discover that every one of them has a strong ability to preach and to teach.

Chapter

41

Shepherding Techniques that Lead to Church Growth

CHAPTER SUMMARY

Jesus Christ was many things to us. He called Himself different things at different times. At one time He said He was the way, the truth and the life. He announced that He was the door. He declared that He was the bread of life and the light of the world. But He also said He was the good shepherd. Learn and apply the shepherding techniques of Jesus Christ from the Book of John chapter 10.

41.1 A good shepherding technique is to be ahead of your sheep.

41.2 A good shepherding technique is to know your sheep by their names.

41.3 A good shepherding technique is to let your voice be known by the sheep.

41.4 A good shepherding technique is to stay with the sheep.

41.5 A good shepherding technique is to know your sheep.

41.6 A good shepherding technique is to be known by the sheep.

41.7 A good shepherding technique is to keep the church family together.

41.8 A good shepherding technique is to notice the problems of your sheep.

41.9 A good shepherding technique is to deliver your sheep from captivity.

41.10 A good shepherding technique is to give your life for the work of God.

What did Jesus mean when He said He was a good shepherd? The word shepherd in John 10:11 is translated from the Greek word poimen. It is this same word, poimen, which is translated pastor in Ephesians 4:11.

> **And he gave some, apostles; and some, prophets; and some, evangelists; and some, pastors [poimen] and teachers;**
>
> **Ephesians 4:11**

The word shepherd is interchangeable with the word pastor. What the Lord was really saying was, "I am the good pastor". Throughout the Bible, Jesus referred to Himself as a shepherd or a pastor.

Jesus said He was a good shepherd. What techniques did He use? He spoke extensively about the techniques of a good shepherd in the tenth chapter of John. What were His techniques? What were His methods? Below are the techniques that made Jesus a good shepherd.

1. A good shepherding technique is to be ahead of your sheep.

> **To him the porter openeth...and LEADETH THEM OUT.**
>
> **John 10:3**

What does it mean to lead sheep? It means to be practically available for them to see and learn from you in every area of life and ministry. Anything you want your sheep to do, you must first do it yourself. They will follow you if they see you doing it first!

A pastor who wants his church members to pray must practically lead them into prayer. When the sheep see the shepherd taking the lead, they are convinced that the ground is safe. A bad shepherd will sit at home and send the members to go for a prayer meeting alone.

In our church, I have always tried to do first, what I wanted my people to do. When we were building a basement in our church, we could not afford to hire the necessary machinery. We had to dig ourselves. I needed the help of the entire church to drill and dig very deep into the ground. After that, we needed to carry tons of red sand out of the pit.

I could have easily delegated the digging to some others, but I decided to dig and carry the sand myself. My decision motivated members of all social standings to get involved.

University students, lawyers, doctors and businessmen all joined in to work. They worked with all their might. Why was that? They had seen their shepherd taking the lead.

Notice what made David popular.

> **But all Israel and Judah loved David, because he went out and came in before them.**
>
> **1 Samuel 18:16**

Why did the subjects of Israel love David? The answer is simple. They could see him practically going in and out with them. They saw him doing things with them. Sometimes we have long periods of fasting with all-night prayer meetings everyday. You would be surprised to see how many people attend every night. I tell my members that I am struggling and suffering in the fast just like them, and they love to hear how I am suffering too. The sheep are always happy to identify with the shepherd when the shepherd identifies with them.

Leadership is very spiritual. Even when people do not see you physically, they follow you spiritually. Sheep have a mysterious way of becoming like their shepherd. They are following him in the Spirit.

Go ahead of your sheep. Do not operate as a super executive, just walking in and out like a "big shot". There is no place for "big shots" in the harvest field. There is no place for "unreal leaders" in the real world of the sheep.

2. A good shepherding technique is to know your sheep by their names.

> **...and he calleth his own sheep by NAME...**
>
> **John 10:3**

You must know the names of your sheep. You must want to know all their names and call them by name. Nobody is a number! Nobody wants to be called "Hey!" or "You there!"

You must get to know new people everyday. Keep asking their names until the name sticks. I am not ashamed of asking somebody his name seven times until it sticks. When you know the sheep by name an important spiritual attachment is formed.

3. A good shepherding technique is to let your voice be known by the sheep.

> **...for they know his voice. And a stranger will they not follow...**
>
> **John 10:4-5**

How do people know the voice of the shepherd? How do you know the voice of someone? It is because you have heard them speak to you time and time again. A good shepherd must speak to his sheep over and over until they know his voice.

I preach to my church all the time. I do not often have guest speakers. I believe in guest speakers, but I believe the best person to preach to my sheep is me because I am their shepherd.

When a woman gives birth to a baby, her breasts are full of milk for the new child. So it is with the shepherd. His spirit is full of the Word to give to his children. No other woman's body and breasts are better qualified to feed her own child. Nature made it that way. Because you gave birth, you are naturally primed up to feed what you have brought forth.

When your sheep are used to your voice, they will not follow strangers. If you call yourself a pastor, rise-up and feed your sheep regularly. Preach to them all of the time, and teach them from your heart. They will grow up and give birth to others.

They will know your voice on the issues of marriage, business, success and life in general. They will only want to hear your voice concerning different aspects of their lives. The voice of a true shepherd always rings in the spirit of his sheep.

I question whether you are a real shepherd if you do not regularly and consistently feed your sheep.

4. A good shepherding technique is to stay with the sheep.

> **The hireling fleeth, because he is an hireling, and careth not for the sheep.**
>
> **John 10:13**

Anyone who calls himself a pastor will want to stay around and mingle with the members, talk with them and be interested in them. David said,

> **One thing have I desired of the Lord, that will I seek after; THAT I MAY DWELL IN THE HOUSE OF THE LORD all the days of my life, to behold the beauty of the Lord, and to inquire in his temple.**
>
> **Psalm 27:4**

David wanted to stay in the house of the Lord. He actually wanted to live there. And you want to rush home! Are you really called?

I question the genuineness of a pastor who has no interest in staying around after service to mingle and chat with the sheep. The Bible says that the hireling flees. This means that he dashes off quickly! He wants to get away from the people!

Such people cannot stand visitors in their homes. They always say things like, "I need my privacy, I need my space" or "I can't stand having all these people around" and "I can't cook for so many people". Remember that a bishop is supposed to be "given to hospitality" (1Timothy 3:2).

5. A good shepherding technique is to know your sheep.

> **I am the good shepherd, and know my sheep, and am known of mine.**
>
> **John 10:14**

Knowing your sheep means that you must know their names, where they live and where they work. You know about their health, their friends, and their school. You know when they are writing exams. You know their family, their spouses and who they live with.

You must know their financial situation and their occupation. Simply know all aspects of their lives. Know means know! It is only when you know more details about your sheep that you can help or advise them properly.

I once asked a pastor about one of his sheep. I asked, "Is he married?"

He answered, "I don't know."

"Where does he work?"

"I'm not sure." He answered.

"Did he come to church last week?"

"I didn't see him," he replied.

In a very large church, you may excuse the pastor if he does not know these details. But in a small community church, the pastor has no excuse when he does not know the details about his sheep.

Brother X, Pastor X

I remember a pastor in my church who used to belong to another church. One day, at a wedding, he happened to meet his former senior pastor. His senior pastor said to him, "Brother 'X', it is a long time since I saw you."

"Did you come to church last Sunday?" the senior pastor asked.

Brother 'X' (who had now become a pastor in my church) smiled and said, "No pastor I didn't."

This senior pastor did not know that this brother had long stopped attending his church. He did not know that this gentleman had even become a pastor in another ministry. How sad!

Jesus said that a good pastor knows his sheep. If God gives you twenty people to look after, make sure you know all about them. Do not let any of them slip out of your hands. Jesus kept saying, "Those that thou gavest me I have kept, and none of them is lost." (John 17:12). It is important to have many junior pastors and shepherds to work with the senior pastor so that none of the sheep get lost.

God will hold us accountable for every single sheep that is lost. Keep the sheep that God has given to you.

6. A good shepherding technique is to be known by the sheep.

A good shepherd "opens up" his life to the sheep so that they can know about him. The sheep are interested in the shepherd's life. Do not be a mystery figure to your sheep. Let them know how real you are and how you experience the same problems and temptations they do.

7. A good shepherding technique is to keep the church family together.

One of the cardinal features of the pastoral calling is the ability to keep many people together throughout the years.

The longer a group of people stay together the more the people step on each other's toes. The conflicts of a family begin to rise. Brothers turn against brothers and sisters against sisters.

It is a good pastor who keeps everybody together. The pastoral gift keeps employers in the same church with employees. The anointing on the shepherd is able to keep the old in the same room with the young. It keeps the married flowing with the unmarried.

As the church grows, good shepherding techniques will keep enemies worshipping together under the same roof. It is good shepherding techniques that will keep debtors and creditors within the same fold and prevent them from tearing each other apart.

But he that is an hireling, and not the shepherd, whose own the sheep are not, seeth the wolf coming, and leaveth the sheep, and fleeth: and the wolf catcheth them, and SCATTERETH THE SHEEP.

John 10:12

8. A good shepherding technique is to notice the problems of your sheep.

> **But he that is an hireling, and not a shepherd, whose own the sheep are not, SEETH THE WOLF COMING...**
>
> **John 10:12**

The Scripture tells us that the good shepherd can see the wolf coming. He sees the problems of his people and is concerned. He knows when they are doing exams. He knows when they are having marital problems.

He knows when their businesses are going through "tough times". When a sheep fails his exams or loses a loved one, a wolf of discouragement and frustration is soon to come. A good shepherd must be able to see the wolf and move into action.

The bad shepherd sees the wolves but says, "That's your problem!" The good pastor will always notice when the sheep are in trouble.

9. A good shepherding technique is to deliver your sheep from captivity.

> **...and the wolf catcheth them, and scattereth the sheep.**
>
> **John 10:12**

Pastors, rise up and pray for your sheep! Minister to their needs. Apart from preaching, pray for their deliverance from witchcraft, demons and diseases. People love to be prayed for by their pastor. Pray for them, anointing them with oil. They need this encouragement and ministration.

10. A good shepherding technique is to give your life for the work of God.

> **I am the good shepherd: the good shepherd giveth his life for the sheep.**
>
> **John 10:11**

A good shepherd sacrifices his life for the sheep. The bad shepherd is only prepared to give two hours of his time on Sundays. He always wants to get away from the crowd.

If a woman desires to be a good wife, she must give herself fully to her husband. If you want to be a good doctor, you must give yourself fully to medicine. Similarly, if you want to be a good shepherd, you must give your life and your time to the high calling of the pastoral office. It is worth it at the end of the day. Decide to use the best shepherding techniques. Give yourself fully to this work. You will soon have a mega church.

Chapter

42

How Wise Management of Church Money Can Lead to Church Growth

CHAPTER SUMMARY

Almost every strategy for church growth will require the use of money. You will need money to organize camps and conventions. You will need money to go on the radio and television. You will need money to do outreaches, crusades and breakfast meetings.

■ Keys to Handling the Money

42.1 Managing money involves a lot of wisdom.

42.2 Over-spiritualizing financial issues is the number one cause for the financial confusion that plagues churches.

42.3 Church employees must pay taxes

42.4 Avoid debt.

42.5. Employ wisely and carefully.

42.6 There is nothing prestigious about having many employees in your ministry.

42.7 Start a building project as early as possible.

42.8 Do not start a grandiose project that is far bigger than your ministry.

42.9. There are many huge building projects which are impressive to men but which God did not initiate.

42.10 Grandiose building projects inflict great stresses on the senior pastor.

42.11 Meet the needs of the church before you meet the needs of the pastor.

42.12 Church members may encourage the pastor to buy the nicest car for himself.

42.13 Since you cannot always explain the source of all your blessings as a pastor, do not openly display everything you have.

42.14 Separate the Pastor's money from the church's money.

Your handling of the church's money will greatly affect church growth. Your handling of the church's money will cause the people to have faith in you or to lose confidence in you. In other words, the congregation will judge you by the way you handle the offerings they entrusted to you. As they see their donations being put to good use, their commitment will rise. They will see you as a wise leader because you used the money carefully. It is important that the church members see you as a wise person rather than as a fool. If they see you as a wise person, they will entrust more money to your care. Without a good supply of money most of your dreams and visions will die in your belly.

Keys to Handling the Money

1. Managing money involves a lot of wisdom.

It is important to use secular principles to manage the money of your church.

2. Over-spiritualizing financial issues is the number one cause for the financial confusion that plagues churches.

3. Church employees must pay taxes.

The church itself does not pay tax. However, individuals who work for the church must pay tax. If a church engages in any kind of business or profit-making activity, it must pay taxes on the income made from that. In other words, churches do not pay taxes on the tithe, offerings and gifts received. However, tax should be paid from income generated from farms, shops and other businesses. Do not spiritualize the paying of tax.

4. Avoid debt.

Although this instruction sounds simple, it is probably the most profound piece of advice I could give to any ministry. Debts have closed down many churches. Debts have deceived many pastors into a false sense of prosperity. Debts have deceived pastors into over-extending themselves. Many borrow until they cross the threshold where they have borrowed too much. You can prosper without borrowing money.

5. Employ wisely and carefully.

The more people you employ, the more salaries you have to pay. As the saying goes, "the fewer the merrier". It is possible to do many things with a few employees. It is possible to accomplish much with fewer but better qualified people.

6. There is nothing prestigious about having many employees in your ministry.

God did not call you to create jobs. He called you to win souls.

7. Start a building project as early as possible.

As soon as your church begins a building project, your finances will improve and you will be surprised at what you are able to accomplish. Do not wait to see huge sums of money before you begin a building project. The building project you embark upon will be the greatest evidence of the financial integrity of your ministry.

8. Do not start a grandiose project that is far bigger than your ministry.

You may never finish it and your church members may be discouraged by the unending nature of your building project.

9. There are many huge building projects which are impressive to men but which God did not initiate.

Unfortunately, many of these grandiose projects are empty or half-filled shortly after completion. Some churches are only filled on the day of their dedication.

10. Grandiose building projects inflict great stresses on the senior pastor.

These stressed-out pastors tend to preach mostly about finances because there is a great and pressing need for money.

11. Meet the needs of the church before you meet the needs of the pastor.

For instance, put up a building for the church before you build a mansion for the senior pastor. Seeing their church building come up generates much confidence and inspires the church members to give.

12. Church members may encourage the pastor to buy the nicest car for himself.

Many members have mixed feelings about their pastor's prosperity! On one hand, they are happy that he is doing well, but on the other hand, they wonder whether money is being used wisely.

13. Since you cannot always explain the source of all your blessings as a pastor, do not openly display everything you have.

14. Separate the Pastor's money from the church's money.

1. It is important to differentiate between the money of the church and the pastor's money. Clear lines of demarcation must be established.

2. There must be an understanding that the tithes and offerings of the church do not belong to the pastor even if he is the unquestionable founder and leader of the church. Because of this, a pastor must not randomly access the church funds for personal needs.

3. The pastor must not receive the church's tithes and offerings into his personal account.

   Offerings must not be kept in the pastor's home. It is wise for the pastor not to count money himself, but to delegate that task to a team of honest Christians.

4. A pastor should desist from taking money directly from the offering. Those who count money will consider you to be an unprincipled thief.
5. Do not borrow money from the church with the intention of paying back later.
6. Do not use your money for church projects with the intention of being paid back later.

Chapter

43

How to Manage Offerings, Improve Tithes and Raise Funds in the Church

CHAPTER SUMMARY

Without a good supply of money most of your dreams and visions will die in your belly. In the following chapter, you will learn the following:

- **How to prevent the loss of offerings.**
- **How to improve tithes and offerings in the church.**
- **How to raise funds in the church.**

Prevent the loss of your offerings by the following measures:

i. Prevent stealing of the offerings by monitoring who becomes an usher.

ii. Keep the ushers in view at all times so that none of them is able to dip his fingers into the offering bags.

iii. Ensure adequate security so that an intruder cannot steal the offerings.

iv. Prevent the loss of offerings by ensuring that two or three people count the money at the same time.

v. Make sure that no one is ever left alone with the money. While they are alone, they can steal the money.

vi. You must have a form that indicates how much money was counted for the day. This form must be signed by at least two people. Whatever is on this form must correspond with the bank pay-in slips.

vii. Keep the money in a secure safe to ensure that the offering is not stolen after it has been counted.

viii. Offerings should not be kept in the pastor's house, as he will be accused of misusing the church's money.

ix. Bank the money at the very next opportunity. In between the time you receive the money and the time you do the banking, money can be misappropriated.

x. Ensure that 100% of your offerings are banked and banked promptly.

xi. Do not take out money from the offering before it is taken to the bank. This will confuse the accounts and open the door to all kinds of malpractices. If you need petty cash, sign a cheque of a fixed amount and enter this as your petty cash imprest.

■ How to Improve Tithes and Offerings in the Church

1. Dedicate enough time during the service for receiving offerings.

2. From time to time, teach the church about giving. Regular and weekly teaching on giving tends to lose its impact. But irregular, spontaneous and Spirit-led teachings on giving, tend to boost offerings remarkably.

3. Show the congregation evidence of judicious use of money. Church members lose interest in giving, when they feel they are just financing the lifestyle of their superman pastor.

   I constantly mention the different projects, which we are engaged in so that my people are motivated.

4. Flow prophetically when receiving offerings. The people respond more to the power of God, than to human efforts to raise funds.

5. Take at least two offerings in each service. Initially, you would think that people would divide their offering into two. But experience has shown that taking two offerings approximately doubles the income realized from offerings. Also, there are many people who come to church late and they must also be given the opportunity to give their offerings.

6. Teach about tithing.

7. Link tithing with church membership. In other words let the people understand that you consider their tithe as the indication of their genuine membership.

8. Establish real differences between the tithe and every other offering. There must always be some indication that the tithe is different from every other offering. For instance, the tithe could be paid through envelopes and cards whereas other offerings would not be.

9. Although opportunities for receiving the tithe should be made at every service, the first Sunday of a month should be set aside as a special Sunday for the receiving of tithes.

10. In line with the concept of distinguishing the tithe, church members can be made to come to the altar to present their tithe, whilst the offering basket could be passed round for all other offerings.

11. Create an index number system for the church. Encourage the members to write this number on the tithing card or envelope. Use a computer to monitor the tithes received. Many people would prefer to have a number on the envelope rather than their names. Not everyone would like people to know how much their tithe is.

12. Separate the record of the names and numbers of church members so that this information is kept private.

    This ensures some confidentiality for members who may not want just anybody to know how much contribution they make to the ministry.

13. Make the tithing records available so that church members can request a statement of their contributions.

14. When the need arises, use these records as a basis to determine who is a member and who is not.

    You can use these records to determine whom the church can assist.

How to Raise Funds in the Church

1. Understand that fund-raising is intended to be a boost to the general tithes and offerings collected.

2. If you do not establish the basic income from tithes and offerings, fund-raising will never achieve its intended effect.

3. Special fund-raising events must not be too frequent in one congregation.

   Members quickly get tired of their pastor's fund-raising gimmicks and will no longer respond to appeals.

4. The fund-raiser must decide on the highest amount to be requested.

   When the amount is too high, he will get few responses. If no one responds to your initial high request, the entire fund-raising event could fall into jeopardy. I have seen this happen many times.

5. It is sometimes better to choose an average amount that many more people can respond to.

   For instance, in many congregations, there are more people who can give a hundred dollars and much fewer that can give a thousand dollars. Simple arithmetic shows us that sixty people giving one hundred dollars yields more than two people giving a thousand dollars each.

6. During fund-raising, give opportunities to all levels of givers to contribute, from the richest to the poorest.

   The poor people may collectively give more than the rich. You may therefore miss your target if you concentrate only on the rich.

7. Pledges are promises of money that Christians make during fund-raising events.

   Generally speaking, the shorter the time given for individuals to honour their pledges, the higher the returns will be. A few days after making pledges, many Christians forget the promises they made in church. I recommend that the period of time to pay up a pledge should be from one week to three months.

8. No matter how much people pledge, a wise pastor should not expect more than 30% of pledges to come in.

   Unfortunately, most Christians are not spiritual and do not keep their word. Many pledge large amounts and do not pay up. If you want to plan successfully you must never budget on what the congregation has pledged.

9. Pastors who budget on promised amounts are usually accused of misusing funds because the full amounts are never realized.

   It is wise to save money towards a project before embarking on fund-raising for it. This ensures that your project comes on whether the people pay up their pledges or not.

10. Never see fund-raising as a means of financing your projects.

    The build-up of your regular tithes and offerings should be the main source of project financing. In other words, see fund-raising as what it really is: a boost to your existing financial situation. God has determined how the church is to be financed: through regular tithes and offerings.

Chapter

44

Define Who Your Members Are

CHAPTER SUMMARY

In this chapter, allow God to birth in your spirit the importance of having accurate data and information. I pray that a data centre will be birthed in your ministry through this book. There is no need to give vague answers about the state of your church anymore. There is no need to tell lies about how many people come to our churches anymore. You can develop a powerful data centre for your mega church today!

44.1 Register all your members using a simple membership registration form.

44.2 The most important fields of information for church membership are the names, ages, gender, telephone numbers and addresses.

44.3 Give every member a life-time index number which will be used as a permanent reference point.

44.4 Do not be deceived! Many church members do not consider their membership as very important.

44.5 The unannounced departure of numerous members without notice, converts your laboriously acquired information into useless data.

44.6 Accept that church membership is fluid in its composition.

44.7 Make it easy to join the church.

44.8 Accept the reality of different levels of member-ship.

44.9 Registering church members can provide important data which is useful in providing programmes and pastoral care to registered members.

44.10 Do not over-extend yourself in the field of computerization and administration.

44.11 Do not inflate figures of membership.

Church members are the most valuable assets of a church. Your vision for church growth is realized as you have more and more church members. It is important to be able to count them and have accurate facts and figures at your fingertips. Church members are difficult to count because they come and go so easily. Many of them do not tell you when they come; neither do they bother to tell you when they are leaving. Because of this, many churches do not have a true and accurate count of who really belongs to them.

Apart from this many pastors cannot tell where they stand in terms of their church growth vision. They cannot tell when the church is growing and whether they are accomplishing their vision for growth. Many pastors cannot tell how many lawyers, doctors, fishermen or teachers there are in their churches. But this is important information because it will guide you in all your interaction with the congregation.

1. Register all your members using a simple membership registration form.

Having a complicated form with all sorts of details often creates useless data that is never used. The church is not the Central Intelligence Agency and does not require such extensive information.

2. The most important fields of information for church membership are the names, ages, gender, telephone numbers and addresses.

Some will argue that further information such as previous marriages; number of children, educational background, etc. are relevant for good pastoral care.

I agree with you, but my experience is that most of this information is never properly used or managed. It becomes piles of useless data that no one knows what do with.

3. Give every member a life-time index number which will be used as a permanent reference point.

This number will be needed by every computer system and programme used. The index number will be used to monitor the individual's tithes. It can also be used by the individual in any activity that requires identification. For instance, if you have classes or examinations in the church, this number will come in handy.

4. Do not be deceived! Many church members do not consider their membership as very important.

When they are moving to another location or country, many church members do not bother to inform their pastor that they are leaving. They see themselves as insignificant members whose absence will not be noticed.

5. The unannounced departure of numerous members without notice, converts your laboriously acquired information into useless data.

This is why unnecessary and lengthy efforts to gather information about each member should be discouraged.

6. Accept that church membership is fluid in its composition.

There are always some stable and unmovable people in each congregation but it is best for every pastor to accept the absolute fluidity of church membership. Church membership can be described as a flowing river in which the water you see today will not be the water you see tomorrow.

7. Make it easy to join the church.

The filling of a simple form is an easy single procedure for joining the church. Some churches insist on people going through various classes and procedures before they are allowed to become members. This is a good idea but the danger is that many will not go through these classes and will assume that they are not members. I believe that as they join the church through a simple procedure, they will then have the opportunity to go through the classes.

8. Accept the reality of different levels of membership.

Within every congregation, there are at least four levels of membership:

i. Members who have filled a simple form.

ii. Members who are tithers.

Tithing indicates a level of commitment and Christian maturity.

iii. Members who participate in small groups and weekday (non Sunday) service.

Such people are even more committed.

iv. Members who are leaders.

There are people who in addition to all three descriptions above, become leaders and workers in the church. This fourth level is a crucial level because it is here that the moral and ethical standards of the church can be enforced. You cannot prevent homosexuals from filling forms. Neither can you prevent prostitutes from paying tithes or participating in church activities. You can only preach to them and pray that the Lord shows mercy. However, you can actually prevent a known or practising immoral person from occupying a position of leadership. This is the only way that the integrity of the church can be safeguarded–at the level of the leader's membership.

9. Registering church members can provide important data which is useful in providing programmes and pastoral care to registered members.

Use computers, databases, and any other gadgets to manage the fluid membership of the modern church.

10. Do not over-extend yourself in the field of computerization and administration.

There are many diversions and time-wasting traps which can cause a pastor to leave his true calling.

11. Do not inflate figures of membership.

The greatest person in Heaven will not be the pastor with the most members; it will be the pastor who was most humble while on this earth.

Chapter

45

What to Expect from the Average Church Member

CHAPTER SUMMARY

A successful mega church pastor is someone who understands the mindset of the average church member. Without a clear understanding of how church members think and operate, you will not succeed in administering the church. In this chapter, learn about the mindset of the average church member.

The following points describe in a general way (of course, there are many exceptions) the mindset of the average church member. Financial planning by an administrator must take into account these realities. A successful pastor must predict certain trends and circumvent them.

The quicker you understand and predict these trends and circumvent them, the more successful you will be in ministry.

Pastors must not have an erroneous impression that their members really love God and that their minds are constantly on the church and its projects.

1. Most church members are not thinking about the church but about themselves.

2. They spend a lot of money on themselves, but very little money on God.

3. Most church members feel that a hundred dollars is little money in a shopping mall but is too much to give as offering in church.

4. Many church members do not pay tithes and they will not do so no matter what you say!

5. If you preach about tithes, some people will pay up for a while but most people will stop when they forget the message. Your financial planning as an administrator must take this into account.

6. Most church members will pledge various amounts of money during fund-raising events. However most of them will not pay what they promise. A wise pastor must expect only a small percentage of the pledged amount.

7. Most church members are irregular in their church attendance.

   These members therefore only contribute irregularly to the ministry. This accounts for the unpredictable and low income of churches. Any wise planner must take into account this unpredictable behaviour.

8. Most church members are ignorant of the sacrifices their pastor makes. Many church members think their pastor's only duty is to rest all week and deliver one Sunday sermon. This makes the average church member unwilling to make many financial sacrifices for the ministry.

9. Most people are inherently ungrateful. They benefit from the church but refuse to express their gratitude through contributions and gifts. The ingratitude of church members is demonstrated by the amounts of money people are willing to give to the ministry.

10. Many church members have commitments to other groups such as political parties, old boys' associations, tribal associations and professional bodies. Their commitment to these groups is often stronger than their commitment to the church. Know that many church members will readily sacrifice you and your church programmes for other engagements.

Chapter

46

How to Choose Helps Ministers

CHAPTER SUMMARY

As a church grows, a new group of people will become important. These are the helps ministers! At the beginning of a church, a helps ministry does not seem very important. The pastor is the jack-of-all-trades and has to help himself accomplish whatever he needs to. But with the growth of a mega church, you will need people to help in many areas. New problems will arise that will require the input of helps ministers. Helps ministers are there to solve problems in different areas of expertise. Find out the principles for choosing helps ministers in this chapter.

- **Principles for Choosing Helps Ministers**

46.1 Employ people that are genuinely needed by the organization.

46.2 Employ people from within the church.

46.3 Readily dismiss people from your organization.

46.4 Employ as few people as you possibly can.

46.5 Make employees carry out multiple roles.

46.6 Wherever possible, use equipment instead of human beings.

46.7 Do not neglect professional and technical aspects of the ministry.

> **Then the twelve called the multitude of the disciples unto them, and said, It is not reason that we should leave the word of God, and serve tables.**
>
> **Wherefore, brethren, look ye out among you seven men of honest report, full of the Holy Ghost and wisdom, whom we may appoint over this business.**
>
> **Acts 6:2-3**

A helps minister is someone who stays in the background but helps you to accomplish great things for the Lord. Such people are usually administrators, secretaries, personal assistants, special aides and special envoys. Although helps ministers are not publicly acknowledged, their role often converts a little known pastor into a fruitful and well-known minister.

Your willingness to accept that you need such helps ministers and your ability to successfully blend them into the ministry will determine how big your church can become. I can remember how I declared that I did not and would not work with any women. Unfortunately for me, many of the helps ministers were women. I had to adapt to and accept their existence and presence in the ministry. My unwillingness to do so would have spelt failure in many areas of ministry.

Sadly, some people posing as helps ministers have destroyed entire ministries. Indeed, helps ministers can make or break an entire ministry.

■ Principles for Choosing Helps Ministers

1. Employ people that are genuinely needed by the organization.

2. Employ people from within the church.

As much as possible, employ people who are church members. Sometimes it is not possible to do so. But it is better to take from amongst your own sheep.

3. Readily dismiss people from your organization.

Anyone who employs people must be ready and willing to dismiss these people in the future if the need arises. Contrary to traditional opinion, it is important to fire non-performing staff members even though they may be members of your church.

4. Employ as few people as you possibly can.

When people are employed for non-existent jobs, they become disgruntled and dissatisfied. Such people complain and create a discontented atmosphere in the church office. It is better not to have an employee than to have an unhappy employee.

5. Make employees carry out multiple roles.

For instance, a pastor could be a lecturer at the Bible school and at the same time do pastoral duties. You may not need to have a secretary as many people can type their letters on their own. You may not need to have a receptionist as you could have a doorbell to announce the arrival of a visitor.

6. Wherever possible, use equipment instead of human beings.

Machines do not get tired! Machines do not develop moods and attitudes! Machines do not ask to be paid for over-time work. Machines do not go on leave. Machines do not go on maternity leave. Machines do not resign suddenly!

7. Do not neglect professional and technical aspects of the ministry.

You should have some knowledge about many professions. Many pastors have a "black-out mentality" and think they are not qualified to discuss certain things.

For instance, as soon as some ministers realize that something has to do with legal work they black-out and call for lawyers saying, "This is legal work, just call the lawyers to take over." In this way, pastors unsuspectingly sell their fate to misguided professionals who do not have their vision.

Whether it is accounting, medicine, law, architecture or engineering, there is a level to which you must be able to understand and discuss issues. You must read a lot and ask many questions. It takes humility to ask questions about things you do not know.

But by asking many questions, you will learn a lot about many things that you are clueless about. You can have sensible discussions with all the professional groups in your church. Bankers, travel agents, lawyers, accountants, human resource managers, carpenters, contractors, engineers, architects and administrators are supposed to be able to explain what they are doing in simple language. With the passage of time they will develop a healthy respect for your ability to engage in intelligent discussions on different subjects.

Chapter

47

Guidelines for Employing Helps Ministers

CHAPTER SUMMARY

- **Guidelines for Employing Helps Ministers**

47.1 **Put everything in writing.**

47.2 **Let education be the basis of employment.**

47.3 **Place people according to their temperaments.**

47.4 **Supervise everything.**

a. **Supervision by meetings**

b. **Supervision by visits**

c. **Supervision by monitoring targets**

d. **Supervision by the "scapegoat" principle**

47.5 **Be a benevolent employer.**

1. Put everything in writing.

Once you begin to employ people, it is important to write letters and contracts where necessary. Discussions are not sufficient basis for dealing with employees even though they may be church members.

2. Let education be the basis of employment.

Although the success of ministry is not dependent on education, it is an important factor. Education greatly refines the natural gifts that God has given to every individual. Any kind of education is often valuable even in the ministry.

Your education does not have to be in a particular field in order to be valuable in that field. For instance, I am trained as a doctor but I function as a pastor, a manager, a doctor and a leader. I was not trained for much of what I do today but my general education in the fields of anatomy, physiology, pharmacology, microbiology etc. have greatly enhanced my managerial skills.

Generally speaking, the more formally educated a person is, the more valuable he is. That is why salaries jump as individuals acquire more degrees.

However, this is not a hard and fast rule. Some people are able to informally educate themselves thus making up for a lack of formal education. Another important effect of education is the establishing of discipline in the individual. The discipline that a person develops to go through exams is important. Generally speaking, an educated person is more disciplined than an uneducated person.

The disciplines of education (having to stay up late, having to pass exams, having to overcome various barriers and hurdles) are all exercises that prepare the individual for the rigours of real life.

3. Place people according to their temperaments.

Know all about temperaments. The knowledge of an individual's temperament is the best guide for placing him. Unfortunately, someone may be educated in an area but does not have the right temperament for that kind of work.

If you do not understand the strengths and weaknesses of the choleric, the melancholic, the phlegmatic and the sanguine you will be a frustrated employer. You will constantly wonder why the work is not done even though you have someone who is a specialist in that field.

Choose a choleric when you need a driving manager. The choleric is good at jobs that involve targets and deadlines. He is also good at pioneering new projects and doing things that have not been done before. He is also good at supervising others because of his natural tendency to take charge. Because he is self-motivated and self-supervising, he is able to drive through the obstacles of a big project. A choleric person will spontaneously work for many extra hours. He or she can handle a number of different functions at the same time. The choleric is not usually good at being an assistant.

Choose a melancholic when the job involves being meticulous and detailed. A melancholic employee will also do well in positions where books and records must be kept. They are also target-oriented and very focused. A melancholic may also be good for jobs that require secrecy. Melancholic people are very intelligent and very loyal. Use them for sensitive jobs that require loyalty. Because they are very analytical and detailed they are also good at jobs that involve technical things. They are usually the best at using computers, machines and other technical equipment.

Choose the phlegmatic when there is a monotonous job. Repetitive work within already defined structures is the best place for the phlegmatic worker. Teaching in a school setting and doing routine work in an established office are good examples of jobs for the phlegmatic. They are usually not good at meeting deadlines and building new projects. The phlegmatic is easy-going and may be the best person to handle difficult people situations. He may not always express the urgency required in sensitive situations and sees no need to hurry about anything. Keep your phlegmatic away from stressful and high intensity work zones.

The sanguine must be employed when the job requires intelligence, skill-giftedness, and the creation of happiness and pleasant conditions. The sanguine is good at jobs that have to do with human relationships. They usually give a good public presentation of your office and what you stand for. They are often good singers because they are uninhibited and therefore give full expression to the music they perform. They introduce life and vitality to almost every circumstance. The sanguine is usually gifted and must be used in his gifted areas and not in the area of organization.

Somehow the sanguine is not very good at meticulous management and organization. Your sanguine employee may look outwardly charismatic, but is often not disciplined enough to carry things through.

4. Supervise everything.

There are four main ways to supervise:

a. Supervision by meetings

Meetings provide a forum for discussion of the work. During these meetings, different aspects are discussed and the employees are made to focus on the important targets.

b. Supervision by visits

There are two types of visits: announced visits and unannounced visits. Announced visits help the individuals to put up their best performance. Surprise visits help the manager to see the real picture.

c. Supervision by monitoring targets

This is the best form of supervision. Ultimately, the worker is supposed to produce results. A result-oriented work place is often more fruitful than others.

d. Supervision by the "scapegoat" principle

In this method, workers who are found to be non-performing can be dismissed as an example to the others. In all my experience, there is nothing that sends a more sombre message than the dismissal of an employee. A tone of seriousness is introduced into the system by the dismissal of one person.

5. Be a benevolent employer.

Be kind and generous to your staff. It is important for people to perceive that you genuinely care for them. Even if you do not have a good salary to offer, show them love. You will be surprised to find out that people will work for *"more love and less money", than for "more money and less love".*

Chapter

48

How to Employ a Helper

CHAPTER SUMMARY

- How to Employ a Helper

Step 1: The application letter

Step 2: Presentation of documents by the applicant

Step 3: The temperament examination

Step 4: The general interview

Step 5: The financial interview

Step 6: The letter of appointment

Step 7: The remuneration package letter

Step 8: The job description letter

Step 9: The orientation letter

Step 10: The general expectations letter

Step 11: The sanctions letter

How to Determine Salaries

Salaries are always determined by the following:

a. The real cost of living

b. The salary which the individual was paid in his previous workplace

c. Comparable salaries

d. The educational background of the individual

e. The value of the individual to the organization

f. The length of time the individual has worked after school

g. The length of time the individual has worked for the organization

h. The ability of the organization to pay the individual

Step 1: The application letter

An application letter is to be written by the potential employee. This is important so that the individual will not say that he was forced to work in the ministry against his will. The application is the evidence of the individual's desire to work with you.

Step 2: Presentation of documents by the applicant

There should be a presentation of CVs and certificates from school. This is important because there are many who claim to have certain backgrounds but in actual fact have no real qualification. Some people attended university but either did not complete their courses or did not pass their exams.

Step 3: The temperament examination

A simple test can reveal the basic temperament of your potential employee. Ensure that you put your employee in an area that is suitable for his temperament.

Step 4: The general interview

Every applicant must be interviewed by a panel. A panel is better able to objectively assess an applicant. The interview helps create a solid foundation for the future. The panel becomes convinced about the rightness or wrongness of employing this individual. The job seeker defends his application and makes a case for his employment. The interview helps the applicant to perceive the church as a professional, efficient and competent organization. This interview establishes whether the individual is the right person for the job or not.

Step 5: The financial interview

This interview centres on the financial package that the newly employed person can expect to receive. Sometimes it is wise to separate financial discussions from discussions centred on the job itself. In a church setting it is important that people work because they believe God has called them, rather than for the money. After this interview, if the individual is still happy to work for the organization then you may go ahead and give him the letter of appointment.

Step 6: The letter of appointment

A letter of acceptance of the applicant must be given to him when he passes the interview. This letter should specify the date of commencement of work. Such a letter would remove doubts concerning his date of employment. The date of employment becomes important when determining benefits that are time-related.

Step 7: The remuneration package letter

This is a letter that indicates the remuneration package that has been discussed at the financial interview. This includes things like the take home salary, and any other housing, transport or health benefits that may exist. This includes what the person will be paid and what the person can expect in the future. It is wise to retain such letters.

Step 8: The job description letter

Give a letter containing the job title and the job description. This should explain in detail the job that the person is expected to do. Explain in your letter how the individual will be assessed and what targets should be accomplished. This letter should be delivered at an extensive and explanatory meeting.

Step 9: The orientation letter

This letter should introduce other existing departments and indicate the functions of other staff members. There will be many questions on the mind of a new person. For instance:

- Where should I go if I need money to complete a project?
- Who do I call on when I need equipment?
- Where do I go when I need equipment to be fixed?
- Where do I go when I personally need financial assistance?
- Who do I see when my computer breaks down?
- Who do I see when I need a car?
- Who do I see if I need to arrange for transport?
- What do I do if I want to resign?
- Who is my boss?
- Who does my boss report to?

Step 10: The general expectations letter

This is a letter that indicates the other general expectations of an employee as well as any staff rules that may exist. In some offices, there may be dress codes and rules about privacy and confidentiality. There may be rules about the use of equipment and the repair of equipment. There may also be rules about visitors to the office and access to the offices. There may be working hours that are peculiar to the office. All these and more need to be spelt out clearly.

Step 11: The sanctions letter

This is a letter that indicates a sanctions package. It should include measures that will be taken against an employee in the event of unsatisfactory performance or behaviour. Such sanctions must always include the possibility of dismissal. You must also include the reality of the need to lay off staff in the event that the church can no longer sustain its staff.

■ How to Determine Salaries

The employer must determine salaries. It is good to use a board to determine salaries. The board must have a formula that guides them in determining salaries.

It is important to establish clear grades and ranks among employees. These ranks must be understood and accepted by all. The basis for rank is the same basis for determining salaries. Ranks amongst the employees become the basis for different grades of benefits.

Salaries are always determined by the following principles:

a. The real cost of living

   There is no point in paying someone less than he can survive on. You will only create an army of petty thieves within your offices. The cost of living varies from country to country. It even varies within a country. It is important to consider these realities. In some places people earn a lot of money but have equally high bills.

b. The salary which the individual was paid in his previous workplace

   This serves as a good measure to what the person has lived on in the past. People often inflate their former salaries. Knowing the previous salary helps to silence individuals who may claim that you are not paying them well. All you have to do is to refer them to their previous jobs.

c. Comparable salaries

   Salaries can be determined by knowing what is being paid to individuals who are doing similar jobs in comparable organizations. A secretary who demands an unreasonable salary must be told what other secretaries earn in comparable organizations. A pastor who demands outrageous benefits must be told about what other pastors earn in other churches.

d. The educational background of the individual

   Generally speaking, the more educated a person is, the more he earns. There are times, however, that the qualifications of an individual must be ignored. There are some people who are good at passing exams in school and therefore have many degrees. Unfortunately, many of such people are of little practical use when it comes to real work. It must be remembered that a certificate is just a piece of paper and does not mean that an individual is capable of carrying out a job.

e. The value of the individual to the organization

   This is the most important factor in determining someone's income. Consider what would happen if a particular employee were absent. Easily replaceable people, such as drivers and secretaries are not as valuable as managers and lifelong assistants!

f. The length of time the individual has worked after school

Usually, the longer an individual has been in gainful employment, the more mature and productive he is. Young people are full of zeal and energy but sometimes lack the maturity that seasoned workers have.

g. The length of time the individual has worked for the organization

The length of time that individuals have worked for you must be recognized. Generally speaking, the longer people work, the more they must be paid.

h. The ability of the organization to pay the individual

It is all well and good to propose very high salaries. Will the church be able to continue paying these salaries? Many organizations are unable to pay their employees at the end of the month. Over-staffing and over-paying people sometimes create this unfortunate situation. The leader must assess carefully whether he will be able to sustain certain levels of payment.

Sometimes, individuals want to be paid as though they work in a bank. I often tell my employees that we are neither a bank nor a gold mine. A secretary working for a gold mine may obviously have a higher salary than a secretary working for a church. A church simply does not have the income that a gold mine has and therefore cannot sustain the salaries that a gold mine pays.

Chapter

49

How Camp Meetings Cause Church Growth

CHAPTER SUMMARY

A camp is a special time when a section of the church goes away to a secluded place to wait on God. During these days, there is usually intensified preaching, teaching and fellowship. These days of intense quality fellowship and spiritual impartation leave indelible imprints in the hearts of the participants.

■ The Special Environment of a Camp

49. 1 A camp has a timeless environment.

49. 2 A camp has a tension-free environment.

49. 3 A camp has an anxiety-free environment

49. 4 A camp has a patient environment.

49. 5 A camp has a humble environment.

■ Powerful Effects of Assembling for a Camp

49.6 Camp meetings allow the Word to be spoken with boldness.

49.7 Camp meetings allow the Word of God to be preached extensively which causes a great increase in the number of disciples.

49.8 Camp meetings allow important interaction between believers.

49.9 Camp meetings allow many hours of prayer to take place.

49.10 Camp meetings encourage oneness and unity so that the whole church has one heart and one soul.

49.11 Camp meetings give room for prophesies at church which charge up the people.

49.12 Camp meetings give room for the manifestation of spiritual gifts which lead to the edifying of the church.

49.13 Camp meetings counteract the devil's work of division.

49.14 Camp meetings fight separation and isolation that comes from pride and sensuality.

49.15 Camp meetings are gatherings which prevent the scattering of the sheep and deprive the devil of meat.

...and the number of the disciples MULTIPLIED...

Acts 6:7

There is something about a camp, which is different from a Sunday or weekday service. A camp has a powerful spiritual impact on all who attend. Camps cause great growth to come to the churches.

The Special Environment of a Camp

1. **A camp has a timeless environment.** The difference in the quality of fellowship is brought about by the timelessness of a camp. A camp is timeless because people do not have to rush home by any particular time. There is no closing time for the preaching and teaching. There is no need to cut down, cut back or cut off anything that is necessary for the people.

2. **A camp has a tension-free environment.** Tension is created by the presence of people who know it all. Proud people do not usually come for camps. They are usually too big to be found at such meetings. A camp automatically eliminates a group of stiff, fussy and difficult-to-please church members.

3. **A camp has an anxiety-free environment.** Anxiety is created by the cares of this world. The cares of this world are the legitimate needs, and concerns of the congregation. At a camp, we are cut off from the outside world for a few days. The worries, cares and problems of the world are suspended for a while as we focus on the Lord.

4. **A camp has a patient environment.** Patience is important when training pastors. Jesus told His disciples to wait for Him and they did. They patiently sat under the trees and slept till Jesus reappeared.

   Without patience, you will not see, hear nor feel many aspects of the glory of God.

5. **A camp has a humble environment.** The need to stay for long hours eliminates proud people from the congregation and leaves you with a group that are more teachable and open to receive.

Powerful Effects of Assembling for a Camp

1. Camp meetings allow the Word to be spoken with boldness.

The absence of the proud know-it-all allows the Word of God to come forth freely.

And when they had prayed, the place was shaken where they were assembled together; and they were all filled with the Holy Ghost, and they spake the word of God with boldness.

Acts 4:31

2. Camp meetings allow the Word of God to be preached extensively which causes a great increase in the number of disciples.

And the word of God increased; and the number of the disciples multiplied in Jerusalem greatly; and a great company of the priests were obedient to the faith.

Acts 6:7

3. Camp meetings allow important interaction between believers.

And all that believed were together, and had all things common;

Acts 2:44

4. Camp meetings allow many hours of prayer to take place.

And when they heard that, they lifted up their voice to God with one accord, and said, Lord, thou art God, which hast made heaven, and earth, and the sea, and all that in them is:

Acts 4:24

5. Camp meetings encourage oneness and unity so that the whole church has one heart and one soul.

And the multitude of them that believed were of one heart and of one soul: neither said any of them that ought of the things which he possessed was his own; but they had all things common.

Acts 4:32

6. Camp meetings give room for prophesies at church which charge up the people.

He that speaketh in an unknown tongue edifieth himself; but he that prophesieth edifieth the church.

1 Corinthians 14:4

7. Camp meetings give room for the manifestation of spiritual gifts which lead to the edifying of the church.

Even so ye, forasmuch as ye are zealous of spiritual gifts, seek that ye may excel to the edifying of the church.

1 Corinthians 14:12

8. Camp meetings counteract the devil's work of division.

> These are the ones who cause divisions, worldly-minded, devoid of the Spirit.
>
> Jude 19 (NASU)

9. Camp meetings fight separation and isolation that comes from pride and sensuality.

> These be they who separate themselves, sensual, having not the Spirit.
>
> Jude 19

10. Camp meetings are gatherings which prevent the scattering of the sheep and deprive the devil of meat.

> And they were scattered, because there is no shepherd: and they became meat to all the beasts of the field, when they were scattered.
>
> Ezekiel 34:5

Chapter

50

How Conventions Cause Church Growth

CHAPTER SUMMARY

Conventions are simply gatherings of God's people. Conventions lift up the name of Jesus and always bring an air of celebration and victory. At these gatherings, many things take place which are spiritually positive and which lead to church growth.

■ Powerful Effects of Gathering for Conventions

50.1 Church conventions are important because the sheep are fed with good pasture.

50.2 Church conventions are important because they allow healing power to flow.

50.3 Conventions of the saints are important because they bring the presence of God.

50.4 Conventions of the saints are important because evil spirits are driven out of people.

50.5 Conventions of the saints are important because they enable praise to go on.

50.6 Conventions of the saints are important because they allow people to be saved.

50.7 Conventions of the saints are important because they allow the power of the Holy Ghost to shake the church.

50.8 Conventions of the saints are important because they cause all needs to be met.

50.9 Conventions of the saints are important because they enable spiritual gifts to operate. This causes the fear of God to be in the church.

50.10 Conventions of the saints are important because they allow revelations, psalms and prophecies to come forth.

... And the Lord ADDED to the church daily such as should be saved.
Acts 2:47

At conventions, the church usually enjoys the ministry of guest preachers. Convention speakers are often well received because they have the aura of a visitor.

Below is a list of powerful things that happen when gatherings of the saints occur. The gathering of the saints is what we call a convention. The more powerful conventions you have, the more your church will grow.

■ Powerful Effects of Gathering for Conventions

1. Church conventions are important because the sheep are fed with good pasture.

I will feed them in a good pasture, and upon the high mountains of Israel shall their fold be: there shall they lie in a good fold, and in a fat pasture shall they feed upon the mountains of Israel.

Ezekiel 34:14

2. Church conventions are important because they allow healing power to flow.

And Jesus departed from thence, and came nigh unto the sea of Galilee; and went up into a mountain, and sat down there. And great multitudes came unto him, having with them those that were lame, blind, dumb, maimed, and many others, and cast them down at Jesus' feet; and he healed them:

Matthew 15:29-30

3. Conventions of the saints are important because they bring the presence of God.

For where two or three are gathered together in my name, there am I in the midst of them.

Matthew 18:20

4. Conventions of the saints are important because evil spirits are driven out of people.

And there was in their synagogue a man with an unclean spirit; and he cried out

Mark 1:23

5. Conventions of the saints are important because they enable praise to go on.

And they, continuing daily with one accord in the temple, and breaking bread from house to house, did eat their meat with gladness

> and singleness of heart PRAISING GOD, and having favour with all the people. And the Lord added to the church daily such as should be saved.
>
> Acts 2:46-47

6. Conventions of the saints are important because they allow people to be saved.

> And they, continuing daily with one accord in the temple, and breaking bread from house to house, did eat their meat with gladness and singleness of heart Praising God, and having favour with all the people. And THE LORD ADDED TO THE CHURCH DAILY such as should be saved.
>
> Acts 2:46-47

7. Conventions of the saints are important because they allow the power of the Holy Ghost to shake the church.

> And when they had prayed, THE PLACE WAS SHAKEN where they were assembled together; and they were all filled with the Holy Ghost, and they spake the word of God with boldness.
>
> Acts 4:31

> In the name of our Lord Jesus Christ, when ye are gathered together, and my spirit, with the power of our Lord Jesus Christ
>
> 1 Corinthians 5:4

8. Conventions of the saints are important because they cause all needs to be met.

> Neither was there any among them that lacked: for as many as were possessors of lands or houses sold them, and brought the prices of the things that were sold
>
> Acts 4:34

9. Conventions of the saints are important because they enable spiritual gifts to operate. This causes the fear of God to be in the church.

> But a certain man named Ananias, with Sapphira his wife, sold a possession, And kept back part of the price, his wife also being privy to it, and brought a certain part, and laid it at the apostles' feet. But Peter said, Ananias, why hath Satan filled thine heart to lie to the Holy Ghost, and to keep back part of the price of the land? Whiles it remained, was it not thine own? and after it was sold, was it not in thine own power? why hast thou conceived this thing in thine heart? thou hast not lied unto men, but unto God. And Ananias hearing these words fell down, and gave up the ghost: and great fear came on all them that heard these things.
>
> Acts 5:1-5

10. Conventions of the saints are important because they allow revelations, psalms and prophecies to come forth.

How is it then, brethren? when ye come together, every one of you hath a psalm, hath a doctrine, hath a tongue, hath a revelation, hath an interpretation. Let all things be done unto edifying.

1 Corinthians 14:26

Chapter

51

How to Have Successful Conventions

CHAPTER SUMMARY

51.1 Conventions should be held three times a year following the pattern of the feasts of Israel.

51.2 Conventions are important events in the life of a church and people must take time off to attend and to participate.

51.3 Everyone in the church must come for conventions. All males were to attend the festivals.

51.4 Conventions must celebrate the salvation that the Lord has given us.

51.5 Conventions must lead to much praise for God's goodness. There should be special times of praise and worship as well as special music.

51.6 Conventions will raise funds for the house of the Lord. There must always be special times of fund-raising in the house of the Lord

51.7 Conventions bring about a feeling of joy, victory and celebration. These are important feelings that inspire church growth.

> **Three times a year you shall celebrate a feast to Me.**
>
> **Exodus 23:14, NASB**

1. Conventions should be held three times a year following the pattern of the feasts of Israel.

If you have more than three conventions, the events will lose their significance. God ordained three main feasts for Israel. These feasts commemorated various significant events in the life of the nation Israel. They were to serve as reminders of significant things that the Lord taught them in their walk with Him. There were seven different events that were grouped into three feast times. The Feast of Passover took place in the first month; the Feast of Pentecost took place in the third month, whilst the Feast of Tabernacles was held in the seventh month of the year.

2. Conventions are important events in the life of a church and people must take time off to attend and to participate.

> **On this same day you shall make a proclamation as well; you are to have a holy convocation. You shall do no laborious work. It is to be a perpetual statute in all your dwelling places throughout your generations**
>
> **Leviticus 23:21, NASB**

3. Everyone in the church must come for conventions. All males were to attend the festivals.

> **Three times a year all your males shall appear before the Lord GOD**
>
> **Exodus 23:17, NASB**

4. Conventions must celebrate the salvation that the Lord has given us.

Altar calls must be made during conventions. Sadly, Christian programmes are being held without altar calls for salvation.

> **And ye shall observe the feast of unleavened bread; for in this selfsame day have I brought your armies out of the land of Egypt: therefore shall ye observe this day in your generations by an ordinance for ever.**
>
> **Exodus 12:17**

5. Conventions must lead to much praise for God's goodness. There should be special times of praise and worship as well as special music.

> **And the children of Israel that were present at Jerusalem kept the feast of unleavened bread days with great gladness: and the Levites and the priests praised the LORD day by day, singing with loud instruments unto the LORD.**
>
> **2 Chronicles 30:21**

6. Conventions will raise funds for the house of the Lord. There must always be special times of fund-raising in the house of the Lord.

Conventions can greatly boost the finances of a church. Christians must be told to come to conventions expecting to give and to support the work of the Lord. They must not appear at a convention empty-handed.

> **Thou shalt keep the feast of unleavened bread: (thou shalt eat unleavened bread seven days, as I commanded thee, in the time appointed of the month Abib; for in it thou camest out from Egypt: and NONE SHALL APPEAR BEFORE ME EMPTY:)**
>
> **Exodus 23:15**

> **And thou shalt keep the feast of weeks unto the LORD thy God WITH A TRIBUTE OF A FREEWILL OFFERING of thine hand, which thou shalt give unto the LORD thy God, according as the LORD thy God hath blessed thee:**
>
> **Deuteronomy 16:10**

7. Conventions bring about a feeling of joy, victory and celebration. These are important feelings that inspire church growth.

> **And thou shalt rejoice before the LORD thy God, thou, and thy son, and thy daughter, and thy manservant, and thy maidservant, and the Levite that is within thy gates, and the stranger, and the fatherless, and the widow, that are among you, in the place which the LORD thy God hath chosen to place his name there.**
>
> **Deuteronomy 16: 11**

Chapter

52

Why Relationships and Friendships Lead to Church Growth

CHAPTER SUMMARY

Churches that do not grow are often isolated. Ministers of the Gospel who have good relationships with other ministers often become successful and take on the characteristics of their friends. It is important to have good friends in the ministry. You become like your friends. If your friends have large and successful churches you are likely to have a large and successful church too.

52.1 **You must have friendships, associations, relationships, affiliations and connections with other ministers of God.**

52.2 **You must have friends and relationships in the ministry because these relationships will give you KNOWLEDGE you do not have.**

52.3 **You must have friendships and relationships because they stir you up for greater works in the Lord.**

52.4 **You must have friends who will tell you the truth in love.**

52.5 **You must have associations in the ministry. Many blessings come by being associated with other blessed people.**

52.6 **You must have friendships, associations, relationships, affiliations and connections with other ministers of God to avoid isolation.**

> **Iron sharpeneth iron; so a man sharpeneth the countenance of his friend.**
>
> **Proverbs 27:17**

Silently living in isolation will not help anybody. It will definitely not help someone who wants his church to grow. Humble yourself and do what it takes to have relationships with those who matter.

Years ago, I zeroed in on Dr. Yonggi Cho and decided to learn from him and get close to him. Perhaps, that was one of the most important decisions of my life as a pastor. I had decided to become close to the pastor of the largest church in the world. That association has affected me in more ways than I can think.

Golf and Lunch

One day, after playing golf and fellowshipping privately with Dr Cho, I sat down to have lunch with him and some other ministers.

An elderly Korean gentleman walked up to me and said, "You have done very well. I remember you. I remember when you first came to meet with Dr Cho in Yverdon, Switzerland. You were unable to meet him, even though you wanted to."

That was almost twenty years ago.

Then he continued, "You have persisted. Do you remember me? I spoke to you then."

I smiled back at him, "I remember you clearly. I remember it like yesterday. I had just started my church and I did not even have a church building."

Then he said again, "You have really persisted."

You see, it had been a long and dogged journey of coming close to a great person. I had come from the outside, from nowhere. And here I was, sitting next to the pastor of the largest church in the world having lunch.

After years of associating I had become a golfer and also received the great spiritual blessing of becoming the pastor of a large church.

1. You must have friendships, associations, relationships, affiliations and connections with other ministers of God.

Every minister and every relationship is a joint that supplies something to your life and ministry. What they supply to you will cause growth to happen in your ministry. Relationships with key ministers of God have greatly contributed to the growth of my ministry.

Relationships cause growth!

Interactions cause growth!

Friendships cause growth!

That is what the Bible says.

New dimensions and new chapters have opened up in my ministry as I have opened up to different people. Read it for yourself:

> **... the whole body, being fitted and held together by that which EVERY JOINT SUPPLIES, according to the proper working of each individual part, CAUSES THE GROWTH of the body for the building up of itself in love".**
>
> **Ephesians 4:15-16 (NASB)**

2. You must have friends and relationships in the ministry because these relationships will give you KNOWLEDGE you do not have.

You are always excluded from certain things because of knowledge you do not have. In the ministry, it is necessary to relate with other ministers who may not be in your church or denomination. God wants to expose you to other ministry gifts.

> **...being darkened in their understanding, EXCLUDED FROM THE LIFE OF GOD, BECAUSE OF THE IGNORANCE that is in them, because of the hardness of their heart;**
>
> **Ephesians 4:18 (NASB)**

3. You must have friendships and relationships because they stir you up for greater works in the Lord.

When you stay in your little world you have no idea of what God is doing elsewhere. You have no idea that there can be something greater and better than what you are doing. Every time I have visited someone's church I have been blessed and provoked to do something greater and better in my church.

> **And let us consider one another to PROVOKE UNTO love and to GOOD WORKS:**
>
> **Hebrews 10:24**

4. You must have friends who will tell you the truth in love.

When the truth is spoken to you in love, it causes you to grow up. Is it not growth you are seeking? Is that not why you are reading this book? Hearing the truth causes you to grow up. That is what the Bible says.

Relationships with external ministers can expose you to the truth that you need to hear. You may not hear that truth in your own world because there may be no one with enough authority or exposure to tell you what you need to hear.

> **But speaking the truth in love, MAY GROW UP into him in all things, which is the head, even Christ:**
>
> **Ephesians 4:15**

5. You must have associations in the ministry. Many blessings come by being associated with other blessed people.

My association with great men of God has been a tremendous source of blessing to me.

One day, I was invited to a foreign country to preach. I wondered why the pastor had invited me. When I asked him why he had invited me, he said, "I saw you on a video with David Yonggi Cho. It seemed you were interpreting or doing something on the stage."

He said to me, "I invited you because anyone who is associated with David Yongi Cho must be a good person."

"Wow", I said to myself, "this is the clearest example of how you can be blessed just by being associated with someone else."

Laban, the non-believer, knew this principle very well. He told Jacob, God blessed me because you were in my camp. He recognized how, where and why blessings were coming to him.

> **And Laban said unto him, I pray thee, if I have found favour in thine eyes, tarry: for I have learned by experience that the Lord hath BLESSED ME FOR THY SAKE.**
>
> **Genesis 30:27**

6. You must have friendships, associations, relationships, affiliations and connections with other ministers of God to avoid isolation.

> **And the eye cannot say unto the hand, I have no need of thee…**
>
> **1 Corinthians 12:21**

Often, isolation occurs because one has been hurt in the early stages of ministry. Many ministers run into a corner to escape being despised.

Isolation can work together for your good.

Isolation helps you to concentrate on your ministry.

Isolation helps you avoid being despised, disregarded and discouraged all the time by other so-called successful ministers.

Isolation helps you to avoid the distractions of inter-church politics.

Isolation helps you to avoid the wholesale adoption of other ministers' mistakes.

Isolation helps you to develop your unique identity and calling.

Isolation helps you to avoid being submerged under the banners of other domineering pastors who are trying to assume lordship over all churches in the city.

Isolation will force you to learn biblical rather than human standards for all aspects of life and ministry.

But isolation can also work against you in the ministry because you will need the input, ideas and gifts of other ministers.

You may be able to learn a great deal from other successful pastors in your city. I have learnt a lot from those directly ahead of me in my city. I have watched and learnt from their mistakes and successes. I do things in my church that I have learnt from other ministers.

Chapter

53

How to Develop Important Ministerial Relationships

CHAPTER SUMMARY

The key to developing ministerial relationships with other pastors is to invite them in an honourable way, treat them well and give them a memorable time in your company. This is the seed that can develop into lifelong relationships.

■ How to Develop Relationships through Invitations

53.1 Treat your visiting minister as a very important person.

53.2 Show honour to your friend by giving him an honourable invitation.

53.3 The visiting minister should be welcomed at his point of entry.

53.4 Welcome your guest when he arrives in the church. Talk to him.

53.5 Invite someone that you genuinely admire and respect.

53.6 Refer to your invited guest by the official designation he has accorded himself.

53.7 Find out the full name of your guest and pronounce it properly.

53.8 Identify and introduce the visiting minister's delegation.

53.9 Know the name of the invited minister's church or ministry.

53.10 Give your visiting minister enough time to minister.

53.11 Introduce your guest minister with excitement. Let the church welcome the visitor with great respect and expectation in their hearts.

53.12 Outline and explain specifically to your guest minister any function or expectation you may have of him.

53.13 After preaching and ministering, the visiting minister should be refreshed briefly and then politely escorted away.

53.14 Ensure that your visiting minister will have good food that he can eat during his stay with you.

53.15 The conditions of your guest minister's visit should be clearly defined prior to his arrival and acceptance to minister.

■ Seven Steps to a Good Honorarium

53. 16 A good honorarium should cover all the expenses of the visiting minister.

53. 17 A visiting minister's rank also determines what a good honorarium is.

53.18 A good honorarium is calculated by the number of days a person ministers.

53.19 A good honorarium is also determined by the impact of the visiting minister's ministry.

53.20 Honorariums should not be given to the visiting minister in full public view.

53.21 The visiting minister may sign a voucher or receipt for the honorarium (for accounting purposes).

53.22 The honorarium should be prepared with an accompanying letter before the meeting.

Most of the important relationships I have in the ministry have developed after I invited them to visit my church. Most of these friendships have grown over the years and become vital relationships for my ministry.

It starts with the invitation to the pulpit and develops into other areas although not all invitations have led to relationships.

Do not be surprised if some visiting ministers shun your friendship. Some people are not very relational and others may not be interested in a relationship with you.

Sometimes, people do not relate with you because they are intimidated by you. They may be afraid of you and will show it by rejecting you.

■ How to Develop Relationships through Invitations

1. Treat your visiting minister as a very important person.

Everyone loves to be pampered and treated specially. The wrong handling of a visiting minister often leads to offences and the destruction of already fragile acquaintances. Give your guest the best possible place to stay. Don't put him in a room with your children. Don't make him share a room with your children. You may not be able to afford the nicest hotel, but you must do what you can afford. Ministers tend to ask where other visiting preachers were hosted.

The Four-Room Hotel

One day, I was invited to a country to preach. I had travelled very far and spent many hours getting there.

When we arrived, we were taken to the dirtiest part of the city. The roads were literally strewn with rubbish. You could not take two steps without stepping into something. There was a big house right on the corner of this filthy area.

When we entered the house I asked, "Where is this?"

I was told that it was a hotel. I was surprised that they were calling it a hotel because it had only four rooms which opened into a common space. Also a family lived upstairs, above the four rooms. Apparently, the pastor saved a lot of money by using this building because his family owned it.

In the morning, a man would come up with a big plate of bread rolls in one hand and margarine in the other hand.

I asked, "What is this?"

He said, "This is for your breakfast."

I have never stayed in a dirtier place than that building. I was afraid to have my bath because I was afraid of the electric wires that were sticking out into the shower. I was afraid of turning in the bed because I did not want to touch more of the bed sheet with my body.

I settled into this four-room hotel and stayed there for a whole week.

I was happy to be there because I thought they were very poor and this was what they could afford.

Later in the week, I got to find out that this same ministry had hosted another man of God. "Wow", I thought to myself, "Did this man of God stay in this hotel?" I did some investigations and found out that he had actually been brought to this same four-room hotel.

As soon as he entered our four-room hotel he struck the table and said, "I am not staying here. Take me to the best hotel in this city!"

The host pastor scrambled to get the man of God a proper hotel.

"Are there other hotels in this town?" I asked.

"O yes, there are other nice places."

Later that week we passed by the hotel where this other man of God had been taken.

You see, people find out how you treated others. They compare. Ministers are very sensitive, always looking out to see if they are despised or respected.

2. Show honour to your friend by giving him an honourable invitation.

Do not invite someone you want to honour to a minor function. Invite the person to an important service that will be well attended. Invite people personally if you can and follow it up with a letter. You must be present at the service for which you invited the person. Do not invite a minister if you know you will be absent (especially when building a new relationship).

The Man in Shorts

One day, I was invited by a man of God to minister in his church. I arrived in the city after a very long journey and it was already time to preach. My host, however, was at home wearing sports shorts and playing table tennis.

He asked that we be taken to the church where I was to speak. I found out that it was a minor programme that my host himself would not bother to attend.

I did not know the young man who introduced me to preach. He did not know me either and I did not know what role he played in the church.

As I preached, I wondered why I had come all this way to a programme that my host would not even attend himself.

3. The visiting minister should be welcomed at his point of entry.

If the external minister is coming from another location, as much as possible a minister of his rank must receive him at the airport, station, etc! For example, if he is a head pastor, then the senior minister of the inviting church must meet him and see him off. In some cases it is not possible for the senior pastor to meet arriving guests at the airport or station. So an appropriate person must do that on his behalf.

4. Welcome your guest when he arrives in the church. Talk to him.

Sit next to him and relate with him! Make friends with your guest and have good fellowship with him. It could be the beginning of a lifelong relationship. Don't spend all the time making excuses about the size of your church and the poor attendance of the convention. Every genuine pastor will appreciate the effort you are making to build the church.

5. Invite someone that you genuinely admire and respect.

Remember that secret criticism kills relationships. Do not criticize or ridicule your guest ministers. Why do you invite someone to your church only to criticize him behind his back? Do not speak evil of any minister or church, especially from the pulpit or in public. Do not entertain negative comments about guest ministers and their preaching whilst they are with you and when they are gone. I have had ministers of the Gospel who invited me and allowed their associates to criticize me after I left. If you have anything to say about a minister, say something positive.

... speak evil of no man...

Titus 3:2

Remember that the way you speak will set the stage for others to criticize you in the future.

The Windowless Room

You must show your guests that you respect them. Once I was invited to minister in a large church. I enjoyed ministering there but I had one problem. I was put in a guest house with a windowless room. The room I was living in didn't have "windows". There were windows but they were permanently closed and permanently covered with curtains. There was also no functioning air conditioner in the room.

This meant that this room was virtually windowless and airless. In the evenings, after ministering, I would go out and sit on the field to breathe in some fresh air. When I was sure that I had enough oxygen for the night, I would retire to my windowless room.

On one of the days, I found out that a great American preacher had also been invited to this church. So I asked, "Where did this American preacher stay when he came to minister here? Did he stay in this same windowless guest house?"

As I expected, the American minister was not put in my windowless room. He had been taken to a grand hotel and treated royally. Naturally, I felt that these people did not appreciate the gift of God and did not care for me as much as they did for their American guest.

Indeed, you must be careful how you treat ministers because they are always asking questions to find out if they are really respected, appreciated or even wanted.

6. Refer to your invited guest by the official designation he has accorded himself.

People have reasons for calling themselves Bishops, Reverends or Apostles. Ministers are sensitive about their titles. If his title is General Overseer, do not refer to him as the General Superintendent. If he refers to himself as an Apostle, do not call him a Pastor.

7. Find out the full name of your guest and pronounce it properly.

You must know the full name of your invited guest. There is nothing more disrespectful than a person who cannot bother to pronounce your name. Many African Americans had their names changed because their white slave masters could not bother to pronounce their African names. Do not refer to him as Reverend Ag when his name is Reverend Agegebodavari.

8. Identify and introduce the visiting minister's delegation.

It is important to acknowledge them as well. Do not disregard people's associates. You may be disregarding a future Elisha. The visiting minister's wife should also be welcomed nicely. She is an important person.

9. Know the name of the invited minister's church or ministry.

Not remembering the correct name of somebody's church makes you look arrogant. Don't give the impression that you are dealing with an unimportant church with an unfortunately laborious name. Don't give the impression that you cannot be bothered to remember the name of his ministry. For instance, do not say he is the Pastor of The Light Church when he is the Pastor of Lighthouse Chapel International. There is a big difference between the two!

10. Give your visiting minister enough time to minister.

For example, do not give a guest minister 10 minutes to minister, when he has travelled long distances to be with you.

The Hand of God

One day I travelled to a far away land to minister. I had been invited by this man of God to be a speaker at a convention. The service was to close at about 8.00pm and I was supposed to start preaching at about seven o'clock.

To my surprise, instead of my host introducing me and handing over the microphone to me he began a teaching on "the hand of God". Indeed, it was a night of revelation as he taught on what the hand of God was. He gave several examples of the hand of God at work in the Old Testament. Then he gave examples of the hand of God in the New Testament. Then he explained how the hand of God could change your life.

Then he taught on where the hand of God can be found today!I sat for almost an hour as I listened to this wonderful message. But I couldn't help wondering why I had come all the way from Ghana. This man knew exactly what he wanted to minister to his people and to say the least, I felt silly sitting there. Then, at the end of his message, I thought he would hand over to me so that I would preach the second message of the day. But it was not yet my turn because he announced that the hand of God had begun to move right there in the congregation.

Suddenly, the hand of God began to move in the congregation and people began to scream and fall down under the power. He ministered powerfully to the people for another twenty minutes.

By the time he finished, there was hardly anyone standing in the congregation. It was indeed a night of power and of the hand of God. Finally, when it was past closing time, he announced that I had come from Ghana to also minister (there were people strewn all over the front of the church). What was I expected to do now?

I was indeed surprised that I was being called to speak after the service had clearly ended with the power of God evident and people lying all over the front. Everyone in my entourage was bewildered. I have never forgotten this strange behaviour of my host. Obviously he did not really want me to come.

11. Introduce your guest minister with excitement. Let the church welcome the visitor with great respect and expectation in their hearts.

12. Outline and explain specifically to your guest minister any function or expectation you may have of him.

For example, if you want him to raise funds, make altar calls, ordain pastors, etc., discuss this with him in detail before he arrives. Do not surprise your guest with unusual ceremonies with which he may not be comfortable. Don't put him on the spot and make him feel silly or inadequate.

13. After preaching and ministering, the visiting minister should be refreshed briefly and then politely escorted away.

14. Ensure that your visiting minister will have good food that he can eat during his stay with you.

Flamingo Stew

One day, I was invited to minister in a large church. We were put in a hotel which had very little ventilation. When it was supper time, the hotel was unable to provide food so the host sent some people to bring food to us.

As we sat around the dinner table, we were served with "chicken". But I was not sure whether it was a chicken because the legs of the chicken were so long and I had never seen such a long chicken leg before. Honestly, I was not sure which bird I had been given. Perhaps it was a flamingo, perhaps it was an eagle, perhaps it was just a local bird. This was not the first time I had been given a local bird to eat. On another ministry trip I had been given a bird which had a completely different colour from what I was used to. Yet on another occasion I was served with a whole bird so small that it could fit into my palm.

Again and again people choose to give you the most easily caught bird in the area. Everybody calls the birds in their area "chicken". But experience will teach you that not all birds are chickens. Try to give your guests food that they can eat and "chicken" that they will enjoy.

15. The conditions of your guest minister's visit should be clearly defined prior to his arrival and acceptance to minister.

Even so hath the Lord ordained that they which preach the gospel should live of the gospel.

1 Corinthians 9:14

The honorarium and all expenses can be discussed in many cases before the minister accepts the invitation. This includes financial, transportation, and accommodation arrangements. The minister must be given the option to decide whether he will come in spite of the conditions that you are offering him. This is especially important if the minister is travelling a long distance. You may wrongly assume that the visiting minister will only incur the cost of his plane ticket.

But you may not know that he had to, for example, travel in a rented car 300km to the airport and sleep in a hotel overnight in order to be able to catch the plane in the morning. All of these are hidden expenses, which must be discussed. It is very sad for a minister to travel several miles, minister from his heart, only to return impoverished and in debt.

The Phone Call Invitation

One day, I received a phone call from a man of God inviting me to his church. He said he would be so honoured if I would come to minister in his church.

Then he asked, "Are there any conditions for your coming?"

I answered, "If you can pay for my ticket and where I would stay that should be fine." He was happy and promised to do that. I travelled on several different flights and eventually landed in this country.

The first surprise was that we were taken to a hotel different from where he had told us we would be lodging. I quickly checked my secretary's notes and asked why we were being taken to a very different place. They mumbled an apology and took us to where they had earlier promised. I enjoyed my visit there and ministered powerfully.

Finally, when I was leaving, I was expecting to receive the money for my ticket. No such luck! He did not pay for my ticket! He did not give me any honorarium! What had happened? I had undertaken this journey entirely at my own expense, without planning to. If you do this to visiting ministers, you will soon have a bad reputation and no one will come to you any more.

Seven Steps to a Good Honorarium

And as ye would that men should do to you, do ye also to them likewise.

Luke 6:31

1. A good honorarium should cover all the expenses of the visiting minister.

   The honorarium must also bless and encourage the minister financially. A good honorarium must be judged by what you would like to receive if you were the guest.

2. A visiting minister's rank also determines what a good honorarium is.

   If the person is a very senior minister, the honorarium must be correspondingly substantial.

3. A good honorarium is calculated by the number of days a person ministers.

4. A good honorarium is also determined by the impact of the visiting minister's ministry.

5. Honorariums should not be given to the visiting minister in full public view. Do not let the visiting minister feel uncomfortable as he receives your envelope in the full view of everyone. Your guest should be given his honorarium in private and by the appropriate person.

6. The visiting minister may sign a voucher or receipt for the honorarium (for accounting purposes).

7. The honorarium should be prepared with an accompanying letter before the meeting.

   This is to avoid very long delays in paying the honorarium. Some churches even forget to pay any honorarium at all. It is often more difficult to pay the honorarium long after the minister has left than it is to pay immediately after the programme.

Chapter

54

How Church Growth Is Affected by Gethsemane

CHAPTER SUMMARY

- **The Principles of Gethsemane**

54.1 **Gethsemane teaches us that the turning points for your life and ministry are determined in the private and personal times you have with the Lord.**

54.2 **Gethsemane shows us the greatest example of waiting on the Lord.**

54.3 **Gethsemane teaches us that you must have a place you go to often to wait on the Lord.**

54.4 **Gethsemane teaches us the importance of going away from your usual environment and to places where you benefit from nature.**

54.5 **Gethsemane teaches us the importance of fellowshipping with your most senior friends and associates.**

54.6 **Gethsemane teaches us the importance of being alone with God.**

54.7 **Gethsemane teaches us the importance of praying, "Thy will be done" for several hours.**

And He came out and proceeded as was HIS CUSTOM to the Mount of Olives; and the DISCIPLES ALSO FOLLOWED Him.

And when He arrived at the place, He said to them, "Pray that you may not enter into temptation."

And HE WITHDREW from them about a stone's throw, and He knelt down and began to pray,

saying, "Father, if Thou art willing, remove this cup from Me; YET NOT MY WILL, BUT THINE BE DONE."

Now an angel from heaven appeared to Him, STRENGTHENING HIM.

And being in agony He was praying very fervently; and His sweat became like drops of blood, falling down upon the ground.

And when He rose from prayer, He came to the disciples and found them sleeping from sorrow,

and said to them, "Why are you sleeping? Rise and pray that you may not enter into temptation."

Luke 22:39-46 (NASB)

■ The Principles of Gethsemane

1. Gethsemane teaches us that the turning points for your life and ministry are determined in the private and personal times you have with the Lord.

The turning point for Jesus' ministry came in the Garden of Gethsemane. Gethsemane was the place where Jesus received strength to accomplish the will of God. The turning point for your church will come when you wait on the Lord. The turning point that will give you church growth will take place in your Garden of Gethsemane.

2. Gethsemane shows us the greatest example of waiting on the Lord.

There is no man that is used of the Lord who has not interacted with the Lord deeply and personally. Moses encountered the Lord by the burning bush. It was that personal private burning bush meeting that propelled him into his worldwide ministry. It will be your personal private burning bush experience that will propel you into the church growth you desire. Jacob's meeting with the Lord also gave birth to his ministry of producing God's nation Israel.

3. Gethsemane teaches us that you must have a place you go to often to wait on the Lord.

It must be part of your life's routine to visit Gethsemane regularly. According to the Scripture it was His custom to visit that garden in the Mount of Olives.

> **And He came out and proceeded as was HIS CUSTOM to the Mount of Olives; and the disciples also followed Him.**
>
> **Luke 22:39, NASB**

4. Gethsemane teaches us the importance of going away from your usual environment and to places where you benefit from nature.

Nature tends to relax you and God's voice will reach you better when your mind and heart are relaxed. Nature itself has many messages contained within it.

5. Gethsemane teaches us the importance of fellowshipping with your most senior friends and associates.

Gethsemane is a place where you can have important life-changing discussions with the most important people in your ministry.

6. Gethsemane teaches us the importance of being alone with God.

Gethsemane is a place where you can receive life-changing revelations from the Lord. The disciples received life-changing teachings about prayer. Without revelation you will not be different from the people you lead.

7. Gethsemane teaches us the importance of praying, "Thy will be done" for several hours.

Some people do not believe in repeating prayers. But if we are to follow the example of Jesus, we will spend hours praying. We will pray, "Thy will be done" for hours and hours on end.

Chapter

55

The Art of Waiting on God

CHAPTER SUMMARY

Gethsemane teaches us that the longer we stay in the presence of God the more we get soaked and affected by Him.

55.1 Develop the art of waiting on God all alone.

55.2 Develop the art of waiting on God with a group of fellow ministers.

55.3 Develop the art of waiting on God with the congregation.

55.4 Develop the art of waiting on God by timing yourself.

55.5 Develop the art of waiting on God in a church atmosphere.

55.6 Develop the art of waiting on God by praying in tongues whilst you read the Bible and other ministry books.

55.7 Develop the art of waiting on God by praying with targets.

55.8 Develop the art of waiting on God by praying with absolute fasting.

55.9 Develop the art of waiting on God by praying and fasting with "no pleasant bread" (instead of not praying and not eating at all).

> **Who hath woe? Who hath sorrow? Who hath contentions? Who hath babbling? Who hath wounds without cause? Who hath redness of eyes? THEY THAT TARRY LONG at the wine ...**
>
> **Proverbs 23:29-30**

Wine changes those who tarry long at it. We are also affected as we stay longer and longer in His presence. The longer you tarry at the wine, the more you experience stronger effects of the wine. When you tarry long at the wine, you begin to babble uncontrollably and act strangely.

As you stay longer at the wine, your eyes turn red and you start to see things differently. Just as people learn to stay longer and longer at the wine bar, you must learn to stay longer in His presence. The longer you stay in His presence, the more you will experience the effect of God's presence.

1. Develop the art of waiting on God all alone.

> **And it came to pass in those days, that HE WENT OUT INTO A MOUNTAIN to pray, and continued all night in prayer to God.**
>
> **Luke 6:12**

Jesus went into the mountain to pray. After this prayer time he chose his disciples. There are times you must pray with others but there are times you must wait on the Lord alone. If you cannot spend long times praying on your own there is something wrong with you.

Remember that a minister is an ambassador of the Lord. You are a representative of Jesus Christ who is supposed to tell others about God. If you have never spent time with Him, what will you know and what will you share? The Apostle John described his ministry as sharing and preaching what he had seen, known, handled and touched. "That which was from the beginning, which we have heard, which we have seen with our eyes, which we have looked upon, and our hands have handled, of the Word of life; ... That which we have seen and heard declare we unto you, that ye also may have fellowship with us: and truly our fellowship is with the Father, and with his Son Jesus Christ." (1 John 1:1-3).

2. Develop the art of waiting on God with a group of fellow ministers.

> **Let the priests, the ministers of the LORD, weep between the porch and the altar ...**
>
> **Joel 2:17**

Jesus is always present in a special way when we come together to wait on Him. The New Testament shows us how prophets and teachers ministered to the Lord and fasted. The Lord will speak when His ministers come together to wait on Him.

> **"Now there were in the church that was at Antioch certain prophets and teachers; as Barnabas, and Simeon that was called Niger, and Lucius of Cyrene, and Manaen, which had been brought up with Herod the tetrarch, and Saul. As they ministered to the Lord, and fasted, the Holy Ghost said, Separate me Barnabas and Saul for the work whereunto I have called them"**
>
> **(Acts 13:1-2).**

3. Develop the art of waiting on God with the congregation.

> **Blow the trumpet in Zion, sanctify a fast, call a solemn assembly:**
>
> **Gather the people, sanctify the congregation, assemble the elders, gather the children, and those that suck the breasts: let the bridegroom go forth of his chamber, and the bride out of her closet.**
>
> **Joel 2:15-16**

All through the Bible, the prophets called the people to come together to wait for His deliverance. This is an important pattern we must follow. If you want church growth you must develop the practice of calling the church together for fasting and long hours of prayer.

4. Develop the art of waiting on God by timing yourself.

> **... saith unto Peter, What, could ye not watch with me one hour?"**
>
> **Matthew 26:40**

Note the time at the start of your prayer session. Decide how long you are going to pray before you start. When you do that, you will be compelled to spend a decent period of time in prayer. Jesus was not impressed when Peter could not pray for one hour. He is the same yesterday, today and forever. He is equally unimpressed that you cannot pray for one hour.

If you do not note the time, you will think that you prayed longer than you actually did. You will tell yourself, "Oh, I must have prayed for two hours" when you only prayed for ten minutes.

Unless you are experienced in prayer, you will make wrong judgments about the length of time you have prayed. Nowadays, I can tell when I have prayed for an hour. Initially, I would pray for ten minutes and think it was an hour. This is why you need a clock when you are going to wait on the Lord.

5. Develop the art of waiting on God in a church atmosphere.

> **...Now bring me a minstrel. And it came to pass, when the minstrel played, that THE HAND OF THE LORD CAME upon him.**
>
> **2 Kings 3:15**

A church atmosphere is created by the sound of preaching and worship music. Playing DVDs of church services also create a church atmosphere. Pray with some kind of preaching or music in the background. *The speed of preaching/music is a hundred times faster than the speed of silence.* This means that time runs a hundred times faster when there is some kind of background preaching or music.

Have you been there when people were asked to observe a minute's silence? Have you noticed how long the period of silence was? Did you know that they never really spend a whole minute of silence? A minute of silence is so long and so uncomfortable that people rarely spend a whole minute in silence.

This is because of the principle I just shared with you: *the speed of preaching/music is a hundred times faster than the speed of silence.*

When you pray with the sound of preaching or music in the background, time runs much faster! Before you know it, you would have spent several hours in prayer with the Lord!

The sound of the preaching of the Word of God creates the best atmosphere for spiritual things. Dear friend, we are constantly bombarded with the godless atmosphere of secular television and radio. That kind of atmosphere actually prevents prayer.

You need something that will keep you in a prayerful mood for at least one hour. Godly music creates a beautiful worship environment. I always play music or preaching in the background when I am praying.

Dear friend, the very atmosphere of our world is charged with demonic entities. The prince of the power of the air pollutes the very air we breathe. It is difficult to pray in such an environment. This is the reason why many Christians do not pray for long hours. They are trying to pray in a hard and difficult atmosphere.

But there is good news: You can have your own little church service wherever you are! The Spirit of the Lord can move over you in your car. Invest in whatever it takes to create the right prayer atmosphere. The Spirit of the Lord will come upon you as you stay in the environment of anointed minstrels and preachers.

6. Develop the art of waiting on God by praying in tongues whilst you read the Bible and other ministry books.

> **For if I pray in an unknown tongue, my spirit prayeth, but my understanding is unfruitful.**
>
> **1 Corinthians 14:14**

Because I pray in tongues for long periods, my mind is unfruitful and free for reading. I constantly read whilst I spend hours in prayer. My spirit prays to the Lord while my mind concentrates on the Bible that I am reading. This helps me to pray for even longer hours.

As you pray in tongues for hours, your spirit man will be edified and charged up.

7. Develop the art of waiting on God by praying with targets.

> **And it came to pass in those days, that he went out into a mountain to pray, and continued ALL NIGHT IN PRAYER to God.**
>
> **Luke 6:12**

Set yourself targets for praying. You can set yourself a target of prayer by giving yourself a number of hours to pray. For instance, you can decide to pray for ten hours, twenty hours, forty hours or fifty hours. With a target of fifty hours, you are likely to need about six days to pray. Sometimes, setting the target in terms of hours is better than setting the number of days you want to wait on the Lord.

I have always felt that unless I spent a long time in prayer, I would not accomplish much. All the prayers I learnt from Jesus were prayers of many hours.

Jesus spent forty days in the wilderness.

Jesus prayed all night in the mountain before He chose His disciples.

Jesus prayed for a great while before day.

Jesus prayed for three hours in the Garden of Gethsemane. These examples must be a guide for your prayer life. They will make you spend many hours of your life in prayer.

If you believe in these examples from the life and ministry of Jesus you will never be satisfied with five and ten minute prayers. You will desire to pray for lengthy periods of time.

8. Develop the art of waiting on God by praying with absolute fasting.

Absolute fasting is when you do not eat anything at all. Absolute fasting is an important exercise that makes you more spiritual and causes you to focus on God. For those who eat a lot and spend a lot of time eating, fasting provides a necessary break from a strong carnal distraction.

9. Develop the art of waiting on God by praying and fasting with "no pleasant bread" (instead of not praying and not eating at all).

> **In those days I Daniel was mourning THREE FULL WEEKS. I ate NO PLEASANT BREAD, neither came flesh nor wine in my mouth, neither did I anoint myself at all, till three whole weeks were fulfilled.**
>
> **Daniel 10:2-3**

Daniel fasted for twenty-one days. Daniel's fast involved eating, but eating what he described as "no pleasant bread". In other words, he stayed away from what he would really have loved to eat.

Staying away from your usual meals and your usual delights is a form of fasting. It is called "no pleasant bread" fasting. It is better to have prayer and eat a bit than to do absolute fasting without praying.

Many people do absolute fasting without praying. Many times, absolute fasting actually prevents people from praying. At the end of their fasting time, many Christians have hardly spoken to the Lord. They use all their energy to survive the absolute fast and make it to 6.00pm when they can eat.

Why do I say it is better to pray and eat than to fast absolutely and not pray? Because all the promises Jesus gave to us had to do with prayer and not fasting. Jesus Christ promised to answer prayers. Jesus never promised to answer fasting. Understand what I am saying! Fasting is important for every Christian. Don't use this as a reason not to fast. Look at the Word of God. Are the promises of reward for our prayers or for our fastings?

Look at just seven of the promises Jesus gave to people who would pray. These promises are the words of Jesus Christ Himself. Did He promise to answer fasting or did He promise to answer prayers? Indeed, if I have to choose between fasting and praying I would choose to pray because Jesus has promised to answer prayers!

1. And whatsoever ye shall ask in my name, that will I do, that the Father may be glorified in the Son. If ye shall ask any thing in my name, I will do it.

   John 14:13-14

2. Ye have not chosen me, but I have chosen you, and ordained you, that ye should go and bring forth fruit, and that your fruit should remain: that whatsoever ye shall ask of the Father in my name, he may give it you.

   John 15:16

3. If ye abide in me, and my words abide in you, ye shall ask what ye will, and it shall be done unto you.

John 15:7

4. And in that day ye shall ask me nothing. Verily, verily, I say unto you, Whatsoever ye shall ask the Father in my name, he will give it you. Hitherto have ye asked nothing in my name: ask, and ye shall receive, that "your joy may be full.

John 16:23-24

5. Therefore I say unto you, What things soever ye desire, when ye pray, believe that ye receive them, and ye shall have them.

Mark 11:24

6. And I say unto you, Ask, and it shall be given you; seek, and ye shall find; knock, and it shall be opened unto you. For every one that asketh receiveth; and he that seeketh findeth; and to him that knocketh it shall be opened.

Luke 11:9-10

7. But thou, when thou prayest, enter into thy closet, and when thou hast shut thy door, pray to thy Father which is in secret; and thy Father which seeth in secret shall reward thee openly.

Matthew 6:6

Chapter

56

Church Growth through a United Group of Branch Churches U.G.B.C.

CHAPTER SUMMARY

Traditionally, church growth is achieved through the swelling up of a single church until it seats thousands and thousands of people. However, there is another way to achieve church growth in our modern and complex world.

- **Advantages of Having a United Group of Branch Churches (UGBC)**

56.1 History has proved that united groups of branch churches are very often the most stable and established congregations everywhere.

56.2 Belonging to a network of churches sometimes eliminates the instability that characterizes young independent churches.

56.3 In a network of branch churches, there are tried and tested principles that are passed on to sister churches.

56.4 In a united group of churches the good name serves as publicity and attracts people to the church.

56.5 In a network of churches, trained members benefit from an established and respected system of pastoral training.

56.6 Members of a network of churches benefit from each other financially..

56.7 Church members readily flow between churches belonging to a united group of branch churches.

56.8 Churches within a network of churches easily benefit from anointed senior ministers of that network.

56.9 Pastors within the network of churches can receive fatherly counsel and encouragement from seniors.

56.10 Churches within a network operate under a particular spiritual covering.

■ Principles for Operating a United Group of Branch Churches (UGBC)

56.11 It is important to distinguish between independent mission branch churches (IMBC) and a united group of branch churches (UGBC) before you start branching out.

56.12 Let the pastors and the congregations understand that it is the same church but in different locations. This means that congregation members are free to move from one location to another.

56.13 Set up an administration which monitors the attendance and finances of every member of the group of churches.

56.14 Maintain your leadership over the United Group of Branch Churches (UGBC).

56.15 Let the church function as one large body (UGBC).

56.16 Let the church function as one large body in different locations with shared leadership.

56.17 Do not allow the branch pastors or branch churches to develop individualized visions.

56.18 Study loyalty and teach extensively on loyalty.

56.19 Be loyal to the branch pastors and churches so that they do not have any good reason or basis to separate themselves from you.

56.20 Encourage the same teachings and books to be taught in the whole group of churches.

56.21 Let the entire group of churches remain connected through the internet.

56.22 Let the entire group of churches stay connected by having the same paraphernalia in every church; using the same offering baskets, banners, signboards.

Laws for Managing a United Group of Branch Churches (UGBC)

56.23 Know

56.24 Communicate

56.25 Influence

56.26 Encourage

56.27 Teach

A United Group of Branch Churches UGBC

Through a network of several churches in different locations, you can achieve the same numbers as you would with a single huge church. You can achieve church growth by setting up a united group of branch churches (UGBC) that are related and considered as one big family. This united group of churches would be the same church but in different locations. This group of branch churches will function as one unit with one team of leaders and pastors managing the church in different locations.

This group of churches will also function as one financial unit with incomes from the different locations. The financial capabilities of this united group of branch churches will be far greater than any single church.

Independent Mission Branch Churches (IMBC)

This united group of churches is in sharp contrast to independent missions that are sent out from the church. Independent branch churches are not the same as "one church in different locations". They are "different" churches in different locations.

These independent mission branch churches have independent leaders and independent financial systems.

They do not depend on each other for anything.

Independent mission churches may remit a percentage of its income to the headquarters.

The pastors of these churches have their own visions and dreams of what they want to do.

The pastors of these independent mission churches do not relate closely to the parent church.

Advantages of Having a United Group of Branch Churches (UGBC)

1. History has proved that united groups of branch churches are very often the most stable and established congregations everywhere. These networks of churches are sometimes called denominations. There are several well-known networks of churches in the world today.

   A united group of churches may be the way God wants to grow your church.

2. Belonging to a network of churches sometimes eliminates the instability that characterizes young independent churches. The institutional stagnation in a denomination may be a lesser evil compared to the advantages that come from belonging to a group of related churches.

3. In a network of branch churches, there are tried and tested principles that are passed on to sister churches.

4. In a united group of churches the good name serves as publicity and attracts people to the church. This name becomes like a franchise and serves as a powerful asset. The good name of a network of churches also has spiritual significance.

5. In a network of churches, trained members benefit from an established and respected system of pastoral training.

6. Members of a network of churches benefit from each other financially. You are not likely to get financial support from outside your network. Through a system of brotherly interdependence, churches are able to accomplish a lot.

7. Church members readily flow between churches belonging to a united group of branch churches. The network of churches is able to keep members within the fold. This enhances church growth.

8. Churches within a network of churches easily benefit from anointed senior ministers of that network.

9. Pastors within the network of churches can receive fatherly counsel and encouragement from seniors. Pastors of independent churches are usually suspicious and wary of external ministers who parade as fathers. There is little trust because independent churches often compete with one another rather than support each other.

10. Churches within a network operate under a particular spiritual covering. The same anointing runs through the entire network because it is really one church.

Principles for Operating a United Group of Branch Churches (UGBC)

1. It is important to distinguish between independent mission branch churches (IMBC) and a united group of branch churches (UGBC) before you start branching out.

It is important to define and describe what exactly you are planning from the outset. If you fail to define these things from the beginning you will have lots of confusion and rebellion.

You must make the following points very clear before starting a united group of branch churches (UGBC):

a) That branch churches are not independent and will be continually monitored and governed by the headquarters.

b) That the mother church's finances will start the church and support it fully.

c). That income will flow into a central fund and ministers are paid from a central fund.

d) That all the needs of the branch churches and the head-quarters will be met by the united group branch churches.

2. Let the pastors and the congregations understand that it is the same church but in different locations. This means that congregation members are free to move from one location to another.

3. Set up an administration which monitors the attendance and finances of every member of the group of churches.

Administer the finances of all the churches centrally; paying expenses and managing the bills centrally so that those who have more do not waste anything and those who have less do not suffer. "As it is written, He that had gathered much had nothing over; and he that had gathered little had no lack. (2 Corinthians 8:15).

This does not mean that all the money has to physically move to one place. The money does not have to move to one geographical location, but decisions concerning the money must be taken centrally. A good church administration will manage the churches that have been created. To be a good administrator, you must have a good knowledge of secular issues.

Church administration requires a combination of the power of God and the wisdom of God. Without good church administration everything that you build will eventually collapse. You need to master church administration otherwise your ministry will be likened to a rocket that shoots off and falls apart shortly after takeoff.

> **But unto them which are called, both Jews and Greeks, Christ the power of God, and the wisdom of God.**
>
> **1 Corinthians 1:24**

4. Maintain your leadership over the United Group of Branch Churches (UGBC).

Churches and branches will be established by teaching and training the pastors constantly and requiring them to come for certain meetings and to meet certain standards.

5. Let the church function as one large body (UGBC).

The church in different locations will share its finances. This means that the money one church has belongs to all the other churches.

6. Let the church function as one large body in different locations with shared leadership.

Shared leadership means that pastors can be transferred from one location to another without destabilizing anything.

7. Do not allow the branch pastors or branch churches to develop individualized visions.

Their vision should be the vision of the UGBC group of churches in different locations.

8. Study loyalty and teach extensively on loyalty.

Fight independent-minded pastors who want to separate themselves and do something on their own. Such independent-minded people destroy the concept of the united group of branches (UGBC).

Loyalty is essential for maintaining a network of churches. The churches you will plant will not be in the same location. It is therefore necessary to teach people to be loyal wherever they are situated.

I once heard of someone criticizing me for teaching on loyalty.

He said, "Why should you teach on loyalty and disloyalty?"

He went on to say that it was not necessary to teach on loyalty because people will be inspired to loyalty by your good leadership.

I was not surprised that this dear critic of mine had never planted a single branch. It is amazing how people criticize something they have never done before.

On another occasion, a dear pastor criticized me for teaching on loyalty. However when his church split, he became an avid reader of my books and even promoted them to other ministers.

Loyalty is the subject which must be taught until the culture of faithfulness and loyalty is established in the UGBC.

9. Be loyal to the branch pastors and churches so that they do not have any good reason or basis to separate themselves from you.

Show interest in and develop the branch churches so that your neglect of them does not become the reason for them to break away and separate themselves.

10. Encourage the same teachings and books to be taught in the whole group of churches.

Conduct special programmes in the different branch churches to establish them.

11. Let the entire group of churches remain connected through the internet.

12. Let the entire group of churches stay connected by having the same paraphernalia in every church; using the same offering baskets, banners, signboards.

■ Laws for Managing a United Group of Branch Churches (UGBC)

Managing a network of churches is different from pastoring a single church. Pastoring a network of churches requires the development of a complex system of management. The laws for managing a complex network of churches are:

1. **Know:** Know what is going on in the different churches.

This is done by developing a system in which reports are sent regularly to the headquarters. Weekly or monthly reports must contain vital information about the churches that you have established. This should include:

i. The real attendance

ii. What is preached and who preaches

iii. The income of the church for the week.

2. **Communicate:** Communicate regularly to maintain a spirit of loyalty and togetherness in the family of churches.

   Reports must be sent to the headquarters by the most convenient method e.g. email, letter, fax, courier or by hand. Gradually, a well-controlled and fully- monitored system becomes established. The information must be used for taking decisions about churches and pastors.

3. **Influence:** Influence what is going on in the different churches. Influence what is going on by having frequent meetings with all the pastors and leaders. Meetings with the leaders are more important than meetings with the church itself.

4. **Encourage:** Churches that are part of the network need a lot of encouragement. Pastors and churches greatly benefit from frequent visits by seasoned ministers.

5. **Teach:** To maintain a spirit of loyalty and togetherness in the network. It is important to teach on the advantages of belonging to the network.

Chapter

57

Anagkazo, *Biazo* and *Anaideia*: The Keys for Advancement

CHAPTER SUMMARY

Sometimes we need to go back to the Greek in order to understand the original meanings of some Bible words. In this chapter, discover the meanings of the following Greek words as the keys for your advancement.

i) Anagkazo: "to compel", to necessitate, to drive, and to constrain by all means such as force, threats, persuasion and entreaties.

ii) Biazo: "to use force" or "to force one's way into a thing".

iii) Anaideia: "to be shameless".

> **... Go out into the highways and hedges, and compel [anagkazo] them to come in, that my house may be filled.**
>
> **Luke 14:23**

What Is Anagkazo?

Anagkazo simply means *"to compel".* It also means to *necessitate, to drive,* and *to constrain* by all means such as *force, threats, persuasion* and *entreaties.* You see, the New Testament was translated from the Greek language and the Old Testament from the Hebrew language. *Anagkazo* is the Greek word that is translated "to compel".

There is another closely related Greek word, *"Biazo".*

What Is *Biazo*?

Biazo is a Greek word found in Matthew 11 that means *"to use force"* or *"to force one's way into a thing".* This is a quality I find lacking in Christian circles. We are forceful about everything else, except God's work. We are forceful about our jobs, our girlfriends, our marriages and our future. But when it comes to God's work we become like timid mice!

When I see commercials on television, I realize that there are groups of people who are very confident about what they have to offer. They are so confident that they boldly sing catchy songs about how good their product is.

Alcohol advertisers are some of the best in the business. We all know that beer and liquor are killers and destroyers of young people. Alcohol has broken up more homes, destroyed more marriages, caused more car accidents, and started more wars and fights than anything else in the world. Yet, it is advertised and promoted constantly. Beer is the cause of many accidents, leading to the deaths of countless numbers of people. And yet there are smiling people on television, telling us that it is the "power" we need. These commercials are being forced down our throats. We are being forced to believe things that are not true.

Even though beer is the "devil in solution" we are being compelled to believe otherwise. When I think of the forcefulness of people who want to make money at all costs, I realize that Christians have a better reason to be forceful. Why then is it that we Christians behave like lame ducks, toothless dogs and helpless sparrows?

I believe that the revelation of *anagkazo* and *biazo* can change that. *Biazo* means to force one's way into a thing. If Christianity is going to spread we are going to have to be a lot more forceful than we are. Whether it is making money, spreading a false religion or selling deadly products, the world is forceful about it. That is why I am teaching Christians to be biblically forceful.

What Is *Anaideia*?

Another related Greek word I want us to study is the word *Anaideia.* Anaideia is a Greek word that is used only once in the Bible. It means *"to be shameless".* In the eleventh chapter of Luke, we learn of a man who exhibited shamelessness in his relationship with God.

I say unto you, Though he will not rise and give him, because he is his friend, yet because of his importunity [anaideia] he will rise and give him as many as he needeth.

Luke 11:8

In 1982, I was admitted to the University of Ghana, the premier university in my country, Ghana. I cautiously entered this new environment wondering what lay ahead. One of the first things that struck me was the shamelessness of unbelievers.

The Kissing Students

I remember one of the first times I walked into Volta Hall, the ladies' hall. When I got to the staircase that led up to the first and second floors, there was a young man and a girl engaged in a prolonged embrace and kiss. I know that in some places this might not look strange. However it looked strange to me.

This couple continued in their long embrace and intimate kissing as we passed by them. They could not care less about who saw them! They were not moved! They were shameless! Perhaps they felt they were in love.

When we got upstairs, I told my friends, "It seems people around here are not ashamed of what they're doing."

Then I asked, "Why are we ashamed of what we believe in?

Why are we ashamed of the Gospel?

Why do we go around like timid mice that don't have anything to offer?"

The Spirit of the Lord rose up within me and I said, "If they are not ashamed of their immoral lives, I'm not going to be ashamed of the Gospel."

For I am not ashamed of the gospel of Christ...

Romans 1:16

It is amazing to see homosexuals boldly speak of their abnormal lifestyles. They come on television and speak confidently about the anomaly of anal intercourse. These people forcefully demonstrate for their rights. How come Christians are so quiet when it comes to speaking God's Word? Many Christians sit in their offices and allow their unbeliever colleagues to shamelessly speak of their evil deeds. The sinners around us dominate the discussions with unwholesome words.

The Apostle Paul practised anaideia. Remember, it was Paul who said, "We are not ashamed of the Gospel." Many Christians are genuine and have a real message to impart. But for a message to have any impact, it must be compelling. It must drive the listener to change! The message of the Lord Jesus Christ must persuade the unsaved to make a decision for Christ. It is so important for us to catch the message of *Anagkazo, Biazo* and *Anaideia.*

Chapter

58

Why *Anagkazo* is Important for Church Growth

CHAPTER SUMMARY

- **Growth through Anagkazo**

58.1 **Anagkazo is important because only a certain type of evangelism will lead to church growth.**

58.2 **Anagkazo is important because the people that will fill our empty churches are not in places where they can receive bourgeoisie invitation cards.**

58.3 **Dear pastor, without anagkazo, your church is going to be empty.**

58.4 **Without anagkazo, many churches are going to die a natural death.**

58.5 **Life is becoming more hectic and people are becoming more busy in the twenty-first century.**

In the fourteenth chapter of Luke, we read a familiar story where Jesus told of an important person who held a party for his friends. I want you to read this whole portion of Scripture so that you will be familiar with the story.

> **Then said he unto him, A certain man made a great supper, and bade many: And sent his servant at supper time to say to them that were bidden, Come; for all things are now ready.**
>
> **And they all with one consent began to make excuse. The first said unto him, I have bought a piece of ground, and I must needs go and see it: I pray thee have me excused.**
>
> **And another said, I have bought five yoke of oxen, and I go to prove them: I pray thee have me excused. And another said, I have married a wife, and therefore I cannot come.**
>
> **So that servant came, and shewed his lord these things. Then the master of the house being angry said to his servant, Go out quickly into the streets and lanes of the city, and bring in hither the poor, and the maimed, and the halt, and the blind. And the servant said, Lord, it is done as thou hast commanded, and yet there is room.**
>
> **And the lord said unto the servant, Go out into the highways and hedges, and compel [anagkazo] them to come in, that my house may be filled. For I say unto you, That none of those men which were bidden shall taste of my supper.**
>
> **Luke 14:16-24**

This man had the unfortunate experience of spending a lot of money on a big party, inviting important people, only to find out that most of them wouldn't come. This man was very surprised about their rejection of his invitation. He became angry as he listened to the excuses of those he had invited. In his anger, he decided to invite anybody he found on the street.

Imagine having a party with people you don't even know! Unfortunately, at that time of the night, there were not so many people around. Even after inviting those on the street, his party was relatively unattended. He then decided to invite the sick, the blind and the handicapped. Imagine that! What an unusual selection of partygoers! His party was full of the nonentities and the down-and-outs of society.

■ Growth through *Anagkazo*

I believe this story is symbolic of the Lord Jesus sending us out to invite people to Him. It is also symbolic of pastors sending out their members to evangelize the world. I have discovered that every time I embark on evangelizing the world (inviting many people to a great supper), I encounter the same things that this man encountered. However, I believe this man was a success. In spite of everything, he had his party and his house was full of guests. It might not have turned out the way he initially wanted, but he had his party anyway. You see, God is sending out His church to invite the whole world to know Christ. Unfortunately, many of those who are invited do not respond. The Jews were the first to be invited to know the Lord. But they rejected Christ and the Gospel moved on to the Gentiles. Many of the elite, who live in large urban centres, hear the Gospel on television and in church. However, they do not receive the message but rather criticize preachers. Again, the Gospel is passed on to the poor and non-elite in villages. They willingly receive the Word because they have no other hope but God.

1. *Anagkazo* is important because only a certain type of evangelism will lead to church growth.

People are not going to be convinced or compelled to know God through our little church games. Our "Mickey Mouse" church programmes and bazaars will not go very far in today's world. We must go out there and drive them to God.

2. *Anagkazo* is important because the people that will fill our empty churches are not in places where they can receive bourgeoisie invitation cards.

If people are going to be touched with the Gospel, a new strategy of going to the gutters, highways and the bushes must be employed. Sitting in church and inviting people has long been an unworkable strategy for church growth.

3. Dear pastor, without *anagkazo*, your church is going to be empty.

Please remember that if this man had not employed the strategy of *anagkazo* he would have had an empty house. Remember this, "A pastor without *anagkazo* will have an empty church."

4. Without *anagkazo*, many churches are going to die a natural death.

What you must realize is that the membership of a church is very fluid. Many people come and many people leave. If you don't have more people coming in than those you are losing, your church will begin to die. If you don't want your church to close down, you must do what Jesus instructed – go out and practise anagkazo.

5. Life is becoming more hectic and people are becoming more busy in the twenty-first century.

Busy working people are going to have more and more excuses. The strategy of anagkazo will help you to overcome these excuses. Through your new driving and forceful attitude you will bring many people to Christ and to church.

Chapter

59

How to Use *Anagkazo* to Induce Church Growth

CHAPTER SUMMARY

59.1 Use anagkazo to prepare a great supper.

59. 2 Use anagkazo to influence many people.

59. 3 Use anagkazo and never cancel your service. Anyone practising anagkazo is not prepared to cancel his service.

59. 4 Use anagkazo to prevent having empty halls.

59. 5 Use anagkazo to overcome people's excuses.

59. 6 Use anagkazo to overcome people's lies.

59. 7 Use anagkazo to make a way.

59. 8 Use anagkazo to go out of your usual circle of friends.

59. 9 Use anagkazo until there is no more room in your church.

1. Use anagkazo to prepare a great supper.

Anyone who wants church growth must prepare for it. Most Christian outreaches are not successful unless there is a lot of preparation. Ask yourself how much preparation has gone into anything you do. If there is a lot of preparation there is usually a lot of success. Crusades, church growth, outreaches depend on your preparation. This anagkazo man prepared for his great programme. Being in the ministry has not happened without thousands of hours of preparation. Sermons I preached to ten people some years ago are the same sermons I am preaching to thousands today.

Preaching to a small group of ten people was part of God's preparation for me. If you want God to use you mightily, you must start preparing now! Take every opportunity you have to do something useful in the church. Years ago, I remember playing the drums and the piano in my church. Though I didn't know it at the time, that was part of my preparation for ministry. Today, I know a lot about music and musical equipment. I can discuss intelligently, all details that concern music, worship and expensive equipment. My experience with the music department has been a valuable asset to me.

2. Use anagkazo to influence many people.

You will notice that this man in Luke 14 held a great supper and invited many people. One of the primary reasons churches do not grow is because Christians keep to themselves. You cannot keep to yourself if you want to be an effective witness for the Lord Jesus Christ. When you sit on a bus, you can decide to be friendly to those nearby. Begin talking to the people around you. I always try to share the Gospel with people around me. I always have some Good News about Jesus. He has saved me and set me free.

During my second year in medical school, we lived on the beautiful Legon campus. We were transported daily to the other side of town where a teaching hospital was located. This involved a one-hour bus drive from one end of town to the other.

Balloons and Condoms

I remember one day as I sat in the bus, I watched some senior colleagues take out condoms, blow them into balloons and fly them in the bus. As these students shouted and laughed over their lewd jokes, I realized how confident they were in what they were doing. We the Christians sat timidly in the bus, trying to concentrate on our books. That day, I decided not to keep to myself. I got the attention of everyone on the bus and began to preach. Although preaching on the bus later became quite common, at that time it was unusual. Some of the students were angry and others were bored. Some looked out of the window in disapproval but I preached on! I decided not to keep to myself anymore. I decided to be like the man in Luke 14.

Clapping on the London Bus

An anagkazo person does not keep to himself. I once lived in London for a period of time. I felt stifled by the stiff atmosphere in England. I was used to preaching anywhere and everywhere. But in England I couldn't easily relate to the people around. Everyone seemed so unfriendly and uninterested. One day, while sitting upstairs in a double-decker bus, the spirit of anagkazo rose up in me and I said to myself, "I can't keep it to myself any longer."I rose to my feet and to the surprise of everyone on the bus, I began to clap my hands to get their attention. I tell you, I may have looked bold on the outside, but I was quite scared on the inside. There were all sorts of murderous looking characters on the bus. But I maintained my cool and delivered a complete Gospel sermon.The bus was quiet for a few minutes as they listened to this young madman preach. I took my seat after preaching and got off at the next stop. One gentleman, who got off the bus with me said to me, "I admire your courage!

But I don't think you got very far." Whether I got very far or not is not what matters. What is important is that I preached the Word. And the Word always accomplishes something when it is preached. ...my word be that goeth forth out of my mouth... it shall accomplish that which I please..." (Isaiah 55:11)

3. Use anagkazo and never cancel your service. Anyone practising anagkazo is not prepared to cancel his service.

Every pastor, in going through the normal processes of church growth, will experience highs and lows. But a pastor with the spirit of anagkazo will never cancel his church service. He will decide to press on no matter how many people attend. One of my pastors told me how only one person attended church on a particular Sunday. He said that he had never felt so low. However, he managed to preach to that one soul and do his best for the Lord.

Anagkazo in the Community

I remember there was a time we had a very low attendance for one of our services. The Lord told me to do what this man in Luke 14 did: "Go out there and invite the community to church."

I said, "How can I do that on a Sunday?"

The Lord replied, "You do it, and you will be blessed."

I continued arguing with the Lord, "What will our Sunday morning visitors think? We will drive away people from the church." However, the Lord insisted, "Go out and compel them to come in."

I obeyed the Lord. I announced to the church that we were going to stop the service, go out into the community and invite them.

I said, "We are going to go out to the community to bring them in."

I announced, "This is not a gentle invitation. Every single one of you must hold the hand of someone you see out there. Physically bring them into the church building."Some were taken aback. But we did it! And we brought in hundreds of "un-churched" dwellers of the community. That day we had several people giving their lives to Christ. We did this on numerous occasions and over a period, that particular service increased in size dramatically. I was not prepared to close down my service because of a low attendance. That is what any pastor with the spirit of anagkazo is prepared to do.

4. Use anagkazo to prevent having empty halls.

A pastor working with the spirit of anagkazo is not prepared to have an empty church service. Many years ago, as a medical student, the Lord asked me to start a church. I had no members in my church. Not even one soul to preach to! But I was not prepared to have an empty church.

Anagkazo and the Dawn Broadcast

I was still a student when the Holy Spirit directed me to the nursing students' hostel. I remember that very first day. It was around 5 a.m. and still dark. Standing outside the hostel, I clapped my hands and woke them up. They might have been surprised but that didn't bother me. I preached to them about Jesus. After I had finished I did something very bold. I said to them, "If you want to give your lives to Christ, change out of your night clothes, wear something decent and come downstairs. We want to talk to you about Christ."

That morning several young ladies gave their hearts to God. Up to this day, many of them are still members of my church.

Preaching at dawn to people in their beds has been one of my favourite methods of implementing this principle of anagkazo. One morning, I preached at the hostel of public health nurses. A lady threw down a note saying she was a backslider and needed help. She wanted us to speak with her. That morning we ministered to her and God delivered her. She has been a faithful member of our church for the last ten years.

Although I started out with an empty classroom, it soon became filled with nurses who had given their lives to Christ from my anagkazo dawn broadcasts.

Dear reader, I want you to understand something; I did not inherit a church from anyone. I have often gone to places where I knew no one, and no one knew me. I have had to go out and win souls, driving and persuading people to the Lord, until the room was full.

5. Use anagkazo to overcome people's excuses.

Many people are full of excuses. The man in the story listened to three amazing excuses for not attending his party. However, he was not impressed by any of them.

The first excuse was about testing oxen in the night. Everyone knows that no one tests oxen at that time of the night.

The second excuse was about somebody who had just gotten married. But we all know that a dinner would have been a nice outing for a newly-wed couple.

The third excuse was about going to see some land in the night. Let me ask you a question. Would you not assess a piece of land before you buy it? How could you inspect a piece of land in the night? Would you even see it clearly? Yet somebody was using this as an excuse for not attending the party.

Any good minister, who wants to reach people, must not be overwhelmed by people's excuses. He must learn to overcome people's excuses.

Even as you minister the Word of God, people form excuses in their minds. They develop reasons why they will not obey the Word. Every good preacher must learn to preach against people's excuses and ideas. Jesus spoke directly against the people's reasoning and excuses. And they knew it!

> **... for they perceived that he had spoken this parable against them.**
>
> **Luke 20:19**

Many excuses cannot be substantiated. A good minister must learn to see through the emptiness of excuses.

> *I spoke to one friend, inviting him to church. He in turn spoke about how the time was not convenient and how he had quite a distance to travel.*
>
> *I said to him, "You are a successful businessman. Everything you want to do, you do. You travel. You get up early everyday. You even have time to visit your girlfriend who lives a few hundred kilometres away. How come you have no time for God?"*
>
> *I told him, "If you really want to do something you can do it."*

Some people do not pay their tithes because they claim they have no money. Watch how much money they spend on other things. You will realize that the problem is not a lack of money, but the spirit of greed.

6. Use anagkazo to overcome people's lies.

> *I remember once, one of my pastors did some fundraising in a branch church.*
>
> *During the fundraising, the pastor asked for those who would like to give some money for the purchase of church instruments. A husband who happened to be a foreigner was prepared to give a donation. Just as his hand was going up, his wife pulled his hand down. She thought the pastor hadn't noticed.*
>
> *After the service, the lady approached the pastor and said, "You know, the reason why we didn't give any money during the fundraising was because my foreign husband didn't want to give.*
>
> *She continued, "You know how these foreigners are. They are so stingy."*
>
> *But that was a lie. It was she who did not want to give anything.*
>
> *Finally she promised the pastor, "I will see what we can do. I am sure we will be able to help."*

All pastors must learn to overcome the lies and excuses of the people we lead.

7. Use anagkazo to make a way.

What differentiates the successful from the unsuccessful is the ability to overcome excuses. Notice that the man in Luke 14 was not moved by any of the excuses and reasons given. He made a way out of every circumstance that was produced by the unwilling guests. I believe in one thing: If you really want to do something you make a way, if you do not want to do something you make an excuse.

They Came to Party

I recall when many young people were unwilling to come to church. The young men especially, made all sorts of excuses. The spirit of anagkazo rose up in me and I said, "If they will not come to church, let us have parties for them."

We organized a party for the young people in one area of the city. We made invitation cards and distributed them to the youth in the community. They were very happy and said to themselves, "This is another opportunity to jam."

I remember that evening in particular, we played upbeat Christian music and danced with the unbelievers. One of them told me later that he wondered why they were not being served with beer. At a point in the party, we switched to slower music and stated we had an announcement to make.

By that time, many of the hardened unbelievers were sitting around. To their surprise, I got up and preached the Gospel to them. They were surprised but they still gave their lives to Christ. Many were born again that night.

I have pastors in the church who were saved during some of these surprise evangelistic parties. The Bible says by all means, "save some".

Anagkazo means to compel and to drive people to God. An anagkazo person is not moved by unfavourable circumstances. We were not moved by the fact that these young men did not want to attend church. We made a way around that! Learn to make a way where there's no way. Find a way to overcome every excuse that people place before you.

8. Use anagkazo to go out of your usual circle of friends.

Everyone has a circle of friends. The usual thing is to stay within your circle of friends and acquaintances. However, anyone who wants to be used by God must move out of this regular group. You will notice that the anagkazo man in this story was forced to move out of his normal circle of friends. This is a reality that we must face if we want to please God!

I Had My Circle

I had a group of friends I grew up with in Accra. A sort of elitist company made up of the children of foreigners and other bourgeoisie. As a child I travelled first class on intercontinental flights and interacted mainly with the so-called upper echelon of society. I stayed in international cities with my father. My hobbies were swimming and horse riding and horse racing. There were just a few people who had such pastimes.

However, there were hardly any Christians in these circles. When I got born again, I found myself moving out of this circle into a very different group. I moved out into better company, different from what I knew.

The fact is, in order to please God I could not spend a lot of time in those circles anymore. There were simply no believers in that group. If you want to please God you will have to move out of your circle and get to know other groups of people.

I know that the rich man in this story would not normally fellowship with people who live in hedges or who stand on highways. I know that the rich man in this story would not normally interact with cripples, the blind and the disabled. However, in order to achieve church growth he had to interact with people of other social backgrounds.

The Nice Little Fellowship Must Grow

I remember in 1984 when I was the leader of a nice fellowship at the university. We loved each other dearly and were good company for one another (actually, I found my wife in that group). Many of the people that I knew in that little group are still my bosom friends up to this day. However, the Spirit of God impressed upon me to move out of our little group and to go to people we didn't know.

I remember some people were not in favour of expanding our nice little clique. "If you bring in more people, we will lose something," they said. "There's something about a small fellowship. It's nice to be petite. It's a cute little family."

But I led this group into one outreach after another, driving and necessitating people to come to the Lord. I was never tired of preaching. People are not tired of sinning, why should you be tired of spreading the gospel?

During the second year of the medical school (which by the way is the most difficult year), I led this group in dawn broadcasts every Saturday morning. Everyone knew about us. They were used to our voices that rang out loud and clear every Saturday morning. "Thank God for our nice little fellowship," I said. "But we have to go out there and win souls." We must move out of our little circle.

After awhile, unbelievers are no longer impressed with our sermons. If you do not rise up with a new approach, a new anagkazo method, your message will lose its punch. As we continued preaching at dawn, I realized that people just turned over in their beds and ignored us. I said to myself, "Our messages are no longer driving people to the Lord." But the Spirit of the Lord gave me a bright idea.

Knock on Their Doors!

Since the people were now so used to our voices, we needed to do something new. I decided to send out a group to stand outside the doors of their rooms. I told the preacher for the morning, "When you get to the altar call, we will start knocking on their doors."

I told him, "Tell the people who are listening to you that they are going to hear a knock on their door. If they want to accept Christ they should open up and we will come in and lead them to the Lord." The preacher followed my instructions. Suddenly, those who were ignoring us had to pay attention. We were knocking on their doors at 5 a.m.! Believe me, many were gloriously born again during those morning broadcasts.

Salvation for the Mocker

I vividly remember one brother in particular; He would laugh at Christians as they spoke in tongues. He made fun of the gift of speaking in tongues. This is someone who would get drunk and lie by one of the many ponds scattered around the beautiful campus of the University of Ghana. That morning as my friend the evangelist preached and said, "Perhaps you are hearing a knock on your door. If you want to be born again open your door and someone will come in and lead you to the Lord", I happened to knock on the door of this young man.

I was surprised when he opened the door and welcomed us in. He said, "I knew you would come here. Today is my day!" We prayed with him and he gave his heart to the Lord that very morning. To this day, this man is serving the Lord. I give glory to God for all the people that have been born again as we have forcefully moved out to speak the Word. Anagkazo works!

9. Use anagkazo until there is no more room in your church.

> **...and yet there is room.**
>
> **Luke 14:22**

A song that I love goes like this: *There's room at the cross for you. There's room at the cross for you. Though millions have come, there's still room for one. There's room at the cross for you.*

Do not be satisfied as long as there is room in your church. The man in this story sent out his servants simply because there was room. I believe that every church should arrange more chairs than the people who actually come. The presence of empty pews should motivate the pastor to reach out until the house is full. The whole essence of church growth is to have a full church.

> **...compel [anagkazo] them to come in, that my house may be filled.**
>
> **Luke 14:23**

Evangelism is directly related to church growth. All our efforts to lead people to the Lord should bear fruit. We must see our efforts filling church buildings. Whatever the case, a minister must see that there is room at the cross for one more soul. I believe that if we have this mind, God will use us to fill the church.

I have never been satisfied with the size of my church. When we had ten people, I wanted twenty. When we had fifty, I dreamed of a hundred. When God gave me one hundred people, I thought to myself, "What would it be like if I had five hundred people?" When the church was numbered in the hundreds, I thought, "What would it be like if we had thousands?" I think a pastor will get tired of preaching to the same few people after awhile. We must be motivated to have a fuller house. These words keep ringing in my soul, "That my house may be filled!" "That my house may be filled!" Dear Pastor, never forget that there is still room at the cross.

Chapter

60

How *Anaideia* and *Biazo* Cause Church Growth

CHAPTER SUMMARY

Anaideia and ***biazo*** are the keys to church growth. Evangelism is the key to getting new people to join your church. Without ***biazo*** and ***anaideia*** you will not have the strength to evangelise.

■ *Biazo*

Verily I say unto you, among them that are born of women there hath not risen a greater than John the Baptist: notwithstanding he that is least in the kingdom of heaven is greater than he. And from the days of John the Baptist until now the kingdom of heaven suffereth violence, and the violent [biazo] take it by force.

Matthew 11:11,12

Multitudes of non-Christians are hurtling down a broad street to Hell. They sing, they dance, and they wine and dine. They do not give a hoot about the Gospel we preach! Many of us Christians live in our nice little world where we are oblivious to the reality of sinners going to Hell.

I once worked as a sub-intern at the mortuary of the largest hospital in Ghana. Something struck me that I want to share with you. Every few minutes a car would park outside the mortuary. In that car was the body of a man sprawled in the back seat, or even sometimes in the boot (trunk).

I would stand at the main door of the mortuary as people brought in their loved ones and relatives who had died at home or on the street. These people were so sad and shaken. You must understand that only a few hours earlier they had been talking to a living person who was now gone forever. They were bringing their loved one to a fridge.

I noticed that there did not seem to be any particular time of the day when dead people were brought to this mortuary. As I stood there, God showed me that people were dying across the city all the time. Death is not reserved for early mornings or late nights. It happens anytime and anywhere.

A person who has never stood at the door of a mortuary will not know how common death is. How frequently people depart for eternity! Just as the Lord spoke to his prophets when they saw certain things, the Lord spoke to me when I stood at that door. He asked, "How many of these people do you think were saved?"

"I died for them; I gave up my life for them, but are they saved?"

Listen to me Christian friend. Our church bazaars, weddings, fellowships and nice choirs are not enough to win the multitudes to Christ. People are hurtling down the road of destruction. They do not even know that they are going to Hell.

They Heard the Music

This reminds me of the Second World War in which the prisoners were taken to large camps. They were stripped of their clothes and herded into huge gas chambers. As they filed in, their captors would play beautiful music for the prisoners. They heard the music. How soothing and refreshing it must have sounded. "Surely nothing evil is going to happen to us," they thought. Little did they know that they were about to be slaughtered by the same people who were playing the music.

This is the lot of unbelievers today. They hear the music of the devil. The melodies and lullabies of this present world charm them. Because of these things, they do not know that they are walking to their own destruction. "...as an ox goeth to the slaughter..." (Proverbs 7:22).

In Matthew 11:12, the Bible tells us that the violent take the kingdom of God by force. What does this mean?

The Twentieth Century New Testament puts it this way, ... **men using force have been seizing it**...

The William's Translation says, ...**men are seizing it as a precious prize...**

The Goodspeed translation says, ...**Men have been taking the kingdom of heaven by storm**...

The Weymouth translation says, ...**the kingdom of God has been enduring violent assault**...

All these Scriptures tell us one thing. Gentle words, nice songs, lame sermons and docile choirs cannot help much in this indifferent and uninterested world. People don't want to know. They are deceived.

Church Games Will Not Help

They don't care whether Jesus comes today or tomorrow. "Leave me alone," they say. "To Hell with this church business of yours." That is why we need what the Bible calls *Biazo*. *Biazo* means to use force and to force one's way into a thing. Many people are blinded by the devil. We must open their eyes to the realities of Heaven and Hell.

...the god of this world hath blinded the minds of them...
2 Corinthians 4:4

Apostle Paul did not only give nice sermons. He was actively involved in turning the heads and opening the eyes of unbelievers. I always know when people are ignoring the message. But I don't want anybody to ignore this important message – I must turn their heads and open their eyes. One particular morning, my group in the university found ourselves in a hall, preaching.

When we have city-wide crusades, I stand on the platform and command my church members to go out into the community. We don't wait for them to come to us; we go out there and bring them from their homes.

One day, we even went to a "Red Light District" and brought a group of prostitutes to the crusade. I was very happy to see these prostitutes coming to the altar to give their lives to the Lord. You see, if we hadn't forced these women out of their "work places" and to the crusade, they would never have been saved. Most prostitutes do not go to church. They would have just gone about their daily routine. We would have ended up preaching to ourselves.

Christian friends, let's stop playing games. If we are going to preach the Gospel, let's not preach to ourselves. Let's go out there and drive them in (*anagkazo* and *biazo*) to the Lord.

Anaideia

> **I say unto you, Though he will not rise and give him, because he is his friend, yet because of his importunity [anaideia] he will rise and give him as many as he needeth.**
>
> **Luke 11:8**

In Luke 11, Jesus told us a story of a man who needed three loaves of bread. This man buried his shame and embarrassment and went to his friend's house at a very odd hour. The master of the house was woken up.

He might have shouted, "What is happening? Are there some armed robbers here? Is there a fire? What is going on outside?" The servant of the house probably replied, "It's the neighbour. He says he wants some bread for his visitors."

Dear Christian friend, most of us would not disturb even our best friends at midnight. How much more to ask for something trivial like bread!

But Jesus' message here is very simple. If you are ashamed to press for certain things, you will never achieve them. If you are shameless in trying to achieve church growth you will accomplish things that others will only dream about! God has shown me that people who are very concerned about their public image cannot achieve much for God.

Are You Ashamed to Pursue Church Growth?

It takes anaideia, shamelessness, to start a church. When I discussed with my friend the idea of starting a church, I remember he looked at me in amazement. He said, "What if people don't come to the church? We will be so embarrassed. People in town will hear that we tried to start a church that didn't work."

By starting a church, I don't mean to break away with a large segment of someone else's ministry. I am talking about moving into a room that has two or three people and preaching to them. It takes shamelessness to tell these few people that they are now in a great church. If you are not prepared to go through the shame and ridicule of standing in an empty room and looking odd, you will never achieve great things for God.

Are You Ashamed of Church Work?

One pastor told me he was afraid to do an altar call (inviting people to give their life to Christ). What if no one responds? Would you not feel ashamed? People will think that you are not anointed and that your message was not powerful enough. It is this very train-of-thought that keeps people away from powerful ministry.

One of my Elders called and told me that for the first time someone in the church had responded to her altar call. You see, she had been shamelessly doing altar calls with no one responding. But with anaideia (shamelessness and persistence) she eventually had results!

Are You Ashamed of the Healing Ministry?

The shameless man, who asked for the bread, eventually accomplished his goal. I remember when I first began to pray for the sick. I was very worried about what people would think about me.

> *Many times whilst standing on stage, the devil would tell me, "Don't even bother to call out for testimonies; no one will be healed."*
>
> *The devil told me, "Do not disgrace yourself any further. Just end the service here and send the people home."*
>
> *But the Spirit of the Lord rose up within me and I said to myself, "I am not ashamed. If no one gets healed this time, I will do it again, and again, and again! One day, someone will get healed." I am glad to say that many have been healed. After I had qualified from the medical school, I worked for one year as a medical doctor.*

Are You Ashamed of Full-Time Ministry?

> *At a point, the Lord began to speak to me about entering full-time ministry. I argued with the Lord, "I will work and bring enough money to support the church."*
>
> *I continued, "What will people think of me, leaving such a noble profession to enter such a controversial one." I told the Lord, "No one knows my church! And no one knows me!"*
>
> *"Worst of all, what a shame it is for me to live off people's offerings."*
>
> *"That's ridiculous! Why should people contribute their pennies for my upkeep? I find it degrading," I thought.*
>
> *However, the Lord told me, "They that preach the Gospel must live off the Gospel."*

> **Even so hath the Lord ordained that they which preach the gospel should live of the gospel.**
>
> **1 Corinthians 9:14**

I had to bury my pride as a doctor and shamelessly enter full-time ministry. Through the revelation of shamelessness *(anaideia),* I have gone far in ministry. I have achieved things, which no one ever thought would come out of me. *Anaideia* (shamelessness) is the key you need to accomplish great things for God!

Chapter

61

Why You Must Become a Hard Leader to Have Church Growth

CHAPTER SUMMARY

What does hardness and strength of leadership have to do with pastoring large numbers of people? As time has gone by, however, I have found out for myself how important it is to be a strong and hard leader if you are to have church growth.

Indeed, this idea of strong, hard leadership for church growth is a totally biblical concept with many supporting Scriptures.

61.1 You must be a hard leader because you can only build a large house on a rock solid foundation.

61.2 You must be a hard leader because Jesus Christ wanted Peter, the head of His church to be a hard rock.

61.3 You must be a hard leader because Jesus recommended John, the greatest prophet, for being a hard person.

61.4 You must be a hard leader because everything depends on the leader.

61.5 You must be a hard leader because the head of the church, Jesus Christ, is a hard leader and He does not apologize for it.

... I will liken him unto a wise man, which built his house upon a rock:

Matthew 7:24

The traditional picture of a pastor is of a soft, kind and understanding man who listens to all the problems of the congregation. This kind pastor is so loving and understanding of all the issues that are presented. He has time for everyone and he cares for everyone's children. He is gentle and friendly to everyone who wants to talk to him.

This is the picture that I also had of a pastor. I was therefore shocked when I heard from Dr David Yonggi Cho, (pastor of the largest church in the world) that to build a large church you need to be a very strong leader. I thought it was contradictory since the pastor was supposed to be a soft, gentle, caring man who loved the people with the love of the Lord.

1. You must be a hard leader because you can only build a large house on a rock solid foundation.

You cannot build a big church on a soft leader. You need a hard leader upon whom you can build a huge ministry. The church is the house of God and equally needs a rock as its foundation. You need a rock because the rain is going to fall, the floods are going to come and the winds are going to blow on the church you are building. If there is no hardness in the foundation there is no hope for the future.

...I will liken him unto a wise man, which built his house upon a rock:

And the rain descended, and the floods came, and the winds blew, and beat upon that house; and it fell not: for it was founded upon a rock.

Matthew 7:24-25

2. You must be a hard leader because Jesus Christ wanted Peter, the head of His church to be a hard rock.

He changed Peter's name into "the rock" because He knew that a hard person was needed to build the worldwide church. Jesus wanted Peter to be a hard leader, not easily moved around. You must also be a hard leader who is not easily moved around.

And I say also unto thee, that thou art Peter, and upon this rock I will build my church; and the gates of hell shall not prevail against it.

Matthew 16:18

3. You must be a hard leader because Jesus recommended John, the greatest prophet, for being a hard person.

People who are soft and wishy-washy do not head great ministries. A wishy-washy leader is someone lacking in decisiveness. He is without strength or character. Great ministries are often headed by hard leaders who are not moved by what people say but are moved by what God says.

John the Baptist could not be bothered by what people thought. He was not even bothered by what the king thought. He took no thought for his life as he rebuked the king for marrying his brother's wife. No wonder Jesus recommended him.

And as they departed, Jesus began to say unto the multitudes concerning John, What went ye out into the wilderness to see? A reed shaken with the wind?

But what went ye out for to see? A man clothed in soft raiment? Behold, they that wear soft clothing are in kings' houses.

But what went ye out for to see? A prophet? Yea, I say unto you, and more than a prophet.

Matthew 11:7-9

4. You must be a hard leader because everything depends on the leader.

... smite the shepherd, and the sheep of the flock shall be scattered abroad.

Matthew 26:31

Everything depends on the shepherd. Everything depends on the leader. When the shepherd is down everyone goes down with him. A whole church cannot lean on something that is soft, weak and indecisive. Unstable, waffling and weak-kneed leaders have no place at the head of a large ministry. To be the captain of the ship means everybody's life depends on you. To be the pilot of a plane means everyone's life depends on you.

The Soft Pilot

I once watched a documentary of such a weak leader who was the pilot of a flight from Colombia to New York. He was asked to delay his landing because of air traffic at the airport. Can you believe that he flew his plane around in circles until he finally ran out of fuel and crashed the plane, killing many people?

Of course, an investigation was launched into this terrible tragedy. The air crash investigation eventually ruled that this pilot had not put sufficient pressure on the air traffic control and had not impressed upon them strongly enough that he was running out of fuel.

That night this weak-kneed pilot killed many people, including himself, because he lacked the strength to impress upon air traffic control that he needed to land urgently.

He also lacked the strength to forcefully (and illegally, if necessary) land his plane when he knew that everyone was in grave danger.

This is what it is like to have a weak and soft person in charge of everything. This is why Jesus wanted Peter to be a rock. He wanted a hard person to be the head of His Church.

5. You must be a hard leader because the head of the church, Jesus Christ, is a hard leader and He does not apologize for it.

> **Then he which had received the one talent came and said, Lord, I knew thee that thou art AN HARD MAN, reaping where thou hast not sown, and gathering where thou hast not strawed: And I was afraid, and went and hid thy talent in the earth: lo, there thou hast that is thine.**
>
> **His lord answered and said unto him, Thou wicked and slothful servant, THOU KNEWEST THAT I REAP WHERE I SOWED NOT, AND GATHER WHERE I HAVE NOT STRAWED:**
>
> **Thou oughtest therefore to have put my money to the exchangers, and** *then* **at my coming I should have received mine own with usury.**
>
> **Matthew 25:24-27**

Jesus told us parables that illustrated His hardness as a leader. He made no apologies for this reality. In this parable, the servant accused their leader of being hard. "Thou art a hard man" they said. In their opinion, this hard leader had benefits they thought he didn't deserve. But the Lord did not deny that he was a hard man. In fact, he confirmed that he was as hard as they thought: reaping where he had not sown.

Dear friend, you will need to be as hard as our Lord if you are going to get anything done for the kingdom.

Chapter

62

The Hardness and the Decisions of a Mega Church Pastor

CHAPTER SUMMARY

In this chapter, I want to share with you a few of the decisions that a strong, hard pastor would probably have to take whilst building a large church.

62.1 A pastor who is building a large church will have to take decisions to put the right people in the right places.

62.2 A pastor who is building a large church will have to rebuke people who are out of order in the church.

62.3 A pastor who is building a large church will have to take the hard decisions not to allow his wife to lead him or guide him in the ministry.

62.4 A pastor who is building a large church will have to take the hard decisions to keep his wife in her place.

62.5 A pastor who is building a large church will have to take the hard decisions to reach out and do evangelism.

62.6 A pastor who is building a large church will have to take the hard decisions to send people out to start branches.

62.7 A pastor who is building a large church will have to take hard decisions to treat people differently.

62.8 A pastor who is building a large church will have to take the hard decision to build something.

62.9 A pastor who is building a large church will have to take hard decisions that make people sacrifice their money and their lives.

62.10 A pastor who is building a large church will have to take a decision to lead the people in hours of prayer.

62.11 A pastor who is building a large church will have to take decisions to practise frugality in the church. It is not easy to be frugal. It is not easy to lead people in a frugal lifestyle. People rebel against hardships. If you are not a hard strong leader, you cannot lead your organization into frugality.

62.12 A pastor who is building a large church will have to take decisions to lead the entire congregation in hard and difficult times of fasting.

62.13 A pastor who is building a large church will have to take decisions to dismiss certain people and replace them with others.

62.14 A pastor who is building a large church will have to take the hard decision to make the people give him his due honour.

The hardness and decisions of a mega church pastor mark out the character of his leadership. A mega church pastor will need strength to drive the congregation forward into the Promised Land.

His strength will be revealed through the hard decisions that he takes and his ability to follow through with what he has decided.

1. A pastor who is building a large church will have to take decisions to put the right people in the right places.

If you go by what the majority think you can never be the pastor of a mega church. Joseph was chosen to be the prime minister and to have authority over the whole of Egypt. Can you imagine how the other departmental heads felt when this Israeli slave was made their boss?

> **And Pharaoh said unto Joseph, Forasmuch as God hath shewed thee all this,** *there* **is none so discreet and wise as thou art: Thou shalt be over my house, and according unto thy word shall all my people be ruled: only in the throne will I be greater than thou. And Pharaoh said unto Joseph, See, I have set thee over all the land of Egypt.**
>
> **Genesis 41:39-41**

2. A pastor who is building a large church will have to rebuke people who are out of order in the church.

If you cannot rebuke people who are out of order you cannot be the pastor of a mega church. People constantly step out of order. They want to see how strong you are. They want to see how far they can go. They want to see if you will address those uncomfortable issues. Everybody is watching to see how strong you can be.

> **But he turned, and said unto Peter, Get thee behind me, Satan: thou art an offence unto me: for thou savourest not the things that be of God, but those that be of men.**
>
> **Matthew 16:23**

3. A pastor who is building a large church will have to take the hard decisions not to allow his wife to lead him or guide him in the ministry.

Adam was guided by his wife into the chaos we now experience in the world. Abraham was guided by his wife into giving birth to Ishmael. In both cases the Bible uses the phrase, "And Adam/Abraham hearkened unto the voice of his wife.... Ahab was guided into murder and stealing by his wife. Ahab, like Adam and Abraham, allowed himself to be guided, influenced and prodded into evil.

Job, on the other hand, was pressurized by his wife to curse God. But Job would have none of it and called her a foolish woman! If you cannot reject erroneous influence coming from your own wife, you cannot be a mega church pastor. A hard mega church pastor must be able to see foolishness in his wife when it surfaces. Your wife is not an angel and she is not God. She is just a human being like anyone else. If you can't distinguish the evil from the good, you cannot be a mega church pastor. You must be able to call your wife a foolish woman if she tells you to curse God and die!

Then SAID HIS WIFE unto him, Dost thou still retain thine integrity? CURSE GOD, AND DIE. But he said unto her, Thou speakest as one of the foolish women speaketh. What? shall we receive good at the hand of God, and shall we not receive evil? In all this did not Job sin with his lips.

Job 2:9-10

4. A pastor who is building a large church will have to take the hard decisions to keep his wife in her place.

A mega church pastor must ensure that his wife does not do anything to destroy the work of God. Michal's comments could have ended the praise and worship ministry of David. But David did not allow it. He would carry on his praise and worship ministry in spite of what his wife thought. He sharply rebuked her and disconnected from her! He continued his ministry of "abandoned praise and worship". Today, we all sing those heart-felt psalms that came from a man who abandoned himself helplessly before his God.

When David returned home to bless his family, Michal came out to meet him and said in disgust, "How glorious the king of Israel looked today! He exposed himself to the servant girls like any indecent person might do!"

David retorted to Michal, "I was dancing before the Lord, who chose me above your father and his family! He appointed me as the leader of Israel, the people of the Lord. So I am willing to act like a fool in order to show my joy in the Lord.

Yes, and I am willing to look even more foolish than this, but I will be held in honor by the girls of whom you have spoken!

2 Samuel 6:20-22 (NLT)

5. A pastor who is building a large church will have to take the hard decisions to reach out and do evangelism.

It takes strength to lead the church out as an army. It takes strength to lead pampered Sunday Christians into the evangelistic mode. It takes strength to preach about the need for the Gospel to money-loving prosperity-seeking congregants.

Then tidings of these things came unto the ears of the church which was in Jerusalem: and they sent forth Barnabas, that he should go as far as Antioch. Who, when he came, and had seen the grace of God, was glad, and exhorted them all, that with purpose of heart they would cleave unto the Lord.For he was a good man, and full of the Holy Ghost and of faith: and much people was added unto the Lord.

Acts 11:22-24

6. A pastor who is building a large church will have to take the hard decisions to send people out to start branches.

It is not easy to send people away. We love staying with the people we love and enjoying their company. But this is the very thing that will kill the growth of the church.

> **And when they had fasted and prayed, and laid their hands on them, they sent them away.**
>
> **Acts 13:3**

7. A pastor who is building a large church will have to take hard decisions to treat people differently.

It is not easy to relate to people according to God's gift. People always compare themselves with others. They ask, "What is this person doing and what am I doing? What is this person getting and what am I getting? Where is this person going and why am I not going? Because leaders are afraid to treat people differently, they often keep the wrong people in the wrong places doing the wrong things.

> **Peter seeing him saith to Jesus, Lord, and what shall this man do? Jesus saith unto him, If I will that he tarry till I come, what is that to thee? Follow thou me.**
>
> **John 21:21-22**

8. A pastor who is building a large church will have to take the hard decision to build something.

Building involves a lot. Nehemiah suffered greatly because he decided to build the walls of Jerusalem. Building the house of God often involves fighting a spiritual war and building at the same time.

> **They which builded on the wall, and they that bare burdens, with those that laded, every one with one of his hands wrought in the work, and with the other hand held a weapon. For the builders, every one had his sword girded by his side, and so builded. And he that sounded the trumpet was by me.**
>
> **Nehemiah 4:17-18**

9. A pastor who is building a large church will have to take hard decisions that make people sacrifice their money and their lives.

It is not easy to make people sacrifice their lives. It takes a hard commander to send people to their certain death.

> **Now when Jesus heard these things, he said unto him, yet lackest thou one thing: sell all that thou hast, and distribute unto the poor, and thou shalt have treasure in heaven: and come, follow me.**
>
> **Luke 18:22**

10. A pastor who is building a large church will have to take a decision to lead the people in hours of prayer.

It is not easy to lead people in long hours of prayer. It takes a hard leader to force the congregation to go through the discipline of long hours of prayer.

> **And he cometh unto the disciples, and findeth them asleep, and saith unto Peter, What, could ye not watch with me one hour?**
>
> **Matthew 26:40**

11. A pastor who is building a large church will have to take decisions to practise frugality in the church. It is not easy to be frugal. It is not easy to lead people in a frugal lifestyle. People rebel against hardships. If you are not a hard strong leader, you cannot lead your organization into frugality.

> **When they were filled, he said unto his disciples, Gather up the fragments that remain, that nothing be lost.**
>
> **John 6:12**

12. A pastor who is building a large church will have to take decisions to lead the entire congregation in hard and difficult times of fasting.

Then the king and his nobles sent this decree throughout the city: "No one, not even the animals, may eat or drink anything at all.

> **Everyone is required to wear sackcloth and pray earnestly to God. Everyone must turn from their evil ways and stop all their violence.**
>
> **Jonah 3:7-8 (NLT)**

13. A pastor who is building a large church will have to take decisions to dismiss certain people and replace them with others.

> **And the king... set the royal crown upon her head, and made her queen instead of Vashti.**
>
> **Esther 2:17**

14. A pastor who is building a large church will have to take the hard decision to make the people give him his due honour.

Many times a pastor has no one to say certain things for him and he will have to say them himself. Learn to say the hard things that you have to say if there is no one to say it for you.

I had to tell the church myself that I was a pastor. I had to tell my church how to address me. On another occasion I had to inform them that I was a Bishop.

And Elijah said unto her, Fear not; go and do as thou hast said: but make me thereof a little cake first, and bring it unto me, and after make for thee and for thy son.

1 Kings 17:13

Chapter

63

The Art of Copying

CHAPTER SUMMARY

All successful pastors copied from someone else. Church growth is accomplished by pastors who are willing to copy from other pastors. There is no shame in copying from someone who has experienced what you need.

In this chapter :

i) **Learn how to copy**

ii) **Recognize that we are all copies of something else**

iii) **Is Copying Biblical?**

Copying is the art of following a pattern or model until you have reproduced a good imitation of the original.

All successful pastors copied from someone else. Church growth is accomplished by pastors who are willing to copy from other pastors. There is no shame in copying from someone who has experienced what you need.

Copying may be a bad word to you, but copying is only bad when it is illegally done during examinations. Copying is the highest form of learning and is the God-given method of learning which babies and children use. "Be an original," they say. But the reality is that everyone copied from someone else. Every great worship leader copied from some worship leader somewhere else. Every great evangelist copied from another evangelist. Every great man of God is a copy of some other man of God somewhere.

Every anointing is a copy of another anointing. The anointing that came on Peter, James and John was simply a copy of the anointing that was on Jesus their master. The anointing that was on Elisha was simply another of the same kind of what was on Elijah.

> *Recently, I was having breakfast in a hotel in an African country and here came along a famous Christian singer whose music and CDs are played all over the world. As we sat together, one of my pastors, asked him a question, "Who has influenced your music ministry?"*
>
> *He answered, "Oh, Andre Crouch has been my greatest inspiration."*
>
> *I immediately understood why this fellow was doing so well. He was simply a copy of someone else. He was proud to be another of the same kind.*

I have noticed that all those who do well in any field, are those who closely follow after someone of the same kind. Whether it is preaching, singing, healing, pastoring; the principle is the same. God is in the business of producing many ministers of the same kind.

Learn How to Copy

Decide to become a pastor of a large and growing church. You can have church growth. Decide to be a great man of God; decide to be become the pastor of a huge church. How can you do this? The answer is simple: copy someone who has done it before you. Do not be mystical about the formula to greatness in God. Do not beat about the bush. Go directly to God's method of producing greatness.

Churches that work are pastored by pastors of a certain kind. Churches that grow are pastored by men and women of a certain kind. Since that is also your vision, why don't you become another of the same kind? Copying is the way to the anointing. Copying is the key to greatness in God. Copying is the open door for you to enter the things of the kingdom.

If there is a great evangelist, another of the same kind will also be great. If there is an anointed pastor, another of the same kind will also be anointed. If there is a powerful apostle, another of the same kind will be powerful.You are not special or different. You are simply going to become another of the kind that God has raised up already. You must find someone with a similar calling and follow hard after him.

It won't be long and we will be going home. You don't have much time for trial and error. You cannot afford time for experiments. You may be in the middle of your experiment when the Lord calls you.

You need to get straight to the point. You need the anointing and you need it fast! You need to preach well and you need to preach well now! You need to heal the sick and raise the dead and you need it to happen within the time the Lord has given you. How many years of experimentation are you going to dabble in until you become humble enough to copy someone's success.

■ We Are All Copies of Something Else

Begin to accept that we are all copies of something else. I am not some rare species whom Christ has chosen for the end-time move. Such thoughts only lead to error. I am a member of the Lord's army. I stand among the ranks and I am glad to be have been able to copy something that one of my fathers has done.

Do you want to raise up a great church?

Do you want church growth?

Thoughts of being unique will keep you away from learning from obvious examples in front of them. God wants to raise up more mega church pastors.

■ Is Copying Biblical?

> **And the earth brought forth grass, and herb yielding seed after his kind…and God saw that it was good. And God created…every living creature …after their KIND…and God saw that it was good. And God made the beast of the earth after his kind...and God saw that it was good.**
>
> **Genesis 1:12, 21, 25**

Almighty God created things to produce after their kind. The grass produces another of the same kind, the herbs produce another of the same kind, and the whales produce another of the same kind. Even man produces another of the same kind. The Lord God saw that another of the same kind was a good thing! Instead of being preoccupied with producing another of a different kind, let us produce fruit that is a good copy.

> **And God said, Let us make man in our image, after our likeness...**
>
> **Genesis 1:26**

When the Lord created man, he created something that was like Himself. He said that let us make something that is like us: another of the same kind, a copy. There are many similarities between man and God because we are made in His image. God is a Spirit and the Father of spirits. Human beings are also spirits living in bodies. God the Father, God the Son and God the Holy Spirit make up the Trinity we know. Man as spirit, soul and body also makes up a triune being. When men walk in their creative and inventive elements they are clearly copying God.

Chapter

64

Why Copying Will Help Your Ministry

CHAPTER SUMMARY

64.1 Copying is a God-given method of learning for children.

64.2 Copying is God's way of making you humble.

64.3 Copying causes you to discover that there is nothing new under the sun.

64.4 Copying is good because you become something that is already successful and working.

64.5 Copying makes things easier for you on this road of ministry.

64.6 Copying helps you to enter new things faster.

64.7 Copying helps to overcome problems.

64.8 Copying is the natural way to increase.

64.9 Copying is the key to great teaching and preaching.

Copying is the highest and fastest kind of learning.

1. Copying is a God-given method of learning for children.

Children use this method of learning effortlessly and that is why they learn anything easily. This is why children learn languages quickly. Many new things are a struggle for grown-ups to assimilate. Young people have no problems learning new things because they have no inhibitions when it comes to copying.

One day, I heard someone describe some people in his church as "BBTs". Then he said, "I myself am a "BBT".

So I asked him, "What is a BBT"? Who is a "BBT"?

He answered, "A "BBT" is somebody who was "Born Before Technology".

He continued, "Such people cannot learn or use computers and other modern technology."

He explained, "When you have BBTs in charge of certain things the church is not able to move forward."

I thought to myself, "What makes someone a "BBT" is his inability to learn anything using the fastest method of learning – copying! He cannot understand the computers, the software and the other modern gadgets because he does not copy easily."

2. Copying is God's way of making you humble.

...that they without us should not be made perfect.

Hebrews 11:40

The world's system teaches that the way to be qualified is to go to school. But the biblical way to becoming anything in the ministry is copying and following. Copying is the natural way by which God reproduces ministers. Pride and presumption will keep us from becoming highly anointed servants. Think about it; if you were able to do as much as certain people, it would be a great achievement. Forget about outshining others! If you can just be as good as some of the guys ahead of you, you would have achieved a lot. The ministry is difficult. It takes a lot of grace to even please God.

And I will pray the Father, and he shall give you another Comforter, that he may abide with you for ever;

John 14:16

The Holy Spirit (Comforter) is the anointing. When Jesus promised another comforter of the same kind, He was promising another anointing of the same kind. He was showing that the same kind of anointing with which He had ministered would be available to the apostles when He left. Most pastors would hasten their progress in the ministry if they would understand this simple truth. There is no new and special anointing that God wants to give you. He is simply going to give you another anointing of the same kind. Even the apostles were promised another of the same kind. It takes humility to admit that you are not an original. When people are impressed with your ministry, it is not easy to reveal that your message is not original. When people are impressed with your style it is not easy to reveal that you learnt it from somewhere else. Copying makes you dependent and sheep-like. The sheep nature is different from the serpent nature. It is the nature of snakes to be independent and solitary. This is the very opposite of how you must be if you want to walk with the Lord.

To be another of the same kind, you will have to depend on someone, you will have to learn from someone and you will have to follow someone. It is a good thing because no one can boast except in the Lord who created all things. Because you are humble, the blessings of God are going to be passed on to another generation. Not only will there be one great man of God for this generation, but there will be another of the same kind for the next generation.

3. Copying causes you to discover that there is nothing new under the sun.

> **The thing that hath been, it is that which shall be; and that which is done is that which shall be done: and there is no new thing under the sun. Is there any thing whereof it may be said, See, this is new? it hath been already of old time, which was before us.**
>
> **Ecclesiastes 1:9-10**

Indeed, there is nothing new under the sun. This is a fact that you must accept. You have nothing new to offer and your life will not introduce anything special. Like most ministers, I once thought I was introducing something new. I thought I had some new gifts and ideas, which no one else had ever had. With time, I discovered that all that I was doing had been done before. Every single thing I am doing and saying I have found people who said them before I did.

The truth about my ministry is that I am simply following hard after others I genuinely admire. I want to be like them and I am not ashamed to say so! I like their spirit! I like their flow! If I can be a copy of something that is working it would be a great achievement for me.

4. Copying is good because you become something that is already successful and working.

Copying sets you free from experimentation. You are free from years of wasting time as you discover principles that have worked over and over again. You do not have to create a new name. Making a name is not easy. That is why names are sold as franchises. A good name is one of the most valuable things on earth. Becoming another of the same kind means you are another with the same kind of name. Copying gives you access to strategies and formulae that have worked for your kind.

When I decide to become another of the same kind, all I need to know are the methods which were used by the one I am copying from. What worked for him will work for me. I simply copy the systems and techniques that have produced the results in him. Since I am going to be another of the same kind, the same kind of methods that worked for him will surely work for me!

5. Copying makes things easier for you on this road of ministry.

Many who are called to the ministry do not know how to walk the road of ministry. They know God has called them but don't have a clue as to how to progress. Many men of God do not know how to climb into higher heights in ministry. They see other men of God accomplishing great things but don't know that they can do the same!

The road to accomplishing the same things is clear now. Humble yourself and become another of the same kind. Don't try to be unique, special or different. Just become a copy of something that is working. Become another of the same kind. Use the techniques they used. Follow them very closely. Preach what they preach. Pray in the same way that they pray. Seek God in the same way that they do. Have as close a relationship to God as they do. You will surely become a marvelous copy of something successful.

6. Copying helps you to enter new things faster.

Copying quickens your rate of advancement in life and ministry. Because you are following a well-chartered road, you have the benefit of those who went on before you. The things that slowed them will not slow you down. You will move through obstacles faster because your kind will give you tips on how to overcome.

Without experiments and trials, anyone would be faster. One day, I was going somewhere with someone. He was in his car ahead and I was in mine. When he got into traffic, he called me and told me not to come the way he had gone because there was too much traffic on his route. I ended up getting there faster than he did because he saved me from having to go through his problem.

7. Copying helps to overcome problems.

Problems of a particular kind usually have the same solution. When you copy someone you will learn from the solutions he has developed. His experience at tackling the same problems will be yours. Have you ever wondered why doctors are calm in the face of apparent emergencies? It is because they are following solutions that have been repeated over and over for the same kind of problem.

8. Copying is the natural way to increase.

The natural way that all of creation multiplies is by producing another of the same kind.

> **And the earth brought forth grass, and herb yielding seed after his kind ...and God saw that it was good. And God created ...every living CREATURE ...after their KIND ...and God saw that it was good. And God made the beast of the earth after his kind ...and God saw that it was good.**
>
> **Genesis 1:12, 21, 25**

The natural way that the church will grow from glory to glory is to shamelessly learn from those ahead. I do not dispute that there are other ways to move forward. But I can share what has worked for me. *Copy! Copy! Copy!* Become another of the same kind. I want to be like my fathers who have gone ahead of me. I want to be exactly like them. I want to be like Jesus. I don't need to have any unique characteristics.

9. Copying is the key to great teaching and preaching.

> **Hear another parable: There was a certain householder, which planted a vineyard, and hedged it round about, and digged a winepress in it, and built a tower, and let it out to husbandmen, and went into a far country:**
>
> **Matthew 21:33**

Jesus taught the Word of God in the most beautiful and anointed way ever known to man. Little children remember his stories long after they stop reading the Bible. His teachings are relevant two thousand years after He gave them. The things that Jesus said are read by more people, quoted by more authors, translated into more languages, set to more music and represented in more art than any book ever written by man.

As someone said, comparing the teachings of Socrates, Plato and Aristotle to those of Jesus is like comparing an enquiry with a revelation!

Years ago, I told my beloved that I wanted to be a teacher of the Word like Jesus was. I thought to myself, "The teachings of Jesus are not easily forgotten, even by children." I decided to copy Jesus. Years ago, before I became a pastor, I decided to teach and preach with stories.

Jesus told so many stories. He would say, "A certain man had two sons..., a certain man made a great party..., there was a certain rich man which was clothed in purple..., a certain rich man died..., a certain man went up from Jericho..., there was a certain rich man which had a steward..., the ground of a certain rich man brought forth bountifully..., a certain noble man went into a far country..."

I decided that I wanted to be a teacher like Jesus. I didn't want to be anything new; I just wanted to be an exact copy of Jesus Christ.

The key to becoming a great preacher is to copy another great preacher. Just find a preacher whose ministry touches lives and become another of the same kind. Learn how to preach by copying! Don't blame anyone for your dry preaching. Don't blame anyone if no one listens to you! You know what to do.

Preach in the same way, teach in the same way and you will be very successful. Don't try anything new because there is nothing new. I don't know how plainer I could be when I say you should "copy"? Shamelessly copy, photocopy, photograph, replay, rewind and repeat what those great men do. You will find yourself becoming another of the same kind!

Those who are too proud to do this deliberately are becoming copies of somebody anyway. Why not choose and become a copy of somebody you admire? Why not choose to be a copy of someone whom God has sent into your life to train and mentor you?

Chapter

65

Church Growth and the Constant Effort to Accomplish

CHAPTER SUMMARY

Church growth is accomplished through constant effort. Without persistence in seeking the growth of the church, you will never have a mega church.

65.1 Pastors who exert a constant effort to accomplish church growth can expect to be found without spot and blameless.

65.2 Pastors who exert a constant effort to accomplish church growth can expect to become rich through their work.

65.3 Pastors who exert a constant effort to accomplish church growth can expect to become men of authority in charge of huge churches.

65.4 Pastors who exert a constant effort to accomplish church growth can expect to be made anointed, prosperous and fat.

65.5 Pastors who exert a constant effort to accomplish church growth can expect plenteousness in church members and church growth.

65.6 Pastors who exert a constant effort to accomplish church growth can expect to gain access to the corridors of power and influence.

65.7 Pastors who exert a constant effort to accomplish church growth can expect to have a great ministry that will last many generations.

Many pastors are unwilling to apply the relentless, unremitting and exacting efforts that are required to accomplish church growth. The church, like a farm, will require you to bestow much labour on it.

■ Diligence

Diligence is the constant and earnest effort to accomplish what is undertaken. Diligence is the persistent exertion of your body and mind towards your goal. People just want hands to be laid on them so that they can receive the magical gift of a mega church. But church growth does not happen that way. Church growth happens by being attentive and persistent in building the church. Church growth happens through diligence. Church growth will be given to pastors who believe in diligence. Church growth will be given to pastors who are relentless in their pursuit of church expansion.

■ Seven Rewards for Your Constant Efforts

1. Pastors who exert a constant effort to accomplish church growth can expect to be found without spot and blameless.

> **Wherefore, beloved, seeing that ye look for such things, be DILIGENT that ye may be found of him in peace, WITHOUT SPOT, AND BLAMELESS.**
>
> **2 Peter 3:14**

2. Pastors who exert a constant effort to accomplish church growth can expect to become rich through their work.

> **He becometh poor that dealeth with a slack hand: but the hand of the DILIGENT MAKETH RICH.**
>
> **Proverbs 10:4**

3. Pastors who exert a constant effort to accomplish church growth can expect to become men of authority in charge of huge churches.

> **The hand of the DILIGENT shall BEAR RULE: but the slothful shall be under tribute.**
>
> **Proverbs 12:24**

4. Pastors who exert a constant effort to accomplish church growth can expect to be made anointed, prosperous and fat.

> **The soul of the sluggard desireth, and hath nothing: but the soul of the DILIGENT shall BE MADE FAT.**
>
> **Proverbs 13:4**

5. Pastors who exert a constant effort to accomplish church growth can expect plenteousness in church members and church growth.

The thoughts of the DILIGENT tend only to plenteousness; but of every one that is hasty only to want.

Proverbs 21:5

6. Pastors who exert a constant effort to accomplish church growth can expect to gain access to the corridors of power and influence.

Seest thou a man DILIGENT in his business? he shall STAND BEFORE KINGS; he shall not stand before mean men.

Proverbs 22:29

7. Pastors who exert a constant effort to accomplish church growth can expect to have a great ministry that will last many generations.

Be thou DILIGENT to know the state of thy flocks, and look well to thy herds. For riches are not for ever: and doth the crown endure to EVERY GENERATION?

Proverbs 27:23-24

Chapter

66

How to Work Hard for a Mega Church

CHAPTER SUMMARY

How do you become an effective, tenacious and tireless minister of the gospel? How can you be relentless in your drive for church growth? This chapter seeks to show you how to work hard as a pastor.

66.1 Work hard by using the most fruitful working hours.

66.2 Work hard by spending a lot of time on the church.

66.3 Work hard by expending your energy and money on the church.

66.4 Work hard by cheerfully doing the same things over and over.

66.5 Work hard under an overseer.

66.6 Work hard when you have no overseer.

66.7 Work hard by working from your heart.

> **Let the elders who rule well be considered worthy of double honor, especially THOSE WHO WORK HARD at preaching and teaching.**
>
> **1 Timothy 5:17 (NASB)**

How do you become an industrious worker, occupied all the time with the Lord's work?

1. Work hard by using the most fruitful working hours.

Every true job has its own working hours. The work of the ministry has its own peculiar working hours. This often confuses people. They think pastors must be in the office from 9:00 a.m. to 5:00 p.m. like everybody else. But those are the fruitful working hours of secular offices. But we are not bankers or accountants. We are ministers of the gospel!

No more banking hours for pastors! Nobody asks pilots to work from 9:00 a.m. to 5:00 p.m. Everybody knows that their working hours are peculiar and everyone accepts that reality. Helps ministers and church administrators may have to work from 8.00am to 5.00pm like secular workers because of the nature of their ministry work. But shepherding pastors will have completely different fruitful working hours.

On Sunday mornings, our church boots into action at 6.00am and we sometimes leave after midnight. Sunday is the church's busiest and most important day for the pastor. A Sunday well spent is like a whole week of work! It should be the case for every church. Pastors counsel, visit, and teach Bible school classes throughout the whole of Sunday. Pastors who are building their churches must rest on Mondays.

2. Work hard by spending a lot of time on the church.

When an activity consumes just a few minutes of your time in a week, it cannot be called your "work". For instance, I drive my car for a few minutes every day but my work is not "driving" per se. It is something that I do on my way to work. However, if driving a car, for example a taxi, were to become my work, I would not spend less than eight hours a day driving. Then, to me, driving would have become work!

You cannot claim to be doing the "work" of the ministry until it actually consumes a reasonable amount of time in your week. If waiting on God, catching the anointing, catching revelation and receiving guidance from the Holy Spirit does not take up many hours and days of your week, then you are not working yet. For a minister of the gospel, praying and waiting on God must take up many hours. If it is work it will take up your time.

When you were not a pastor building a large church, you could afford to spend a few minutes catching the anointing. You could afford to spend twenty minutes receiving a revelation from the Word. But now that you are a serious professional mega church builder, you need to spend several hours and days waiting on the Lord!

3. Work hard by expending your energy and money on the church.

Everyone must realize that doing the work of the ministry involves spending a lot of energy. Do not be surprised if you get tired doing the work of a pastor. It is only a sign that you are working well. Most good jobs leave their employees exhausted.Do not be surprised if the ministry leaves you tired and worn out. Another thing that you will expend is money. Does it not cost you money to go to work everyday? Do you not spend money at work for lunch everyday?

It is the same thing with the work of ministry. Why should you complain if you have to pay money to travel to wait on the Lord? Why should you complain if you have to spend money buying books and CDs that you need? Make no mistake about it. Waiting on God, catching the anointing and revelation by the guidance of the Spirit is hard work. Praying, visiting, counseling and interacting with people is hard work. As you do the work of God, you will expend your energy and money. When you begin to feel tired, just remember it is a sign that you are really working.

4. Work hard by cheerfully doing the same things over and over.

By nature, all real work is repetitive and regular. If you are working hard you will do the repetitive and regular chores cheerfully. Even if you are bored you must keep doing the "work" - praying, visiting, counseling and interacting (PVCI). Even if you are tired you must keep doing the "work" – waiting on God, catching the anointing, catching the revelation and guidance (WAR).

Many pastors don't pray much because they feel it's repetitive and boring. But when prayer becomes your work you will have to repeat your prayers and you will have to pray regularly. When visiting becomes your work, you will have to visit repeatedly and regularly.

There is a difference between a social visit to a friend's house and a pastoral visit. Pastoral visits must be conducted repeatedly by pastors. Mega church pastors must intentionally go to the homes of their members on a regular basis. Don't we do our secular work when we don't feel like it? Don't we all go to the same work place repeatedly and regularly although we don't feel like it?

In the same way, anyone who claims to be doing the work of the ministry must rise up and repeatedly do the important tasks of a pastor. We don't pray just because we feel like it. We pray because we have to! We must rise up early and cheerfully intercede for the people God has given us.

5. Work hard under an overseer.

> **To Titus, my true child in a common faith: ...For this reason I left you in Crete, that you might set in order what remains, and appoint elders in every city AS I DIRECTED YOU,**
>
> **Titus 1:4-5 (NASB)**

Paul directed Timothy and Titus in the ministry. He told them what to do, where to stay and even what to say. He sent them on errands and missions in the ministry. Timothy and Titus are good examples of ministers who worked under the oversight of an apostle. They received detailed instructions on how to behave in the church. The reality is that most ministers need to be supervised.

Unfortunately, some people develop an attitude when they are supervised. They frown and sulk when they are instructed or corrected. They threaten to break away when they are told off. They say, "The church structure is too rigid, too tight and too inflexible. We need space to operate and develop our ministries."Because supervised people are paid less than the unsupervised they often break away because of money. Working diligently under an overseer will only lead to your promotion.

6. Work hard when you have no overseer.

> **For I would have you know, brethren, that the gospel which was preached by me is not according to man.**
>
> **For I neither received it from man, nor was I taught it, but I received it through a revelation of Jesus Christ.**
>
> **Galatians 1:11-12 (NASB)**

Paul is the best example of a minister who had no overseer. He did not need to be supervised. No one told him where to go or what to say. Your calling may be such that you do not need an overseer. When you have no overseer, you need maturity in hearing the voice of the Holy Spirit. You need accuracy in hearing the voice of the Holy Spirit. You need to be able to judge yourself since there is no one around to judge you.

Nobody will tell you are wrong. No one will tell you when to pray, study or visit anyone. God will have to tell you directly. When you are not supervised, no one will speak to you about the changes you have to make in your ministry or the decisions you have to take.

No one will tell you when you are going astray or when you are moving into error. You have to judge yourself. And your judgment had better be right. If you have not been called into this kind of unsupervised position do not venture into it because it will destroy you. Many ministers have become independent and self-governing when they should have lived and ministered under the supervision of a true apostle like Paul.

7. Work hard by working from your heart.

> **For I have no man likeminded, who will naturally care for your state.**
>
> **Philippians 2:20**

There is nothing like doing a job from the bottom of your heart. Work for God until it becomes your second nature. Work for the Lord until it is a pleasure for you to work. Work for the Lord until you cannot distinguish between working and resting. No one ever told me what to do in ministry. I have naturally wanted to pray, to visit and to counsel my people. I have naturally wanted to wait on God, catch the anointing, revelation and receive guidance from the Holy Spirit.

Our church is larger today and I struggle to know the names of everyone and to remember who they are. It is almost an impossible task! I wish I knew everybody's homes. I wish I could attend all their important family events. It is a natural desire. Anyone who is a true pastor has what I call "natural care".

Chapter

67

Church Growth and the Work of a Pastor (P.V.C.I.)

CHAPTER SUMMARY

- **Three Reasons Why Ministry Is Hard Work!**

67.1 **Ministry is hard work because Paul taught that ministry was work.**

67.2 **Ministry is hard work because Epaphras laboured in ministry work.**

67.3 **Ministry is hard work because Jesus described the workers in ministry as labourers.**

- **The Pastor's Work: PVCI**

67.4 **Prayer**

67.5 **Visitation**

67.6 **Counselling**

67.7 **Interaction**

> **... LET HIM LABOUR, working with his hands the thing which is good...**
>
> **Ephesians 4:28**

I remember when I first started out in full-time ministry. People would often ask my wife, "Where is your husband? Is he at home?"

One lady, a lawyer friend of hers said, "Oh, so your husband doesn't work anymore!"

My wife would answer, "You have no idea how hard he works."

They thought that because I was no longer practicing medicine, I was no longer working. Many people think that all that the pastor does is to prepare one sermon a week and then deliver it on Sunday morning. Afterwards, he is free to sleep until the next Sunday.

Many times people have called either late in the morning or in the afternoon and have said, "Hullo, how are you pastor? Sorry to disturb your sleep."

I would think, "This man thinks I sleep all day and all night as well."

Then I would politely answer, "I was not sleeping."

I have never bothered to explain what I was doing. "It is a waste of time," I thought to myself.

These and other remarks have made me realize that some people think that the ministry is a very restful occupation—an easy alternative to real and difficult jobs.

■ Three Reasons Why Ministry Is Hard Work!

1. Ministry is hard work because Paul taught that ministry was work.

> **And he gave some, apostles; and some, prophets; and some, evangelists; and some, pastors and teachers; For the perfecting of the saints, for the WORK of the ministry, for the edifying of the body of Christ:**
>
> **Ephesians 4:11-12**

The saints are to be perfected for the work. This means that pastors are to perfect the saints so that *they* can join in the hard work of ministry.

2. Ministry is hard work because Epaphras laboured in ministry work.

> **Epaphras, who is *one* of you, a servant of Christ, saluteth you, always labouring fervently for you in prayers, that ye may stand perfect and complete in all the will of God.**
>
> **Colossians 4:12**

There was a man called Epaphras, a servant of Christ "always labouring fervently for you in prayers". Epaphras was not playing games. He was not on a holiday. He was labouring, working and fighting for the kingdom of God.

3. Ministry is hard work because Jesus described the workers in ministry as labourers.

When Jesus saw the multitudes who were fainting because of lack of a shepherd, He said, "The harvest is plenty but the labourers are few." The Greek word translated labourer is the word "ergates", which means a toiler, teacher, laborer and a worker.

The ministry is toil and sweat. I have found that out practically. Anybody who wants to have a mega church must realize that he is not embarking on a game but real work. You will soon realize that church growth is not a joke and neither is it a game. It is real toil and labour. If ministry is work, what does it involve? What type of work is ministry work?

■ The Pastor's Work: PVCI

PRAYER (P) VISITATION (V) COUNSELLING (C) INTERACTION (I)

1. PRAYER

Prayer is the sustaining force of the church. I believe in praying for hours for the church. There is a correlation between the amount of prayer put into the church by the eldership of the church and the growth of the church. In Korea, it is well known that the pastors pray for long hours. It is no surprise then that the largest churches in the world are found in that nation. I believe that every full-time pastor should try to pray for at least three hours every day. Lay pastors and shepherds should pray for at least one or two hours a day. There must be long times of prayer.

2. VISITATION

In Jeremiah 23:2, God makes it clear that one of the principal duties of pastors is to visit.

> **Therefore thus saith the Lord God of Israel against the pastors…Ye have scattered my flock...and HAVE NOT VISITED THEM…**
>
> **Jeremiah 23:2**

It is quite clear from this, that pastors are expected to visit their sheep in their homes. This is different from counseling them in the office. It is also different from preaching and teaching from the pulpit. It is a special ministry. The greatest visitor on this earth was Jesus Christ. Since his visit, the world has never been the same again. There is a difference between church members who have been visited and those who have never been visited. Church members who have been visited in their homes become stable and hardly ever leave the church.

3. COUNSELLING

It is important to minister the Word of God, especially in teaching. Churches based on solid Bible teachings tend to grow. As the years go by, these churches grow larger and larger. It is like a flock that has been exposed to fields and fields of green grass. The natural response is that the flock will be healthy, multiply and grow. You will find greater growth in churches that have strong teaching and preaching than in churches that emphasize miracles. I believe in miracles but these can never take the place of the Word. Sheep don't feed on miracles. They feed on the Word!

4. INTERACTION

A shepherd is supposed to interact with his sheep. How can he interact properly if he is detached and aloof? Pastors and shepherds must do what I call *"Deep Sea Fishing".*

Deep Sea Fishing

What is the deep sea? The deep sea is the mass of church members who stream in and out of church every Sunday morning. Many people attend our churches and nobody knows them or even talks with them. Some come in and out for a while and then drop out.

It is the duty of shepherds and pastors to plunge into what I call the deep sea and conduct Deep Sea Fishing. They are to move into the crowd of unknown faces and interact with them. They must befriend unknown people, talk with them, find out where they live, and establish a line of friendship. Everybody wants to be known and to feel important. When people are not known, they move away to a place where they can be known and made to feel important. All human beings have a psychological need to be identified and recognized!

It is that need that we try to meet by doing *"deep sea fishing"*.

When all the pastors do deep sea fishing, they will get to know the people who do not belong to small groups within the church, but still need pastoral visits and care. *Deep sea fishing* helps to establish floating visitors in the church. That is why it is important for lay pastors and shepherds to be in church on Sunday and involve themselves in this all-important interaction - deep sea fishing. It is not only the pastor who is preaching who has work to do.

I like to linger in the church for hours after the service, interacting with different people and meeting different groups. I am neither a Prime Minister nor a pop star. I am a pastor. Pastors are not film stars. They are shepherds who are supposed to mingle with their sheep. The Bible says that the sheep know the voice of the good shepherd. How can they know your voice if they don't even see you?

Chapter

68

Church Growth and the Work of Taking Heed to Yourself (W.A.R.)

CHAPTER SUMMARY

Take heed to yourself so that you can become a mega church pastor. The ministry depends on you because you are the shepherd. If you go down everything will go down with you. You must invest in yourself. You must protect yourself and you must help yourself.

- **The Work of Saving Yourself: WAR**

68.1 Waiting

68.2 Anointing

68.3 Revelation

i) Revelation for Preaching

ii) Ten ways to Receive Revelation

iii) Revelation for Guidance

- **Two Missing Ingredients**

68.4 How to Minister with the Manifestation of God

68.5 How to Minister with the Presence of God

> **Take heed unto thyself, and unto the doctrine; continue in them: for in doing this thou shalt both save thyself, and them that hear thee.**
>
> **1 Timothy 4:16**

The work of taking heed to yourself involves four main things just as the work of pastoring a church involves four main things. The four main things we need to do to take heed to yourself are: Waiting on God, catching the Anointing, catching revelation and receiving guidance from the Holy Spirit (W.A.R.)

The Work of Saving Yourself: WAR

WAITING (W) ANOINTING (A) REVELATION (R)

1. WAITING

We must wait on the Lord! Learn our lessons well. In His timing He will tell where to go, what to do and what to say. Pastors and shepherds should make it a point to get away from their busy schedules and wait on God for even longer periods. Jesus himself retreated to the wilderness and mountains to pray. Praying for whole days on retreats is a very important aspect of a pastor's schedule.

Waiting actually involves pausing, slowing down and not rushing headlong into things.

The ministry is spiritual from beginning to end.

Full-time ministry always involves prayer and ministry of the Word.

> **...It is not reason that we should leave the word of God, and serve tables... But we will give ourselves continually to prayer, and to the ministry of the word.**
>
> **Acts 6:2-4**

Peter made it clear that his work was not arranging tables nor organizing food for his church members. His duty was to pray and minister the Word.

2. ANOINTING

> **How God anointed Jesus of Nazareth with the Holy Ghost and with power: who went about doing good, and healing all that were oppressed of the devil; for God was with him.**
>
> **Acts 10:38**

You will receive several anointings in the course of your life. Different gifts will be imparted to you at different times. These different gifts are given to you at different times depending on what you are doing in the ministry. You cannot go around doing the good work of building large churches unless you are anointed to do so. The anointing is the Holy Spirit and Jesus taught us to pray for the Holy Spirit. You must spend hours and hours praying for the Holy Spirit. God will give you what you ask for.

Apart from receiving the Holy Spirit on the day of Pentecost, (Acts 2:4) several other impartations of the gifts of the Holy Spirit took place. Jesus breathed on the disciples at a meeting and asked them to receive the Holy Spirit (John 20:22). On another occasion when the disciples were assembled they were filled again with the Holy Spirit and empowered for miracles, signs and wonders (Acts 4:31).

3. REVELATION

> **That the God of our Lord Jesus Christ, the Father of glory, may give unto you the spirit of wisdom and revelation in the knowledge of him**
>
> **Ephesians 1:17**

Revelation for Preaching

Revelation is an instance of communication and disclosure that God gives to His servants. God discloses His word and His will to those that He loves. Have you ever thought about it? Revelation is the one thing that sets you above your congregation and enables you to lead them.

Think about it. If God has revealed something to you that He did not reveal to others, He must regard you differently. Revelation is what sets you apart from the ordinary Christian.

Kenneth Hagin shared how he had prayed for the spirit of wisdom and revelation for years and years on end. It also became my prayer as I sought after the Lord.

> **Study to shew thyself approved unto God, a workman that needeth not to be ashamed, rightly dividing the word of truth.**
>
> **2 Timothy 2:15**

Receiving revelation is key to the success of your ministry. Revelation has several parts to it. Revelation can be from the word of God or from visions and dreams. A pastor must spend his time seeking revelation from God. The spirit of revelation is evident when a person preaches or teaches the Word of God. Revelation from the Word of God is the most beautiful kind of revelation and you must spend time seeking for it. "No man ever spake like this man," is what they will say when the Spirit of revelation is upon you.

Ten Ways to Receive Revelation

1. You receive revelation when you listen to anointed messages from preachers and teachers of the Word of God. (Ephesians 4:11-12).

2. You receive revelation when you study the Word of God in relation to sermons and messages you have recently heard. (2 Timothy 2:15).

3. You receive revelation when you study the Word of God and search for the deeper meanings of words in the Bible. (2 Peter 1:21).

4. You receive revelation when you have discussions with fellow pastors, teachers and prophets. (Acts 13:1-3).

5. You receive revelation when you read the real life stories of men of God that have gone ahead of you. (Acts 1:1).

6. You receive revelation when you study the dreams and visions of well-recognized prophets. I have received much revelation for my life by studying the visions and dreams of Kenneth Hagin and Rick Joyner. (John 20:17-18).

7. You receive revelation when God reminds you of something important. Don't take it lightly when you suddenly remember something you have forgotten. (John 14:26).

8. You receive revelation when the Lord puts a burden on your heart. (Jeremiah 23:32-40).

9. You receive revelation when God impresses something on your heart through the inner witness. (Romans 8:16).

10. You receive revelation when God speaks to you through a dream or a vision. (Acts 16:9).

Revelation for Guidance

For as many as are led by the Spirit of God, they are the sons of God.
Romans 8:14

One of the key aspects of revelation is the guidance that it brings. You must be led by the Holy Spirit in all that you do for God. Every detail matters to God. He wants to know and He wants to direct. You cannot just have a radio programme because everyone is doing it.

When you are led by the Spirit of God, you become a son of God. A son of God is a supernatural being who operates under the powers granted by his heavenly father. Being led by the spirit of God makes you have a supernatural ministry. It is supernatural to have thousands of people gathering every Sunday to listen to your wisdom.

Kenneth Hagin said the difference between ministers is their ability to be led by the Spirit of God. One of the key duties of a minister is to wait and seek for supernatural guidance concerning everything that he is doing. Waiting on God for supernatural guidance is no small task. It is a big job and will take up hours, days and weeks of searching for the will of God.

Two Missing Ingredients

There are two things that are often missing in a minister's life: the manifestations of God and the presence of God. Supernatural guidance and obedience to God's will are the keys to the manifestations and the presence of the Lord. You must relate with ministers not just by their good doctrines. You must relate with them because you sense the presence of God in their lives.

Why should you bother to get close to ministries that have no spiritual glory on them; from whence the glory of the Lord has departed? Why do you have something to do with someone whom God is not with?

How to Minister with the Manifestation of God

The key to the manifestations of God is obedience to His Word. Whether this Word came through the reading of the Bible or through a dream, you must obey it. It is the only thing you can do to show Him that you love Him. God will manifest Himself to you when you obey His instructions. Read for yourself the promise of the manifestations of God:

> **He that hath my commandments, and keepeth them, he it is that loveth me: and he that loveth me shall be loved of my Father, and I will love him, and will MANIFEST myself to him.**
>
> **John 14:21**

How to Minister with the Presence of God

You must seek to obey the will of God when He shows it to you. It is the key to the presence of the Lord. The presence of God will come on you because you are obeying the words and instructions to your life. Read for yourself the promise of the presence of God:

> **Jesus answered and said unto him, If a man love me, he will keep my words: and my Father will love him, and we will come unto him, and make our abode with him.**
>
> **John 14:23**

Chapter

69

Church Growth and Outward Impressions

CHAPTER SUMMARY

The Bible teaches us to have something to answer those who glory in outward appearances. There are always people who live and take decisions purely by the outward appearance.

■ Ten Areas Where Outward Impressions Are Important

69.1 **The outward appearance of your church building will affect your church growth.**

69.2 **The outward appearance of the location of your church building will affect your church growth.**

69.3 **The outward appearance of your stage will affect your church growth.**

69.4 **The outward appearance of the pastor will affect your church growth.**

69.5 **The outward appearance of the pastor's wife will affect church growth.**

69.6 **The outward appearance of the pastor's children will affect church growth.**

69.7 The outward appearance of the associate pastors will affect your church growth.

69.8 The outward appearance of the pastor's car will affect your church growth.

69.9 The outward appearance of the ushers will affect your church growth.

69.10 The outward appearance of the choristers and musicians will affect your church growth.

> **... that ye may have somewhat to answer them which glory in appearance, and not in heart.**
>
> **2 Corinthians 5:12**

The Bible teaches us to have something to answer those who glory in outward appearances. There are always people who live and take decisions purely by the outward appearance. Most of the people in our churches are carnal people. Carnal people usually judge by outward appearances because they are not spiritual. Whether you like it or not outward appearances matter in church growth. To have a mega church, you must be able to relate with and impress many carnal people who judge by outward appearances.

Once you are dealing with men you will be dealing with outward appearances. Indeed, the Lord does not look at these appearances but men do. "... for the LORD seeth not as man seeth; for man looketh on the outward appearance, but the Lord looketh on the heart" (1 Samuel 16:7). If man looks on the outward appearance then you need to get your outward appearances in order.

■ Ten Areas Where Outward Impressions Are Important

1. The outward appearance of your church building will affect your church growth.

Is your church housed in a ramshackle and decrepit building? Is your church building painted? Is it neat? Is there rubbish everywhere? Is there a refreshing and well-designed sign directing people to the service? Is your church building hot, stuffy and airless?

2. The outward appearance of the location of your church building will affect your church growth.

Is your church located in a disreputable or dangerous place? Are people afraid to come to that area? The location of your church will definitely affect the people who come there.

3. The outward appearance of your stage will affect your church growth.

Is your stage well lit and well organized? Or is it overcrowded? Are the instruments properly arranged and positioned on the stage? Is there symmetry on the stage? Is the stage simply a collection of odd items, many of which are not used during the church service? What is the character of your decorations? Does your stage have an international feel to it? Or have you allowed someone with poor taste to decorate your stage according to the low standards that she knows?

4. The outward appearance of the pastor will affect your church growth.

Do you dress nicely? Is your suit two sizes bigger than you are? Have you ironed your clothes until they are stiff and shiny phantoms of the original? Are your shoes dusty? Is your shirt falling off your shoulders? Are your teeth yellow? Do you have missing teeth that make you look like Dracula when you smile? Are any of your teeth sticking out or pointing in the wrong direction that make you look like a predator when you speak to the congregants? You may need to get a dentist to correct all that. You will be surprised at how improving the appearance of your teeth can lead to church growth.

5. The outward appearance of the pastor's wife will affect church growth.

Does the pastor's wife have a nice hairstyle? Or is her hair simply a black oily rag that has been dumped on her head? Does she bother to make herself beautiful? Does she have nice dresses and shoes? Does she smile? Is she friendly? Is she hospitable? Or is she ill-natured and quarrelsome? Does she look like a witch? Does she have a grim and unfriendly look? Does she constantly fall into depression and black moods?

The negative outward characteristics of a pastor's wife will definitely affect church growth.

6. The outward appearance of the pastor's children will affect church growth.

Barefooted, scruffy little ragamuffins running all over the place will not help your church grow. If the pastor's children are constantly wear ill-fitting and dirty clothes, it will not improve the outward image of your church. A thriving prosperous church does not have little children who look like beggars or beggars' children running all over the place.

7. The outward appearance of the associate pastors will affect your church growth.

Do your associate pastors look like a group of nobodies? Are they significant leaders in the congregation? Do they dress well? Do your associate pastors act like wimps constantly exuding timidity and false humility? Do they constantly have sheepish smiles? Are they constantly trying to please the richer members of the congregation?Do your assistant pastors have cars? Are they happy people who breed confidence, loyalty and unity?

8. The outward appearance of the pastor's car will affect your church growth.

Is your car the oldest model of its type? Is it always breaking down; making you have to beg for lifts and favours? This will not help church growth. Is your car the most expensive car in the church? Why do you want to look like the richest member of your church? Are you a business tycoon or a pastor? Why don't you rather blend into the congregation and be seen as an average person, neither the richest nor the poorest?

9. The outward appearance of the ushers will affect your church growth.

Do your ushers look like lean hungry foxes ready to steal offerings from the basket? Or do they look like dignified gentlemen who are humble servants in the house of the Lord? Do they know how to walk and carry themselves?

10. The outward appearance of the choristers and musicians will affect your church growth.

Do your choristers and musicians look nice? Do they do their hair and wear nice clothes? Are they so clumsy that they cannot fit into their clothes nor walk up the stage? Do they have nice voices or do they shriek through the microphone every Sunday? Are they smiling, happy worshippers of the Lord?

Chapter

70

Ten Reasons Why Women Make a Church Grow

CHAPTER SUMMARY

Women believe more quickly and are more ready to flow with God's servant. When churches are being pioneered, women are often the greatest treasure the apostle could have.

70.1 Women will make your church grow because they helped Jesus in His ministry. In the Bible women followed Jesus and helped Him.

70.2 Women will make your church grow because the apostle Paul used women in his ministry.

70.3 Women will make your church grow because they recognize the anointing and believe in it quicker than men.

70.4 Women will make your church grow because God has destined to destroy the devil through women.

70.5 Women will make your church grow because women are the producers of children.

70.6 Women will make your church grow because women are good pastors.

70.7 Women will make a church grow because women they are good helpers.

70.8 Women will make a church grow because they are more permanent and loyal workers.

70.9 Women will make a church grow because they are less concerned about money than men.

70.10 Women will make a church grow because the largest churches in the world have used women to build their churches.

Women are one of the greatest assets a church could ever have. Satan has deployed his weapon of deception to keep the women out of the workforce. Women have been depicted as the most dangerous group of people ready to destroy the man of God and his ministry. Indeed, many strange women have done just that!

However, this same group of apparently dangerous people hold the key to church growth.

1. Women will make your church grow because they helped Jesus in His ministry. In the Bible women followed Jesus and helped Him.

If women helped Jesus I would like them to help me too. If Jesus needed the help of women, you will too. Jesus had a worldwide ministry. He travelled to many cities and villages preaching the gospel. The twelve disciples were with Him on these preaching tours as well as certain women who ministered to Him. Women are always present where fruits are being borne!

> **And it came about soon afterwards, that He began going about from one city and village to another, proclaiming and preaching the kingdom of God; and THE TWELVE WERE WITH HIM, AND ALSO SOME WOMEN who had been healed of evil spirits and sicknesses: Mary who was called Magdalene, from whom seven demons had gone out, and Joanna the wife of Chuza, Herod's steward, and Susanna, and many others who were contributing to their support out of their private means.**
>
> **Luke 8:1- 3 (NASB)**

2. Women will make your church grow because the apostle Paul used women in his ministry.

If women helped the apostle Paul to achieve so much for God, they must have some importance other than making meat pies, serving tea or frying fish! Women can be fellow labourers with apostles in the ministry.

> **And I intreat thee also, true yokefellow, help THOSE WOMEN WHICH LABOURED WITH ME in the gospel, with Clement also, and *with* other my fellowlabourers, whose names are in the book of life.**
>
> **Philippians 4:3**

3. Women will make your church grow because they recognize the anointing and believe in it quicker than men.

Indeed, women are the live wires of the anointing. They receive, they detect and they believe ten times faster than the average man. Abigail recognized that David was going to become the king and she honoured him whilst her husband was hardened and resistant. The woman with the issue of blood received the anointing whilst Peter, James and the others felt and received no healing anointing at the crusade. Mary Magdalene went to the graveside on Easter Sunday to experience the resurrection first hand whilst Peter, James, John and the other powerful apostles were huddled away in unbelief and depression.

You may have heard of the Azusa street revival whose leader was William Seymour. There was a man called Charles Parham who was William Seymour's spiritual father and the principal of the Bible School William Seymour attended.

Pentecostalism was born when Charles Parham taught his Bible students (including William Seymour) about receiving the Holy Spirit and speaking in tongues in his Bible school although he himself did not yet speak in tongues.

Agnes

A lady called Agnes pressurized Charles Parham to pray for her to receive this Holy Spirit. Charles Parham was reluctant to pray for her but she pressed him to. When Charles Parham prayed for her, a glow came over her and she received the Holy Spirit and began to speak in fluent Chinese tongues. She even received the ability to write in Chinese. This was apparently documented by the government.

Amazingly, the Azusa street revival and the worldwide Pentecostal movement began through this lady being the first to believe and receive this gift of speaking in tongues. It was after this that William Seymour moved to California and began what we know as the Azusa Street Revival. Indeed, William Seymour himself had not yet received the Holy Spirit when he moved to California.

4. Women will make your church grow because God has destined to destroy the devil through women.

Women will destroy the devil. The ancient prophecy that attests to this fact is that women will bruise the head of the serpent. Through women you will destroy the devil, that old serpent that deceived the world.

> **And I will put enmity between thee and the woman, and between thy seed and her seed; it shall bruise thy head, and thou shalt bruise his heel.**
>
> **Genesis 3:15**

5. Women will make your church grow because women are the producers of children.

Wherever there are women there are children, off springs and fruits. In the natural, women bring about and nurture young ones. In the ministry, the same pattern is seen. Wherever there are women there are lots of spiritual children. Somehow, women attract other people to the church and convince many to join. They are the first to believe and the first to convince others to join in.

6. Women will make your church grow because women are good pastors.

Women have the natural gift of talking. They have this gift because they are always talking to children as they bring them up. This gift of talking can be perfectly transposed into the ministry as counsel, teaching and interaction.

I have watched as women have cared for others and built large churches. God used Aimee Semple McPherson to build the Four Square denomination of churches which is a thriving ministry today.

7. Women will make a church grow because women they are good helpers.

Women are natural helpers because they were created by God to help. Every woman has an inbuilt engine that makes her a natural helper. Women are looking for someone to help. Many women entered their marriages hoping to fulfill their divine calling of helping someone. Unfortunately, the hurts and confusion of marriage do not allow them to use their helping gift. In the church many women are able to express this natural helping gift.

8. Women will make a church grow because they are more permanent and loyal workers.

A church grows proportionately to the number of permanent and loyal people it has. Men are known to change their jobs at least four times in their lives whilst many women keep their jobs for a lifetime. A church filled with faithful and loyal people is a great blessing.

9. Women will make a church grow because they are less concerned about money than men.

Women are usually not as interested in money as men. They seem to be more content if they feel safe, secure and happy. Generally speaking, I would prefer to have women counting the church money. Generally speaking, I would prefer to have women in certain sensitive positions.

10. Women will make a church grow because the largest churches in the world have used women to build their churches.

Pastor David Yonggi Cho speaks about how women have served faithfully as cell leaders and helped to build his church. I once preached in a large church that seated twelve thousand people. It was one of the largest churches in that country. In that service, I was amazed to find not more than twenty men amongst twelve thousand women. Amazing women!

Chapter

71

How Radio, Television and Buses Make a Church Grow

CHAPTER SUMMARY

- **Ten Steps to an Effective Radio Ministry**

71.1 Believe in the radio ministry.

71.2 Be led by the spirit.

71.3 Have a radio programme early in the morning in your town or city.

71.4 Have a radio programme everyday.

71.5 Prepare for your radio programme as you would for a sunday sermon.

71.6 Minister to people on the radio as though they are in front of you.

71.7 Pray for people on the radio.

71.8 Never forget to invite people to come to your church.

71.9 Do altar calls for salvation and healing.

71.10 Ask for support at the right time.

■ Steps To An Effective TV Ministry

71.11 Recognize and believe in the powerful influence of television ministry.

71.12 Decide to do television ministry only when the Lord has led you to do it.

71.13 Spend the time to find out exactly what is involved in having a television ministry.

71.14 Buy inexpensive equipment when you are a beginner in the television ministry.

71.15 Train your own people to slowly learn the technical aspects of the television ministry.

71.16 Produce a quality television programme!

71.17 Always keep the name of your ministry on the screen.

71.18 Develop an excellent website that will complement your television ministry.

71.19 Invite people to attend church, at the end of your programmes.

71.20 Have telephones and internet facilities available to respond to calls and requests that come from your television programme.

■ Steps to an Effective Bus Ministry

71.21 Be aware that the bus ministry could be the missing key from your church growth strategies

71.22 Know that buses help POOR PEOPLE to come to your church.

71.23 Know that many of the largest churches in the world run effective bus ministries where they transport people from all over the city to their churches

71.24 Deploy buses to strategic points where you do outreaches.

71.25 Give free buses when you recognize that the people cannot pay for the service.

71.26 Charge enough to cover your cost when they can pay for it so that the bus ministry does not ruin the finances of the church.

... according to the prince of the power of the air...

Ephesians 2:2, KJV

A Vision

A prophet shared a vision. In the vision, he found himself out on the street witnessing. No one was listening to him and he was not getting far with his evangelistic outreach. Then he met an angel who asked him what he was doing. He explained to the angel that he was on outreach doing house-to-house evangelism and door-to-door witnessing.

Then the angel said to him, "Follow me, I will show you another way."

The angel took him to a very long pole stuck in the ground and climbed with him to the very top. The angel said to him, "Call out the people from here and speak to them from this place."

As the pastor sat on the top of the pole and ministered, crowds began to gather and come to him. He was amazed at the response that he was getting by speaking from the top of the pole.

The Lord said to him, "Move away from door to door evangelism and call out to the people through the airwaves. I will bless your ministry as you summon the people through the airwaves."

This vision is a revelation of the importance of radio and television ministry for church growth. The media has an important role to play in our current world. Satan is the prince of the power of the air. He has dominated the airwaves and the church must rise up to take control of the airwaves and dominate it through the gospel of Jesus Christ. The media ministry is a fight against the prince of the power of the air!

Ten Steps to an Effective Radio Ministry

1. **BELIEVE IN THE RADIO MINISTRY.**

   Whatever you do that is not of faith is sin. What you do out of faith will work out. Mountains will be moved and rivers will be crossed as you press into the radio ministry. Understand the advantages and blessings of a radio ministry. You must know that you will reach people through the radio whom you will not reach in any other way.

2. **BE LED BY THE SPIRIT before you embark on a radio ministry.**

   Pray about the radio ministry and put it before the Lord. If He gives you peace about it then go for it. If it is not his will or his time then stay away from it. If you are led by the Spirit to be on the radio, it will be a blessing to the church. If you are not led by the Spirit to be on radio it will not help you.

3. **Have a radio programme EARLY IN THE MORNING in your town or city.**

   Your voice must be heard every morning in your city. Your voice must be heard preaching, praying for people and ministering to all who tune in.

4. **Have a radio programme EVERYDAY. For your radio ministry to be effective it must be every day or every weekday.**

5. **PREPARE for your radio programme as you would for a Sunday sermon.**

   In all labour there is profit and your diligence will cause you to stand before kings. Do not come to the studio unprepared and fumble through the programme.

6. **MINISTER TO PEOPLE on the radio as though they are in front of you.**

   Speak as though you were speaking to thousands. Do not wonder to yourself whether people are listening or not. Many people are listening to you.

7. **PRAY FOR PEOPLE on the radio.**

   People love to be prayed for. Pray powerful prayers using the King James language, the Psalms and the Synonyms.

8. **Never forget to invite PEOPLE to come to your church.**

   Use your time on the radio wisely. Tell people what to do and they will obey you. Invite them to come and see you so that you can continue ministering the power and the anointing to them.

9. **DO ALTAR CALLS for salvation and healing.**

   Salvation must never go to the background of your ministry. Jesus Christ came to this world purposely to save sinners. Use the radio to lead people to Jesus Christ. All ministry flourishes on the foundation of Jesus Christ.

10. **ASK FOR SUPPORT at the right time.**

    Do not be ashamed to ask for money. Ask and you shall receive, knock and the door shall be opened unto you. The work of a pastor includes asking for support for the ministry. But remember that there is a time for everything. Do not start your radio ministry by asking for money. The first thing you do must be to minister the Word of God.

Steps to an Effective TV Ministry

1. **Recognize and believe in the powerful influence of television ministry.**

   Know that being on television makes you known and makes your church visible. Being known and visible makes your church a good option whenever people are deciding to find a good church. There are times when people will attend your church as a direct response to your television programme. Be aware that your television programme will not necessarily cause more people to attend your church.

2. **Decide to do television ministry only when the Lord has led you to do it.**

   Always be led by the Spirit of God. Do not do things because everyone is doing them.

3. **Spend the time to find out exactly what is involved in having a television ministry.**

   There are many hidden costs in a television ministry.

4. **Buy inexpensive equipment when you are a beginner in the television ministry.**

   Do not listen to technical people who advise you to buy super expensive stuff that is not really necessary.

5. **Train your own people to slowly learn the technical aspects of the television ministry.**

   There is no rush. After you have trained ordinary people to do a television programme, your production cost will be almost zero. If you do not train your own people, you will have a very high production cost which will kill your television ministry.

6. **Produce a quality television programme!**

   Compare your programmes with other successful television ministries and try to match them. Emulation is the key to catching up and surging forward. Don't be ashamed to be a copy cat.

7. **Always keep the name of your ministry on the screen.**

   Show people how to reach you and make it easy for them to do so. Many people watch TV programmes for twenty minutes and do not know who is speaking or which ministry is being presented.

8. **Develop an excellent website that will complement your television ministry.**

   If you cannot be on television, you can have a website that shows your programmes. You may have more success on the website than on television. The internet will soon take over from what we know as television today.

9. **Invite people to attend church, at the end of your programmes.**

   Many people will come because you specifically asked them to. Use your time on television wisely. Tell people to come and see you in your church.

10. **Have telephones and internet facilities available to respond to calls and requests that come from your television programme.**

    Set up a system to respond promptly and eagerly to the people who call in. If you tell them to call in and they cannot reach you they will soon lose faith in your TV programme.

Steps to an Effective Bus Ministry

1. **Be aware that the bus ministry could be the missing key from your church growth strategies**

2. **Know that buses help POOR PEOPLE to come to your church.**

   Be aware of the blessings that come to people who help the poor. A church that considers the poor will receive many blessings.

3. **Know that many of the largest churches in the world run effective bus ministries where they transport people from all over the city to their churches.**

   Doing a bus ministry is simply following the example of many other mega churches in the world today.

4. **Deploy buses to strategic points where you do outreaches.**

   Let the people who have been saved and won to the Lord through your outreaches have an easy way of coming to the church.

5. **Give free buses when you recognize that the people cannot pay for the service.**

   Seek support for your bus ministry from the wealthier members of your church. In so doing the rich will be helping the poor.

6. **Charge enough to cover your cost when they can pay for it so that the bus ministry does not ruin the finances of the church.**

Chapter

72

Twenty Diverse Tests and Temptations of a Pastor Who Seeks Church Growth

CHAPTER SUMMARY

Many things that happen in our lives are actually tests! Your desire to have a mega church will lead you to a road that has many painful testing experiences.

■ Twenty Tests

72.1 **As you build a mega church, you will be tested so that you can be promoted. Without these tests you cannot be promoted.**

72 2 **As you build your church, you will suffer persecution because you want to do something so godly as to build a big church.**

72.3 **In your quest for church growth, you will go through tests that are designed to humble you.**

72.4 **In your quest for church growth, you will go through tests that will reveal what is in your heart.**

72.5 **In your quest for church growth, you will go through tests that will show whether you are really obedient.**

72.6 In your quest for church growth, you will go through tests to show whether you really love the Lord.

72.7 As you grow into a mega church pastor, you will go through tests that are like fiery trials.

72.8 As you become a mega church pastor you will be tested by bad winds, bad storms and floods.

72.9 As you grow into a mega church pastor you will be tested with grief and sorrow.

72.10 A mega church pastor will be tested for his ability to withstand pressure.

72.11 A mega church pastor will suffer temptations.

72.12 On your road to church growth, you will meet with wicked and unreasonable men.

72.13 A mega church pastor will be tested by people who desert him.

72.14 In your quest for church growth you will be tested by people who do not support you.

72.15 In your quest for church growth, you will be tempted with the personal weaknesses of your life.

72.16 To become a mega church pastor, you must pass the test of handling disloyal people.

72.17 In your quest to become a mega church pastor, you will struggle with your personal needs and the church's needs.

72.18 In your quest to become a mega church pastor you will be tested with your ability to fast and pray as well as your ability to watch and pray.

72.19 In your quest for church growth you will be tested with your willingness to expose yourself to danger.

72.20 In your quest for church growth you will be tested for your susceptibility to delusions.

Nothing is going to come to you easily. You must consider your life to be one long series of tests, trials and temptations. There is a purpose for each test that God takes you through. Because spiritual tests do not take place in a classroom they are not easily recognized. Many things in a pastor's life look like coincidences but they are not. Many people you meet and interact with look like they just happened to come by. Indeed, they did not just come by; they were sent by the Lord. Some people you meet today are the newly arriving tests, trials and temptations of your life. You will be expected to pass the tests of relating with them. So what are the tests that a pastor of a mega church should expect to go through? What trials will a pastor desiring church growth experience?

Twenty Tests

1. As you build a mega church, you will be tested so that you can be promoted. Without these tests you cannot be promoted.

In school, you cannot move to the next level unless you pass your tests. The scripture says that you become perfect and complete after you have successfully gone through trials, testings and temptations. O mega church pastor, don't you want to be perfect and complete? Don't you want to be fully qualified for all the increase that is coming to you?

> **Consider it all joy, my brethren, when you encounter various trials, knowing that the testing of your faith produces endurance. And let endurance have its perfect result, that you may be perfect and complete, lacking in nothing.**
>
> **James 1:2-4, NASB.**

2. As you build your church, you will suffer persecution because you want to do something so godly as to build a big church.

Expect persecution from your friends, relatives, colleagues and bystanders. Don't complain because you are being persecuted. It's part of the package. Expect to be persecuted because of your mega church.

> **Yea, and all that will live godly in Christ Jesus shall suffer persecution.**
>
> **2 Timothy 3:12**

3. In your quest for church growth, you will go through tests that are designed to humble you.

You need to be very humble to be a pastor of thousands of people. You must not think too highly of yourself. Expect troubles, persecutions, difficulties that will bring you to your knees.Expect situations that you cannot do anything about to break you down, and bring you to your knees. O mega church pastor, these things are intended to help you remember that you are but a man.

> **And thou shalt remember all the way which the LORD thy God led thee these forty years in the wilderness, TO HUMBLE THEE, and to prove thee, to know what was in thine heart, whether thou wouldest keep his commandments, or no.**
>
> **Deuteronomy 8:2**

4. In your quest for church growth, you will go through tests that will reveal what is in your heart.

No one knows what is really in your heart. You don't even know. But there are circumstances that can bring out what is in your heart. God will allow those tests to reveal what is in your heart. You may say, "I love the Lord" but you really love a man. When the man is gone you will find out whether you really love the Lord.

> **And thou shalt remember all the way which the LORD thy God led thee these forty years in the wilderness, to humble thee, and to prove thee, TO KNOW WHAT WAS IN THINE HEART, whether thou wouldest keep his commandments, or no.**
>
> **Deuteronomy 8:2**

5. In your quest for church growth, you will go through tests that will show whether you are really obedient.

"I love the Lord and I will obey Him" is the song of the average minister of the gospel. But there are certain things that will really reveal whether you are obedient to the Lord. It is easy to say, "I will go anywhere, I will do anything". Then the command will come, "Now go to the uttermost corner of that poor country!" Suddenly, all the obedience is thrown out of the window and you realize how unwilling and disobedient you really are. I have people who call me "Daddy" and answer every sentence with "Yes, please". They present themselves as the most humble and obedient servants. But one instruction can reveal how truly detestable and disobedient they really are.

People profess, confess and claim things, but their deeds reveal that they are actually disobedient, detestable and worthless to you. "They profess to know God, but by their *deeds* they deny *Him*, being detestable and disobedient, and worthless for any good deed" (Titus 1:16, NASB). These are strong words but they are true.

6. In your quest for church growth, you will go through tests to show whether you really love the Lord.

Do you really love the Lord? I love Jesus! I love the Lord with all my heart! I will do anything for Him. One day, something will come to your life and that thing will reveal what you love. Do you love the Lord, do you love money or do you love the fame of ministry? It will all be revealed through the tests that are coming your way.

> **Thou shalt not hearken unto the words of that prophet, or that dreamer of dreams: for the LORD your God proveth you, TO KNOW WHETHER YE LOVE THE LORD YOUR GOD WITH ALL YOUR HEART AND WITH ALL YOUR SOUL.**
>
> **Deuteronomy 13:3**

7. As you grow into a mega church pastor, you will go through tests that are like fiery trials.

Fire makes you lose everything. When you go through a trial that makes you feel that you are losing everything, don't be surprised. Don't think it is strange.

People have lost their wives, their children, their money and their self-respect through the fiery trials they experienced. Some people have lost as many as three wives in the fire. Some people lost as many as five children. You have to believe that these fiery trials are necessary for your promotion to a mega church pastor.

> **Beloved, think it not strange concerning the fiery trial which is to try you, as though some strange thing happened unto you:**
>
> **1 Peter 4:12**

8. As you become a mega church pastor you will be tested by bad winds, bad storms and floods.

One day, the pastor of a large church said to me, "A bad wind is blowing on our friend."

He continued, "We must pray for him because if that bad wind turns in our direction, it will not be good for us!"

You see, as you build a mega church and work for God, you may think that only good winds will blow in your direction. The fact that you are doing the right things and building your house on a rock does not mean that a bad wind will not blow on you.

Amazingly, the bad wind that blows on the person who is doing all the wrong things is the same bad wind that will blow on the good person's house.

> **Therefore whosoever heareth these sayings of mine, and doeth them, I will liken him unto a wise man, which built his house upon a rock: And the RAIN descended, and the FLOODS came, and the WINDS blew, and beat upon that house; and it fell not: for it was founded upon a rock. And every one that heareth these sayings of mine, and doeth them not, shall be likened unto a foolish man, which built his house upon the sand: And the RAIN descended, and the FLOODS came, and the WINDS blew, and beat upon that house; and it fell: and great was the fall of it.**
>
> **Matthew 7:24-27**

9. As you grow into a mega church pastor you will be tested with grief and sorrow.

Sadness, mourning and grief are tests that will meet every man desiring to be a mega church pastor. These are things that a mega church pastor must experience. By the time you have had a few heart-rending times of grief you will be wiser and more humble. You will become an eternity-oriented pastor because you *lay to heart* the times of mourning and grief. Without all these experiences your mind will gallop towards delusions that only end in more deception.

> **It is better to go to the house of mourning, than to go to the house of feasting: for that is the end of all men; and the living will lay it to his heart."**
>
> **Ecclesiastes 7:2**

10. A mega church pastor will be tested for his ability to withstand pressure.

A pastor of a big church is under a lot of pressure: pressure from the congregation, pressure from financial problems, pressure from his wife, pressure from his children, pressure from his associates, pressure from the dropping attendance, pressure from the projects, pressure from the employees, pressure from the press and pressure from the general public.

> **For we would not, brethren, have you ignorant of our trouble which came to us in Asia, that WE WERE PRESSED OUT OF MEASURE, above strength, insomuch that we despaired even of life:**
>
> **2 Corinthians 1:8**

11. A mega church pastor will suffer temptations.

O mega church pastor you will not be exempted from temptations because of your lofty ambitions. You will be tempted in every way on your journey to achieving church growth. You will be tempted with finances to enrich yourself and to misuse money. You will be tempted with lustful things and strange women. You will be tempted with divorce. You will be tempted with disloyalty. You will be tempted with pride. You will be tempted with discouragement. You will be tempted to give up. You will be tempted with unforgiveness and bitterness. You will be tempted to misuse your power. Do not be deceived. The higher you go in the ministry, the more you should expect to be tested and tormented.

> **For we do not have a high priest who cannot sympathize with our weaknesses, but One who has been tempted in all things as we are, yet without sin."**
>
> **Hebrews 4:15, (NASB)**

12. On your road to church growth, you will meet with wicked and unreasonable men.

O mega church pastor, get ready to meet unreasonable men and women who will oppose you and make things difficult for you. I have met men with an intractable dislike for us. There are people who have opposed the development of our cathedrals and church buildings. These unreasonable men are temptations and testing's on the way to your victory.

> **And that we may be delivered from unreasonable and wicked men: for all men have not faith.**
>
> **2 Thessalonians 3:2**

13. A mega church pastor will be tested by people who desert him.

When people desert you, you will have to depend on the Lord. Along the journey of ministry, there will be many who will abandon you. Don't cry too much when people leave you. I can tell you about quite a number of people who have deserted me especially as I went deeper into full time ministry. It is not because you are a bad person that people abandon you. It is because of your calling and the tests that go with it.

> **For Demas, having loved this present world, has deserted me and gone to Thessalonica...**
>
> **2 Timothy 4:10 (NASB)**

14. In your quest for church growth you will be tested by people who do not support you.

What a painful thing it is to have people withholding their support when you need it most.

> **At my first defense NO ONE SUPPORTED ME, but all deserted me; may it not be counted against them."**
>
> **2 Timothy 4:16 (NASB)**

15. In your quest for church growth, you will be tempted with the personal weaknesses of your life.

Every pastor has personal weaknesses. Some have temperamental weaknesses which lead to moodiness, depression, and poor communication. Other ministers suffer from disorganization, mismanagement of money and poor personal judgment. All these personal weaknesses show up as time goes on and present great temptations to the aspiring mega church pastor.

You will also be tempted with distressing situations. Many ministers have distressing marriages. The usual problems of marriage are heightened by the pressures of ministry and the pressures of pinnacle leadership.

> **Therefore I am well content with weaknesses, with insults, with DISTRESSES, with persecutions, with difficulties, for Christ's sake; for when I am weak, then I am strong.**
>
> **2 Corinthians 12:10 (NASB)**

16. To become a mega church pastor, you must pass the test of handling disloyal people.

How you handle disloyalty will determine how big your church can become. Disloyal people can scatter what you are building and make nonsense of your church growth efforts. You will be tested on whether you can be drawn into confusion by strife-causing leaders.

Your understanding of loyalty and disloyalty will be revealed by your ability to improve or worsen complicated situations in the church. You will be tested on your ability to silence the voice of the devil amongst your leaders. You will be tested on your ability to handle your accusers. You will be tested on your ability to dismiss people who bring division. You will be tested on your willingness to mark and avoid dangerous people.

> **Now I beseech you, brethren, mark them which cause divisions and offences contrary to the doctrine which ye have learned; and avoid them.**
>
> **Romans 16:17**

17. In your quest to become a mega church pastor, you will struggle with your personal needs and the church's needs.

You will have needs that must be met and these needs and desires can become a test and a snare to you.

> **But in all things approving ourselves as the ministers of God, in much patience, in afflictions, in necessities, in distresses,**
>
> **2 Corinthians 6:4**

18. In your quest to become a mega church pastor you will be tested with your ability to fast and pray as well as your ability to watch and pray.

Fasting is the painful activity of not eating so that you can pray. Watching is the painful activity of staying awake so that you can pray.

> **In weariness and painfulness, in WATCHINGS often, in hunger and thirst, in FASTINGS often, in cold and nakedness.**
>
> **2 Corinthians 11:27**

19. In your quest for church growth you will be tested with your willingness to expose yourself to danger.

Many people have ended their journey to a great ministry because of dangers they did not want to expose themselves to. "Is it dangerous to go there?" they ask. In so doing, many people cut off themselves from the fields God expects them to work in. It is the poor who are often open to the preaching of the gospel. These poor people who will come to your church, often live in dangerous and deprived areas. If you are not prepared to go to these poor and dangerous areas, there is very little you can do for God.

> **I have been on frequent journeys, in dangers from rivers, dangers from robbers, dangers from my countrymen, dangers from the Gentiles, dangers in the city, dangers in the wilderness, dangers on the sea, dangers among false brethren**
>
> **2 Corinthians 11:26 (NASB)**

20. In your quest for church growth you will be tested for your susceptibility to delusions and deceptions.

As your church gets bigger and you have more money, you will be tested by the deceitfulness of riches. You will be tempted to despise small ministries and pastors of smaller churches. If you pass all these tests you will truly be ready to handle a mega church.

> **And for this cause God shall send them strong delusion, that they should believe a lie:**
>
> **2 Thessalonians 2:11**

BIBLIOGRAPHY

SECTION 1

Dake's Annotated Bible Reference Bible. *Eleven Complaints of Moses,* page 66.

Walter McCleary. *Classic Books for Today No. 196, An hour with David Livingstone.* Public Domain

SECTION 2

Ahn ed, Ché. *Hosting the Holy Spirit.* Ventura: Renew Books, 2000.

Anderson, Gerald & Thomas Stransky F. *Mission Trends No. 2: Evangelism.* New York, New York: The Paulist Press, 1975.

Cho, David Y. *Successful Home Cell Groups.* Gainesville: Bridge-Logos Publishers, 2001.

Chung, Chin Hong. *Phenomenon of Rapid Growing Megachurches. "A case Study of Yoido Full Gospel Church."* Religions Study Vol. 16. Korea: Seoul National University.

Conn, Harvie M. *Planting and Growing Urban Churches.* Grand Rapids: Baker Books, 1997.

Duah, O. K. *Parting Words of Rev James McKeown.* Accra, Ghana: Blessed Publications, 2001.

Evans, Tony. *God's Glorious Church.* Chicago: Moody Publisher's, 2003.

Foli, Richard. *Towards Church Growth in Ghana.* Accra, Ghana: Trust Publishers, 1996.

Haggard, Ted. *The Life Giving Church.* Ventura: Regal Books, 2001.

Hagin, Kenneth. *Understanding the Anointing.* Tulsa: Faith Library Publications & Kenneth Hagin Ministries Inc., 2004.

Hamphill, Ken. *Bonsai Theory of Church Growth.* Nashville: Broadman & Holman, 1991.

Harrel, David E. *All Things Are Possible.* Indiana: Indiana University Press.

Heward-Mills, Dag. *Anagkazo.* Accra, Ghana: Parchment House, 1999.

------*Loyalty & Disloyalty.* Accra, Ghana: Parchment House, 1999.

Holland, Roger. *The Revived Church.* Reepham, Norfolk: Clay's Ltd, St. Ive's plc., 1988.

Joyner, Rick. *Mobilizing the Army of God.* Charlotte: Whitaker House, 1994.

------*Visions of the Harvest.* Charlotte: Whitaker House, 1998.

Kahne, Gary W. *The Dynamics of Personal Follow-Up.* Michigan: Zondervan Corporation, 1976.

Laurie, Greg. *Upside Down Church.* Wheaton: Tyndale House, 1999.

Loveland, Annie C. & Otis Wheeler B. *From Meeting House to Megachurch: A Material and Cultural History.* Missouri: University of Missouri Press.

McNeill, John. *Modern Christian Movements.* Philadelphia: The Westminster Press, 1950.

Osbourne, T. L. *Tragedy, Trauma, Triumph - Why?* Osfo International.

Oyedopo, David. *The Release of Power.* Dominion Publishing House.

Rainer, Thom. *Effective Evangelistic Churches.* Nashville: Broadman & Holman, 1996.

Schaller, Lyle E. *The Small Membership Church.* Nashville: Abingdom Press, 1994.

------*The Very Large Church.* Nashville: Abingdon Press, 2000.

Silvoso, Ed. *Prayer Evangelism.* Ventura: Regal Books, 2000.

Spader, Dann & Mayes Gary. *Growing a Healthy Church.* Chicago: Moody Publisher's, 1991.

Stonebraker, Robert J. *Optimal Church Size: The Bigger the Better.* Journal for the Scientific Study of Religions.

Stowell, Joseph M. *Shepherding the Church.* Chicago: Moody Press Edition, 1997.

Wagner, Peter. *The Importance of Prayer in Leading People: Leaders on Leadership.* George Barna, California: Regal Books, 1997.

Warren, Rick. *Purpose Driven Church.* Grand Rapids: Zondervan, 1995.

Whitaker, Colin. *A Passion for the Gospel.* Eastbourne: Kingsway Publications.

SECTION 3

Florence Littauer. *Personality Plus.* Albuquerque, NM. A Division of Baker Book House Co. Grand Rapids